PUNCHES, PINTS, POLITICS
AND PENSIONERS

Punches, Pints, Politics and Pensioners

PETER AND KATE ALDRIDGE

WITH A FOREWORD BY
DAVID A. HILL

The Pentland Press
Edinburgh – Cambridge – Durham – USA

© Peter and Kate Aldridge, 1995

First published in 1995
by The Pentland Press Ltd
1 Hutton Close
South Church
Bishop Auckland
Durham

British Library
Cataloguing in Publication Data.
A catalogue record for this book
is available from the British Library.

ISBN 1-85821-253-7

Typeset by Carnegie Publishing Ltd, 18 Maynard St, Preston
Printed and bound by Antony Rowe Ltd, Chippenham

To our mother, Mary Agnes, for all her love and dedication.

To John Jaques for all his patience.

Contents

Illustrations

Foreword

WHEN I first met Peter Aldridge I was less interested in his exploits among the high life and low life of the West End of London in the fifties and sixties than I was in his ability to run a very difficult pub for which I, the local manager for a brewery, needed to find a man (and a woman) in a thousand.

Having found them and quickly established a respect for their courtesy, humour and hard work, I began to realize that Peter and Shirley had led no ordinary life before we met in 1970. I began to hear tales of London mobsters; meetings with Marlene Dietrich, Trevor Howard, Kim Novak and dozens of other stars. Over many a friendly pint I heard of encounters with Henry Cooper in the ring, parties with Freddie Mills; monumental punch-ups in London pubs; incredible stories of posh night clubs and sleazy strip joints and the equally incredible ladies therein.

Although battered by more than their fair ration of trouble, Peter and Shirley, he the tough, determined heavyweight boxer from the South Yorkshire coalfield, she the pretty, equally determined and hard-working wife, always seemed to have retained the humour and humanity which lesser people would have lost very early on.

Like Peter, this book pulls no punches, makes no pretence and is uncompromising.

In the same chapter the book can be hilarious, violent, exciting and tender but is, like the author, never dull.

Those whose lives have been relatively ordered and ordained but who have known, liked and respected someone who has travelled a different route, will know Peter and Shirley well by the end of the book, and you will be all the better for it—if slightly bruised.

David A. Hill
of Carlsberg/Tetley

David A. Hill of Carlsberg Tetley.

PART ONE

Seconds Out

Chapter 1

M Y first recollection of this world is locked in a colliery-owned house, within the mining village of Armthorpe, the centre of the Yorkshire coal fields. I was born in the mid-thirties, not a propitious time in that part of the country. They were hard times for the British working class, harder still for those unemployed who lived north of Peterborough, that invisible line dividing Britain into what most Northerners have always maintained, is a preference by both Business and Government for the southern half of our islands.

I was to be the youngest of six surviving children. When an excited seven year old brother, Allan, hurried to inform my eleven year old sister, Kate, of my arrival, he was rebuffed caustically with, 'send him back, there are enough of us.'

Poverty paints a harsh picture in which there is little room for the softer shades of sentiment. I learned quickly just how stern a teacher it could be.

My father was not a miner, but a Sheffield man, an out of work steel-worker. A prideful fellow who had not learned to live with unemployment. His only asset was a magnificent tenor voice, good enough to have made him a wealthy chap today. Then, it earned him a few bob, singing in working men's clubs and public houses. Together with his friend Swifty, they worked the South Yorkshire area. My dad said of his mate, 'he could croon before Bing Crosby was out of napkins, he boo-bo-booed every time he forgot the words and that was pretty frequently.' Swifty used to warble the modern songs of the day, Pop sang the classical stuff.

My mother's brother was the miner, unmarried but nonetheless he still qualified for the tenancy of a colliery house. This man put a roof over my family's head, saving them from the humiliation of the Workhouse—the fate of many during the traumatic years of the Depression. My mother often told me stories of those days, how she had pushed a pram from Rotherham to Armthorpe, with my brother Allan and all their worldly possessions aboard. My brother Harry and my sister Kate clung to the sides, adding their not inconsiderable weight to the vehicle. My two elder sisters had been heartbreakingly handed over to my father's mother to rear.

Just as everyone else around us, Dad's best suit went into the pawn shop on Monday morning, to be retrieved on Friday, ready for his weekend stint singing. The buses into Doncaster were full on that day, crowded with women all carrying similar brown paper parcels, conversation being sparse. These were not happy times.

Years later, Kate sat on a Monday morning bus into town and listened to the animated discourse which filled the air. The talk was of holidays abroad. One lady obviously full of herself, said, 'we are going to Venice next week.'

Her companion, not to be outdone, replied, 'we haven't made up our minds yet, we are tossing up between Majorca and Yugoslavia.'

A far cry from our parents' day, when the only vacation known was the annual day out to Cleethorpes with the local working men's club. Mr Ghitto a neighbour, would collect the few pence each week which would pay for the yearly outing. It often rained and turned the front into a sea of mud, no place for paddling and sand castles, yet far from ruining the day, we would all repair to the amusement park, the men to the pubs.

My father's mother at no time knew such pleasure. To my knowledge her life revolved around the fish and chip shop she owned in a nearby village. Her relaxation came every Tuesday afternoon, when she visited Doncaster Market, enjoying tea and toasted teacakes before going to see a film then, refreshed, she returned home to open the shop for the evening trade. She died in that shop, aged seventy-six years, and still to the last, handling and cutting up frozen fish.

Armthorpe was always a sizeable village, although it has grown in recent years. The houses, smoke-encrusted, stood in terraced ranks, broken by gennels (alleyways), so one didn't have to go through the houses to reach back gardens. Handy for us children, for the homes opposite backed on to a lovely sand quarry, ideal for daring leaps from hill tops; it was also a short cut to Mere Lane School, the local primary. And a battle ground for men to let off steam. Mr O'Reilly a life-long neighbour of Mam's, used it regularly as he took on all comers. He bore the scars heroically, yet as my father said many times, 'he would be better leaving it to men who knew how to defend themselves.' Dad didn't argue, neither did he make appointments for duels, nor face up and prance around as Mr O'Reilly. Oh no, he just belted whoever dared to upset his equilibrium. It usually needed only one blow anyway. About five houses away from my uncle's, lived a family who'd moved to Armthorpe from Rossington, another pit village close by. Their son went to grammar school and spoke French, we thought fluently. He may well have been speaking his own version of Double Dutch, we would not have known, yet the respect we held for him was awesome.

Dr Hart was the village doctor, a good man who lost the use of his fingers through his research in radium. He volunteered to go to Finland with a medical team, when Russia attacked that country. Dad said, 'he needed his head examining.' Then Pop had had his fill in the battlefields of France, during World War One.

My mother's sister, Kate, who also lived in the village, but in a small street of council houses, had cause to send for the doctor who had just arrived in the village to take up practice. She said, 'there was a sharp knock on the door, and in walked this sight for sore eyes. Unkempt hair topped an ankle-length overcoat which was in need of renewal or cleaning or something drastic. Well, I ordered him out, only to be told, "I'm the bloody doctor".'

Hart had just come out of the Royal Navy and this was his first sortie into general practice. He said later, 'I nearly made it my bloody last, after I had met Kate.' He stayed in practice in the village until his death many years later.

Dr Hart gave me the examination for the Boxing Board, to enable me to obtain a Boxing Licence. He encouraged me to give it my best; a great man. He was a good friend of my father's, I learned in later years. Never a man to mince his words, he once commented to Dad, 'there's only thee, me and the vicar married.' A summation of the villagers hardly fair, yet there were a goodly number who had forgotten to tie the marital knot. A practice condoned today, though even in my time it was a sin kept well hidden.

The village was full of characters, my Aunt Kate being not the least of them. She lived next door to a councillor, Mrs Paling, a woman who, besides her civic duties, ran the village choir.

During the General Strike, my aunt became aware of nocturnal doings in the vicinity of Nellie Paling's backyard. Kate, as you will have gathered, was also a pretty straightforward woman in her actions. She went on the attack the next day, 'Nellie, there had better be a ton of coal in my coalhouse tonight. We, also, need to cook and keep warm.'

And there was, though to all accounts, her relationship with my aunt was not quite as warm as heretofore.

In mitigation of my relation's blackmail, one must remember, in those days there were no electrical appliances; cooking and warmth came from the family hearth. In the General Strike it was the survival of the fittest. Machination is not the brain child of modern society.

Another well-loved man of the village, was the Catholic priest, Father O'Flynn. He owned an old rattletrap of a car, an extreme rarity of any age at that time. We would race to the other end of the village, to the bridge at the entrance of the estate, and wait for him to appear on the Doncaster road. He'd pack so many kids into the vehicle, it was a miracle it ever started, let alone ran. Not for him the penny-pinching ways of later priests to cross my mother's path. I remember how upset she was shortly before her death. She had inadvertently given the priest a higher denomination coin, for her candle, than the customary two shillings. He accepted it as a donation, though he must have realized she could not afford such benevolence.

When Father O'Flynn died, Doncaster and its precincts turned out to honour the man—no matter what their religious affiliations were.

I grew, and the Second World War came, bringing with it financially better times for those not called into the Armed Forces. Nothing else changed much. Women still dressed in floral, cotton pinafores, their hair screwed up in curlers, doing their shopping in the village stores. The men always clean and tidy, remained dressed in collarless shirts fastened with a stud, scarves wrapped tightly around their necks, the ensemble completed by a flat cloth cap pulled firmly on their heads. It was almost a uniform with both sexes. There were the odd exceptions, who stirred the air with comment as to their reasons for such flagrant violation.

One, Kate remembers very well, Mrs Bentley, who lived close by my uncle's house and so became the focus of my sister's attention. She was known locally as the Blue Lady, for her habitual wearing of that colour. Always well-dressed in the very latest mode, which prompted speculation from the feminine population, how she managed to afford same? To my sister, who was still a child, she represented what everyone called her, a Lady.

With the advent of war, father managed to get a job in a munitions factory. I was too young to understand the wrath of my dad, as my two elder brothers voluntarily joined the Navy and Army respectively. Dad had survived the trenches and horror of the First World War, to be repaid with the degradation of unemployment and the ensuing poverty. From where he stood, his sons were repeating his mistake by offering their lives for King and Country. A country which didn't give a damn, once they had served their purpose.

My elder sister married an airman. His death and the heroic way he died, caught my young imagination. He was one of many flyers who volunteered to go after three German battleships escaping from Brest into the English Channel. There was no known grave for my brother-in-law, 'last heard of off the Dutch Coast', was the official obituary. I watched my sister grieve, war suddenly becoming very real. She joined the Women's Auxiliary Air Force. Shortly after,

Peter Aldridge, aged 10, and pets.
V.E. Day 1945.

our small street cried for another airman, this time a neighbour's son.

There were to be many other losses within our village before the nightmare ended, husbands, sons and boyfriends, which left us all that much poorer.

The end of the war saw my father again unemployed, this time the pain more deadly . . . He had pulmonary tuberculosis, the dreaded consumption, which so many people who had suffered the deprivation of the pre-war years developed. If only penicillin and streptomycin had been made available immediately after the war, many poor souls might have been saved. It was not to be. My mother became a widow.

It was now my turn to know abject poverty. Whereas my brothers and sister experienced similar conditions, everyone around them was in the same plight. There were no outward shows of wealth to draw comparisons. In my time, people were enjoying an affluence unknown previously, black gold (coal) was in demand as Europe rebuilt itself.

Mary Agnes Aldridge.

My brothers had been demobilized, had married and left home. My elder sister had remarried, and gone to live in Australia. My sister Joan married and went to live in Hull, her husband's home town. Kate had also married and had migrated to Australia.

Just before the outbreak of hostilities between England and Germany, my uncle had also married. We were re-housed by the council in a small cul-de-sac of semi-detached houses. A place where everyone shared each other's joys and sorrows. At least that is, when they weren't fighting their children's battles for them. These were generally bloodless. Venomous though the anger may have been, it did not last long. Mother at no time missed the rent. Until she died, the fear of losing her home was uppermost in her mind. If it meant going without food, clothes or fuel, then so be it, the rent had to be paid at any cost. There were no debts either, beyond those considered to be strictly necessary.

Life insurance payments were never allowed to run into arrears. A penny or twopence per week on all her children and herself. Enough to ensure us all a Christian burial. I can hear her now, 'if we don't pay these, we will all end up in paupers' lonely, unmarked graves.' We were barely above pauperism, yet her staunch Catholic faith could envisage nothing worse, than to lie forgotten when dead, as if she had never existed.

In later years she insisted on my sister Kate promising, out of mother's insurance pay out, she would have a stone for her grave, adding contentedly, 'there will be enough left for a stone, black marble with white chips.' She had asked for nothing in life, in death she feared oblivion. This strong show of wealth would guard against that.

I remember too well for my own good, how she had bought from the

Army and Navy stores, an ex-RAF tunic top and heavy studded boots, assuring me worriedly, yet placatingly, 'those will not wear out so quickly.'

'Oh, Mam,' I remember saying, the feeling of utter shame, knowing I would have to go to school in those clothes, overwhelming me beyond further protestations.

That was when I learnt to fight. By the time I was thirteen I was Cock of the School, physically. A school bully. Anyone who tried to usurp me was soundly thumped into obedience. This was to stand me in good stead in later years, when I began amateur boxing. I became used to taking hard blows and fighting back.

At that time I was determined to better my lot. With no father to guide me, I relied on my fists to secure the life style I could only dream about. At fourteen I was victor ludorum of the school, best fighter, best runner and best overall sportsman. Coming second had no place in my plans.

Believe me, to be best fighter, one had to be bloody good, those pitmen's sons knew how to fight. They asked for and gave no quarter. Looking back on my early days, I understand better, the urgent need and longing I felt to gain respectability. Money and clothes, although much desired, were lesser considerations. I was certain those things would automatically follow.

I left school armed only with a secondary education. My sister Joan then came to the fore, dragging me around Doncaster, single-mindedly bent on securing me a position.

She did well, finding me an apprenticeship as a plumber with the reputable firm of John Holmes Ltd. The wages were the equivalent of £1.76 per week. My mother and I went hungry that first two weeks, to buy the required overalls and boots for the job.

What a woman Mary Agnes Naughton was. Sacrifice seemed to be a way of life for her. Her mother died when she was a young child and, from then on her very existence was just a fight for survival.

My apprenticeship, too, proved to be a hard, rigorous training ground. I was put to work under the foreman plumber, a man named Jock Goldie, a loud mouthed braggart and bully, who made my life a literal hell for two long years.

About a year after beginning work, I started as an amateur boxer at Elmfield House in Doncaster.

Jock had never been a coward. He didn't have to prove himself for he

Peter Aldridge, aged 16, 1951.

had been a rear gunner, in the Royal Air Force; the most unenviable position in the aeroplane. He was a clean good-living man, who owned a good home, better than most in those days. Nevertheless, young as I was, I surmised his conduct could only be due to one thing—jealousy. Surprisingly, he bought a ticket for my first fight, which was to be staged in the Corn Exchange, Doncaster, the venue for many of my later engagements. Jock, true to character, told everyone, 'I am only going to see him get a hiding.'

I was by this time a gaunt six-footer, boxing as a middle-weight, (Senior). I had not fought as a Junior, nor as a Schoolboy. George Topham, at twenty-four years of age, was my first opponent. I entered the ring as nervous as hell, I wasn't frightened of him, but of the bloody noisy crowd. George came at me with gusto the instant the bell sounded, intent on putting a swift end to my aspirations to be a boxer. He had been boxing a number of years, and was about to brush me off as he would an annoying fly.

It went, as the local newspaper headlines read the next day, 'a tall, raw-boned sixteen year old, who had taken up boxing less than six months previously, under Malcolm Woodcock; his first appearance in the ring and he won in twenty seconds.' They went on to say, 'a vicious right cross that K.O.d G. Topham, British Railways.'

I stood in the centre of the ring, bewildered as Topham went down. I was probably more confused than the man on the floor. Then I heard above all the uproar, the shout, 'good punch, young un.' It was my brother Allan, yelling gleefully, beside himself with pride and excitement. He was the only member of my family to watch the fight.

We went home elated to a mother who had been worried sick with fear. The next day she bought every newspaper she could lay her hands on, and went to every house in that tiny street, boasting of her son's prowess.

The following week I repeated my success. Headlines screamed, 'Boy Hope wins again, inside distance.'

The referee had stopped the fight against W. Ball, Y.M.C.A., at the Corn Exchange. This time I had had good support from my family, Allan, Harry my other brother, and sister Joan were there to cheer me on. Mam was unbelievable, she went around like a peacock displaying its feathers, marching up and down our street again with the newspapers, sending the cuttings out of those news-sheets to my sisters in far off Australia.

However, the situation was far from happy at work. Jock Goldie became more impossible to get along with. My success in the ring had only served to exacerbate the situation. He now took every opportunity to ridicule or chastise me whenever he thought he had a likely audience.

My luck was to change there, too; it came in the shape of a man named Frank Gibson, a lovely, funny little chap, who was a master plumber. I was transferred to him as his apprentice.

'So, you are the soap wrapper!' he said with a twinkle in his eyes.

'Soap wrapper?' I asked, puzzled

'Scrapper,' Frank answered, laughing at my obvious bewilderment. Thus began my introduction to two very happy years together. Although Jock continued to lay on the stick every chance he had, it didn't seem to matter so much. He had apparently taken a dislike to Frank, too, and I must say there was little love lost so far as Frank was concerned. He detested Jock. He could do little about it. Frank with a large, young family to support was finding it hard to make ends meet, so had to step carefully to keep his job. Of course, this made him fair game for Jock.

At home, mother was going without food so that I could eat to build my strength for boxing. I often think how very hungry she must have been sometimes, as she watched me dining. And still the rent and insurances were paid, as she lived on bread and butter.

My brothers and sister could do little to help. They, too, were struggling to keep their heads above water. Apart from the odd food parcel from Louie or Kate in Australia, all substances ingested in our household were, to say the very least, basic and sparse.

My boxing career progressed steadily, I had a return fight with George

Topham, proving it was no fluke the first time we fought, I K.O.d him in the third round this time. The match was again held in Doncaster's Corn Exchange.

'That is it,' said George, 'when a sixteen year old kid does you twice, it's time to quit.' True to his word, he never fought again.

By now I was invincible, or so I thought. All the early success with no defeats gave me, to put it mildly, one hell of a swollen head. I was too young to cope intelligently with all the adulation I received from fight fans and girls.

Then I met a *boxer*. His name was Willie Sevens, a former Youth Club Champion. I fought him at the Corn Exchange and he gave me a boxing lesson I wouldn't forget in a hurry. I lost on points; my vaunted right hand could not touch him. That night I was taught the difference between a scrapper and a *boxer* and how.

Fortunately, it was early in my career, and I was always a fast learner, particularly if the instruction had been a painful one. I went on to win five more fights in 1951, but lost again to a more experienced fighter, Fred Britton, at King's Lynn in Norfolk.

It was about this time, I decided I needed professional help. I resolved to enlist the aid of John (Basher) Bell, a Geordie ex-fighter, who was training one or two other boxers in my own village of Armthorpe. John resided in the village and I went to his home. I knocked on the door, and as John opened it, I asked without preamble, 'will you train me to fight?'

'Come into the back garden,' he said, unperturbed by my brash request. He led me through the house into the back yard, where there was an old punch bag filled with sand.

'I'm going to swing this at you.' With no further warning, he swung the bag in my direction.

Trying to impress, I let go with all the power I could muster in my right hand.

'Fucking hell's fire! you'll knock down anything that lands on,' John swore. Plainly, I had achieved the desired effect. I soon learned that as John became excited, his accent became broader, his language that much more colourful.

With the combination of Malcolm Woodcock at Elmfield House, and Basher Bell at home, I had the best of tuition. I did not lose a fight until the Amateur Boxing Association finals in London. I ran up fifty-two fights without a loss. As Basher repeated gloatingly, 'f'ing hell's fire, you've knocked down everything you've hit, I f'ing knew you would.'

In 1951 I also met and fell head over heels in love with a pretty, blonde nurse, named Shirley. At the time she was working at a children's home called Wynthorpe Hall, in Dunsville, a small hamlet not far from Armthorpe. From my school days I had kept a number of friends, among the staunchest were Tommy Penrice and George Meehan. Both were also courting nurses from the Hall. Even though we had little money, we all counted these as being among the happiest days of our lives.

Peter and Shirley, aged 18 years, 1954.

Proudly I took Shirley home to meet Mam, who received her with little enthusiasm, polite, as she always was with visitors, yet cautious. Asked her opinion after Shirley had left, she replied in the same vein, 'h'mm, she is good-looking, but you have to watch the good-looking ones.'

Yet they were to become firm friends over the years. If truth be known, Mam would often take Shirley's side against me. Particularly when I wandered off the straight and narrow as wander I did. When I ventured to take other girls home, Mam would give me a long, cold stare, as only she could, and say chillingly, 'Shirley is the right girl for you.'

A prophecy? Or by intent, for she knew full well how to manipulate her off-spring if she considered it to be in their own best interest. Her Irish ability to foretell some events, alas, did not extend to horse-racing, for her sixpence each way hardly netted her a fortune, despite long hours perusing the racing columns of the *Sporting Pink*.

Almost everyone in the sixteen to twenty age group, were racing bike enthusiasts. We were no exception. George, Tommy and I purchased a bicycle of our choice. Mine was a Hercules Racer. It cost me one pound down and five bob a week on the never-never. I soon realized why Mam was so dead set against hire purchase. Oh God, what a struggle to pay it off, I had. The going without that five measly bob entailed!

Tommy did the same as me, yet with little or no trouble to meet the repayments. Both George and he were working at Markham Main Colliery, earning far in excess of my wages.

I really should correct the above statement, for George was not a lover of work of any kind, and dodged it whenever possible. He'd much sooner be pedalling his bike around the streets of Armthorpe. The fabulous chrome Daws bicycle he had chosen, which was far

George Meehan, 1951.

more expensive than Tommy's or mine, remained unpaid for. He missed the payments until it became a habit, or it ceased to worry him, I am still not quite sure which of the foregoing is correct. The finance company, tiring of their efforts to rectify this anomalous situation, decided upon repossession, underestimating my friend George. He had been well groomed in the art of like matters, his mother being a past master at it.

Mary Meehan would obtain all kinds of newfangled household appliances, that by no stretch of the imagination, could she possibly afford. Here was where her mastery came into play. As soon as one was repossessed, she would obtain another from a different source. In those halcyon days of no debtors' register, her strategy was faultless. In today's more-awake-to-sinners environment, his mother would have to invent shrewder tactics. So would George.

Then, George had no intention of allowing his beloved bike to be repossessed. He concealed it behind the hut in our garden, telling my unsuspecting mother, 'I have to keep it away from my brothers or they will ruin it.' A simple subterfuge, yet clever enough to fox the hire purchase bods. Subsequently, the firm must have tired of trying to retrieve the bike, at least that was how George explained their loss of interest. Whichever was the truth, George kept his ill-gotten gains.

George is the funniest man I have ever met and that includes professional comedians. None of the humour was ever intentional, this probably being the reason why it was so devastating. My brother Allan boasted, 'I could put that bugger on the stage, and earn a fortune.'

In the autumn of 1951, George, Tommy and I, now almost inseparable, decided to visit the Hull Fair. Our only means to get there was by bicycle. Hull is a long way from Doncaster, but Hull Fair was the largest in Britain, making it an irresistible magnet for the three of us. Allan, who after demobilization had become a long-distance lorry driver, mapped out the best route for us to take.

We intended to ride to Hull, stay overnight at my sister Joan's house, then catch the ferry to New Holland on the Lincolnshire side of the river, thence to Brigg and down the Scunthorpe road to Doncaster. We made it without mishap to Hull and the Fair, albeit more than a little saddle-sore. We had a splendid time, trying our hand at every knock-em-over, shoot-em-down stall in sight.

George won a watch with an expanding bracelet. Tommy and I were green with envy. To own a watch in those days was really something, one with an expanding bracelet was something else. To make matters worse, Tommy and I had absolutely nothing to show for our efforts.

George drove us mad with his repeated question, 'do you want to know what time it is?' He flashed that confounded watch under our noses, probably sensing our jealousy. He fiddled with the bracelet whenever Tommy and I were close, 'does it look all right on?' he asked sickeningly, until we felt like choking him with the blasted bracelet, not daring to answer for fear of being carried away with the idea. Joan and her husband must have been as heartily sick of that watch, as we were by the time we left their house.

The following day we caught the ferry to return home. Crossing the Humber we all leaned far over the side of the boat, enjoying every minute of this special treat, watching the great swathe of water sweeping away from the bow of the ferry, in a flurry of foam. This was living, forgotten was the long ride awaiting us on the other side, or the darkening, foreboding heavens.

Allan Aldridge, the author's brother, in 1951.

I can picture the scene as if it were yesterday. George was winding his watch for the umpteenth time that day, making sure we were both given a good view of the proceedings. Suddenly the boat gave a wallowing heave, George's prized possession slipped from his grasp into the murky waters of the River Humber. We were close to the bow of the boat and I can still see George, all these many years later, running from the prow of the ferry to the stern, up and down, backwards and forwards, all the while screaming, hysterically repeating, 'my watch, my watch.'

Cruelly we laughed and fell about, as George cried bitter tears. It started to rain, as if the Gods were in sympathy with George, even though he became as wet as Tommy and me. It bucketed down, continuing the cloudburst as we splashed our uncomfortable way home. Past Brigg we trundled down the Scunthorpe road to the end, and to the transport café which Allan had recommended. Wet and bedraggled we entered the warm, invitingly dry building. Allan had previously told us about the ample food, which could be obtained for your money here. 'You will get a good substantial meal for two and sixpence, it more than satisfies the truckies, and they're hungry-nosed buggers.'

Sure enough, for our money we received an egg, a pile of chips, sausage, mushy peas and toast, plus a steaming, outsize mug of tea. It was worth saving our last half-a-crown for. I have never had a meal which tasted as good as that since. But after all we were bloody hungry, wet and very tired.

The café was furnished with long, wooden benches and tables. Practicality had been the watchword of the owners, definitely not style. It was very well patronized; eventually we succeeded in finding seats which enabled us to sit next to each other. Seated on the bench opposite were two extremely heavyweight lorry drivers who studiously ignored our existence.

George had a long, prominent nose, a big hooter we used to call it, much to George's annoyance. The wet, cold weather outside, coupled with the snug, heated atmosphere inside, had given George his usual heavy sniffle.

As we tucked into this huge meal, he continually sniffed a long, nasty runner of mucus back up his nostril . . . Tommy and I were used to George and his less refined habits and it affected our appetite not at all. However the same could not be said of the two truckies, one of whom unable to stand it any longer, reacted violently, 'for Christ's sake, wipe your bloody nose,' he shouted at him.

He banged his knife and fork down on the table, and leaned threateningly over George.

George appeared not in the last perturbed by this intimidatory behaviour and bravely answered, 'you wipe it, you're bloody nearest.'

I fell off the end of the bench, as Tommy collapsed backwards with uncontrollable laughter. George had surpassed himself, ever quick at rep-artee. Unmindful of the obvious danger, he had replied with his customary aplomb. This was my mate, at his unwitting best.

Probably not wanting to strike an idiot, and who could hit laughing men? the two bewildered drivers left their meal and walked out. They had never met a George before, their bulk deterring all but a halfwit from stepping out of line, yet here were three boys who refused to be bullied. The fact that it was George's disgusting habit which caused the furore, was beside the point.

He provided us with many laughs over the years, the sad part was, he at no time intended to be funny. In fact on a lot of occasions he would appear very hurt at our mirth. He was a walking disaster, things invariably went wrong for him, and nearly always in a comical manner.

My boxing career continued on its successful way. In 1952 I had twenty fights and won them all. Seventeen by knock outs. I was by then fighting as a Light-heavyweight and stayed predominately in that division until the end of my boxing days. Now and again I ventured into the Heavyweight class, unsuccessfully, for they were just too big for me.

I was indeed a lucky young man, I had a loyal following of fans from the surrounding districts of Doncaster. I had a happy home, despite the fact of it being a very poor one, and friendship from mates who followed me loyally for years, through the ups and downs of the fight game.

There was one such occasion, which I think is worth recalling on paper. I was booked on the Bill at Pudsey Baths, a village near Leeds. It was a grand affair, most of the spectators in the front rows were in evening dress. We were all highly impressed, and not a little overawed by all this opulent splendour. Our world was singularly lacking in these showy refinements.

I was to fight a Liverpool man named Simpson. Malcolm Woodcock was again unable to be present to second me, an occurrence which was not unusual when I fought away from home.

Basher Bell was also absent, he had caught the flu. It must have been a very bad dose to keep him away. So there I was with no second. My brother Allan, soldier that he is, volunteered to fill in. I wasn't overly concerned as he had gained enough knowledge of the procedure involved in the fight game during the previous two years as he followed me around the venues. George as usual, was the bucket man. His job was to pass the bucket of water up to the ring at the end of each round.

The first round was a tough one, Simpson was by no means going to be a pushover. Returning to my corner as the bell signified the end of the first skirmish, I found Allan fully prepared and quick with the necessary advice.

'Stay away from him,' he whispered, as he washed my gumshield out, in the bucket George was proudly tending.

'Box him, stay out of reach,' he instructed quietly, as my gumshield was replaced and my face wiped.

'Watch him, box him,' he repeated in my ear, as I rose to leave the corner for the second round.

As I approached Simpson an almighty roar reverberated around the Baths. I hadn't laid a glove on him, nor he on me. Simpson's face was probably a reflection of my thoughts. He appeared absolutely dumbfounded. When you are within that roped square, you can see nothing other than your opponent and the referee. Inside this brilliantly lit ring you are in a world consisting of three people, one of whom is out to nail you to the floor. The usually howling mob outside the ropes is not the least interested in your health; all they ask for is a good scrap for their money. They can be inordinately rowdy when frustrated.

There is normally a quietness that descends at any match until the first blow is struck, apart from the odd over-exuberant fan urging the boxers on. This night was definitely different. I wondered what the hell was going on out there. The noise had barely abated as the fight continued. I began to get on top of Simpson, and knew I was hurting him badly at the close of this round. I boxed with only half of my mind assessing my opponent for openings. I couldn't wait to get back to my corner to find the cause of all the hullabaloo.

'What's happening down there?' I asked Allan, as soon as I was seated. There was a whole heap of people milling about behind me, the disturbance seemingly emanating from there.

Allan threw a towel over my head, covering most of my face, 'don't you worry about that, keep your mind on the fight,' he reprimanded harshly, pushing me out toward the centre of the ring for the third and last round.

Early in this round I caught Simpson with a good right hand. It was all over, the referee stopped the contest.

I returned to my corner and a jubilant Allan. 'Now then,' I demanded belligerently, 'what the bloody hell is going on?'

'All right, calm down, it doesn't affect you.' He started in to tell me about the accident which had occurred, almost immediately on my leaving the corner for the second round. There is a lip which runs around the edge of boxing rings. The bucket man has to lift the bucket of water up and over this lip. George had inadvertently pulled the bucket towards him, instead of lifting it over the rim of the ring. The whole contents had spilled completely upon a man and woman seated at the ringside, saturating them to the skin, evening dress and all. The man highly agitated, had leapt to his feet to have a go at George. Allan laughingly went on to say, 'here I was trying to watch you, and holding this lunatic off George. The fool continued to try to free himself, all the while yelling, 'I'll kill him'. George didn't help by not telling the man he was sorry.'

Pete Platts, another great friend and ardent fan of mine, remarked afterwards, 'there was a good fight going on in the ring, but a bloody better one outside it,'

George had struck again in his own inimitable fashion.

We finally managed to get the state of affairs calmed down somewhat, when George nearly stirred it all up again.

The wet man, still seething at not being able to vent his anger, shouted at George, 'You've spoilt our night completely.'

'Well, you don't think I am happy, do you?' my friend plaintively replied.

High from my victory in the ring and George's calamity, we laughed until our sides ached. Then when our individual recollections of the incident had been well and truly sated, Allan asked, 'would you like to go the York way home?'

We were all in favour of this, particularly as he had hired the car, squeezing six of us inside, until it was literally on its axles the whole way. Conscious that we may be harbouring feelings of indebtedness Allan, the lover of history that he is, enthused 'you will be able to see the Roman Wall.'

We all said, 'yes' most emphatically, in our youthfulness not the least bit tired. The laughter and sheer joy of each other's company, and life in general, still held us on that exultant peak, drowning any reservations we may have had about sight-seeing in the early hours of the morning. Little knowing the consequence of this decision would last for many frightening weeks, away we drove, a noisy, merry band of nocturnal tourists, until we ran out of petrol, right in the middle of Selby.

Selby is a sleepy place at any time. At 2 a.m. even the cats had gone home to bed. There we were stuck outside a jeweller's shop with absolutely no sign of life anywhere. Something had to be done.

Jimmy Abbot and Pete Platts came up with the best idea, out of a load of rubbish. This was to wake up the proprietor of a garage we had passed further back along the road.

Which act turned out to be a story unto itself.

The two of them set off, boastfully promising they would be back shortly with petrol. Finding an empty oil can outside the garage, they proceeded to bang on it energetically until the irate owner appeared at the door. After what Pete said was a swearing match, and a terrific argument between him and them, ending with Pete threatening, 'I'll bang on this bloody tin all night, unless you get out here and serve us,' the man unwillingly served them, albeit verbally abusing them throughout the procedure.

Uncaring, for they had got what they wanted, the pair of them swaggered back to the car with enough petrol to get us all home.

I went to work as usual the next day, very tired, yet resisting the temptation to call in sick, as Frank Gibson was on a roof job and needed me there for safety's sake.

Tommy Penrice, George Meeham and Peter Aldridge, 1953.

I arrived home at the end of the day, utterly bone weary. As I approached the corner of our small street I saw a police car standing outside the house. Three very large policemen advanced towards me.

One of them inquired sternly, 'Peter Aldridge?'

'Yes,' I replied, 'what's up?'

Immediately I wondered what Jimmy and Pete had done at that blasted garage, they had omitted to tell us about.

'Get in,' one policeman said, pointing at the car.

'What for,' I asked. Thoroughly shaken, I turned from the car door.

'Get in,' he growled. Bending my head down he forcibly thrust me into the car, repeating as he did so, 'in.'

From the rear seat of the car, I pleadingly asked again, 'what have I done?'

The policeman at the side of me remained silent, the vocal one turned from his seat alongside the driver, and snarled at me, 'shut up.'

I was driven to the police station and escorted up the steps into what I learned later was called the Operations Room. There to my surprise sat

Jimmy Abbot, Pete Platts, Tommy Penrice and George Meehan, all looking totally fed up.

'Sit down,' the police sergeant said commandingly.

I sat. Turning to my friends I asked the straightforward question, to which I had been unable to get an answer to from the police, 'what are we here for?'

'We are here for robbery,' blurted out George.

'Shut up, no talking allowed,' the sergeant commanded.

'Where is our Allan?' I asked, ignoring the sergeant's warning.

'We are picking him up now,' the sergeant answered for them.

It wasn't long before they had us all assembled. As Allan entered the room, George, incapable of containing himself further, jumped to his feet. 'They have got us for robbery, Allan.' His addiction for exaggeration, and the cinema, coming to the fore, 'they're not going to frame me, for something I haven't done.'

'Shut up, George,' Allan snapped unkindly, 'give me a chance to find out what is happening.'

The sergeant then spelled out the reason for our detainment for questioning.

It appeared that, during the time we had been sitting outside the jeweller's shop, it had been robbed. Jewellery worth £15,000 had vanished overnight.

We were Johnny on the Spot.

Even we were confused. We had not seen anything, nor heard anything while outside that shop. We only knew not one of us were guilty, we had been together throughout. I knew we were going to have a job proving it wasn't a conspiracy, and my heart sank. In spite of our protestations of innocence we were taken, at first separately, then two at a time into an office and questioned. It was midnight before they released us.

Our ordeal lasted for three extremely frightening weeks, the police never leaving us alone for long. Turning up constantly, they came to Mam's house at all odd hours, to ask yet more questions. Occasionally picking me up, and the others, at work to take us in for further interrogation, cajoling, before resorting to threats, certainly not satisfied with the answers we could give them.

Suddenly, when we were hopelessly convinced we were about to be charged with the robbery, it was all over. As quickly as the nightmare had began, it had ended. Our ill luck at being outside that particular shop that night, was compensated by our unbelievable good fortune now.

They had caught the thieves who'd committed the crime, and in actual possession of the stolen goods.

The police collected us together at the police station, for the last time. We stood in front of the C.I.D. inspector as thoughtfully he eyed each one of us, before saying, 'I was totally convinced it was you lot, although I must admit your story was ridiculous enough to be true. However, I am very pleased for your sake it has turned out well.'

One incident I find amusing, but only on recollection, occurred during an interview with the inspector held with Allan and myself. It is probably the story the inspector alluded to at the end.

After being told by Allan and myself, the reason why we were in Selby, the inspector drawled sarcastically, 'so, you decided to go from Leeds to York to see the Roman Wall at one in the morning?'

'Well, he hadn't seen it before,' Allan said unhappily.

'Tut, tut, tut,' jeered the inspector, pointing his finger at me.

'Can't you think of a better excuse than that for being in Selby?' I could not, apart from planting one on him for his sarcasm, I was devoid of ideas. Our story of why we were outside the jeweller's seemed pretty far-fetched even to us.

Free of the worrying, nagging fear, our small gang sat discussing the whole sorry mess in retrospect.

George added his own thoughts to our perception of the past few weeks' trauma, giving an entirely different slant to the general one.

'I tell you, I was scared stiff in the police station, but I bet those buggers inside the jeweller's shop were shitting themselves, when we were sitting outside for all that length of time.'

The year 1953 turned out to be another good year for me in boxing. I beat the National Coal Board Heavyweight Champion, Ken Booth, knocking him down four times and giving away five stone in weight. He was seventeen stones four pounds, I weighed in at twelve stones two pounds. I fought seventeen times that year, winning all fights, stopping fourteen of them inside the distance. I was then Top Amateur in the Doncaster area.

My life at work remained unchanged, the wages still pitiful in comparison to the norm, Jock Goldie still seeking opportunities to have a go at Frank or me. Yet the time spent with Frank was a wonderful period in my life, a time I will never forget. He owned an ex-army motorbike, and it wasn't from the later years of the war either. We would drive from job to job on this machine, regardless of the weather. Always Frank was able to keep my spirits high, with his sharp dry wit, delivered deadpan. On arrival at the site, Frank would invariably introduce me proudly, 'this is Peter Aldridge, the *boxer*.'

Stroking my ego? Yes, but I was a young lad trying desperately to better myself, in the only way I knew how. Confidence boosting I badly needed, for in spite of my early success I was lacking in self-assurance. I realize now Frank was well aware of this.

Nevertheless life was great. I professed, and firmly believed I was deeply in love with Shirley, though I was still able to flirt with every good-looking lass I came in contact with.

When not training for fights, Tommy, George and I spent most of our spare time at Wynthorpe Hall. George making everyone laugh as usual, his customary flair for unfortunate accidents and *faux pas* undiminished. The nurse he was courting, a girl named Hazel Pask, laughed no less heartily than any of us at George's antics. It was probably this natural ability of George's to make her laugh, which attracted her to him. Of course, we were not supposed to be there, for any unauthorized person to be inside the perimeters of the Wynthorpe Hall grounds, meant they were trespassing, no matter their reason for being there.

This fact carried little weight with us. The nurses lived in. The only way we could see and talk to them, was through the downstairs windows of the Hall. There was an added attraction which, it would be unfair to say, was the primary reason for our being there—we were being fed fairly substantially. I admit in our youthful, every-hungry state, this alone would have been sufficient itself to draw us to the Hall. We would hang around those windows, from which Shirley, Hazel and the other nurses would feed us surplus meals from the kitchens.

The police made regular patrols of the grounds. However, we soon became familiar with the set times of their rounds, and timed our visits accordingly, becoming more daring as we remained undetected.

One evening the police arrived unexpectedly early, for reasons known only to themselves. When the Law arrived, we scattered, Tommy and I running for a low fence separating the Hall grounds from a large meadow. We cleared the fence easily, but there was a drop of around five foot on the other side, which we hadn't been aware of. We landed heavily. Shaken but not hurt, we dropped flat and lay very still. George followed seconds later. We heard him groaning as he hit the ground, 'oh, bloody hell. Oh, shit.'

'Christ, be quiet,' Tommy and I hissed in unison.

The police searchlight came over the top of the fence, missing us, yet illuminating the field beyond. The police finally moved on, and we stood up, stepping out of the shadow of the fence.

'Oh, God,' George said, with such anguish we both turned to gaze at him.

In the moonlight we could see the cause for his obvious distress. George had borrowed his elder brother Sydney's best gaberdine raincoat, albeit without Sydney's consent, to impress Hazel. As he jumped over the fence, he had landed flat in the middle of a pile of cow-clap. Oh, shit, indeed. The recently passed, slimy green excrement oozed its way down the front of Sydney's prized possession.

'Oh, bloody shit,' repeated poor, unlucky George.

For once we didn't laugh. It could have happened to any of us.

We hurried homeward, away from the Hall. There was little point in risking going back to the girls, besides I hardly believed they would appreciate the aroma George was giving off.

As we neared the end of our street and George's home, he piteously pleaded with us to stay with him. 'Please come in with me and explain to our Syd how it happened. He's not going to listen to me. I think he'll kill me for this. It's his best coat, he only wears it on special occasions.'

How could we refuse? Admittedly he had brought it on his own head by borrowing the coat when he knew the value Syd placed on it. All the same who could envisage what would happen?

We were mates, and as such we stuck together, unless it got too dicey. In we went, the three most downcast young fellows you could imagine, full of remorse and disquiet. Sydney was a hard-working youth, who was also noted for his easily aroused, fiery temper. Small in stature, yet with a heart as big as a lion when it came to scrapping.

As we entered the house, George's mother stared at him aghast. Mary Meehan had a large family of seven girls and three boys, and a husband whom my sister Kate always referred to as Andy Capp, maintaining throughout her association with Mary, that the character had been modelled upon him. Whenever Mary had got into too much debt, he would take off and work the showgrounds. My mother assumed Mary had used his name to obtain credit. Do not get me wrong, Kate always liked Mary Meehan, saying her conniving was so transparent only a fool could be taken in by it. It was all done for the benefit of her large brood.

Mary would pinch from Jesus Christ, to give to her children. Kate came home one Christmas time, to find my mother very worried. Mary Meehan had asked for and got Mary Agnes's Co-operative Society book, to buy in some necessary groceries. Mam had felt sorry for her, it being Yuletide and everything. Kate dashed immediately to the local Co-operative store, to find Mary at the check-out, her trolley laden with Christmas goodies. Large boxes of chocolates, crackers, the real necessities of life were sparse indeed in that barrow. She was brandishing Mam's pass book. Her only regret was that Kate had caught her before she had got her craftily acquired Christmas shopping home. Kate gave Mary Agnes the talking to.

Mary Meehan tried and worked very hard, she laboured in the fields, long back-breaking hours, picking peas, potatoes and whatever else the farmers could find for her to do. This money would go to feed her hungry family. Mary retained nothing for herself. Andy Capp provided little in that household, only his occasional presence and more children. In spite of this Mary would defend him to the death. Not only did she protect her husband and progeny against outsiders, she supported them against each other in the constant battles which raged within her castle.

This was to be one of the latter occasions.

'Whatever will our Syd say when he comes home?' she wailed.

Fortunately for us, Sydney had gone to Lincoln, to see his girlfriend, travelling there on his old motorbike. George again begged us to stay. Tommy was on the early shift, and much as he would have like to stop, if only to see the outcome of this shemozzle, he was forced by tiredness to return home to bed.

I was left with no alternative except to remain to stand by George. To be perfectly honest with you, I wouldn't have missed it for quids. Nevertheless, I had a horrible feeling of apprehension as I heard the familiar chug, chug, chug, of Sydney's worn-out motorbike.

George had wiped the thick smelly mess off the coat, leaving a large nasty green, pungent stain across the front and down one sleeve of the garment.

Mary had placed the coat on a hanger and suspended it from the door of a large storage cupboard next to the fireplace in this family-sized kitchen. I waited with bated breath for the explosion as Sydney entered the room.

It didn't come. Cheerfully Syd acknowledged me, 'all right, Peter?' he asked, then his gaze fell on the coat hanging in front of him. He let out one almighty yell and rushed from the house, leaving all of us speechless. Moments later he reappeared, swinging a hatchet like a Mohawk Indian. I really though he intended scalping George. I dived at him, trying to grab his axe-swinging arm, while big, fat Mary hung desperately on to him. All the time Syd was screaming at the top of his voice, 'I'll bloody kill him.'

Sydney didn't need to be told who was responsible for ruining his beloved topcoat.

George had curled up on the settee in a foetal position, his arms covering his head and face, making no attempt whatsoever to defend himself from the onslaught. It took the combined strength of both Mary and me to hold Syd off George, who reiterated sobbingly, 'keep him away from me, Mam.'

After at least a half-hour of punishing struggle, we managed to disarm and calm Syd down. It really showed the extent of the pride of ownership of that garment, when Sydney would most definitely have murdered his brother for damaging it.

'Keep out of my sight, George, or I might still bloody kill you,' Sydney warned his brother in a cold, clearly bitter voice. He really meant it, too. George, white and shaken, backed away from the settee and Syd.

I went home to Mam, and the mirth it caused when I told her what had happened. We laughed until our sides ached.

Mary had the coat cleaned six times, yet the stain remained plainly visible for all to see, including Sydney, who needed no excuse after then to belt George at every possible opportunity.

Things improved for me on the boxing scene. I was rated sixth in the Amateur Boxing Association Ratings of Great Britain. I was now boxing all over the country. London, Cardiff, Glasgow, et cetera, I went a winning way, yet was missing my friends and fans, George's light relief especially, for they just could not afford to follow me.

I also made the headlines for something other than boxing in 1953. Frank and I were working on a roof using a roof ladder. Frank left me to return to the ground to fetch other material for the job, when the gutter suddenly collapsed . . . I was left high and dry lying on a steep, slate roof of a building, four storeys from the ground in the Main Street of Doncaster.

Every time I moved to try to gain a firmer purchase, I slipped another foot further down. Frank began screaming at me from below, 'for Christ's sake, Peter, do not move, keep still.'

Frightened out of my wits, I attempted to remain motionless, a very difficult feat on a slippery slate roof. It seemed for ever before the fire engine arrived, its horns blaring, an ostentation quite unnecessary as far as I was concerned. I just wanted to feel the earth beneath my feet again.

They managed to hook a rope around me, without my having to move about too much, then by means of a telescopic ladder, fulfilled my dreams of being on terra firma once more.

The newspaper headlines, with deliberate hyperbolic phrasing, read, 'Boxer in dire peril, plucked from roof'.

It was an experience, and publicity I could well have lived without. When I arrived back on the ground, Frank looked at me, obviously moved, for tears welled in his eyes. Nonetheless he still quipped, 'thank God. It looked for a time, as if I would have to carry my own tools back to the yard.'

I laughed, forgotten was the terror and the ultimate shock. Frank had again put everything to rights.

Then one day the bottom dropped out of my world at work. Frank had decided to leave John Holmes to take up another position elsewhere. I couldn't go with him. I was to be left to cope with Jock Goldie on my own. Frank advised me to leave and arranged an interview for me with the large plumbing firm of Nicklins. I obtained the position and my apprenticeship papers were then transferred to that company. My final day was to be on a Friday, week's end, when most of the men employed at John Holmes would return to the yard, to finish up for the week.

I arranged with the foreman joiner, Tom Scoldy, to have as many workers as he could muster, above the plumbers' shop in Holmes work-yard. Tom and I had become firm friends, for he had complained repeatedly about the harsh, uncalled for treatment I was receiving from my own foreman.

At least fifteen men stood silently as I said my piece to Jock Goldie, listening to every word as I packed my bits of tools into my plumber's bag.

'Well, Jock, I am bound apprentice here no more,' I began, before getting to the point. 'Now I am going to see just how good you are, against someone who can hit back.'

The colour drained from his face, as I continued, 'I am going to pay you back for all the misery you have caused me, and others, by giving you a bloody good hammering.'

Jock Goldie stood there a quivering hunk, stammering excuses. His former cocky cleverness gone, he was very much aware of the silent men watching, and listening to his bleating pleas.

I didn't hit him. I didn't have to. I had beaten him out of sight. Walking out of John Holmes yard for the very last time, I felt ten foot tall. I turned to look back at Tom Scoldy. He was grinning from ear to ear and waving vigorously to me.

I knew, then, the humiliation of Jock Goldie would be general knowledge among the workers of John Holmes Ltd.

It was now 1954, I was still winning my fights and in my eighteenth year. It was also the year for me to have a tilt at the Amateur Boxing Association Championships. My call-up papers for conscripted Army Service had been deferred until I was twenty-one, and out of my apprenticeship.

This, without a doubt, was the greatest mistake I have ever made, one which I still rue all these many years later. I should have gone into the Army at eighteen and served my conscription period, instead of doing what I did.

I heard of a position going at Markham Main Colliery, I applied and obtained the job. I still missed Frank and I hadn't settled at Nicklins, besides I would be earning more down the mine. It proved to be yet another massive error of judgement.

I left Nicklins and joined the maintenance staff on day work at the pit. I loathed the job from the word go.

I had become used to working outside in the fresh air and this was the direct antithesis. Going down the mine turned out to be the most depressive period of my life. Wages earned that way is money well and truly deserved. I doubt there is a harder way to make a living. Now I could understand George's reluctance to go to work a lot better.

Regardless of all this stress, I reached the A.B.A. quarter finals by beating Dave Rent of Liverpool, at Bellevue, Manchester. All my friends and fans were present, including brother Allan.

It was Dave's first defeat in his boxing career. He was later to go to America to be managed by Al Weill, Rocky Marciano's manager.

We had taken a bus-load of people to Manchester, including Kate's young son, Tony. It was midnight by the time I had changed, and we had made the much debated decision to return home via the Snake Pass and Sheffield, crossing the Pennine Range. It was a much quicker route home, yet a risky one, for the pass often becomes blocked during the winter, and this was in December.

By the time we began the journey it had started to snow quite heavily. We pig-headedly gave the driver instructions to cross the range. We soon became too committed to turn back, being well up into the pass by then. It wasn't long after that before we became firmly wedged in a rising mountain of snow.

We all turned to with hands and tools in the freezing, driving snowfall. All in vain, it was farting against thunder. As fast as we cleared a stretch, the drifts closed in behind us.

We moved back inside the bus, the driver restarting his engine periodically, trying to warm us a little. We were in fearful trouble. As the driver switched off the bus's engine to conserve fuel, the temperature dropped rapidly, convincing us in our frightened state that someone must go for help.

God help Allan and me as well, for if anything happened to Kate's son, she would hang, draw and quarter us for certain.

Allan told us he was sure there was a large transport café, about a mile further along the road, around the next bend. Saying convincingly to everyone on board, 'a man would make it there quite easily, if he left without delay.'

'I will go, Allan,' George volunteered immediately.

Knowing his penchant for bravado, plus his unquestionable ability to land in trouble without really trying, against our better judgement we agreed he should go . . . Besides, no one else had come forward.

The driver loaned him a large pair of wellington boots, a big hat and a warm pair of mittens. Looking something like Scott of the Antarctic, George left the bus, being almost directly lost to view in the swirling snow and darkness.

We huddled together to keep warm, full of misgiving. To let George out at any time without a lead was asking for trouble.

'What can possibly go wrong?' asked Allan, evidently as concerned as we were. He added appeasingly, 'he's got strict instructions to return, if he has any doubts about not being able to make it.'

One hour later our anxiety intensified, help should have arrived, or at the very least, George ought to have returned.

'We were fools to let him go,' Allan snorted angrily.

'He is a bloody lunatic, of course he shouldn't have gone,' Pete Platts burst out. He had been a dissenter from the beginning to George's leaving the bus. Now it was a case of, 'I told you so', after the event. Tommy added his consolatory pennyworth, 'he's probably sitting there drinking hot tea, and playing the bloody hero, instead of getting some help back here.'

Silence descended on the bus, each one of us unwilling to admit Pete was probably right. There was a distinct possibility George could be in trouble somewhere out there.

One hour and a half after George had left the vehicle, we heard a slow, muted thumping from the rear of the bus.

Not having said a word to each other, the driver, Allan and myself leapt from the omnibus, ploughing our way through the heaped snow-drifts to the back of the vehicle.

George was leaning against the rear of the bus, in an extreme state of exhaustion. He was stiff with cold and barely able to move. He had lost one mitten, his hat and one wellington boot. We dragged him forcibly inside, rubbing vigorously his hands and feet to restore circulation; covering him with all the blankets we had to keep him warm. In the meantime George had passed out. As he came round, he looked up at all the worried faces clustered above him. Turning his head to look at Allan, he said dejectedly, 'Oh Allan, I went for more than two miles up that hill. There was nothing there.'

'Up the hill? You stupid bastard I said along the road, which is down the hill, not up the bleeding hill. That is the bloody direction we came from.'

Whether from sheer relief that George had survived, he could so easily have lost his life on that wild, snow-blanketed moor, or from hysteria, we laughed ourselves silly during the coldest night any of us had ever spent.

We took it in turns to walk up and down the aisle of the bus, stamping our feet, plus shaking or arms, in an effort to keep some warmth in our bodies, not letting each other sleep, by going over and over George's characteristic bloomer in heading the wrong way.

As morning came so did the bulldozers, clearing a path through the pass, for the stupid humans who had ventured through there on a night such as that.

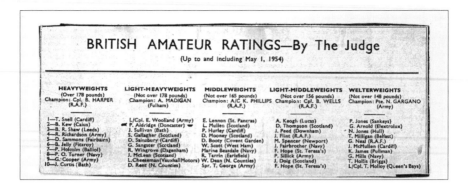

Amateur Boxing Ratings, 1954.

Thirty-odd frozen people were inside that bus as it wended its way back to Doncaster, including our intrepid adventurer, now ensconced in blankets up to his eyeballs, pretending not to hear Allan's scathing comments as we passed the transport café. 'Here it is, just as I said. A mile along the road, around the bleeding bend.'

In 1954 I fought Peter Bates, he was then the Imperial Services Heavyweight Champion. The fight was to take place on Bentley Cricket Ground, near Doncaster. Without any doubt he was the best fighter I was to meet as an amateur. (In 1957 as a fully-fledged Heavyweight Professional, he stopped Henry Cooper in the Fifth Round.)

My brother Harry, who shortly afterwards emigrated to America, warned Allan, 'he is too big, too good and far too heavy for our Boy.'

Boy was the nickname my family had given me at birth. Kate and Allan were the only other members who were dubbed with names other than those they were christened with.

Basher Bell listened to Harry's comments quietly, knowing my brother was only concerned for me. He had differing views to Harry. He had seen Bates fight and knew both our styles. 'We will beat him out of sight with speed,' was Basher's only remark. We not only beat him with speed, I dropped him twice in the last round. Peter Bates never fought again as an amateur; it was my best performance as an amateur, too.

I represented the North of England against Scotland, to knock out Sammy Gallagher in two rounds. This win put me into the semi-finals at Wembley Pool, London. I was now ranked Number Two in the Great Britain Amateur Ratings. And were my family and friends pleased with that!

Mam never watched me fight. I think she preferred to be alone at that time.

Things had become a little better financially, too. I began to plan my future.

I was Northern Counties Amateur Boxing Association Champion, while still working at Markham Main Colliery. Shirley was still employed at Wynthorpe Hall, but we minded our P's and Q's after being almost nabbed there.

Shirley and I would spend hours discussing what we'd do, after the A.B.A. Championship finals. Hopefully, I would become Light-heavyweight Champion, then turn professional, thus fulfilling the gnawing hunger for Fame and Fortune.

All boxers have this dream of reaching the dizzy heights of success, otherwise none would ever enter the ring. And yet very few are successful in achieving their aims. I was determined I would be one of the latter breed.

I would buy a house for Mam, in part-payment for all she had done without. If rewards for unselfishness had been standard practice, Mary Agnes Naughton would have been well up there in the queue. Never again a rent-man calling, or the putting to one side the money needed to keep the roof over her head.

Far from being martyr-like in her altruistic lifestyle, distrustful of displays of sentiment, at all times her sense of humour lay not far below the surface. Even through the toughest periods it came to the fore, probably at its wryest, yet it would be there.

She was born in Roscommon, Ireland, and had a coat of arms to prove it. Very proud of the name Naughton in life, we gave it back to her in death. I think Dad would approve.

As the proverbial Irish she was also prone to malapropism. The unknowing dropping of howlers added to her endearing qualities. One instance of the latter springs to mind. She was informing some race-week visitors about a pub, which is close to Armthorpe. This reputedly had connections with Dick Turpin, the highwayman.

'Dick Whittington stopped here on his ride to York,' she said proudly.

'Did he have his cat with him?' one sharp gentleman quickly asked. Ever the humorist, Mam laughed along with the rest of us.

She had nothing to laugh about for most of her years on this earth, yet laugh she did, and cause much mirth.

A heavy-faced girl would earn the quiet aside, 'you could chop sticks on her face.'

Whilst an odd-looking couple, or mismatched pair, would see Mary Agnes shaking her head ruefully in addition to saying, 'God makes them, the Devil matches them.'

Her devastatingly winning ability to categorize people and things, are among the many facets of Mam we miss. I have never forgotten her almost fanatical instructions to all of us. 'Get your shoulders back, stand straight, walk tall. You are as good as anyone else in this world.'

'Manners maketh Man, not clothes,' was another truism of hers, yet how she would have loved to be able to provide these clothes for us.

To Mary Agnes a publican epitomised all the security one could ever desire. 'Get a pub,' she would say repeatedly, 'you will always have five bob in your pocket.' A goodly sum to my Mam in those days.

Her father was a publican with the Home Brewery in Nottingham, a fearsome man he was too, believing firmly that children should be seen but not heard. He kept pigs as a sideline. Showing another face to him, he would lift Kate, Harry and Allan on to a box, so they could have a stir at the pig-swill. Mam's sister Kate also ran public houses in Sheffield. At heart Mam envied her sister, although she was more than adept at hiding the fact. Borrowing Kate's fur coat for weddings proved to be the only chink in that solid coat of armour.

At last the day dawned for the Amateur Boxing Association's Boxing Finals in London.

There were four Light-heavyweights: Tony Madigan, an Australian who had been beaten by Henry Cooper in the 1953 final; J. Sullivan from Bath, England; Corporal Eddie Woolard of the Army and, of course, myself, the Northern Counties and Scottish Champion.

I drew Woolard for the semi-finals.

Madigan beat Sullivan easily, then I stepped into the ring with Woolard. For this my big chance, both Malcolm Woodcock and Basher Bell attended me. Oh, how I wished they hadn't. For the first time their advice was faulty, their first mistake ever.

I was told to box Woolard who couldn't punch, yet he was bright enough to make the A.B.A. finals. To save myself for Madigan in the finals, who was a clever boxer, and a much tougher proposition altogether. I wasted the first two rounds, intending to finish him off in the third and final round. I would have done, too, if I could have caught him. We underestimated Woolard by a mile, he skittered around that ring like a runner. Knowing he only had to keep me at bay to win, I just couldn't nail him.

I had thrown the fight away. Little solace to know at eighteen I had the following year, whereas Woolard, at twenty-four years of age needed to win that year.

I felt I had let a bus-load of people down, friends and family who had travelled to London, and could ill afford it, to cheer me on to win the A.B.A. Light-heavyweight Champion of Great Britain title. For them, as well as for myself, I was sorry indeed. I had been defeated for the first time in three years, and not by a better fighter. Through my own stupidity I'd lost the chance to be up there. It hurt badly, doubly so as I mentally whipped myself, over losing the prize I had striven so long, and worked so hard for.

Mam greeted me sympathetically on arrival in Armthorpe, counselling, 'go out with the lads, try to forget it, there will be another day for you.'

Taking her advice, I joined Tommy and George for a night's fun on the Town. We went to see a reasonably good film, good enough to take my mind off my woes, yet for the life of me I cannot remember what it was called. After the cinema we decided to visit a café on the North Bridge. This place kept open until midnight. There were few late-closing spots in that era.

The café was crowded, it being the only meeting place for the young in Doncaster, with, as I have said, late-closing hours. We stood shoulder to shoulder, our backs against a tiled wall, chatting away quite happily, while speculatively eyeing some of the girls clustered around us.

It is a magic moment as I sit here, going back in time to the café, and the incident which occurred there. What a silly thing to happen to anyone. Yet with George anything could eventuate, and invariably did so.

In that tightly packed room, where we were minding our own business, causing trouble to no one, to this day I marvel how, or why they all had to pick on George. The only conclusion I can come to is, my friend George must carry his own poltergeist around with him. A bloody extra mischievous one at that.

I leave you to draw your own conclusions.

There we stood laughing merrily, when suddenly a woman appeared from out of the blue. She was in her mid-thirties and extremely agitated. She came and planted herself directly in front of Tommy, pointing her finger accusingly in our direction.

'That's him,' she yelled.

In the milling throng, one or two people had eased in behind us as we had turned to talk to each other. We assumed wrongly the woman meant one of them.

'That's him,' the harridan screamed again, her finger now seemingly pointed at George.

In seconds a giant of a man burst forward out of the crowd, grabbing George by the front of his jacket, crashing him backwards into the wall. Before Tommy or I could intervene he had banged George's head repeatedly at the tiles. We heard distinctly the thump, thump-thump as his head hit the wall.

'Eh, what the hell is going one?' I shouted.

Too stunned to do much else, I couldn't believe what I was actually seeing anyway. I tried to reach the man, to stop this brutish attack on George. Before I could, the woman grabbed hold of his arm fiercely, this time yelling, 'not him, *him*,' pointing clearly to a dishevelled man standing slightly to the rear of George.

This fellow having witnessed what had happened to my mate, wasted no time in bolting for the exit, closely followed by the enraged giant. Poor George, released from the big man's hold, slid down the wall slowly, into a collapsed heap resembling a straw doll.

He was out to the world.

We found out later, the scruffily-dressed man had felt the backside of the irate woman who, not being of Latin origin, was far from flattered by his attentions. Just prior to our arrival she had gone in search of her husband, the giant, to complain about the unsolicited familiarity from the slovenly would-be Casanova. Out of at least 150 people, it had to be George who became so violently a victim of mistaken identity. George sported a lump the size of a cricket ball at the back of his head, besides not feeling very well at all.

The proprietor of the café, a man I knew well, was full of apologies, even though the incident wasn't due to mismanagement. He offered to drive us home to Armthorpe, as George was certainly in no condition for further entertainment. We gladly accepted the offer. It hadn't been our day.

Talking to Pete Platts the following afternoon, I told him of the incident at the North Bridge café.

'Now you know why I won't go out with the silly sod, you are liable to get bloody killed. He is a bloody, walking catastrophe,' Pete chortled.

To me George was better than any tonic obtained from a doctor. He had the ability to cheer me up just by being present. He could make me laugh even when my spirits hit rock bottom. I reckoned he was the best mate any man could wish for, and I still do. My boxing boots were polished by George to a mirror-like slick sheen. His prideful way of following me to the ring, saying stupid things, they automatically took my mind off the coming event. All the butterflies vanishing when he was in attendance. The worried look he wore when he thought the fight wasn't going my way, the sunny splendour he exhibited when he thought it was. To me George had made himself indispensable.

I was coming to the end of my amateur boxing career. Bruce Woodcock, the former Heavyweight Champion of Great Britain, Doncaster's home-bred hero, wanted me to turn professional. I was to have only four more amateur fights.

One of those was in London. I won by a knock-out in the second round. At the very last moment the prizes were presented by George Raft, film star and famous American tough guy. He handed me my award, saying in the gangster-like drawl he'd made so very much his, 'you are good.'

I was amazed at how small he was. I realize now they fit the scenery better, most top-flight stars being around five and a half foot tall. However, it does destroy the image a little, when you realize that any tall man need only to hold out his arm, and let them play with that. No matter how good a boxer they couldn't reach him.

I met George Raft again many years later and shook his hand. I like to think he had remembered me, the star-struck kid that had a punch. My lovely Mam ran around our street, telling everyone our Boy has met George Raft.

In the next fight I represented the National Coal Board against Birmingham Industries. This was in the era of Sir Bernard Docker and the effervescent, flamboyant Lady Docker, of the gold Rolls Royce fame. Lady Docker was a former barmaid who hadn't quite lost the common touch, I do not mean that facetiously, for whatever Lady Docker was, I believe it to be due to her sheer exuberance for living. The lifestyle which both she and her husband enjoyed so openly motivated all her actions.

The night I met the Dockers I was to fight and beat a boxer named Moran, at the Crystal Palace, Sutton Coldfield, Birmingham. After the events all the boxers had been invited to a dinner in Birmingham.

As soon as the sumptuous meal was over, Lady Docker jumped up on to the table, and began to dance along its full length high spiritedly. She danced directly above me, her skirts flaring widely. Admiring the view, I remarked appreciatively to Ernie Baker, who was a very good Middleweight boxer, and was also sitting next to me, 'she has a smashing pair of legs, for a woman in her late forties.' Oh, the arrogance of youth, I considered that time of life almost qualified her for the old age pension, I don't think she would have been flattered by my rudeness.

Far from being written off in the age stakes, she vivaciously presented all the prizes. Her energy continued boundless throughout the evening, putting me and a few others into the shade as far as staying power is concerned.

Sir Bernard looked on with warm affection, though to this day I still believe he must have had a hard time keeping up with his lady in all spheres. She lacked most inhibitions, cuddling and kissing you on the cheek. It was virtually impossible not to be affected by her friendly, so vibrant personality.

My penultimate amateur fight was against a boxer by the name of Dougie Swain, an experienced Heavyweight. George Meehan provided the *coup de grâce* to my amateur career, as only he could.

Malcolm Woodcock had started to allow George to take into the ring, and to second boys in the ten to twelve year old division. George had undertaken the mantle of officialdom easily, and with a great deal of self-important flourish. He was unfortunately harassed by Pete Platts, who without fail, whenever George led his lad into the ring, bellowed, 'good Old Gunga.'

Now this was not only in reference to Gunga Din, but also poking a stick into George's wounded vanity over the spilled water fiasco at Pudsey Baths.

The people present thought they had come to watch a boxing match in the Corn Exchange, Doncaster. They were in for much more sophisticated entertainment, slapstick of the first order.

George upstaged the boxers as only he knew how.

I was having my legs rubbed down by Malcolm Woodcock and Basher

Bell, when George left the dressing room carrying his bucket, and escorting the young contender to the ringside.

In amateur boxing all boxers wear a red or blue sash to differentiate between the fights. It is the second's job to see the sash is in place before leaving for the ring.

On this occasion George had forgotten to tie this around his young charge. The fight was well under way when the referee noticed its omission. According to Pete Platts, the referee yelled, 'stop the fight, this boy has no sash.'

George embarrassed beyond measure, grabbed his boxer, bunging him on to the stool in his corner, and tore off up the aisle back to the dressing room. Hot and flustered he dashed into the room shouting, 'give me a bloody sash quick.'

Grabbing the offending article, he pelted back to the ringside, all the while being hassled and bullied by the hundreds of impatient fight fans. Pete reckoned poor George looked close to tears. The Corn Exchange was packed to capacity as usual. Most of those present were Yorkshire stalwarts, well known for their inability to suffer fools gladly.

George, after running the gauntlet of jeering supporters, climbed back into the ring and tied the sash around his protégé, leaving the ring again as the timekeeper called, 'seconds out . . . Time.'

The poor boy tried to obey the command, but couldn't move, George had tied him very securely to the ring post.

The Corn Exchange erupted at this hilarious pantomime being enacted before their disbelieving eyes. George, back inside the ring again, tried to undo the knot, all the while shaking like a leaf. To a stream of laughter and catcalls, the sash had to be snapped, another sash being hurriedly brought from the dressing room for the discomfited unfortunate lad.

In spite of having George for a second, the boy won his match. More than likely being fighting mad at the crowd, he had taken it out of his opponent. Some good always comes out of misfortune, or so they say. Though I don't think my mate would have seconded that.

George came back to the dressing room with his victorious ward, apparently unmoved now by the continuing ribaldry as he left the room.

His only concern now was the media, 'I hope this doesn't get into the newspapers,' he said seriously, as everyone in the dressing room fell about with uncontrollable mirth. I knocked out Swain in the first round, in front of a crowd who would have preferred to see George performing.

Peter Aldridge, 1954. Age 18 years.

My last amateur fight was in Hull. Again I knocked out my opponent in the first round.

To large headlines in the Doncaster papers, I turned professional with Bruce Woodcock as my manager, another move I was to wholeheartedly regret later.

Basher Bell berated me, 'you should have waited for another year. One more bloody year, that's all. You could have been A.B.A. Light-heavyweight Champion of Great Britain next year.'

'It's too late for that, I am ready now,' I asserted arrogantly.

'I'm good enough to take on the best of the professionals, you wait and see.'

What a foolish young man I was.

Chapter 2

THE year was 1955 and this was a different world, amateur and profes- sional boxing are poles apart. The code of honour and sportsmanship does not apply. It is kill or be killed, a cruel, unrelenting, mercenary game where one tries to pummel one's opponent into oblivion long after they are capable of self defence . . . All try to satisfy the spectators' insatiable blood lust.

My first professional fight was at Willenhall, near Wolverhampton, the local boy, Ray Evans, my first opponent. I won by a knock-out in the first round, returning to Doncaster to a blaze of newspaper headlines. I had dropped Evans with the first punch of the fight. Cockily I thought if they are all going to be this easy, my fortune was already in the bank.

They were not.

My sister Kate heard recently a boxer of world repute state on television, 'no one would enter a boxing ring purely for money.'

I'm sorry, I beg to differ. Unequivocally, and most emphatically I state, only a bloody fool would go in for any other reason.

My next antagonist, an old campaigner called Denis Fewkes, gave me my first insight of what lay ahead of me as a professional boxer. The fight was staged in Nottingham, at the Nottingham Ice Rink. I tried to nail him from the very beginning, frustrated to all hell as he broke every rule in the book. Hanging on, using his weight to turn me away from the referee, he thumbed me in the eye. In short, proving to me that life was going to be decidedly tougher in the world of professional fighters.

I won easily on points, yet he was a professional survivor. I was to meet many more of his ilk before my fighting days were over.

Bruce Woodcock had placed me on a very good Bill for my second match. Top of the agenda was Jack Gardener versus Johnny Williams, both former Heavyweight Champions. Other notables appearing that night were, Henry Cooper, Peter Bates and Joe Bygraves. However my purse for the four rounds amounted to £25. Twenty-five quid well earned, I thought ruefully, my eye still smarting from Fewkes' thumb.

I had much to learn, that was only Lesson one. Lesson two came next.

My third fight was against Peter Woodward at Birmingham. It was held in the Birmingham Indoor Stadium. I set about Woodward, determined this would not be another Fewkes underestimation. So much so I left myself wide-open. I put him down and stood back for the count, until he regained his feet, ready to put him down again should he do so. When, Bang, I was hit by the hardest right I have ever taken. Down I went, I got up almost immediately but stood uselessly, with my hands down. The referee stopped the fight.

After 104 fights as an amateur, winning 101 of them, I had been t.k.o'd, (technical knock-out) for the first time.

Returning to Doncaster, feeling as if the bottom had dropped out of my world, I was greeted by large headlines in the *Yorkshire Evening News*, 'Aldridge stopped in First Round.'

Everyone loves a winner, I took more of a ribbing from my workmates than I thought any man should be asked to endure. I was a big, burst balloon, a tall poppy cut down to ground level. Full of self-pity and bewilderment, yet getting angrier by the minute.

Bruce Woodcock arranged a return bout with Woodward, at the Corn Exchange in Doncaster, my old happy hunting ground. I trained under Basher Bell as I had never trained before, determined to avenge myself on both opponent and fans alike.

To a packed house I savoured that revenge, and how wonderful it felt to vindicate myself. I hit him with all the power I had in my right hand, down he went. This time there would be no getting up, he just lay there, beyond caring.

It was all over in the first round.

Entering 1956 I began training with professionals, this way getting more experience, which hopefully would gain faster for me, that elusive prize of fame and fortune.

One night around ten-thirty, my mother woke me up. It was early to bed in those days, for after training Basher's instructions were always, 'bed.'

'There is someone here to see you, Boy. They are downstairs,' Mam said. Throwing on some clothes, I hurried down to see who my visitors were. In Mam's front room stood Bruce Woodcock with his brother Billy.

'How about Hugh Fearns tomorrow night?' Bruce wasted no time in asking, as I entered the room.

'He's too big for me,' I answered nonplussed.

Fearns was the Scottish Heavyweight Champion. He had just beaten Dick Richardson, who later became the European Champion.

'You will run rings around him,' Bruce flatteringly asserted.

I knew Fearns was to have fought Brian London and that London had withdrawn because of an ankle injury. They weren't kidding me for a moment, I would fill the void left by London; no more, no less.

'You will be Top of the Bill at St James's Hall, Newcastle,' Bruce coaxed. 'Two hundred and eighty quid. You can get the Crombie overcoat you have wanted for so long,' Billy chimed in.

Did these men know me! Two hundred and eighty quid, my mind boggled. I had never seen that much money, let alone owned it. It was also common knowledge, plus being a cause for joshing, how I envied Bruce and his beautiful Crombie coat.

I had asked unashamedly, how much a coat like that would cost eyeing the garment covetously on every opportune moment. Most successful boxers owned one at that time. It became a symbol of their status and prosperity. How very hungry I was for the success which could buy that prestige.

I agreed to fight Fearns. There was one obstacle to surmount first. I was a Light-heavyweight, weighing just twelve stones six pounds. Fearns weighed fifteen stones seven and a half pounds. The British Boxing Board of Control would never allow such a massive weight difference. Billy had an answer for this dilemma. He suggested I wore a lead window-sash, equivalent to fourteen pounds, tied around my waist to hang down my groin, under my shorts.

This was a brilliant scheme accepted by all, until we found out the weigh-in was to be in the centre of the ring, in St James's Hall. Undeterred, I agreed to go through with the subterfuge. I walked stiff-legged up the aisle to the ring, climbing awkwardly through the ropes.

An astute reporter noticed my ungainly movements, and asked sharply, 'something wrong, Aldridge?'

Bruce jumped in front of me, blocking the reporter's view, 'he is just stiff after travelling on the train,' he assured the man.

As I climbed on to the scales, the announcer shouted, 'Aldridge, thirteen

Bruce Woodcock and Peter Aldridge, Woodcock's Gym, Doncaster, 1955.

stones six pounds. Fearns, fifteen stones seven and a half pounds,' as my opponent stepped on to the scales.

The fight was on.

I hurried as fast as I could go to the dressing room, to remove the bloody weight, for it had rubbed the whole of my groin raw.

I really hadn't believed Bruce, when he'd said I could run rings around Fearns. I believed it expedient for Bruce to find a replacement for Brian London, and I was it.

I was wrong again. He was right, I gave Fearns a boxing lesson that night, even though I was going backwards for eight rounds. He did all the pressing, all six feet four inches of him. I had no choice but to pack-pedal and try to out-box him. He was far too big in every way for me.

At the start of the contest when the referee called us together, there was an outburst of laughter at the difference in size. Beside his bulk I must have resembled a bloody midget.

At the end of the fight there was very loud booing, as the referee raised both our arms aloft to signal a draw. I had clearly won, yet Fearns' constant attacking pressure earned him a draw.

Bruce gloated, 'what did I tell you? I said you would run rings around him.'

That night, on the train travelling back to Doncaster, I found out at first hand the truth in the gossip about the Woodcock's tightness, as far as money was concerned. All the expenses came off the top, before division of Prize money. Train fares for three, meals for three, transport, et cetera. The manager then takes his cut, twenty-five per cent. The fellow who has probably taken the thumping, receives what is left. In my case it was about £150, almost half of the carrot offered to persuade me to fight such a massive fellow. Nevertheless, it was still more money than I had ever possessed. To my sorrow it was still not enough to buy that beautiful Crombie coat.

The next morning I awoke to voices outside my bedroom window. It was 10 a.m. and Mary Agnes was doing her usual thing of informing the neighbours about my recent achievement.

'How did Peter go on?' came the voice of Mrs Oller, from across the road. She had obviously missed Mam's earlier narration.

'Oh,' Mam said, enjoying going over it all a second time, 'it was a draw, and do you know he had to box with a fourteen pound lead weight inside his trunks.'

'Oo'er, what did they make him do that for?'

'Some sort of handicap,' Mam answered, no doubt having racehorses in mind.

Good old Mam, she had got it all wrong again, in spite of my telling her it was only for the weigh-in.

I got out of bed and shut the window. Chortling, I tried to go back to sleep. It would have done no good at all to try to explain. Once Mary Agnes had got the bit between her teeth, it was her story and she was sticking to it.

After the Fearns fight I fought Ted Williams in the Town Hall, Leeds. I was disqualified for a low punch.

I exonerated myself later by defeating him over eight rounds, that fight being broadcast by the B.B.C. as the Fight of the Week.

In 1956 I was Top of the Bill at the Yarmouth Hippodrome, Great Yarmouth, fighting Neville Rowe, a very tough fighter from Australia. It was the end of the summer season, and so very hot and close in that Hall. The fight was over eight rounds. Towards the end I just stood there pushing

Peter Aldridge in 1956, aged 21 years.

Rowe off me, and landing yet another punch. He refused to go down, he took an incredible amount of punishment, an extremely hard bloke to beat. I won on points.

This match earned me a fight against Tony Dove at Harringay Arena, in London. I lost on points. I felt so disgusted by this decision, for Dove also thought I had won, looking extremely surprised as the referee held his hand high.

It was around this time things started to go really wrong for me, I broke the forefinger of my right hand in two places, whilst at work. It was the originator of long frustrating months, squeezing a rubber ball with my right hand to make the forefinger bend to form a fist.

Looking back I am convinced that was the end of the powerful punch I had packed into my right hand. No longer would Basher say, 'hell's fire, you will knock down whoever you hit.'

Regardless I resumed my boxing career.

I was on the same Bill as Randolph Turpin and Alex Buxton. They were Top of the Programme at Granby Hall, Leicester, for their title fight. I fought Abe Stanley over eight rounds and again I only managed to draw. However Stanley had remained undefeated after twenty fights. He was not a pushover by any means. I calculated the experience could only do me good.

Yet there were other worrying things wrong with me physically. I was aware of abnormal sensations in my nose and eyes, my right hand still troubled me. In spite of all this I still persisted in chasing the dream.

In 1957 I was paid sparring partner to Henry Cooper for two of his title fights. One was against Ingamar Johannson in Sweden. Cooper was knocked out in the fifth round. The other fight was against Joe Bygraves, who beat Henry over eight rounds.

Really you couldn't exactly say I was a good luck charm for Cooper. I wasn't employed as a talisman though. Jim Wicks, Henry's manager, hired me for speed. Henry did his real sparring with the heavy mob, Nosher Powell, Owen Brady, George Nafugh, a Tongan Heavyweight, plus his brother Jim Cooper. I was the only Light-Heavyweight among them, going into the ring last each day, when Henry was beginning to tire. I was fast and I was glad of my speed too, it proved to be easy work for Cooper just couldn't catch me. I made sure of that.

The other poor bastards got the shit knocked out of them. Henry was a bloody hard man in the ring. Owen Brady quit, going home early, fed-up. It wasn't only the punishing routine. Jim Wicks was a poor payer. At the Thomas-à-Becket in Old Kent Road, London, I received two pounds a round, for my three rounds per day. Six pounds daily, hardly a fortune for getting my head knocked off if Henry caught me.

Henry Cooper, the original nice guy outside the ring, remained that way to this day they tell me. A good-living quiet, hard-training man it remains impossible to be envious of.

He lost a lot of fights and still made a fortune. I do not think he won a match in 1957. Then the Heavyweight scene changed. He hung in there, cleaning up against poor opposition, and of course the money improved out of sight.

To my knowledge Peter Bates and I are the only two boxers to have been in the ring, with both Bruce Woodcock and Henry Cooper. Peter Bates was also managed by Bruce. I sparred with Bruce long after he had finished boxing of course. Peter Bates did the same, only with Henry he fought him as a professional in 1957, knocking him out.

Believe me, I like Henry Cooper but he would never have seen the day, when he could have beaten Woodcock. Henry was a one-armed bandit. Bruce boxed with both hands and both hurt. Henry's jaw and face could not have stood up to Woodcock's savage hammering. The fight would have been a very short-lived bloody one.

Bruce is still alive and well, still living in the Doncaster area, and quite financially sound. He was a fighter who looked after his money. No one kidded Bruce into throwing lavish parties after a fight, as they did with the ill-fated Freddie Mills. Bruce's words over the national radio, still recalled by those who knew him, were uttered from the ring after every big fight. 'won't be long, Mam. Get the tea ready.'

Bruce's matches with Mauriello, Baxi, Savold, Lesnovitch and Mills brought him big money. Never a lady's man, he was married to Nora, a girl who was just as careful with money as he was.

A story told by Ted Greenslade, his main sparring partner for years, went the rounds joyously.

They were in London for the Savold fight, Bruce always stayed at the five-star Regent Palace Hotel in Piccadilly. (Why not—the tax-man was paying, through expense allowance.) He had bought two heavy leather suitcases in America, and as Ted said:

'He had everything except the kitchen sink in them. I carried them off King's Cross station, I wouldn't want to carry them again anywhere. On our arrival at the hotel, a small bell-boy hurried to the taxi to carry the baggage inside.' Ted continued, 'I looked at the poor little bugger, and thought this is going to be funny. Wait until he gets hold of those bloody bags. As he grasped the handles of the suitcases, his face changed, he staggered to the reception desk followed by Bruce and his entourage (Billy, me and old Sam Woodcock). The latter was Bruce's father, who puffed and blowed asthmatically as he moved.

'The bell-boy tottered to the lift, then along a long passage to Bruce's suite of rooms. On entering the lad dropped the loaded bags, standing with heaving chest, red-faced and shaking, the veins in his small hands stood out as if varicose. I could see the pressure welts the cases had left on those hands,' Ted said pityingly.

'Bruce dug deep into his trouser pocket, pulling out sixpence he placed it on the waiting boy's outstretched palm. The lad looked unbelievingly at the tanner still on his sore, open hand as he left the room, patently expecting more from the British, Empire, and European Heavyweight Champion.

'All were silent apart from Sam's wheezing, when Billy's sharp voice came echoing from the bathroom, "eh up, Bruce! Our old man could have carried the bags, he can do with all them tanners."'

To his dying day Ted Greenslade swore it was a true story. Knowing the Woodcocks as I did then, it would not surprise me in the least.

This aside, Bruce was a shy man, who disliked the back-slapping, hand-shaking part of being a celebrity. I think he held it in deep distrust. Money was the only recompense asked for what he did. An instance comes to mind to underline the above. We were travelling by train, first-class to Newcastle. Bruce, as tight as he was reputed to be, refused to travel any other way, not because of comfort or snobbery. It provided anonymity, the most important criterion. Besides, the tax-man would no doubt be footing the bill.

Although he had been retired for six years, he still received a whole heap of adulatory attention. As we sat in our first-class isolation, a small boy knocked on the window leading to the corridor. I pushed the sliding door open, the smiling child stepped forward, asking, 'please, Mr Woodcock, can I have your autograph?'

'This is Mr Woodcock,' I answered pointing to Bruce.

Woodcock without a word to the boy, signed his usual, 'Best Wishes Bruce Woodcock'. As soon as the lad left the compartment, Bruce snapped 'get them blinds down, Peter, and the door jammed.'

We sat in the half-light all the way to Newcastle, my foot holding the door shut. Bruce, the retiring man, even if it meant discomfort for him and others, determinedly intent on preserving his privacy at any price.

There was still another side to Bruce's character, just as illuminative. Years later, as I stood with him among the mourners, at Freddie Mills funeral, Jack Solomons came up to us crying his eyes out, he fell sobbing on to Bruce's shoulder, 'three weeks ago, Freddie asked me to loan him some money.'

'Then why the bloody hell didn't you lend it to him?' snarled Bruce contemptuously.

Solomons snubbed, stared at Bruce amazed, before walking away still snivelling.

'He bloody got it,' Bruce grated, 'Freddie helped to make his sodding fortune.'

Everybody loved Freddie Mills, the nicest, friendliest chap imaginable. Bruce had also a strong dislike of Solomons, he never trusted him. I think it stemmed from the days when Solomons promoted all Bruce's big fights. Never a man to mince words, Bruce is and was, a bluff outspoken, yet truthful Yorkshireman to the core.

My boxing career now on the wane, I lost with a cut eye to Neville Rowe, the Australian, in a return bout. My right hand wasn't good, the peculiar sensation in my nose and eyes becoming steadily worse. After sparring with Henry Cooper for the second time in 1957, I was matched against Ted Williams for the third time, this time the contest was to be held at Doncaster Race Course. Joe Erskine versus Peter Bates topped the Bill.

I had beaten Williams pretty easily the last time we had met and I was more than confident I could repeat that performance.

Something went terribly wrong. After the first punch Williams caught me with I immediately had double vision, the most physically frightening experience of my life.

I saw two Ted Williams, two referees, plus two of everything else. There was no way I could defend myself, let alone go on the attack. I went round after round, backing away from the double image of Ted, who, sensing victory, tried to catch me long enough to put me down. Each time I returned to my corner, I heard Basher Bell, from his seat below me, urging my second, 'pull him out. What is the matter with him?'

In the end he resorted to shouting his protest, insisting the second should throw in the towel. All in vain, I fought to the bitter end, or rather, I tried to keep out of the way of the two Williams who were intent on putting me on the canvas.

I went the distance, losing on points.

Back in the dressing room, my sight returned to normal and I insisted I could drive myself home. I stubbornly resisted all attempts by Allan and George, to play chauffeur for me, yet in the end I was forced to concede.

Driving along Sandringham Road, a major connecting route from the racecourse, my sight went again, causing me to swerve wildly all over the place. Allan grabbed the wheel. Fiercely rejecting all argument, he drove straight to Doncaster Infirmary.

I was admitted to hospital there and then. I had a swollen blood vessel pressing on the optic nerve between my eyes. An operation the next day put it right. I was more fortunate than others, although I wasn't aware of the fact at the time.

Something else had happened during the previous evening's boxing bouts. A young fighter named Jackie Tiller, collapsed during the course of his fight with Eric Brett. He was rushed to the Infirmary, later to be transferred to Sheffield in a vain attempt to save him. He died there three days later.

Two serious injuries on one Bill, one of them fatal. It was inevitable there would be repercussions.

The British Boxing Board reacted with speed, as the newspaper headlines screamed out for boxing to be banned, before there were other deaths. At an annual meeting in London, a Mrs Dora Cussins, a chairwoman of the

Yorkshire Federation of Townswomen's Guild, obtained 4,000 pledges to have boxing made illegal.

All hell appeared to have broken loose. Mam's house and garden being literally taken over by news-hungry reporters. Though what they thought Mary Agnes could tell them, God alone knows.

The Boxing Board, anxious to save the sport, responded. Two promotions were cancelled as they undertook a full inquiry. Meanwhile I was to be suspended. I never boxed again. Dr McIntosh, the examining doctor, a tough, no nonsense, straight-talking man, giving his opinion said, 'it could happen again, and you would most probably die.'

Mam, all the family, and Shirley, to whom I was now engaged, wanted me to leave the fight game. Reluctantly I accepted their advice though I was heartbroken. It seemed like the end of the world, hope gone, I hadn't realized how I loved the sport. I had seen it only as the means to an end. Now it was over and everything it stood for was lost. It enabled me to meet people which ordinarily I could never hope to meet. Boxing, in its way, had been good to me and I would miss it sadly. I did not know then it would open the door to another career, a no less exciting one.

However that was in the distant future. Then, I hated the job at the colliery, constantly searching for an alternative method of earning a living.

Shirley and I married in 1958. We bought a semi-detached house in Dunsville, a few houses away from Shirley's mother, both of us working all hours to meet the mortgage repayments.

We had a daughter, Jacqueline, born in 1959, Shirley working up to the last few days of her pregnancy. We could afford very little in the way of furnishings. It took a long, long time to furnish that small house, and even then only meagrely.

Yet we loved each other and were happy, going without to keep our roof. As with Mam and everyone else around us, for even as today, it was the accepted norm.

Who worries about such things anyway, when every waking moment one thinks about what may have been. I still had an unquenchable fire in my belly to reach the top of the heap. All my life I have striven to climb the insurmountable. In my own way I guess I have reached the apex of the mountain which I have had to climb.

My mother worried constantly because of my working down the mine, and not without due cause. My brother Harry, the only member of our family to become a miner, had got out of the pit after losing part of a finger at the coal-face. My own career was brought to naught, mostly attributable to my breaking of a forefinger down the mine.

Far from least, my cousin, Tommy Naughton, had been killed by a runaway wagon, only three years earlier. A quiet lad who wouldn't say boo to a goose, and a favourite of Mam.

The compensation paid to his parents, for the loss of this loving son, a boy barely out of his teens, was duly cut because Tommy answered a question put by one of his colleagues, while being carried from the mine. The man asked solicitously, 'are you all right, Tommy?'

Not really an appropriate enquiry, yet one full of concern.

Apparently Tommy had answered, 'yes.'

Far from all right, his inside terribly crushed, Tommy died on the way to the hospital. His father wanted the pittance he would have received, to erect a gravestone over his son. He bought the stone, but it meant many more hours down the pit for Uncle Jimmy. Double shifts and all the danger that implied, for he wasn't a young man.

The same as his sister, Mary Agnes, he too wanted remembrance after death for his son. Puzzled still by the inconsistency, Kate always visits her uncle's own marker, a rose bush. Jimmy was cremated. She doesn't know the answer, and neither do I.

The criterion for compensation for being killed in the mine, when Tommy died, was in exact accordance with the letter of the law. One must die within the confines of the pit. Modest, polite Tommy had spoken.

When people judge miners for their actions, they must take into account the treatment meted out to them over the years by ruthless mine-owners, from the Lock-outs to the Buttie-system; to the government owned industry, with mindless men making the rules. Consider well the dangers they face every time they enter the black hole; corroded lungs and maiming, being just a part.

In 1960, my mother the best friend a man could ever wish for, received an insurance pay-out of £1,250. 'If this will get you out of the mine, you can have £1,000 to assist you in getting started in some kind of business,' she said. Who ever had a better mother than that?

The three of us pondered for days, Mam, Shirley and I coming up with lots of different suggestions, only to have them thrown out because of insufficient capital, high-flown ideas or their unviability.

At that particular time, a motorway to bypass Doncaster was under construction, we had heard lorries were required to remove the rubble from the site.

This appeared to be our best option. We decided to buy a couple of old tipper trucks. I was to drive one, and employ George to operate the other.

I can guess what you are thinking, one could envisage no more unlikely candidate for such a position than George. He had left the mine some time previously, acquiring a heavy vehicle driving licence, and most importantly he was available. Whereas Allan, by then, was earning very good money long-distance lorry driving for a local company; I really could not expect him to throw away his job to join a risky new enterprise like ours.

Looking back I am glad he didn't join us. It was a fizzle from the beginning, although Allan's expertise may well have delayed the inevitable, helping to keep it afloat a little longer.

Pete Platts was by then an insurance salesman and I promised him he could have the insurance of the trucks. When he heard George was to be the other driver, he was incredulous. Committed to insuring the lorries, he pleaded, 'oh, no! You must be out of your bloody mind, he will run over somebody. He will kill somebody for sure. Do not do it, Peter.'

Well, George did not do that. Mind you, it is about the only bloody thing he did not do.

Chapter 3

THE haulage business was a highly competitive business. To get an 'A' licence was far beyond our means. Breaking into the trade, which was a desirable, extremely lucrative profession, either with an 'A' or 'B' licence, we found to be well-nigh impossible. It was a closed shop, the large established companies cutting out the little man. One was left with no alternative except to sub-contract from them. However, before we could do this, we had to obtain road licences to carry. These were in three categories: A, B and C.

With an 'A' one could transport goods anywhere; 'B' you were licensed to carry within a radius of thirty to forty miles; 'C' was to haul your own goods only.

We worked very hard to gain and buy two 'B' licences, with authority to transport within a radius of thirty miles from our home point. Thus making sixty miles as the crow flies. We went deep into debt to buy two new vehicles. To get the sub-contract we had to prove we had reliable lorries.

At home, Shirley worked feverishly to secure work for us, for we would be unable to meet the repayments on the trucks if they weren't earning. The only work available was sub-contracting construction site haulage. We were soon to learn the hard way why this was procurable too. We had originally wanted to buy two old tipper trucks and do this type of work. Alas, one couldn't set oneself up as a haulage contractor. As I have said sub-contracting was the only way in, with the larger companies calling the tune.

The business soon became a nightmare beyond all one's comprehension. On top of the normal running repairs, we had busted half-shafts, backends, gear-boxes, mostly due to the type of carrying we were engaged in. Huge rocks and ungraded rubble loaded by uncaring, earth-moving equipment operators, were only part of the cause. The rough terrain of the construction site also took its toll creating incalculable damage, the tyres being just a part of this.

Then we had George's driving to contend with, compounding an already precarious situation. If ever there was an understatement, worthy of mention, then I have just made it.

Flogging ourselves to death, working impossible hours, willing to do almost anything, carry anything, in our desperation. Yet it was still not enough to make ends meet.

Paying George's wages was an added worry, for he, too, was married with a young family to support, and so could not take a cut in pay. All the while we were sinking further and further into debt.

George provided a little light relief, as was his wont. This we needed, yet I have to look back at the incidents with barely a smile. Humour had little place in our lives at that time, and even now the hurt remains, a constant source of sorrow.

On this particular day, Shirley had managed to gain work for both trucks, hauling loads of sand from a quarry near Finningly Air Force Base, to a building site in Doncaster. George and I would pass each other half-way between each point, I would be watching anxiously until he drove into view; for I never knew what he would get up to when I was out of sight. Everything went swimmingly, until mid-afternoon, George failed to appear at the place expected; I scanned the road intently all the way to the site in Doncaster, worried in case he had broken down, hit something, or hopefully just skived off for a few minutes.

On arrival at the site, a large empty field, in the centre of which stood a massive cement mixer, our instructions were to tip the sand around the perimeter of the meadow, a good hundred yards from this machine. Yet George's truck, my Bedford, was leaning against the mixer. I tipped my load in the allotted place and walked over to George and the foreman of the site. A right royal argument was under way between the two of them. Turning from George, the foreman addressed me, his voice carried the utmost disgust.

'He is a bloody idiot. He has managed to hit the only bloody thing in the whole field. Ask him how he did it?'

Now I could see the side-wing of the Bedford was crushed in. Angrily I whipped on George, 'what the bloody hell were you doing in the middle of the field?'

'Peter, I only drove past it, to see what it looked like close up.'

The mournful expression of old, deepened on his face as he continued, 'the lorry slid into it as I passed.'

'I put the bloody thing in the middle of the field, to keep it out of harm's way,' the foreman swore. 'Christ, I didn't reckon on a bloody imbecile showing up.'

'You had no right to go anywhere near it,' I rebuked George furiously.

'I have never witnessed anything so bloody daft,' the foreman marvelled, looking scathingly at George.

George, unabashed, answered in his unmistakable way, 'well, what did you put it in the field for? You haven't started to build yet, have you? If you hadn't put it there, I couldn't have hit it, could I?'

There was just no answer for that kind of logic. Looking at me in exasperation, the foreman shook his head and walked away.

As many before him, and even more unfortunates after, he had learned the uselessness of trying to understand George's cock-eyed reasoning. George could always find an excuse to shift the blame, no matter how ridiculous it sounded, for every calamity he brought about.

In spite of all the trouble, what a smashing fellow he was. I mean that figuratively, besides his being a smasher literally.

Again we had been working from a quarry, on this occasion George ran his lorry in between two stone bunkers, instead of going around them. Needless to say he got the truck stuck, stopping production for a whole half a day.

An irate boss told me, 'if you send that maniac here again, I'll strangle the silly bugger.'

George seemed unmoved by such venomous passion, 'how did I know I couldn't get the tipper through?' he asked the boss.

Yet another quarry incident occurred during the winter months.

I arrived at the quarry to find George stripped naked in the foreman's office, his clothes hung over a fire drying. He resembled a drowned rat.

'What's happened?' I asked foolishly.

'I was working with our lorry, waiting to be loaded, and looking at the ice covering the pond. I just walked on to it to find out if it would hold me.'

'Well, now you know, you silly bugger,' I swore at him.

Still more work and time lost, yet I could never have fired George, he was worth his keep if only for light relief.

It wasn't long after the latter incident, we had been running between Alverly Hall Quarries and Thorpe Marsh Power Station with white stone.

George and I were working together, as I had learned it was by far the best method to keep him in line.

At around 4 p.m. the foreman asked me, 'Peter, will you make your last run with small graded stone, to Selby?' Selby was a distance of about thirty miles from the quarry, I could easily load, make the run and unload, while it was still daylight.

'Let me do it, Peter,' George chimed in, 'I need the overtime badly.'

Ever the consummate soft-touch for a hard luck story, I agreed.

'Go on then, you should be back by 6.30–7 p.m. Watch what you are doing and keep out of bloody trouble,' I cautioned him. What a stupid thing to say or expect of George, whose middle name should have been trouble—a man, who seeing a chasm open in front of him, wouldn't accept it as a hole in the ground. Child-like he'd step into it as a place to be explored.

Do not mistake my meaning, George was not mentally retarded in any way. As some people cannot differentiate between right and wrong, so George lacked the normal ability to foresee the consequences of his own actions. Curiosity would get the better of him every time. The over-sized chip on his shoulder meant he couldn't admit to fault either. The subsequent loss of face, would have destroyed his own mental image of himself. That sounds a bit heavy, yet to this day I believe it to be true.

That night with George doing the Selby run, I had an early night. It was around 6.30 p.m. and we had just sat down to dinner, when the phone rang. It was George.

'Can you come to Selby straight away, Peter, I've got trouble. You will have to sort it out, I can't.'

He gave me the address. It was the same place he was supposed to deliver the stone to, a private house where they were having a driveway installed.

'What's up, George,' I shouted, but to a disengaged line. George had hung up.

I ran for the car, leaving my dinner, and shouting to Shirley, 'he's in bloody trouble again.' I didn't have to say who *he* was.

Selby was roughly sixteen miles from where we lived. For all of that distance I repeated hopelessly to myself, 'George, what the bloody hell have you done this time?'

There was no mistaking the house, a pile of white stone led me to it. As

I approached I could see a very large man gesticulating at George, the latter trying very hard to keep a group of people between himself and the man.

As I stopped the car, George ran over the road to me, 'watch this clever bastard, Peter,' he said worriedly.

I noticed he kept behind me as I approached the growing crowd of onlookers.

'You his boss?' the large man asked.

'Yes,' I replied, asking politely, 'What's the trouble?'

'What about this stone?'

'What about it, is it the wrong kind?' I assumed he was objecting to the quality of the load.

'It's not bloody mine, and I don't bloody want it,' he spat at me.

'What do you mean, it's not bloody yours? You ordered it, didn't you?'

'I never bloody ordered any stone.'

'Hang on a minute,' I said, 'let's hear what my driver has to say.'

'Him, he doesn't know his arse from his elbow.'

'What's he on about, George?' I asked. There was obviously more to this than the wrong type of stone.

'A simple mistake, that is all it is, and he has done nothing but threaten me since he arrived,' George moaned.

'What kind of bloody mistake?' I asked, not really wanting to know.

'A simple mistake!' the big man butted in, 'I have just got home from work and I cannot get up my own bloody driveway. How do I get into my own garage? Where do I put my car? You cunt,' he swore at George, glaring at him with bulging eyes and suffused face. He looked fit to burst.

'Have you looked in the mirror lately?' asked George, braver now that I was present. Unable to bear any more insults, he hit back, 'anyway cunts are useful.'

'I don't know how I've managed to keep my hands off him, and he's really pushing it now,' the man growled at me.

'Well, you will have to put them on me first,' I resignedly said. There was no way I was going to get to the bottom of the mystery of the Simple Mistake, until I got these pleasantries out of the way.

The man decided I looked a tougher proposition than George. After eyeing me balefully, he snarled, 'what are you going to do about that bloody lot?' hooking his thumb at the white heap.

Enlightenment came in the shape of the next door neighbour, who had been quietly watching the whole argument from his own gateway. Now he decided it was time to join in, 'look, I understand the mistake, but I want the stone where it is supposed to be, on my driveway. I am Mr Stevenson, this is number nine.'

For the first time I looked at the number of the house, it was number seven. George's simple mistake was to deliver to the wrong house.

Mr Robinson, for that is what they called the large man, butted in again. 'I don't care whose it is, I want it shifting,' he said belligerently.

'I want it on my driveway,' repeated Mr Stevenson, 'and I'm not shifting it. I know my rights.'

I would have loved to have given both of them their rights. There was only one thing we could do, we had to move nine tons of stone manually. And without the help of the two aggrieved gentlemen.

They did have three barrows between them, which they allowed us to borrow without charge, for which we expressed our grateful thanks.

There were a couple of young lads who had been standing among the crowd, enjoying what looked as if it could turn out to be a possible bout of fisticuffs. By offering them ten bob each, I enlisted their aid in moving the mound of stones to their rightful place; the unhelpful Mr Stevenson's front garden. They earned their money the hard way, it had turned 11 p.m. before we had finished transferring the huge pile of stones from one gateway to the next.

Throughout this back-breaking job, George muttered endlessly to himself, 'all this for a honest mistake, anyone could have made.'

I doubted the veracity of that. No one but George could compound a simple mistake into a bloody big bloomer.

Finally I could stand his mumbling no longer. Tired, dirty and very hungry, I snapped, 'for God's sake, shut up. Give it a rest, or do you know that name he called you. I will be bloody agreeing with him. In any case, working like this makes us into a couple of burks. There has to be an easier way to earn a living.'

George stunned to silence, stopped work to look at me, then his face broke into a wide grim before he chuckled gleefully, 'I like his word better, Peter. As I said, they are useful, two are more handy than one.'

One of the last remembered contretemps we had with George as a driver, occurred when I was forced to send him to work alone, at Steel, Peach and Tozer's steel yard in Sheffield. He had to load in the yard and empty at a tip on the outskirts of the factory. I had sent him there without too much worry, for I thought there was no way he could get himself, or the lorry, into bother. How wrong can you be?

I was working on a building site in Doncaster. At around 3 p.m. I received a telephone call from Shirley.

'George is in trouble in Sheffield, he has lost the truck keys and he is holding up the work at the yard. Can you leave there to sort it out?'

'Bloody hell, how has he managed to do that?'

'I don't know, he says he doesn't know either. He's searched everywhere. During his lunch-break he stopped at a park, sitting on a bench to have a cup of tea from his flask. After his rest he went back to the lorry, but couldn't get in as he couldn't find his keys. He said, "Even if he got in, he wouldn't be able to start the engine." Are you going?'

'I have no bloody choice, have I? This time he will really bloody get it, I am sick to death of him.'

When I reached the park it was to find an extremely apprehensive George, afraid of me in a way which pulled me up sharply, driving the anger out of my mind leaving only a sense of loss. Had I lost my mate?

'Calm down,' I said, as George's words tumbled out of his mouth, in an incomprehensible rush.

'Let's start at the beginning, we'll trace your movements together.'

We crossed over to where George had parked the truck, searching the ground under and around it, fanning out to the park bench where he had taken his break.

'What did you do next?' I asked.

'I went over the road to the shop, to buy some cigarettes.'

We again retraced his steps, this time to the shop. The shopkeeper was an Indian, and a very impatient one at that.

'He has been here ten times already, I have looked and searched, they are not here.'

Ignoring the protestations of the shop-owner we searched the place again.

'What else did you buy, George?'

'I only bought the fags, nothing else, ask him.'

We left the shop and went back to the park, where testily I demanded. 'Now what did you do? You must have done something else?'

'I only went back to the lorry, that is when I missed the keys. I have looked everywhere, I have been back to Gunga Din's shop ten times.'

'Have you talked with anyone else besides the shopkeeper?'

'Shit,' George answered loudly.

'Shit indeed, and we are right in it. Now what are we going to do?'

'No, I mean I went for a shit.'

George took off, running for a clump of bushes in the background, with me hot-footing it behind him. Into the bushes I scrambled, to come upon George who was standing seemingly admiring a pile of excreta. Beside which, lying neatly as if they had been placed there, were the bundle of lost keys.

'You bloody idiot,' I yelled, besides myself with relief and anger. 'I have a bloody good mind to rub your bloody nose in it.'

'It's something you never remember doing,' George whined. 'Who remembers going for a shit?'

I had lost hours of work and money, beside the hassle of driving from Doncaster to Sheffield on very busy roads, all the while wondering what the hell I was doing with my life.

Shit was the word and I was getting deeper into it.

Years later George passed the test for a Public Service Vehicle Licence, a P.S.V. as it is known, allowing him to drive the general public. Amazing but true. He, as far as I knew, never had an accident. What else he did I wouldn't know, but he drove buses for a number of years. I swear to the truthfulness of the following incident, with witnesses galore, who watched and listened with some amusement.

Allan was standing waiting for a bus to take him to Doncaster. The Corporation bus pulled in at the bus stop and waving gleefully from the driver's seat was no other than George. Allan put one foot on the step to climb aboard, then shaking his head ruefully, he stepped back on to the pavement, saying loudly, 'no, bugger it I'll wait the half hour for the next one.'

A mate of mine, accompanied by friends, was already on the bus. He laughingly related the incident for months afterwards.

In the bad winter of 1961 Britain's arterial transport systems came to a grinding halt, enveloped in a frost-laden white isolation. It was virtually the last straw for my aspirations to eventually building a haulage business. Work became unobtainable. I was soon in deep financial strife. Without regular employment for the trucks, I could barely see a way of survival for any length of time. Now my plight worsened alarmingly, something had to be done and quickly. The bank manager applied pressure. I took my books home to my mother to try to explain the predicament the company was in. We had formed a limited company with Mam, Shirley and me as directors.

Mam was unable to grasp why, or how, we had come so close to bankruptcy after working so hard and for such long trying hours. As with most enterprises we needed working capital to carry us over the initial establishing period. This we had never had and it contributed to our downfall in no small way.

After discussing the dire situation, plus the options left open to us, I returned home to Shirley in despair and with nothing resolved. The weather looked set to keep its implacable arctic hold for the rest of the winter. Spring never seemed so far away. We daren't borrow more money to any extent. It would just have been borrowing from Peter to pay Paul. We were incapable of meeting the payments due as it was, without adding more. Most certainly bankruptcy would have been the inevitable outcome of such rash folly.

Shirley continued to search frantically for work for the lorries, managing to find a half-day here and a few hours there. The quarries were at a standstill, as was the building industry, most roads were hardly navigable. Winter mercilessly covered the northern roads with snow and ice faster than the snow ploughs could clear them. This forced the large transport companies to change their policy of sub-contracting work out, having little enough for their own fleets.

Then by sheer unadulterated bad luck, or maybe carelessness—who knows—I dropped the side of the lorry on to my foot, breaking two toes. It spelt the end. We were left with no alternative. We had to get out from under before the banks moved in; or worse still, the trucks were repossessed by the finance company.

To clear the millstone of debt from round our necks, and to keep what still remained of the business, we opted for the only chance left open to us. Which was to sell our house and one truck then move in with Mam. A hard heart-wrenching step it turned out to be, in more ways than one. I had the difficult task of breaking the bad news to George. Surprisingly, he took it extremely well. Helped no doubt by the fact of unemployment being no stranger to him, he said gloomily, 'I have been expecting it, Peter, only a blasted fool wouldn't have seen it coming. It was great while it lasted.'

That is not how I saw it. Once again George had shown me how unflappable he was. In my self-pitying state of mind what a salutary lesson he gave yours truly. If only I had grasped the nettle of knowledge that fatalism has some merit, and stopped beating my head against the brick wall of inevitability.

The house sold, on a depressed property market, for the best attainable price at that time. We sold George's lorry, complete with 'B' licence, to pay off the amount still outstanding on the original purchase cost. As in most hire-purchase agreements, the sum owed was almost the same as the amount asked when we bought it, all money paid to the finance company having been swallowed by the interest charges.

We moved in with Mam. Once again I was reliant on Mary Agnes, this time bringing the added burden of my wife and daughter. At some period or other in their lives, the rest of her family would return to her fireside. Not once to my knowledge did she tire, or turn any one of them away.

The months passed. Although the weather improved and work was easier to come by, things did not improve financially. I drove my only truck yet we could scarcely eke out a living; crippling repayments, running repairs and fuel eating the takings almost entirely.

Finally, with no choice left we came to the agreement to cut our losses and sell the remaining lorry. The bank and finance company wanted all that remained after the sale to clear our debts. Our excursion into the world of entrepreneurs had not been successful. In fact it had been a bloody fiasco from beginning to end. I was broke, no job, a family to support and no means of attaining even that meagre ambition.

I had left plumbing before my apprenticeship was completed. I had not a thing to fall back on. Labouring seemed the only road open to me, but jobs were hard to come by. I was forced on to the unemployment queues. My accursed pride in tatters, I wallowed in despondency. My only saving grace was that I was not bankrupt, though I owed my mother a great deal of money. Not once did she indulge in recriminations on that score.

From first hand experience, I can think of nothing more soul destroying to a man, than to remove his ability to support his family. I defy anyone to gainsay me.

As a child I had watched my father in similar circumstances, not understanding until it happened to me, the depths of despair he must have known. The testiness, the unreachability as he withdrew into himself, as the weeks and then months of unemployment dragged on. Leaving a man devoid of hope, angry at an unjust world, and at his own incapacity to rectify an intolerable situation.

We tell ourselves that was a different generation, a different breed, the circumstances wouldn't apply today. They do, they have, they are. We have the Welfare State which our parents didn't have. I can but state my case. I would not join the dole queue again if they paid me in gold bars. I know that the ignominy has been removed, but the stigma remains for all right thinking men.

We are not a nation of bludgers or parasites on the tax-payer. Most want to be left alone, to be allowed to earn their own keep, to have governments to get on with the job they were elected to do. Govern. The aged, sick and real needy, to be cared for. Families are a man's own responsibility.

Mary Agnes didn't approve of family allowances, 'they will be spent in the pubs, the kids will feel no benefit from it,' she said, airing her vast knowledge of humanity.

Then, she did not approve of my bemoaning my lot either, treating with derisive contempt, my defeatist attitude.

My mother may well have been a descendant of the Stoics. On one occasion she looked coldly at me, saying chastisingly, 'pick yourself up, Boy. You aren't beaten yet, you have only just begun. What about taking a pub?'

'What with?' I asked, her scorn forcing me into sarcasm.

'Be a manager. That way you will not require capital, if you do it will only be minimal, a surety. We could raise that for you.'

The minor fact that I had no experience of any kind to offer, mattered little to Mam. I was Peter the Great.

Kate who had returned from Australia, and was then a catering manageress in the West End of London, suggested if we were even considering entering the Licensed Trade, to take ourselves to London, saying wisely, 'if you have any sense at all, you will go where you will be taught properly. You will gain the type of experience it is impossible to gain in the North.'

How very right my sister was. For good or bad, the time spent in London was time well spent. I regret not a moment of it, the opposite in fact. I still miss it beyond explanation.

PART TWO

They're Open!

Chapter 4

WASTING no time, we bought the *Morning Advertiser* as it covered the licensed victualler's employment vacancies. We answered several advertisements before receiving a reply, granting us an interview appointment.

It was from B.W. Franks, a subsidiary of Levy and Franks. We were to learn later that all their houses were in the West End of London, with the exception of one. Elated because we had at last received a reply, Shirley and I set out for the Big Smoke dressed to kill. Hope had finally returned to dispel our wretchedness. Before we left, Mam said, 'I will keep my fingers crossed for you, just for luck,' she added, 'not that it will matter, you will get the job anyway.'

We believed her, we had a feeling our luck had turned for the better.

Our interview at B.W. Franks was with two young directors, Mr Richards and Mr Barrett. We appeared to have made an impression on them, my boxing career and our ability to chat, enhancing our chances of becoming mine hosts. Shirley's blonde attractiveness also did not go unnoticed by those two very shrewd, yet well mannered men.

We won the position.

We were destined to become the youngest publicans in the West End of London.

Beginning as relief managers with the company, setting afoot fourteen months of ridiculously happy, vying with miserably unhappy, truly difficult times.

Back in Doncaster we made all the necessary arrangements for moving South. Jacqueline had to stay with Mam, which upset Shirley greatly, there just was no other option open to us. The job entailed long hours and constant relocation. . . It was no life for a small child.

It was not what one would call an auspicious start to a career which was to last for the rest of our working lives. Yet it was a beginning, one we truly appreciated, then and now.

The position didn't include accommodation, we had to find our own and that was a story unto itself. Walking for miles to view flats, only to find they had been let, or were in such an unspeakable mess no one would lease them. Eventually with the aid of a very kind lady, Peggy, we had a friend for life, and a flat in Chalk Farm, North London.

This we moved into on a Saturday, starting work on the following Monday. It was a regime of constant change, at least we couldn't say it was boring. A day here and a day there, or a week here and a fortnight there as we covered holiday reliefs. It meant we lived out of suitcases, never caring, for the places we relieved were beyond our wildest dreams— the fabulous houses belonging to B.W. Franks which included Snows Chophouse in Piccadilly Circus and the Holyrood of Oxford Street that was right in the centre of the Rag Trade. The Sussex and the Old Mitre in St Martin's Lane, the Oxford and Cambridge at the end of Oxford Street, were just some of them.

B.W. Franks were a Licensed Catering Company, both Shirley and I had to attend school one day a week, Shirley for catering tuition, myself for liquor and beer keeping. We quickly gained a reputation as good reliable managers, capable of handling the best of houses, proficient in our chosen profession.

We tasted the Good Life, we met the Beautiful Set who frequented the select houses we relieved. We also ate the best of food which those places specialized in. It was Company policy that we reported every Monday to Mr Richards or Mr Barrett for their instructions as to whom we relieved. The managers of most of their houses were long-service employees, and very good people to deal with as a rule. Mr Boncey of the Holyrood was nothing short of a gentleman, as was Mr Verrell of Snows. Both men we owe so much to, for their willingness to give help and advice. There were the exceptions, Mr and Mrs Crockett of the Sussex we are certainly not in debt to. He was a bastard of the first order, who became sarcastic and a smart arse every time we relieved them. His wife was cut from the same cloth, 'when you order your lunch, choose an item from the bottom of the menu,' she would say nastily to Shirley. The bottom of the menu specified the cheaper meals available.

Things came to a head one particular instance, when we were their day-off relief. He had instructed an Irish barmaid to lock all the toilets, he always locked up his flat, which was his prerogative on his day off. However the locking of all the public toilets in the afternoon, was quite a different kettle of fish. It meant we were unable to wash and change ready for the evening session at 5.30 p.m. . . . We were forced to go down to the Leicester Square public toilets to wash. This cavalier treatment of us by a manager we had been instructed to relieve, really put me on the boil. It wasn't over either. At the close of business that night I started to check the tills. It was my job to count the takings, after separating the floats ready for the manager the next day. There were three tills in this house and this night the head barmaid, obviously under instructions, began counting the money from a till. So angry I could barely speak, I managed to tell her to leave the till alone, I was responsible for all takings when her boss wasn't present. She literally stormed out of the pub, in one hell of a huff. Shirley and I had by this time had enough. We locked all the tills, without checking them, and sat to await the return of the gruesome twosome. It was well past midnight when they came back, with no change in their attitude towards us, after their evening on the Town.

I started in straight away, telling them we had been forced to go to Leicester Square toilets because of the closure of their facilities. I told them about their barmaid counting my till, and my refusal to be responsible for all three, which remained unchecked. Then I recapped on all the old irritants we had endured, when we had been sent to relieve him on previous occasions.

He listened, as if not sure of what I was saying to him, then he yelled, 'get out, I will personally see to it that you are fired. We have never liked either of you. Get out,' he repeated loudly.

Shirley and I were worried sick the next morning, while we waited to be ushered into Mr Richards and Mr Barrett's presence. We were eventually summoned into the office where both Richards and Barrett, sat grim-faced staring at us.

'Explain, if you will, exactly what happened last night at the Sussex.' My brain panicked. My God, what had I done, running through my mind the horror of again being unemployed, and possibly unemployable. This is it, this is your last chance down the drain for that blasted pride. Extremely upset I narrated the whole sorry episode from start to finish.

'The Leicester Square toilets?' Mr Richards almost exploded, as he grabbed the phone, shouting down it to his secretary in the next room; he really didn't need a phone.

'Get Mr Crockett from the Sussex, round here now, at once,' he demanded.

My wife and I sat uneasily as Crockett entered the office. I would not have liked to change places with him, at that moment. In no uncertain manner they told him what they thought of his conduct, giving him the biggest dressing down I ever want to witness. I believe he thought we were enjoying the spectacle. I can assure him neither of us were.

'You will not get a day off at all, if you continue to treat my staff in this way,' Mr Barrett stormed at Crockett in conclusion.

He left the office, his tail very firmly back between his legs. Gone was the arrogance he had treated Shirley and me to since knowing him. We could only hope he passed on the warning to his haughty wife, for she was equally as bad as he was.

Ten days later the day relief for the Crocketts turned up again, in the shape of Peter and Shirley Aldridge. I felt ill, for his approach to both of us was decidedly slimy. His wife hardly said a word, probably not trusting herself to speak. They now had cause to dislike us.

Shirley, ever the irrepressible, at lunch time ordered her meal from the top of the menu. Fillet steak with all the trimmings, where ordinarily she would have settled for cold cuts and salad. We received them with no comment, the chef accepting the fact that for the day we were the managers. We had no further problems with the barmaid, either. Notwithstanding, we had made implacable enemies of the Crocketts.

That night my wife cried herself to sleep, the Crocketts and the worry of Jacqueline being away from us, proved just too much.

Every two months we were given a long enough break to go north to see her. Making Mam's day too, for we would relate incidents in our dealings with staff and clientele. She would remain silent until we had finished recounting our stories, then the questions would start, a demand really for more of the same. The juicy bits, especially if they involved famous people, gave her enough gossip, particularly after she had added her delightful embroidery, to keep our small street humming for weeks.

Nevertheless the inevitable question always came, 'when are you going to get your own pub?'

There were to be a lot of hard work, difficult times and water under the proverbial bridge, before that would eventuate.

We were making a lot of friends, some of them to stand us in good

stead over the years, others unusual to say the least. One of the latter was
Harry Hollis and the Roadstars. They were buskers, well known to both
the police and the public alike. The Roadstars worked London's West End,
more often than not in Leicester Square. Harry, by his own admittance,
was Britain's most oft arrested man. He was actually arrested and fined 600
times. That is some record, dubious or otherwise. It must have been a
paying game, for it didn't deter Harry in the slightest. Harry and the
Roadstars used to run regularly through one door of the pub and out of
the other, with the police in hot pursuit. He became a good, amusing
friend over the years, saying to other customers in his very colourful way,
'saved my f'ing skin many a time, this guy,' pointing at me. No doubt
referring to the time I played the innocent to the police, when they asked
if I had seen him.

I once hid him down the cellar of a pub I was relieving, while a
bewildered young constable scratched the back of his head, saying, 'well,
I am sure he came in here.' Then, after failing to find him, 'I was sure he
came in here.'

Over the months we had been asked repeatedly, by other Franks management, 'have you been to the Camden Head yet?'

As we shook our heads in negatory fashion, tired of saying no, we
became more curious as they refused to enlighten us as to their interest.
They merely laughed and said intriguingly, 'wait until you do, you will
find it different.'

We were quite happy to stay where we were, in the marvellous West
End. We weren't that curious about the Camden Head.

Outside of London's heart in Camden, it was another world away from
the Oxford and Cambridge. What a splendid house that was. It boasted a
full-sized reproduction of a racing boat used in the University Boat Race,
suspended from the ceiling in the centre of the pub. The theme was further
carried out with the use of light and dark blue colours throughout the
public areas, the university's and racing team's colours. We thoroughly
enjoyed every moment of our relief periods there.

The Old Mitre in St Martin's Lane, was another favourite pub of ours.
It was used frequently by the theatre people, actors and management alike.
In fact it was the regular watering hole for some. We managed it for a
period of two months, until another manager was appointed to our extreme
sorrow.

We lived in of course. Both my wife and I prayed we would be given the place to manage permanently. It was not to be. Maybe it was our age? Then again, it would have been the length of time we had been with the Company, with no previous background in the trade? Whichever, it was very disappointing for Shirley and me to be left out of consideration.

As you entered the pub, you faced a long carvery, which ran across the length of the room. A chef named Bob, was in charge of this service area. He was a delightful little fellow, almost as broad as he was long, his face invariably wreathed in a broad cheery smile. He spoke with a deep gruff voice, surprising for his height.

One morning as he was setting up his usual display of hams, turkeys, cold-cuts, et cetera, he turned to me saying extremely worriedly, 'Guv'ner, there's one customer owes me a very large bill, do you think you could ask him to settle his food account?'

With hindsight, I understand Bob was also a very cunning little chap. This customer possessed a powerful, intimidating personality. A tall, impressive figure of a man, always dressed in immaculate pinstripes. A man whom I had quickly deduced, was better treated with a servile attitude. Why create waves. He was executive concerned with T.V. advertising.

A book under the bar recorded his outstanding drinks account, this stood at £200. When you remember this was in the early sixties you can estimate it was a great deal of money, yet the standing instructions were 'he will settle when he sees fit to do so.'

This was a warning to leave well alone, his credit was good.

However the food bill was a different matter, the books had to be balanced every fortnight, with no exceptions being made.

The carvery books were Bob's responsibility, yet I could appreciate his reticence and disquiet at tackling this forbidding person.

'Now Bob, the next time this fellow comes in, just ask him nicely if he will settle his account.'

'You have to be kidding, Guv'ner, you don't know him. He's a right bastard. I'm scared of him. Why don't we let the manageress ask him for the money? That's a much better idea.'

He pointed at Shirley, who hadn't a clue as to what was going on.

'That is out of the question, Bob, and you know it. Do as I have told you, ask him politely for the money. If you are worried I will be on hand, but I cannot see what you are worried about.'

'You will Guv'ner, he's a bastard,' Bob repeated.

The following morning, having only just opened up the bar, we had at most, a handful of customers spread around, when Bob shouted to me, 'Guv'ner, he's coming.'

He had seen the approach of the dreaded man through the window. In a blue funk he had called me, for he had no intention of facing the man without backup.

The executive walked into the room, snapping his fingers at me. He said in his customary, condescending way, 'three bottles of champagne for 1.30 p.m. . . Cooled.' He turned briskly and made to leave.

Bob, his gruff voice shaking, asked mumblingly, 'please, would you mind settling your food account, sir?'

In a flash the executive had grabbed the poor chef by the lapels of his white jacket. 'How dare you ask me for money? How dare you? How dare you, you wretch?' All the while shaking Bob as if he were a rag doll.

I must admit my courage deserted me. I quickly bent below the bar and started to rattle a few bottles. Anyway, it wasn't the type of pub where one goes around thumping the customers. Not that kind of client in any case.

When I surfaced, he was literally throwing the chef towards the wall, then he shot out of the door, his face livid.

'I told you, Guv'ner,' tears were running unchecked down Bob's rosy cheeks. 'He's a f'ing bastard, that one.'

Shirley had stood aghast at what had happened. Now she demanded to know what it was all about.

I finished telling her the whole sorry story, before the realization hit me, our job could again be in jeopardy.

'Oh God, I think we have just lost their best customer, we are for the high jump now.'

I still hopefully put the three bottles of champagne on ice. It wasn't required.

Prior to closing at 2.30 p.m., the lunch session finished, we were clearing the bar. Bob was scrubbing down his food counter, when Shirley yelled from the dining room, 'watch out, he's coming back.'

My wife had a good view of the lane from the dining room windows. Only a few seconds later, into the pub strode the T.V. executive. Back ramrod straight, he marched up to the bar, then in a surprisingly courteous tone, he asked, 'how much do I owe you, Old Boy?'

Slapping his chequebook on the bar he added, 'put that degenerate's bill on the account also,' pointing at Bob, who was doing his best to hide behind a fully glass-fronted counter. The cheque covered all outstanding accounts.

'Everything alright, sir?' I asked tentatively

'Certainly, Old Chap.' he answered cheerfully.

Be that as it may, on leaving the bar he gave a cowering Bob, a most vicious look, before heading for the door.

We did not lose his custom, he came in that evening. As we opened at 5.30 p.m. he strode in, accompanied by Michael Redgrave, the actor. Back to his old endearing self, he snapped, 'champagne.'

'Yes, sir,' I said with alacrity, bringing quickly forth the cooled Bubbly. I would have balanced it on my nose, had he asked.

In spite of that little contretemps our stay at the Old Mitre was unforgettably enjoyable. All too quickly our time there came to a close, with the installation of a new permanent manager.

Again we were on the treadmill, a day here, a week there and so on.

One Monday morning we arrived at the office for our instructions for the week. Mr Richards looked at the two of us with some concern.

'Mr and Mrs Aldridge, we want you to cover the holiday relief at the Camden Head, Islington.'

We knew it was the only house they owned, which was not in the West End. Yet surely that wouldn't account for his odd manner, after all we were there to do his bidding. Mr Richards continued.

'We would like you to spend one or two days with the manager first, the trade is very different from any you have encountered so far.'

We didn't like the ominous tone his voice had developed. Worried, we left the office. Once outside Shirley mirrored my thoughts aloud, 'I do not like the sound of this.'

'Neither do I,' I answered, 'If truth be known, I am worried.'

Memories of managers laughing as they'd inquired if we had relieved the Camden Head, crowded our minds. However in all fairness, nothing anybody could have said, would in any way have prepared us for the Head.

We arrived at the Camden Head acutely apprehensive, to say the least. It had the appearance of any large pub, which could be found on any High Street, in any town, anywhere. The difference lay therein.

The catering, apart from bar-snacks, was non-existent. There was just one large circular bar in a central position, of this cavernous room. The manager spoke with the strong accent of the Geordie. We were surprised. B.W. Franks' management were all laid-back city types, very suave.

For all that this man was a very nice fellow indeed. A typical mine host of the northern pit villages, warm, friendly and very chatty. The clientele left us gasping in shock. There were prostitutes of the very low order, pimps of the same class, petty crooks who could have been picked out, even in a Dickens novel setting. And the League of Nations in nationalities. All the same the last were similar to their British counterparts in their lifestyle. Purple Hearts were commonplace as we were to learn later, and I am not referring to the kind worn on the chest of heroes.

Shirley had paled at the sight of the above, yet far worse was to follow rapidly.

The manager introduced himself as Joe Short. 'I'll take you upstairs to meet the wife,' he said, 'you will want to see the flat in any case.'

Again, nothing could have lessened the effect. It was the utter antithesis of everything in our lives, to which we had become accustomed. As we ascended those stairs to the private quarters, Shirley's eyes met mine. Hers were filled with horror and disbelief.

There was a kiddie's pottie on one step, with the faeces still inside it and the place stank to high heaven. The cooker in the kitchen was laden with pans, as filthy as the stove itself. I doubt if any had ever seen heated soapy water, nor for that matter had any other part of this pigsty. If I am wrong and it had suffered previous cleaning, then it had been so long ago it didn't matter.

My mind was unable to register anything except total panic, every part of me rebelling and screaming silently, 'oh, my God, what have we landed into now?'

It was left to my wife to take command, for we certainly couldn't nor would we, live in that incredible filth for two long weeks.

It was a far cry from the West End, and even further from the safety of home. I turned from the squalor of the inside, to the windows, yet they offered little solace, being as dirty as the rest of the accommodation. So begrimed in fact, one could barely see the light of day.

Mr Barrett was a kindly man, his parting words had been, 'If you have any problems you feel you cannot handle, ring me.'

Problems we had. Shirley wasted no time in ringing him from the public bar. Begging him to send someone to examine the state of the living quarters.

Mr Barrett came himself. On seeing the flat for the first time, he exclaimed loudly, 'it's unbelievable. It's nothing but a hovel.'

He threw the book at the Shorts. 'Get it cleaned up,' he snorted, 'you will not be given holiday relief until this place is in a liveable condition. Who do you think would consent to stay here, while you are away?'

The Shorts had booked a holiday in Spain. For a while it appeared as if that would be out of the question. However, a compromise was arrived at. The head barmaid, a woman named Joan, agreed to live in the hurriedly cleaned up accommodation. Shirley and I would travel daily from our home in Chalk Farm.

This concession to allow the Shorts to take their much-needed holiday, also meant longer days for us; yet anything was better than staying in that unspeakable hole. The cleaning up of the flat had barely scratched the surface, the whole bloody place needed fumigating. The Shorts never understood our reaction to their way of life. They were happy living as they did. Really we were a pain in the arse with our petty complaints.

We were to spend one more day with the Shorts, before taking over for our two week holiday relief. The couple decided to take advantage of our being there, on that Friday evening, and went out for the night, up to the West End.

All went well, the house started to fill with its usual assortment of dubious characters. One part of the lounge being reserved by a group of lesbians, regular customers. They had met with no resistance from the landlord over this practice. I had no intention of trying to change things, my stay was to be of short duration. As far as I was concerned it couldn't be short enough.

One of these mixed up half and halfs, whom everyone referred to as 'Billie', would strut up to the bar, thumbs hooked in her belt in a classic Western manner, and say gruffly, 'give us a pint, Mate.'

One could quite easily mistake her for a young lad of eighteen years or so. Really she was a woman of twenty-six. Her short back and side haircut, man's suit coupled with collar, tie and polished laced shoes, undoubtedly led to the following mayhem.

I was in conversation with two young coloured blokes, also pub regulars. The conversation as usual was boxing, something we would need before that night was out. As we talked I kept a weather eye open on the unhallowed motley, which, like it or not, was to be my charge for the next two weeks.

A group of four people, two couples, sat at a table close to the ladies' toilet. Getting their drinks in, they then settled down for a night's enjoyment. Not long after the men had seated themselves, Billie went to the ladies', as she came back into the room, one of the men shouted, 'eh, you. My wife's in there. What were you doing going in there?'

There was only one answer which Billie ever gave to anyone, who had the temerity to question or accost her. She had used it on me, as the new guv'ner to be broken in.

'Get fucked,' said Billie with her usual sang-froid.

How the devil that young woman had survived intact as long as she had, had me beat. Knowing trouble was imminent, I moved fast from behind the bar, almost running across the room to the seated men.

'Let me explain,' I began, 'it isn't a man, it's a woman.'

The two rather hefty gentlemen looked at me scornfully.

'Don't give me that, you f'er,' swore one of the men, 'any silly bugger can see that's a feller.'

I do not object to bad language. Over the years I have heard it in all its infinite variety. But this mongrel had a way of using it, which ruffled my equilibrium more than somewhat. In short this pair had lost my sympathy.

I don't really know what happened next. The men were on their feet, one or two punches had been thrown at whoever was closest. I was the nearest. More of the customers joined in, some were trying to convince the men, that Billie, despite outward appearances and apparently inward makeup, was actually of the female gender. Others had no such honourable intentions grabbing, with delight, the chance to join a free-for-all; they got stuck in and fists and feet flew.

You will have seen, *ad nauseam*, Western bar brawls on television or the wide screen. This was for real. Glasses, bottles, tables and chairs flying through the air, and the unholy din was something else. The screen versions of which I am very fond, are tame by comparison, besides no one gets hurt. There was real blood flowing here and a lot of it was mine.

Shirley and the rest of the staff cowered on their hands and knees behind the bar. All the optic measures hung free as the bottles shattered, gin, rum, brandy, whisky, vodka, et cetera, cascaded down over the helpless bodies of the staff. My wife smelt as if she had bathed in alcohol.

This was a punch-up to eclipse all others, if it hadn't been for the two coloured chaps coming to my aid, things for me would undoubtedly have been far worse.

Billie, the whole cause of this mêlée, was content to just foul-mouth anyone who came within earshot, including yours truly, who had gone to her aid in the first instance.

After what seemed to be an eternity, Shirley managed to reach the phone and dial emergency for the police.

They charged into the Camden Head, batons at the ready, bouncing them off the more wilful of the noisy, blasphemous rioters. Make no mistake this was a riot in full blooming maturity, not just a rowdy pub fracas, to be easily subdued.

As the police burst through the door, I dropped my guard for the first time, and thump, I was hit with a chair leg on the back of my head. I had just planted one on the nose of a villain, who had been intent on showing me his boxing prowess. I had broken his nose, the blood spurted down and out, all over the front of my shirt as he fell across me. One of the sleeves of my shirt had been ripped off in a previous skirmish and I was literally blood-spattered all over. Now blood was dripping down the back of my shirt from the wound in my head.

I was utterly out on my feet, my clothes in tatters, covered in gore, a lot of it my own, staggering about, still trying to land one on some of the flailing figures around me as the police attempted to restore some kind of law and order.

The Black Maria (prison van), had been conveniently placed outside the front entrance of the Camden Head. It was fast-filling with a yelling, abusive mob. A young copper grabbed me and pushed me violently outside to another waiting policeman, 'put him in,' he said contemptuously.

Shirley came running through the doorway, shouting, 'not him, he's the manager.'

Confused I stared at the copper's reaction, as he said in amazement, 'are you sure?'

'I should be, I am married to him,' my wife said sarcastically.

One couldn't blame the constable, anything less like a licensed publican, you would not have been able to find.

After it was all over and we had the place to ourselves, apart from the staff, we sat among the debris of what had been the lounge quietening our shattered nerves with coffee.

No one was interested in strong liquor, we were all getting drunk from the fumes off our clothes.

My head was fit to burst from the wallop I had taken, and yet it was the least of my worries. Whatever were we going to say to the Shorts? What explanation could we give the Company?

Finally the Shorts returned from their evening out and I greeted them with profuse apologies for something over which I had had no control. An apology seemed rather an ineffectual way to express the extreme regrets I felt over the absolute shambles confronting this man. Inanely I stumbled on, 'I am sorry, it was completely unstoppable. I gave it my best shot. It wasn't enough. That bloody villainess Billy caused all this.'

Joe Short looked at me with a wry smile, 'Don't worry, Old Son, this happens every two months or so. There is always something which will trigger it off.'

'Christ!' Amazed, I asked, 'why do the police leave the bloody place open? Why don't they close it down?'

'I asked that when I first came here, there's method in their madness. This way they know where all the bastards are, when they want them.' Now we knew why all the management of B. W. Franks had asked, 'have you been to the Camden Head yet?'

It also explained the odd behaviour of Messrs Richards and Barrett. It was not the state of the accommodation, as we had thought, or the clients of doubtful quality. Oh no, it was the obvious risk to life and limb which one took on stepping inside this pestilential den of iniquity.

By the following Monday morning the pub was open once again to the low-lived drop outs they flattered beyond reason by calling them customers.

B.W. Franks had refurnished it from their stores. They must have had several sets of entire refurbishments continually in stock, just to keep the doors of the Camden Head open.

The Head had undergone a massive clean-up. A huge plate glass window broken during the conflict, had been replaced. Most things had been put to rights, including my head, which now sported six stitches. Mr Richards asked concernedly, 'do you feel fit enough to take on the next two weeks relief here?'

Belligerent in anger, I answered very stupidly, 'they are not beating me, we will do our fortnight. Won't we, Shirley?'

My wife given no chance to state her case, nodded her head, not sure enough of herself, to give a verbal answer. I knew she was more than fed-up at the thought of another two weeks, among these nefarious worthies, yet still willing to follow me to hell and back regardless. Surprisingly, I had won a great deal of respect from the regulars of the Camden Head. Some, no doubt because of my handiness with fists and feet. Others on account of the fact I had stood my ground, and given as good as I had received. However it was more than likely they considered I had been bloodied enough. I agreed with the latter, for I had, in more ways than one.

So followed a reasonably quiet two weeks. Apart from the headache which persisted long after our sojourn there, I can honestly say I enjoyed the rest of our time at the Head, for it was certainly different if nothing else.

We had our amusing moments too, one instance comes to mind of a conversation overheard at the bar, between two prostitutes.

'Walked all f'ing night, not a punter in sight,' one said.

'I had two,' the other replied. 'One silly old bastard said he couldn't get a hard on, only in sea air. Wanted me to drive to f'ing Brighton, all for a tenner.'

'What did you tell the f'ing mucker?'

'I told him I was a f'ing working girl, not a f'ing floozy.'

At the time I didn't know which I found the funnier, their discourse, or my wife's face. Then she hadn't heard or seen anything like it. Today she pretty well rides with the punches.

One prostitute of the lesser order, by the name of Sheila, was a cheery wench with a fast lip. As I stood behind the bar admiring her smashing legs, she remarked impudently to me, 'Guv'ner, you can look there for nothing,' lifting her skirt, she added, 'if you want that, it's a f'ing fiver.'

I didn't want that, they turned me off. Even though one couldn't help liking some of them, their limited vocabulary got to you by the end of the day.

It was in this fashion that our stay at the Head passed, and we returned to the West End, wiser but not sorrier for our time in Islington.

While at the Camden Head, I would often walk down to the Star and Garter, which was also in Islington. This pub was owned by Len Harvey, the famous Triple British Boxing Champion. I loved to spend at least an hour, listening to Len reliving memories of his time in the ring, besides reminiscing about people we both knew.

During the second week of our stay at the Head, Len said to me, 'Peter, I have two tickets for a boxing dinner at the National Sporting Club. I don't feel inclined to go on my own. Would you like to go?' Then he asked casually, 'have you a dress suit, Peter?'

He was a thoughtful man, he'd suddenly remembered the cost of my having to hire one.

'Yes, Len, I have a suit, I would love to go,' I replied. I was absolutely over the moon at the opportunity of attending such a dinner. I did have an evening suit. I'd had to buy one for Snows in Piccadilly, one had to change into formal attire for the evening session there. By 7 p.m. sharp, the management had to be changed and on show in the bar, for all to see. I reckon it added class.

On arrival at the Sporting Club, Len was made a great fuss of, making me wonder about the real reason for asking me along. He was a legend of a man, who was as popular with his peers as with his fans. If he had attended the event on his own, he wouldn't have remained that way for long.

Len wore a dress suit, which although still very smart, was dated. After dinner we were enjoying drinks when Billy Walker came over to us. He was dressed to the nines, gleaming evening suit, immaculate frilled shirt. Len introduced him to me. After a few words in general, Billy walked away. As soon as he was out of earshot, Len remarked sadly, 'he makes me feel like a poor relation.'

This really gives one pause for thought, the great Len Harvey feeling like a poor relation of a man who could not have laced his boots in his time.

This truly painted a picture of the changing world of boxing, money was literally being shovelled at Billy Walker at that period of his career. In Harvey's era, the purse was well and truly earned, not just for staying power either . . . fierce competition and meagre by comparison prize money, makes today's game a walkover for top-flight boxers. Len Harvey would have played with Walker, six days a week, and twice on Sundays.

After completion of our relief at the Camden Head, we were given a weekend off, enabling us to travel north, to see Jacqueline and Mam. Our daughter was pining for her mother, refusing to eat, which was worrying Mam greatly, who was doing her best to pacify her.

'How long will it be before you get your own pub?' Mam asked. 'Jacqueline is fretting terribly. I have told her, once you are in a place of your own, she can then join you.'

Worried we answered. 'Soon, it won't be long now, before we are given a house to manage.' This wasn't really true, we honestly had no idea when, or if we would be given a pub of our own. We had met one couple, employed by Levy and Franks the larger company, who had been on their relieving staff for two and a half years. In the same boat as my wife and me, they also had no idea if they'd get a managerial position permanently. Our morale was very low indeed when we returned to London. We badly needed the pick-up we would in all probability receive on our next assignment.

We were to cover holiday relief at Snows in Piccadilly. Mr Verrell, the manager, planned to go abroad for a three week vacation. It meant we, again, would have to travel from Chalk Farm. Mr Verrell had a private flat in the Strand which, of course, would not be available to us. Snows was a lock-up, there was no accommodation on the premises. Verrell was the only pub manager I ever knew, who was also a member of Lord's. Cricket was his abiding passion in life, he would hold forth for hours on the merits, and demerits of players. Particularly the English Eleven.

What a class place Snows was in those days. For three heavenly long weeks it was to be ours. The best of food, cooked to perfection, a better class of people and life as lived smack in the centre of Piccadilly Circus.

'Get your suits cleaned and pay with petty cash,' Mr Verrell instructed. Mrs Verrell counselled Shirley, 'take £10 a week from petty cash for flowers. If you don't spend that amount, buy something for yourself with the remainder.'

Even with this small financial help, we found it very expensive to do the job. Shirley had to wear black dresses and dark suits, while I resembled a tailor's dummy for most of the time. Both of us having to change for the evening session, it was indeed a far cry from the Camden Head.

The week following our departure from the Head, there had been a murder committed in the place, which I might add, surprised us not at all. Joe Short and his wife, in spite of their leaving much to be desired, personal way of living, deserved medals for managing that infamous house. I was to handle much before I was through in London, nothing came close to the Head in sheer, raw, brutal vulgarity.

The days at Snows were to be long ones . . . they had just been granted midnight closing for the restaurant. Yet it mattered little. We were back in the West End, and life we would dearly love to become accustomed to.

I would leave home for work before Shirley, throughout our relief period at Snows, arriving at about 8.30 a.m. to let the staff in, and also to watch the buggers.

My first run-in with them came early in the piece, the assistant manager, a man named Royle, was the first to try me for size. Most staff will attempt to pull a fast one with relief management, when the resident manager is away. It was expected, and they never failed to live up to my expectations. I had spotted Royle doing a little bit of fiddling with the head waiter. This I stopped dead, by taking them into the office and giving them the Gypsy's warning.

All went swimmingly, the other staff had tapped into the grapevine, and decided the relief management wasn't as half-baked as they had at first thought. We were well into the second week when an incident occurred which would literally stop the traffic in Piccadilly Circus. Besides putting the fear of God into yours truly. Leaving me very wary of strange, beautiful ladies, who profess to be badly smitten at the first sight of myself. No matter how bloody good-looking they are. Well, that is what I tell my inner self. Every calamity that hits, be it self-inflicted or otherwise, I maintain I have learnt something. If it is only to pull my head in, when rain threatens.

Snows employed a young barmaid around nineteen years of age, in their Dive Bar. Her mother, a woman in her early forties, worked part-time for Verrell on a petty cash basis. I didn't use her in my time there, although she would often drop in for a drink.

She was a very attractive lady and a personal friend of Verrell's. On this score I didn't put up any objections when I found she was drinking after hours, which was then between eleven and midnight, the supper licence running until the restaurant closed at twelve. In this case it was simple to break the licensing laws, without fear of intervention from the police.

We were working such outrageously long hours, Shirley would leave at 11 p.m., after then the supper trade quietened down. The barman regularly stayed behind to assist me in setting the alarms and locking the place up.

This particular Wednesday night, trade was very slow, the chef and the waiters were ready to leave by midnight. Sam, the barman, asked, 'can you lock up alone tonight, Guv'ner. I'd like an early night if I can.'

'O.K., Sam, off you go,' I said, like the gullible fool I was.

The Dive barmaid's mother, whose name was June, had been sitting at the bar accompanied by a young good-looking woman, since around 10.30 p.m. After the staff had all left, these two ladies lingered on. I really didn't think anything of it, as June had often left with Sam and me, after we had locked the pub up.

We had a drink together after I had done all I had to do, then June suggested we all have a coffee before going home. Being a staff member, albeit a part-time one, she knew her way about so I promptly agreed. Chalk Farm was a fair distance away.

It was a steamy, hot summer's night. After closing I had removed my jacket and placed it on the chair back, at the table where I was now seated with this lovely woman, named Jackie. June had gone to the kitchen to make the coffee.

'I have been watching you all night,' Jackie murmured, flapping her eyelashes at me. Leaning forward to look into my eyes, she gave me a good view of two splendid breasts. Her hand closing over mine to squeeze gently, she asked huskily, 'would you like to come home with me? I have a lovely flat close by.'

It would be hard for a man, even in his dotage, to turn down a proposition as good as that. I was far from being impotent, nor was I yet senile, but alarm bells as loud as a fire alarm rang in my head. Beads of sweat on my forehead had me groping for a handkerchief in my jacket pocket. Suddenly I realized I had been set up as a chicken ready for plucking, I lunged for the other side pocket of my coat. My keys which had been in there were there no longer. I never let them leave my possession, only the damned heat, and my sitting down relaxed at the table had made me remove my jacket. The keys were there when I sat down. My pocket had been picked professionally, and by the only person able to reach it, June.

I leapt to my feet, shaking off Jackie who was desperately trying to hang on to me. She made a grab at me as I jumped up, saying 'kiss me, darling.'

That convinced me, I left running for the stairs and the Dive Bar below. I bounded down the stairway, hardly touching the steps, and into the Dive Bar. The bar security grill had been unlocked and pushed up. The office door leading to the bar was open and I could hear activity inside. I stepped quickly inside the room where June had been extraordinarily busy. She had opened all four tills, the contents lay scattered everywhere, why I will never know for sure. I can hazard a guess, what she had expected to find was not there.

The procedure in Snows was that all bank notes were removed from the tills at close of business, and placed inside the safe. The change, plus the floats, were left inside the tills to be counted and separated the following day. There was roughly £200 in all, most of strewn about the floor. June had been unable to open the safe. This required a sequence of numbers, only Mr Verrell and I knew the combination of.

As I entered the office, she changed completely from the woman I thought I knew, into a wild-cat. She flew at me with long nails extended like claws, all the while screaming inanely, the only intelligible words were, 'you bastard, you bastard,' throwing heavy coins at and around me, as fast as she could pick them up, once she realized her nails couldn't reach the target.

I dodged and kept out of harm's way, for she was uncontrollable. Eventually I closed on her. As we struggled she changed her tack and began shouting at the top of her voice, 'assault, assault.'

I don't know who was assaulting whom. There was only one thing to do. I needed both hands free so I rammed my foot into her diaphragm pinning her to the wall thus freeing me to grab the phone and dial for the police.

'Snows, Piccadilly,' I yelled, slamming the phone back down, as June almost broke free.

She turned the air blue as we waited for the law, and I watched for any intervention from her friend upstairs. God knows what she was doing, for she couldn't get out, the doors were locked, and she didn't come down the stairs.

The screaming of police sirens heralded the arrival of the boys in blue. I learned later the incident actually stopped the traffic in Piccadilly Circus. The police had no idea of the seriousness, or otherwise, of the situation and they had come in force.

It was unbelievably chaotic. There was I trying to explain the predicament I had found myself in, all the while shouted down by two convincing crying women; amidst a room bursting with blue uniforms.

I phoned Shirley, she could handle this better I consoled myself, besides I needed other help.

'Get in touch with Mr Barrett at his home, and get yourself to the West End Police Station. Because that is where we are all heading. I cannot explain now what has happened, so don't ask . . . I doubt if even you will believe my version anyway.'

June and Jackie were still screaming, 'he is a liar, he threw all the money about, when we started shouting for help. He tried to rape us.'

We were bundled into the Black Maria and driven to Central Police Station, where questioning continued until Shirley and Mr Barrett arrived. I have never been so pleased to see anyone in my life. Although from the look on my wife's face, even if I got away with this, I'd still have to explain what I was doing alone with those two excuses for females. The two women, still alleging assault and attempted rape, Mr Barrett, Shirley and myself were led into an office, where an inspector sat staring stony-faced at us all. We were seated at the opposite side of the desk to the two women, before further interrogation began.

'He's a punch-drunk boxer,' June alleged. 'He forced sex on my friend, then came downstairs to assault me while I was trying to make coffee. I never touched a penny, I was in the kitchen, not the office.'

'It isn't true. It's not true,' I uselessly tried to defend myself. How very inapt that sounded, in the face of such serious accusations. Yet it was the only answer to the charge I was capable of giving. Both my wife and Mr Barrett were far from impressed, giving me peculiar glances, as I repeated for the umpteenth time the evening's events. As I concluded my story, for what was to be the last time, the inspector called in a policewoman to escort June and Jackie out of the room.

'As it stands, it is your word against theirs,' he said coldly.

I was almost at my wits end. How do you prove your innocence in a case like this? I felt I had been completely suckered by those two plausible reptiles. Was it coincidence when Sam asked for an early night? I had a terrible feeling of *déjà vu*. Then, I had staunch friends to sustain me, now I faced the consequence of my stupidity alone.

Just as I was sinking into fatalistic hopelessness, the door opened and the woman constable came into the room. With both hands she placed two piles of sweet-smelling half-crowns and two-shilling pieces in front of the surprised inspector. As they were dropped on the desk, a cloud of perfumed talcum powder arose from them.

'She has broken down, sir,' the woman constable said, with absolutely no expression on her face. She continued, 'those were hidden on her person, sir.'

Again the nightmare had ended, it was all over. This scheming, avaricious woman had brought about her own undoing . . . settling for a few paltry quid when she had found no pound notes in the tills.

In the small hours of the morning, as we were driving home in Mr Barretts's car, Mr Barrett said sternly, 'put this down to experience, Mr Aldridge.'

He went very quiet for a while, before breaking into a chuckle, saying, 'they were two good-looking buggers, weren't they? Didn't that talcum powder smell?'

I was very relieved he was not going to throw the book at me and cared little that I had only three hours sleeping time left, before I had to be back at Snows to let in the staff.

Down to experience it went. The village youth who considered himself worldly-wise, was losing his naivety, and fast becoming just that, well street-wise at least.

We had our relief time to finish at Snows, and much leg-pulling I received from the regulars too. Thank God, there were no further earth-shaking events, everything going smoothly until the Verrells returned. Then I had to tell him about June and her amorous friend, I think he still had a soft spot for her, which I most surely hadn't . . . the only spot I thought suitable for that lady was Holloway Jail.

Our next assignment was at an equally favourite place, the Holyrood, off Oxford Street. Alas, our reputation had preceded us. Mr Boncey would introduce us henceforth as, 'this is the couple who stopped Piccadilly Circus.'

We didn't know if that made us into Celebrities or Notorieties, which-ever, it seemed good for business. The gossip had spread like wildfire, and, as is wont, became more fanciful in the telling.

After the Camden Head and Snows, our fame spread among the West End Houses. It became a regular thing to be asked to relate both incidents over and over, for special customers. In the end we enjoyed it as much as the pub's clients. In retrospect it wasn't half so bad.

After the Holyrood relief we moved on to the Spread Eagle, further up Oxford Street. This was another reputable eating house. So time went by. As we became more experienced, so we became more discontented with living out of suitcases; and being perpetually on the move.

Twelve months had come and gone, Jacqueline was still in Doncaster with Mam, thoroughly disillusioned. Feeling used, we took over the holiday relief of the Devonshire Blue, which was on the fringe of Soho. It was a nice pub with two bars, snack bar and silver-service restaurant. The manager left us with the use of a small bedroom, next to which was the storeroom, where he kept his stock of liquor and cigarettes.

A very busy house, by the Sunday of the second week we were tired and ready for our bed by close of business. We wasted no time in retiring. About 1 a.m. I woke to a sound which appeared to emanate from the room next door, the storeroom.

As the slight noise was repeated, I knew someone had broken in there. I carefully nudged my wife awake, quietly saying, 'don't make any noise, don't touch the lights, try to ring the police in the dark. Tell them we have a break-in.'

The last people I ever wanted to see again were the boys in blue, yet once more I was left with no alternative.

I went stealthily on to the landing. Opening the still locked door with its yale-key, I immediately dropped to my hands and knees. My eyes by now accustomed to the dark allowed me to see, silhouetted outside the window, the shape of a man.

The security bars had been forced apart, the window itself was wide open. I soon realized I wasn't alone inside the room. Understanding the danger in this, I had to act quickly or I could be in serious trouble. There was only one thing to do, get rid of the man outside first. I could see him and it wouldn't be long before he'd be able to see me. I came up from the floor and caught him flush on the jaw. It was a good punch. With all that extra momentum he fell screaming two storeys down to the alley-way below.

I fell upon the dark figure now advancing swiftly towards me, visible now that my back was to the light. We rolled about the floor amid cartons of fags and bottles of liquor. Putting punch after punch into the struggling, yelling mass, I couldn't see where they were landing. Only from his sudden shout of capitulation I knew they were. 'I've had enough, I've had enough, Guv'ner,' he repeated.

I jumped up and away from him to the light switch. As the light flooded the room I could see the complete shambles we had caused, as we had thrashed around. Broken bottles and crushed cartons lay everywhere. Christ, I pleaded to myself, why the hell does it keep happening to me? Angrily I grabbed the man, forcing his arm up his back I frogmarched him down the stairs. A white-faced Shirley who, having done her job, backed away from us to the door as the police belatedly arrived.

As they grabbed hold of the one I had brought downstairs, I told them 'there is another miscreant in the alley-way. He fell from the window of the storeroom.'

I was to bitterly regret telling them about him, how I wished I had kept my mouth shut. With the fall alone he had paid his dues.

Much later during the court case, after I had testified, I learned that the man who had been inside the storeroom, an Irishman, had a criminal record as long as your arm. An out-and-out villain he was sentenced to three years' jail. It wouldn't change him; as soon as he had the opportunity he'd be up to his old tricks again.

The man who had taken the fall into the alley-way, had broken his leg in several places, and was very lucky to have escaped with that. It was his first offence. He had a spastic child and was desperate for money, allowing the Irishman to talk him into the break-in for those reasons. He was given a six month sentence.

It left a sour taste in my mouth for weeks on end, poor sod. If I had only known, he would never have been turned in by me.

On the Monday after the holiday relief was over, we were told to cover a management day-off at the Oxford and Cambridge.

The following day we were to report to Levy and Franks Head Office, for an interview with Harry Franks—the big Boss-man himself.

Not knowing what to expect after our recent misfortune at the Devonshire Blue, my wife and I entered the magnificent office of Mr Franks. We were seated facing the great man. To our relief Mr Barrett was also present.

All kind of images crossed our minds as to the reason for this summons, without exception all were gloomy and foreboding. We had good grounds for this pessimism, ill luck having dogged our footsteps, whether through our own misjudgment, or the unpitying, impish chance of always being in the wrong place at the wrong time. A trait not likely to endear us to Mr Franks.

Shirley sat bolt upright, her fingers stiffly crossed under the silk scarf she held, not looking at anyone, just staring fixedly ahead. I suppose my demeanour also gave both men the same impression, for we were two very frightened young people.

Mr Franks gazed at us blankly, giving nothing away.

'Mr and Mrs Aldridge,' he began, 'Mr Barrett informs me you have had an eventful, although very successful, relief programme for more than a year with us.'

He paused and studied some papers on the desk in front of him. It appeared for ever before he looked up again, and at the two of us.

'We are going to allow you to manage one of our prestige houses, in the West End.'

My hands tightened on the chair seat. I had been unknowingly gripping the seat so hard my hands hurt. An involuntary silly grin was forcing my jaws apart. I looked at Shirley who was smiling at me with a warmth I hadn't seen for a long time. Still we were barely able to grasp that we had made it, the pub of our own which we had so covetously desired for so long was actually going to be ours.

'You will take over the Porcupine, one month from today,' Mr Franks said smilingly. 'Good luck in your new position.'

We were ecstatic, we couldn't thank Messrs Barrett and Richards enough for giving us this chance.

We had a further three weeks of relieving other management before we were to have a week's holiday ourselves. Then we would take over our own house as resident managers. What a marvellous thought that was. We would even have done three weeks in the Camden Head if they had asked. Fortunately it was never again required of us.

Mam was over the moon with the news, she dashed up and down the street telling her neighbours of our good fortune. We were greeted like conquering heroes everywhere we went, all my mates saving every penny to visit us in the big city.

Best of all we were to be reunited with our daughter.

We made the preparations for her to start school, it was an infants' pre-school actually, situated behind the famous Windmill Theatre, on the edge of Piccadilly Circus. One she was to enjoy attending, for even then she was a very determined young lady. She always knew exactly what she wanted out of life.

Chapter 5

THE day for taking over the Porcupine arrived at last, our little family of three strutted around the outside of the building, surveying proudly what was to be our new home.

The leaving manager escorted us around the premises, introduced us to the staff, for we had never relieved this house, then he officially handed over. Finally, it was ours. Shirley and I watched him go, so pleased we completely forgot our manners, omitting to ask the man where he was going, or why he had decided to leave.

The Porcupine had a good class restaurant on the first floor, with bar snacks being served downstairs. We were not the only things around there which were being changed, or on the verge of being so. Probably this was the reason why the manager had left.

Levy and Franks were about to be taken over by the Chef and Brewer Company and it wasn't too long before the change came about. Almost overnight the Porcupine became an Ind-Coope house, with a massive tightening up of the catering side of the business.

Chef and Brewer demanded a sixty-five per cent return on all food purveyance. In this instance it was a very high profit margin indeed, as all supplies had to be obtained from them, at a much higher cost to us than they would have been had they come from a free source. Tied to them, meant they received both wholesale and retail benefit, at a higher rate than could be obtained if both sides were free.

In spite of this disadvantage, and our chagrin, we made the percentage required of us. My name now being duly inscribed over the front door of the Porcupine, as the licensee.

My wife and I had discussed the tactics we would use in the Porcupine, agreeing to try to emulate Snows of Piccadilly. Starting with the staff we set about this task. The barmaids were to be dressed in the same colour and style of dress, the barmen were attired in striped jackets and dicky bow ties; giving what we hoped would be an urbane atmosphere. For in those

The Porcupine, Charing Cross Road corner of Leicester Square, 1990. Our first management position in London, 1961.

days the West End was still a classy place to be, and not least in the pecking order was The Porcupine.

Next door stood the Pickwick Club, then being owned by Harry Secombe and Wolf Mankowitz. The Talk of the Town was across the road, Max Rivers' studios were in Newport Street, as was a large block of luxury flats, Newport House, where John Lennon, Diana Dors, Tommy Steele and a host of other top-notch stars lived. The Porcupine, being just twenty yards or so away, was the local for many of those household names. A lot of the big shows were running in our vicinity too, most starring the names of show business; many of whom we saw inside the Porky.

The village which consisted of Leicester Square, Trafalgar Square, Piccadilly Circus and their environs became our playground as well as our workplace. The Aldridges as licensees, were well-known and accepted by their peers in that exclusive neighbourhood, during the fabulous era in which we all shared.

The Pickwick Club, was an actors' Equity place. Of course, this meant one had to be in Show Business to get in. Being the licensee next door opened this Aladdin's Cave of entertainment for both Shirley and me. I knew the manager, Angelo, and was also a good friend of the head doorman, an ex-boxer named Bert Ireland. It led to many a magic night, for after the Porcupine had closed at 11 p.m. we would, on occasion, go next door to be more than entertained by the best in the world. A little way along Charing Cross Road was Soho with all the clip joints, prostitutes and pimps which go to make up this collective sleaze area known as Soho. They became familiar to me as I took a nightly promenade into their stamping ground. I would walk around Piccadilly, back through Leicester Square and so home to bed. I also became well-known by the denizens of the night, which no doubt saved my bacon from time to time. An unfamiliar person being at risk to muggers and others of that ilk.

The bouncers, callers outside the strip joints, and the newspaper vendors, greeted me as I passed with, 'evening, Guv,' or 'hello, Guv,' a salutation which in my youthful arrogance I found stimulating to my ego.

Celebrity I was not, known I most certainly was, and not always in respect of my intelligence.

An incident of my early days as a publican comes to mind. It was a stifling, summer's evening, the end of a very hot day, when the sun-rays had bounced back off those concrete alleys of inner London. The heat unable to escape had clung to the walls of those old buildings, mingling with the diesel and petrol fumes discharged by the traffic. It hung in poisonous vapours we laughingly called heat-haze.

I stood by an open upper window in the Porcupine, hoping vainly for a cooling breeze . . . but inhaling instead the smells associated with the city during warmer weather.

Over the road, at the end of Newport Alley, a group of people had slowly gathered. Curious as to what was going on, I left the Porky and hurried to join them. They allowed me to get within fifteen yards or so from them, then they suddenly bolted in every direction, all that remained was an empty orange box.

Still puzzled, and no wiser, I returned home to the Porcupine.

Later that night, after re-opening for the evening trade, three men came in and stood at the bar, they stared belligerently at yours truly. 'All right?' I asked worriedly, for they looked far from all right.

'You fucking bastard,' one of them snarled, 'you broke up the best school I'd had all day. I had two bloody good Yank punters until you showed up. What's your bloody game?'

It turned out this man, known as Ronnie, ran Find-the-Lady schools in the West End, Petticoat Lane and Covent Garden, besides all major race tracks. I had unwittingly walked into one of their games, causing it to break up when their men, posted at vantage points to spot the police, mistook me for a copper and gave the signal to flee.

I apologized profusely, for I had cost them money. Despite my stupidity we became good friends. After all, his men had mistaken me for the law, so were nearly, if not quite to blame for their loss.

One of the men with him that night had only one arm, yet he was Ronnie's best dealer and aptly named, One Arm Luke, a man I was to get to know very well. Dexterity would have been just as apt a name for him, he was more adept with one arm than most people are with two.

Luke could have made a decent living working for himself. For a bet he would take on the gamblers in the Porcupine. The wager was that he could tie his shoe laces faster with one hand than they could with two. Simple, and they fell for it in droves. Another popular bet involved tying a windsor knot in his tie faster than the punter. I never knew him to lose a stake. With the tie he was so fast and slick. He would start with one end in his mouth, his only hand flicking the material like lightning over, in, and pulling the tie taut, faster than your eyes could follow. Sometimes he would catch an American tourist who would unbelievingly pay up on losing, they had been taken by the best and usually were very proud of the fact. Pleased as punch to have met him, for he was a character in his own right, and part of the London Scene.

Discussing the game of Find-the-Lady one day, Ronnie told me, 'no one wins. The only folk who seemingly win, are plants we put in to fool the watchers into having a bet.'

They would come into the Porcupine at night, laughing and in a good mood if they had struck lucky that day. Laughing even louder if they had caught someone famous like Bruce Forsyth whom, they boasted, had been taken for £200. That the stories were probably as big a 'con' as the game itself made them no less entertaining.

The Porky did well, we increased the turnover in both the liquor and food departments. Shirley managed the catering side of the business. I stuck with the side I knew, the beer and liquor trade.

Then calamity struck; our very good chef left us. We had to find another of equal standing, fast. A hard task in a place like London, where first rate chefs are at a premium. Shirley stood in until we could fill the vacancy.

I had been bemoaning our loss to all who would listen, then one day a local jeweller, who was also a good customer, asked to see me. 'Would you save a man's life, Peter?' he asked.

Is there really an answer to a question as dramatic as that? I wondered how by any action of mine, a man's life could be saved?

I knew it wasn't a hypothetical query, the jeweller had asked to see me in private. Without further ado I burnt my boat. Nevertheless, with fingers crossed, I said, 'certainly, if I could. How?' all in the same breath.

From the moment he asked, he knew there were no other answer anyone could give. If I am wrong and there is another reply, without being bloody-minded, I don't really want to know; thereby saving myself much further grief.

The jeweller had me in his trap, he now sprang it. 'By giving him the chef's job here.'

Dumbfounded, I gazed at him askance hardly believing my ears. Surely he didn't expect to pull that one off? Thinking my best bet was to equivocate, as he had hardly come to the point with me. I answered, 'I am sorry, my wife handles the catering side of the business, which includes all hiring and firing of staff. I will have to discuss it with her.'

'It will be too late, he is going to commit suicide unless I can get him this position. You see, Peter, I have told him I could fix him up here, to stop him killing himself. He is determined to do it, if he doesn't find work. Please help.'

I remember thinking, Christ, how do I manage to continually get myself into this kind of shit? I didn't air my thoughts. Instead I took the coward's way out and said, 'wait a moment I'll fetch Shirley.'

I dashed up to the kitchen, where Shirley was setting in motion the menu for the day. After explaining the situation to her, she said, 'leave it to me, I will think of something.'

Shirley followed me downstairs in very quick time. The first question she put to the jeweller was short and to the point, 'has he had previous chef's experience?'

Neither my wife nor I expected the kind of answer we received to that broadside.

'He was a contortionist on the stage,' the jeweller said, without batting an eyelid, or having the grace to look a bit sheepish.

This was getting worse by the minute. Flummoxed, my wife may have been, angry she most certainly was at the moment. She brusquely said, 'I must have an experienced chef. I have 200 meals of very good quality, to produce every day.'

'He is a very good cook, it's his hobby,' the jeweller said, then he capped everything that had gone before, by adding the rider, 'I suppose I had better tell you, I'm afraid he is a queer, and you know what they are like. He will kill himself. Give him a week's trial, please, I beg of you.'

We never knew for sure, but we both wouldn't have taken any bets the jeweller wasn't the man's boyfriend. This would explain his anxiety for the ex-contortionist, yet I had not suspected him of being one of those in the time I had known him.

We were in a difficult situation. Short of giving him an outright no, which we were both loath to do, we asked instead, 'can we have a few moments alone to discuss this?'

'Look, give him a week's trial. What have you got to lose?' he pleaded, as I almost shoved him out of the office.

'Only our flaming jobs,' I said in an aside to Shirley.

My wife sat quietly just looking at me, as if trying to read my mind. 'We will give him that week, I will oversee everything he does in that time. That is all the time he will get, if he's no good, out he goes,' she finished decisively.

I knew the decision had been made partly because, as I've intimated, chefs were hard to come by in the West End. We had as much chance of discovering one, as the Irish have of finding gold in the streets. We broke the news to the waiting jeweller. He nearly shook my hand off. 'You will not regret it, Peter,' he repeated himself, 'you will not regret this.'

I sincerely hoped he was right. Well, I thought, if he wants to go there are plenty of knives hanging in the kitchen, to help him on his way. Then enormity of it struck me.

How the hell do I explain giving an unstable, possible suicide, a position as a chef?

The following Monday our new chef, Mr Geoffrey de Vere, presented himself for work. Considering we had given him, a possible fruit and nut case, a job sight unseen, we hadn't done badly at all.

He was of good appearance and hardly looked the type to take his own life. That is if there is a type which will do such a thing.

He was to stay with us throughout our time in the Porcupine. He proved to be not only a jolly good cook, but with a culinary flair to match most chefs. Unflappable too, which is a great asset in a pressure-ridden kitchen.

We had a vegetable cook named Ivy, who lived in Brixton. She was born in the East End of London, and had the quick wit and ready repartee of the true cockney; plus the colourful language which adorned it. We all appreciated the wit, yet could have done without some of Ivy's vast vocabulary of swear words. She liberally endowed every sentence with more than its fair share of colourful expletives.

On first sighting of Mr de Vere she reacted true to form, 'fuck me,' she said explicitly, 'he's as queer as a f'ing nine bob note.'

Yet it was a strange relationship which developed between those two extremes of personalities. They would continually bicker and fall out, all the time working together to produce excellent fare. Eventually, they became firm friends, although they persisted in their arguments for as long as I knew them. Ivy opted to stay with us throughout our term at the Porcupine, too.

On occasion Geoffrey would baulk at Ivy's superfluous oaths, saying, 'she is coarse, that woman, she is very coarse.'

I agreed with him, yet for all that she had her winning ways, and so was a favourite of mine. Notwithstanding, at times the unnecessary addition of all those adjectives did irritate the old ear drums. In that case I would be compelled to tell her to cut it out, enough was enough.

Regardless of this, she was the mould within which the proverbial rough diamond had been cast. Her heart was pure, unadulterated gold. At no time did the woman ever let us down, ever present, and always more than willing to help out in whatever capacity. Her only fault that abominable profanity.

Sometimes the dumbwaiter door in the restaurant had to be hurriedly closed, and a profuse apology given to the startled customers seated near the lift-shaft. You could bet your bottom dollar something had gone wrong in the kitchen, and Ivy would be exercising her ability to never repeat a swearword twice in the one sentence.

This would send Shirley dashing for the stairway to the kitchen to restore order. One could then hear my wife yelling, 'cut it out, Ivy, they can hear you all the way downstairs.'

The Porcupine was a four-storey building. We hadn't an elevator, just one main staircase to serve all floors. The entire top floor had been converted into the manager's quarters. The kitchens were on the third floor, the restaurant on the second floor, and the bar occupied all the ground floor space.

Every morning I had to pass the busy kitchens, coming down from our flat after changing my work-clothes, before opening the bar. Often Geoffrey would remark as I passed the doorway to his work area, 'oh, you do smell lovely.'

Without fail Ivy would mutter under her breath to me, 'watch him, Guv'ner, he's an arse bandit.'

I had many a smile at the antics those two got up to in the kitchens. I know they kept the rest of the staff amused and contented. We had a very small turnover of employees, which helped our reputation with the Company.

The Porcupine was actually built over the top of Leicester Square Underground Station. It was the only thing I disliked about the Porky, for when trains came in or out of the station, we would know by the rattling of glasses behind the bar. Our main entrance was next to the Tube passageway, and the paper-stand where Charlie, the paper man, stacked his incredible range of magazines and newspapers. I marvel still at the speed with which he served the seething mass of people, that swarmed unceasingly up and down the thoroughfare. Yet he remained calm and collected at all times, his sense of humour always to the fore. In his place, I would have been flat on my face tearing up the pavement with my teeth.

His cheery shout of, 'morning, Madam,' or 'morning, Guv,' brightened up many a dismal day for Shirley or myself. How the hell he had time to notice us has me beat.

Shirley's first job in the morning was to get Jacqueline ready for school. We would take it in turns escorting her along Charing Cross Road to Cambridge Circus, then left down Shaftesbury Avenue to the small school behind the Windmill Theatre, on the fringe of Piccadilly. It was a colourful walk we all enjoyed, past the theatres putting on most of the top shows, the dress shops and jewellery stores, the red double-decker buses and taxi-cabs jostling for position in the crowded streets. The good-natured bantering, the shouts and laughter ringing out, and the hustle and bustle on the congested pavements, as commuter, tourist and shopper alike moved along as if on a conveyor belt—all the area's wonderful ambience, unmistakable, inimitable anywhere in the world. It is something which never leaves you, a warm pervasive memory clinging to the senses.

Old London Town, and we were part of it. At times I would stand still in those streets reflecting on just how lucky we were. To have our first pub in what most people acknowledge as the centre of the world, the West End of London.

The Porcupine was an extremely busy house, throughout its opening hours. The morning session was from 10.30 a.m. to 2.30 p.m., re-opening at 5.30 p.m. and closing for the day at 11 p.m. Unless we were going out, my wife and I would sit at our fourth floor window, drinking a cup of tea and literally watching the world go by. From this magnificent vantage point we had a continuously, entertaining show, like the Windmill, it never closed. Constantly changing, yet the established stars stayed on. The prostitutes plying their trade in Soho, the pimps aimlessly standing yet ever watchful. The owners of the strip clubs and their employees, all the underworld shadows which tend to thrive on others. All were players on this our own stage, amid the glamour of neon-lit Leicester Square and Piccadilly Circus, tourist-crowded and all hungry for the pleasure the night would offer.

At the top of Charing Cross Road stood Freddie Mills' Night spot. I would periodically spend an evening with him there. He was, and will always be, the set standard of a Boxing Champion. He epitomized everything which I had longed to be.

At the end of the Second World War, when Britain needed a boost to its jaded morale, when the victor appeared to have become the vanquished, struggling to pay war debts and watching the conquered climb to the top of the world's financial heap, along came Freddie Mills, a champion of their own loins. He gave them the colour which Bruce Woodcock was unable to provide. Brash extrovert Freddie was, yet a modest man too. For being both he won the acclaim of boxing fans and others alike. Everyone loved Freddie Mills. I would ask my friends when they visited, 'would you like to meet Freddie Mills?'

Without exception they jumped at the chance, for he was a living legend. I would take them along to his club, where Freddie would duly make a great fuss of them, shaking their hands. Chatting to them as if he had known them for years, putting them completely at ease. What a man! He fought Bruce Woodcock twice, both fights being won by Woodcock. The difference between the two men was astronomical. Bruce shy, reserved, cautious, no one word describes the man adequately, tight with money and more often than not, blunt to the point of rudeness. Freddie bubbled over with confidence, his personality truly magnetic, money to him was easy come, easy go, it didn't appear to be important to him either way. His manners were impeccable at all times. I spent many happy hours in his company. Sometimes I would find him sitting in his car at the rear of the club, if business was quiet. He died in that car, in that place, from bullet wounds.

To this day, I cannot accept the verdict of suicide. There is a great question mark, too many imponderables. This life-loving, happy family-man who loved his children so much, would not take his own life in such a cowardly fashion. It is only sad, frightened people, unable to cope, or to face up to the world, who do such things.

Two weeks prior to his death I had been in Soho getting my hair cut. Freddie used the same shop. This day he bounced in and out, everyone he knew received either a cheery wave, or an effusive hello. He greeted me normally, yet I will never forget his last words to me, mundane as they were. He could put a lot of feeling into his speech. 'So long, Old Son,' he said, as cheerfully as usual.

It was to be so long, I never saw him again. So long, Freddie.

As I have told you, the Porcupine was next door to the Pickwick Club. Bert Ireland, the head doorman, told Shirley and me they were holding Marlene Dietrich's sixty-fifth birthday party on the coming Friday night. It was the end of her week's show at a theatre in Shaftesbury Avenue, Bert Bacherach had accompanied her on the piano. He was also going to be at the party, with his wife, the gorgeous Angie Dickinson. She, in my humble opinion, is the most beautiful woman imaginable.

The Friday we had awaited so eagerly arrived, but Angelo, the manager, came to see us with sad tidings, 'sorry, Peter, there is no way I can let you in there tonight.'

My wife and I were bitterly disappointed. It sometimes happened that their guests would request privacy, one had to abide by that.

We waited outside our side door, along with all the staff, craning our necks to see the fabulous Marlene. The chauffeur-driven Daimler, absolutely chock-a-block with roses, pulled in to the kerbside. We managed to catch a glimpse of the star as she alighted and went into the Pickwick Club.

We then had to resume our duties inside the Porky for business as usual, and did not see Bert Bacherach and Angie Dickinson arrive.

We had just finished cleaning down, when Bert Ireland appeared in the bar, looking really pleased with himself. 'Angelo says you can come down, if you want to, Peter.'

Want to! Wild horses couldn't have kept us away. Put it this way, we needed no second invitation. Shirley was into a long dress, and I into evening clothes, faster than we had ever dressed before.

We hurried next door. The standing rule in the Pickwick was, one must not talk to or in anyway pester the stars. Asking for autographs was considered *infra dig*. However one could sit and watch through the mirrored walls a lot of what was going on in the club.

Most of the time, Marlene was surrounded by a constantly moving horde of people. Eventually, a small gap appeared against the bar, where she was sitting holding court and we then had a clear view of this stunning person. 'If she is sixty-five, I will eat my hat,' I said to Shirley. 'That makes her the same age as my mother.'

'Yes, but remember all she has to worry about is keeping her face and figure. In that case we could all be beautiful at her age.'

That's as maybe. That night there wasn't a red-blooded male in that room, who wouldn't have made a pass at Marlene, given half a chance. It seemed lascivious somehow to me to contemplate such an idea. Yet contemplate it I did, in great detail.

She was the only 65-year-old I have ever fancied. Even today when I am pushing it, I still remember that elegant lady.

I told Mam later and did she laugh. I think I have told you, I had a lovely Mam.

I walked over to the bar to get drinks for Shirley and myself, trying to catch the barman's eye I turned slightly, to look straight into the inquiring eyes of the film star. Nonplussed I said the first thing which came into my head, brilliant it was, too. 'Happy Birthday.'

She held me with the longest stare, a do-I-know-you look in those eyes, which were the sexiest I have ever seen, before she answered in that well known seductive drawl, guaranteed to turn anyone's head, 'thank you.'

Then the mob closed around her again and I returned to Shirley, trying to balance our drinks while floating on air.

'You know you shouldn't talk to people in here,' Shirley angrily said, as I seated myself.

'What did she say to you?' curiosity getting the better of her as I didn't appear to be forthcoming.

'Get lost,' I answered.

'That jolly well serves you right,' a satisfied wife settled back in her chair, pleased that I had got my come-uppance from the lady.

We laughed all night about the imagined blow to my self esteem. Until now my wife has really thought Marlene actually told me to get lost. I watched through the mirrors as celebrities and unknowns alike, fêted this lone, lovely lady. Among the guests was the beautiful Angie Dickinson, chatting animatedly to the people clustered around the star of the night. Far from being swamped by Marlene's beauty she shone in her own right.

Later, in the early hours of the morning, I made my usual promenade of the village. As I passed through Soho I met, and stopped to talk to a strip club bouncer I knew, named Ted.

'I met Marlene Dietrich at the Pickwick,' I bragged exaggeratedly, 'you would never believe she is sixty-five, she is out of this world.'

'Use our club, Guv'ner,' he said, unimpressed by my story, 'they are a lot younger in here.'

I laughed all the way home to many a passer-by's amusement, who probably thought my dog had done something.

The following day I phoned Mam to tell her who I had seen.

'I was fancying a woman of sixty-five yesterday,' I told her jokingly.

'She looked thirty at the most,' I added.

'Stay away from that sort,' she admonished, 'they are bad women.'

Mam was so straightlaced when she assumed the mantle of protectiveness, over her offspring.

When I explained who the lady was, she laughed fit to burst at my foolishness, then as the name registered with her, she repeated it several times lovingly, 'oooh, she is my favourite star,' she finally gasped.

I would have given my right hand to have been able to introduce her to Miss Dietrich, what pleasure she would have derived from that. I pictured her later that day, running around Ash Grove, like the town crier. By nightfall there'd be very few people in the vicinity, who hadn't heard about my meeting with the famous. Knowing Mam's penchant for exaggeration, I had probably been in conversation with Marlene for hours.

I was to have more visitors from Armthorpe, hoping they would catch sight of the notables, and notorieties which used the area. Some of them did, a few would sit in the Porcupine and observe the clientele, entranced. Mam was apt to do so when a celebrity stayed awhile within the walls of the Porky.

The Porcupine went on increasing its trade on the pub side, while the restaurant, although now using a set menu, not an à la carte as previously, we still managed to keep a good-class trade, the variety of dishes, being cut to obtain the percentage of profit demanded by the brewery. Downstairs in the bar we served both hot and cold snacks, where the business man with little time to spare, or the office worker, could obtain a substantial meal for a very low cost . . . shepherd's pie, ravioli cheese, toad-in-the-hole, meat pies, salads, sandwiches were available plus other quick bites, all were popular.

Less popular with me were the bloody luncheon vouchers. Hundreds of the pestiferous things weekly. These were handed out by employers as a type of perk, a tax-free gratuity to their employees. The winner of course being the boss, the loser the Inland Revenue. Plus of course those in the catering industry, who had to administer the blasted scheme. Whosoever had thought of this idea, should, in my opinion, be put to the stake, or meet some other dire end for all the trouble they have heaped upon the innocent.

To say they were a nuisance was the understatement of all time, regular customer and stranger alike, asked to exchange the benighted voucher for cigarettes and booze. The stranger posed no problem, with my regulars I dare not offend by refusing. Even though it was illegal to exchange them for anything other than food, this went on all over Britain. Despite the penalties being high, none dare risk offending their best clients. Not only did we risk losing our licence, we had the added work of separating the money from the food till into the bar till to cover the cost of the tobacco and liquor we had swapped for the luncheon vouchers.

A strict tally had to be maintained. The profit margin on the bar side, being much lower than the catering percentage.

The West End of London still had a prestigious reputation then, as the sixties progressed, it declined rapidly. Before the downturn, one saw most hotels and public houses opening and closing their grilles, at the start and close of business. Nowadays these are an extreme rarity, in fact, I think they have hit the antique market. And more's the pity. I am not opposed to change for progress, but to my way of thinking, we have achieved little in the post-war years to commend us to future generations.

My sister Kate returned to England recently, after ten years abroad, this was in 1989. She was livid at the wholesale destruction, and the indescribable filth everywhere. She exploded, 'architects, they are not. Philistines and dyed in the wool Vandals, they are.'

She searched in vain for the places where she had worked, and others she had loved. One of the latter was the Hudson's Bay Company building, by the side of London Bridge. It was a stripped edifice, the sou'westered fishermen gone, the whole being flanked by glass and steel monstrosities.

Coming off the bridge to the Dickens steps, they were closed and wrapped in sheets of hoarding, the approach to the station vastly changed and not for the better.

Snows of Piccadilly was also encased in hoarding, it, too, was in line for destruction, so it seemed was most of Old London. This in spite of the fact that it was midsummer, and therefore high-season for the tourists. I wonder if the powers-that-be know the world traveller comes to Britain for its history, and historical buildings. They have the high rise eye-sores at home, they do not need to visit Britain to see them.

I hate to rub salt into the wounds inflicted, yet people in this busy metropolis appeared friendlier then. They had more time for the man in the street, their jocularity, and their innate ability to see and feel the funny side of everything, left a warm feeling.

It was a cold, hard city, as most capital cities are. However, good manners was a London unspoken code, and remarked upon by visitors to this fascinating part of the globe.

An incident which occurred during our early years at the Porcupine, happened at a time when pubs in the West End were choosy about the type of customer they served. One, without fail, kept an attentive eye on the clientage, riff-raff were quickly ousted, dress was carefully monitored. Though Snows we were not, I still insisted on a suitable type of dress and behaviour in the customers. Anybody who appeared even slightly dishevelled was soon sent packing.

Shirley and I had a signal which we used if either was in the flat upstairs, and there was urgent need for both in the bar. We would click the phone once, we would answer that one click and so would know what was going on downstairs. If the phone clicked three times, it spelt trouble, or the bosses were in. Without further ado we would make our way quickly to the bar, not bothering to answer the phone.

This particular day I was in the bathroom when the phone pinged three times. In *déshabillé*, I grabbed the phone to find out how urgent the summons was, Shirley answered, 'quick, get down here, there is a dangerous man in the bar.'

I went as is, almost breaking my neck on the stairs in my desperate haste, past the kitchens, running by the restaurant and down the last flight of stairs, finally dashing into the bar breathless, expecting God knows what kind of bother.

'Where,' I gasped out to Shirley.

'Shush,' she said, she put her finger to her lips. 'Be quiet, look there.'

There were all the bar staff ogling surreptitiously this tall, straight-backed man, sitting at the bar harmlessly demolishing a generous serve of shepherd's pie, and a pint of beer. Apparently oblivious to all the attention he was attracting, he was reading what appeared then to be a printed script. It was Patrick McGoohan, the star of *Danger Man*, a television series, at that time running to top rating. And also a favourite show of mine.

My wife, her sense of humour overriding her better judgement, had decided to pull my leg.

'I might have broken my bloody neck getting down here,' I swore softly at Shirley. 'Look at me, I am half bloody dressed.'

'Well, you would have been more upset, if you had missed him.' She was right, I would have hated missing him, his acting and the show I really liked.

I told him later how she had hoaxed me, and I had almost come down the stairs head first. He thought it very funny. Laughing, he waved his finger waggishly at Shirley, then pointing to me he said, 'dangerous man, indeed, I am glad he wasn't armed.'

Sometimes during a working day we would be alerted to men holding hands under their table, or being overly affectionate towards each other in a mild way. Remember, homosexuality was still illegal. Not as openly prevalent as today's permissive society, homosexuals still existed and on the whole were very nice mannered people. Lesbians were more apt to break the house rules than the men, having a tendency to show off by soliciting, or going over the top with their advances to their soul mates. At times it was extremely difficult to pick them out, both Shirley and me getting more than our fair share of propositions, on occasion astounding the pair of us, for we certainly hadn't realized they were homosexuals. Immediately this happened I would take them to task, making it quite clear, although we tolerated them, we most certainly were not of their ilk, telling them that activities of that nature would not be accepted within the Porcupine. They must keep their soliciting, and all other behaviour which would be offensive to other users of the Porcupine, outside the boundaries of the house.

In this manner we earned the respect of the Gay community, which frequented the West End. They quickly adapted to our rules, knowing they were more than welcome in the Porky, as long as they behaved themselves, and didn't attract unnecessary attention.

Once this maxim passed through the ranks, we had little further trouble with the regulars.

It was about this time Jack Spot's wife started to use the Porcupine. Jack Spot had reputedly run London's gangland. Rumour had it, the Kray brothers took over from Jack.

It was truly remarkable how two young, virtually unknown, East End boxers, appeared to spring from nowhere into prominence in a comparatively short space of time. Maybe it was true, I wouldn't know, despite getting to know the Kray brothers later on.

Jack Spot's wife was a very attractive lady, usually elegantly dressed in black and loaded with expensive jewellery. She would sit at the bar for hours and talk to either Shirley or myself. We found her to be very good company, yet I think she was a very lonely lady, sitting at a bar for the length of time she did, with just the odd drink and us for company. When it was time for her to go she would say, 'well, I must go, or else.'

I often wondered what the or else meant for she went so reluctantly. I knew my wife gained the same impression. It was very intriguing and we would speculate about the reason for her reluctance, neither of us accepting the loneliness as a cause. The woman did not give that impression. It was far more sinister.

I frequently ruminate about past events and people, trying to guess where and what they are doing now. I know where the Kray brothers are, where, in my humble opinion they should no longer be, but that is another story.

The Porcupine saw a lot come, and just as many go, some were real baddies, others just slightly bent. Most forced into crime by circumstance, not many from choice.

About 1963 I was introduced to Susan Shaw, a member of the post-war stable of starlets at Elstree Film Studios, among whom were numbered Margaret Lockwood, Valerie Hobson, Diana Dors and Susan Shaw.

Of course by this time Susan was no longer a household name, nor was she in films. She had been one of the unfortunates in life, and really wasn't equipped to deal with it. Her husband, the film star Bonar Colleano, had been killed in a car crash some years previously. Not surprisingly, as a result, she started to drink heavily. With her money gone, she lived in a one room flat, close to the West End she loved.

Susan would sit up at the bar in the Porky, talking of her days on the big screen, she always included the bit about her agent digging up new parts for her. There was little likelihood of that, she was a shadow of her former self, her beauty gone with each sip from the bottle. We accepted her and felt sorry for her. Listening to her talking, I think things went wrong for her with the death of her husband.

I often would speak softly to her, when the drink was taking its toll, coaxing her to leave, and escorting her over busy Charing Cross Road. We saw her mostly at night time. But one morning around 11 a.m., we had just opened and the Porky was gearing itself for another busy day, when in walked Susan with Trevor Howard, the actor. We all sat at the bar laughing and joking, for at least an hour and half. Susan in her shabby coat covered with pieces of fluff, her hair in its usual mess, grasped my hand tightly and said, 'Peter, Trevor is going to get me a part in his new film. Isn't it great?'

She was deliriously happy. I looked at Trevor who put his arm about Susan giving her a hug, then slowly and seriously winked at me. When Susan went to the ladies' room, in apparent distress, he said, 'Susan is very ill you know,' then he added, 'I bumped into her, and you know she has dragged me halfway across the West End to meet you.'

What a great fellow, I would have done that distance on my hands and knees just to know him.

This was Susan back to her former self, her eyes glowing, elated at the prospect of being before the cameras again.

She was one very sick lady, dying of cancer, unable to control her drinking. This once very beautiful person was withering before our eyes. It was with great sadness that we read in the newspapers of her death, shortly after we had left the Porcupine.

Often Shirley and I will say Susan Shaw is in this, when an old film is shown on television. We will not forget her. She particularly loved her role in *London Belongs to Me* with Richard Attenborough. She played the part of his fantasy lover and neighbour.

I remember well taking her upstairs in the Porky, after we had closed, to watch that film on our television. She completely ruined our enjoyment of the late night special, by talking throughout the film. Telling us where it was shot and how, what did and didn't happen on the set, and who was the real star of the film. Leaving us in no doubt as to where the honour fell. Attenborough wouldn't be amused.

We met Ronald Lewis around that time too. He came into the Porcupine one day with that other fine actor, Ronald Fraser. Both were in plays in the West End and both were the worse for wear drink-wise.

During our conversation Ronald Lewis pulled out a large map from his pocket. It was a plan for a public house and restaurant, he was intending to build somewhere in the south of England.

He asked for ideas for the project, telling me he had a bit of money and was looking for another arrow for his bow, besides acting. Ronald was to use the Porky many times, and invariably the discourse would get around to his old farmhouse he intended to convert into a really plush eating house. A smashing chap, he indicated he would like my wife and I to run this place when it was completed.

He went on location for a film somewhere abroad. We didn't see him again, so never knew whether he completed his dream palace, or not. Although his film and acting career appeared to be still active, over the years he dropped out of the picture. Many years later we learned Ronald Lewis had committed suicide. The film world must be a bloody sight tougher than the licensed trade. I hope he built his Shangri-La and it was successful before he died. Drink has been the downfall of many of the great names of show business. I have often wondered if they had trouble coping with the real world after having to live in the fictitious one day in and day out.

Two very sad people, Susan Shaw and Ronald Lewis, who brightened many lives unknowingly, yet ended their own in despair.

The Porcupine was still steadily increasing its sales, on both the bar and catering fronts. Obtaining new heights in takings is one thing, sustaining those achievements is quite another.

Chef and Brewer, our new owners, wanted more. They continued their push, push-push tactics, forcing us in turn to even greater effort on both sides of the business. Our social life became almost non-existent, although we never considered ourselves anything less than fortunate, in being managers of the Porky in the West End of London.

It is very doubtful if we would have stuck it out in any other place except there. As you will have grasped, we were full of life, young, eager-to-go people. Yet constantly being harassed in the name of profit. The more we made, the more the Company wanted.

Being in the West End boosted our flagging morale in lots of ways. During our very infrequent days off we were able to see some of the current top shows then being presented. *The Mousetrap* still running to packed houses, the cinemas showing such spectaculars as *Lawrence of Arabia*, *The Fall of the Roman Empire*, and *The Sound of Music*, The Talk of the Town where international stars headed the Bills. The stars more often than not would visit the Pickwick Club, and we would see them, sometimes getting to know them as they called into the Porcupine before and after rehearsals.

My wages were a measly £25 per week, hardly allowing a grandiose life style. Shirley received £4 for her seven day week, in the position of 'wife to assist' role. This was the great cheap-labour trick of those days, all the catering companies being party to it, where the wife was employed on a pittance, supposedly working part-time assisting her husband. In actuality she was expected to manage the catering side of the business full time.

With the occasional free ticket for one of the shows, our contacts next door at the Pickwick, we lived life far in excess of our earnings. There was just no way we could have afforded cinema tickets in the West End, and for sure the theatre was out finance-wise.

Next to the Pickwick Club stood Newport House, the flats therein very up-market. As I have already told you, they were mostly occupied by the eminent and titled and the show-biz celebrities of the day. A Scot named Jock was the caretaker of the building, a nice chap in many ways and we became good friends. Though there was a darker side to his personality, I was to get to know in the coming months.

It was a period in my life I am not proud of, one by writing about I just may expurgate from my conscience.

A fellow Scot and friend of Jock's, was John Lennon's chauffeur. He told me Jock had a job for life there, no matter what he did. Jock had been the chauffeur for a famous titled man. During this period he had done some mysterious service for his master which resulted in his being banned from driving for life. His livelihood gone, his employer placed him in the position of caretaker of Newport House.

There must have been some substance to this story, for he got away with everything short of murder.

To boost his salary he was in the practice of using a vacant flat, or even one that was in possession with its owner away. None of those celebrities were ever aware that during their absence their flat was regularly used by high-class call girls.

Jock made a lot of money this way, making a habit of boasting about it. Then one night when we were enjoying a late drink together, he made his clever approach.

'Peter, your wages are bloody rubbish, how the hell you manage I do not know. Why don't you bolster them a bit?'

'How the devil can I do that in here?' pointing jokingly at Shirley.

'By getting me some suitable ladies,' Jock replied seriously, 'when I give you the wink, you tell the girls.'

'You must be bloody joking, there is no way I am getting involved in that game. Thanks but no thanks.'

'Think about it, Peter, what can you lose?'

I was appalled at the very idea of becoming a pimp, for that was what Jock was offering me. Yet within days the concept had taken hold. I told myself I would have the money to give my little family the small luxuries they deserved. This way I dispelled any qualms still lingering through my puritan upbringing.

I knew a lot of the 'working girls'. Though soliciting in the Porky was strictly taboo, they used the house socially. Two of them were, by any standard, strikingly good looking females. One was a bleach-blonde, the other had jet-black hair, I nick-named them Black and White Whisky; for they reminded me of the two Scotty dogs on that advert. Do not ask me why.

Those two girls earned me in the region of £40 a week eventually, a small fortune to me then. All I had to do was to tell them when Jock had a vacancy, when as he put it, he tipped me the wink. One famous star was in America for three months. I know for a fact, his bed was used every night of that period, sometimes three or four times a night.

Years later I watched him on television, the poor sod never knew what Jock had been up to in his apartment during that time. He would probably have thrown several types of fits. It was just as well he was not aware of it or he would never have used the flat again.

Of course Jock kept the laundry, and the flats immaculately clean. The owners at no time suspected anything was going on in their property. Jock once bragged to me he was earning around £250 a week out of the deal. Now that was real heavy money in those days for a working man. Take into account it was all tax free and his overhead expenses were minimal.

I never dared to tell my mother about my extra-curricular activities, or anyone else for that matter. Shirley found out purely by accident, well into the period it covered.

It was certainly nothing to brag about, besides being immoral it was damned illegal and carried stiff penalties.

One morning Jock came into the bar, 'can you spare me a few minutes, Peter, to come next door?'

I hadn't opened the bar, still having a half hour to go before opening time. I followed him to the Newport, wondering what could possibly have gone wrong. On our arrival at the apartments, he said, 'come upstairs, I have something to show you.'

Again I followed in his wake, up the stairs and into this sumptuous flat where, in a badly rumpled bed, lay Black and White Whisky. Both were lying face down, Jock pulled back the sheets exposing the girls' naked bodies.

'If you fancy getting into them, you can,' he said coarsely.

As I have mentioned before, I have all the normal urges of any man, yet somehow I didn't fancy those two. My imagination ran riot, visualizing all who may have been before me. Professionals are not my cup of tea. I declined Jock's offer of one on the house firmly.

'Okay, dokay,' he said, giving each girl two resounding smacks across the backside.

'Get moving,' he snarled.

'All right, all right, give me some time to come around,' Black growled at him. 'You Scots bastard,' White yelled, 'aren't you getting enough out of us? Give us a bloody minute.'

'Get moving,' Jock repeated, 'the fucking owner comes back today, now you f'ing move.'

God, I have never been so ashamed of myself. I was beginning to feel more like a pimp every day. Not having seen any of the action before kept their sordid world away from mine. That no longer applied. I wasn't well pleased with Jock.

The girls by now had hurriedly dressed, cursing solidly as they left the apartment, both glaring at me in passing as if I were to blame, for Jock's callous treatment of them. Which, if you think about it, I was.

After they had gone, I turned on Jock. Furious at being involved so committedly, I shouted, 'do not ever treat them like that again, or the whole bloody deal is off. There is no need for it, and I won't stand still for it.'

In reality I was loath to stop. I needed the money, we had become accustomed to all the little extras we could now afford. Black and White were extremely attractive to men, they were not the coarse common or garden variety of prostitute, regardless of their expletives on being mishandled. They knew how to behave, and did so very well, truly fooling all but the street-wise as to their calling. Both worked very hard, some weeks the money I received from Jock was almost double my salary. Jacqueline was as well dressed as her class-mates in her beloved school. My wife and I could afford the odd meal out after a show. This way I quieted what I referred to as my conscience.

I did try to square myself with Black and White, after the Newport incident, by telling them I had warned Jock and asking them to let me know if he mistreated them again.

'That's all right, Guv, forget it,' Black said, 'the bastard doesn't worry us.'

White had nothing to say, she gave me a speculative look, before turning her back to me, summarily dismissing me and my ridiculous attempt to acquit myself of any guilt.

Once Shirley knew of my activities she worried constantly.

'I hope you realise the risk you are running, getting mixed up in the Game,' she warned.

The Game being a euphemism used by the British in reference to the world's oldest profession. I have never told my wife until now but I, too, was shit-scared most of the time I played the part of a pimp. No one could have been more pleased than I when that chapter in my life ended. I know it doesn't exonerate me, yet I do feel a certain amount of relief by putting it on paper.

Jock's friend, Tom, had been John Lennon's chauffeur for about twelve months. He used to spend most of his working day in the Porcupine, Lennon spent most of his time cooped up in his apartment, much to Tom's disgust.

'He has no idea, in fact not a bloody clue, how or what a Rolls Royce is, or should be used for,' Tom would moan to Shirley and me.

The Rolls, famous in its own right for its psychedelic colours, spent its days parked outside the Newport, on double yellow lines. Receiving a parking ticket every day that dawned. Tom would leave the ticket on the car, saying, 'once you have got a ticket, you may as well leave it on, they won't give you another one that way.'

Tom's only real cause for complaint, was he had insufficient work to do, being bored out of his mind most of the time.

'This is my schedule for the week,' he would lament, then mocking Lennon's Liverpool accent, he would repeat his Boss's instructions. 'Go to Liverpool and fetch me Mam.'

Reverting to his own mode of speech Tom bewailed, 'his next sodding order, you wouldn't believe is, "take me Mam back home". It is a criminal waste of a good Rolls Royce.'

In the latter stages of his employment by Lennon, he would say, 'give me a pint, Guv, I am in for yet another day of bloody leisure. I cannot stand much more.'

As a rule he drank only lemonade during working hours. He was an affable, conscientious man, who really thought he was wasting his time with Lennon, and it was beginning to wear him down.

One evening when it was raining cats and dogs outside, I had to get my weekend returns into Head Office. These I always posted from the Trafalgar Square all-night post office. I was going to get very wet indeed, walking in that downpour.

Tom offered to run me there and back, saying, 'you are not going out into that bloody lot.'

I climbed into the front seat of the colourful Rolls, next to him.

'Get in the back, Mate, we will do this properly,' he laughed.

So I went in magnificent style to the post office.

On our arrival the deluge had stopped, and I moved to leave the car.

'Stay where you are,' Tom commanded, 'I told you, this is being done in the correct manner.'

Donning his matching grey, chauffeur's cap, he went around the vehicle to the rear. Standing stiffly to attention, he opened the door to allow me to alight in style.

I stepped on to the pavement feeling a real charlie, as a large crowd gathered about the Rolls, parting only to admit me to the building.

'Who is it?' I heard them asking each other.

I posted my letters, walking back down the steps through the throng to the waiting car. Tom was still standing to attention, door held widely open.

'To the Porcupine, Leicester Square, sir?' he shouted, as if I were deaf. Sliding into the front seat, he laughingly said, 'thought we could get a little free advertisement out of that, Peter.'

It was a spur of the moment trick, which worked. It had been a quiet rainy Sunday evening with listless trade, now the Porky quickly filled to capacity. God knows what those people thought, as they watched me behind the bar, with Tom and Jock sitting laughing their heads off at the success of the innocent deception.

It was a great boost for the Porcupine that night, one I wished we could have used again, for the people thus conned had a good night, too. John Lennon's mother finally had Tom fired, they were on their way to Liverpool and she was acting up in her usual manner. Tom lost his temper and told her a few well chosen home truths. He said he scored more than one bull's eye. I know he'd had more than enough of the job, patently becoming more disgruntled every day.

Their peculiar, unpolished life-style was not to Tom's liking. He had been used to driving the *crème de la crème* of society and in his inverted snobbish way he considered he had come down in the world.

Basically a down to earth Scot, he nevertheless was of the opinion that the senior Mrs Lennon was upstartedly pretentious.

'She suffers from the illusion she is a lady, and she is the one who is bloody famous.' Adding waspishly, 'she loves to queen it over other people.'

Tom wasn't unemployed for long, he obtained a position as a chauffeur to a city shipping magnate. It was more to his liking, with the extra bonus of being back among the set he had become used to.

I was still to see him frequently, and to continue to receive his unsolicited help in the years ahead.

Weekdays were always very busy in the Porcupine, especially during the lunch period. On this particular day, in spite of having plenty to do, my attention had been caught by a chap seated at a table close to the bar. He appeared highly agitated; being unaccompanied I could see no reason for this disquiet. I told myself he would bear watching. About ten minutes later a well-built, very smartly dressed man entered the Porky. He stood just inside the doorway looking around the room, obviously in search of someone.

Then moving swiftly, he pushed past me as I stood against the bar, advancing on the chap at the table, he literally dived at the disturbed man. Grabbing the front of the chap's jacket, he hauled him to his feet and a sharp scuffle broke out.

This sort of behaviour I most definitely discouraged in the Porky. All who broke this rule of conduct, were forthwith expelled. More often than not they found it a permanent eviction.

This expensively attired gentleman was treated to the same swift justice and I pounced on him from behind. Believing never to give the buggers a chance, meant one can live to fight another day. I had this law-breaker's arm up his back before he realized what was happening. Dragging him to the main double doors, I forced them open with his head, slinging him bodily to the pavement outside.

He gathered himself together before turning to point a finger at me, his dark Italianate, or was it Greek, face suffused crimson with anger.

'You are dead,' he stated. Coldly venomous he repeated, 'you are dead.'

'Piss off,' I crudely answered, fed up with his seemingly empty, posturing threat and with him.

To my surprise he turned on his heel. Without another word, he moved away at a fast pace.

I looked towards Charlie at his paper stand, as he shouted, 'just a minute, Guv.'

I waited while Charlie, leaving his business unattended, hurried in my direction looking very worried.

'For Christ's sake, Guv, do you know who that is? You are in real bloody trouble now.'

'What are you on about, Charlie? I am not worried about that bugger.'

'Then you bloody well should be, bloody hell Guv, don't mess about with them it's fatal. That is one of the Kray gang you have just bloody manhandled.'

Charlie's face, as white as a sheet, expressed his concern for me and the gravity of the blunder I had committed.

My superficial knowledge of the underworld plus my crass inexperience, had landed me in a very sticky, dangerous situation.

All the same, with my limited understanding of the criminal element, I knew better than to tangle with the Kray brothers. I honestly doubt if there was anyone in London, or for that matter Britain, who hadn't heard of those bad lads. Most had gathered their knowledge from the media, others more unfortunate had found out at first hand. It seemed that I might end up being one of the latter.

Had I known of the man's connections, I would have handled the whole fiasco in an entirely different way, and I am far from being a coward.

I stared at Charlie and putting on a brave face shrugged, 'I see what you mean, can't help things now it's done, there is no way to undo it.'

I went back inside the Porky; there would be others in there who knew who the dapper man was.

I returned to my place at the bar just in time to watch the sly, silent exit, of the very nervous chap. I wondered what the hell he had done, to upset the Krays? He hadn't the appearance of the brash, foolhardy sort he needed to be to buck the terrible twins.

Unbelievably managing to put the whole episode out of my mind in a few hours, I was forcibly reminded when a man introduced himself as a detective sergeant from the Bow Street Police Station.

'Mr Aldridge, can I have a quiet word with you?' he asked.

'Sure,' I replied, wondering to myself what was wrong, I led the way upstairs to the restaurant. It had only just closed, the only people present were the waitresses still cleaning down after the lunch session.

We sat at a table overlooking Charing Cross Road. I remember very clearly his refusal of a coffee or drink. He looked at me studyingly, before clearing his throat and saying, 'Mr Aldridge, it has come to our ears that you are marked down for a going over.'

'Me! Rubbish,' I snorted loudly. 'What have I done?'

'Not rubbish, Mr Aldridge, fact, just the downright, factual truth.' He spelled out the occurrence of two days ago. He was well informed, he missed out nothing, ending with, 'we want you to take a different route, and time, every time you go to the bank. Do not leave this building, unless it is completely unavoidable, Do you understand?'

Understand? I was bloody petrified. I understood that all right.

I called my wife upstairs and told her the whole sorry story, in front of the detective. I hadn't wanted to bother her before. Now it was imperative that she knew what we were up against. She had to be put on her guard, if they couldn't reach me, they might try through her.

All my wife said in a resigned voice to the detective was, 'hell, trouble again, it seems to search us out.'

'Stay in,' he warned. 'Don't go looking for trouble, it is looking for you, in a very nasty way.'

He gave us a telephone number to ring in case of emergency, and wished us well before making his departure.

Wishing us well worried us even more than the thought of gangsters hot on our tails. It seemed like a very bad movie, only this was bloody real. Things must be ominous if they'd spared a detective to warn us. Shirley is not a worrier by nature but this affair disturbed her greatly. We stayed close to home, only venturing out to the bank, one of the staff taking Jacqueline to and from the school. This regimen lasted for over two weeks, in which time Shirley and I were almost reduced to nervous wrecks, jumping at any unusual sound.

Then Charlie came to see me.

'Peter, you are an ex-boxer, Ronnie and Reggie Kray are ex-boxers. You have something in common. Why don't you get in touch with them? It can't do any harm and it just may get you out of this fix.'

'How the hell do I get in touch with blokes like that? I don't know them or anyone else who does.'

'I can put a word in the right ear for you, if you like? I am very worried about you, Guv. Those blokes don't threaten unless they intend to carry it out. They have their position to maintain.'

'*You* are worried,' I said exaggeratingly. 'I wish the buggers would show, it's getting us both down this waiting for God only knows what.'

'This is bloody serious, Guv, don't leave it to fester. I'll get cracking on it straight away.'

Charlie, the good friend that he was, did get cracking, though some time was to elapse before anything came of it.

At around seven-thirty one evening, I was busy rearranging chairs and tables for that night's business. There were only a handful of customers in the bar.

I looked up from my task and there just a few yards from me, were a group of five men. In the middle of them stood Ronnie Kray.

Christ, I thought, this is it. I wanted them to get it over with. My wish had been granted, but how I longed to be somewhere else at that moment in time. They all looked very ugly and life-threatening to me.

'I am very pleased to see you, Ronnie,' I said, lying in my teeth. If truth be known, I was frightened out of my wits.

'Thought I'd call in and see you,' he said nonchalantly, stepping forwards to grasp my hand and shake it firmly.

'I am bloody glad you have, I have been worried to death.'

Relieved beyond measure, I told him of the incident and its aftermath. Of our being confined to the house in fear of our lives, even down to the visit from the law. I think that is what put him on side. I was hiding nothing, I'd done my job as a publican by throwing his man out. He should have told me who he was but he didn't and paid the penalty for that error. So did I.

'I knew nothing about it,' Ronnie laughed, 'it's trivial to me.'

'It wasn't bloody trivial to us,' I assured him seriously.

I brought Shirley down to the bar to meet him. We all sat to have a drink together, and we started talking boxing. The Krays loved the game as much as I. We were to meet many times over the years with both brothers, the topic of conversation nearly always boxing.

I liked the Kray brothers. Villains they may well have been, we saw just two friendly men, tough, because their upbringing had been tough. They wanted wealth and all it brought with it and they got it in the only way possible for such as they. They were punished for those crimes against our society, as we so genteelly put it.

I firmly believe their long, uncommuted prison sentences, are a grave miscarriage of British justice. They did not kill babies, women or the average man in the street. They killed the trash in our community, namely Jack 'the hat' Mcvitie, George Cornell. Men the world is well rid of, men with whom our society cannot deal. The do-gooders have fixed that, so now the innocent die instead. Mindless men who deserved the fate meted out to them. So what if other crooks deliver the *coup de grâce*. Better that way than others should die when these killers are released after their life sentence of eight years expires. The Krays killed vermin and it sticks in my craw when they are classed alongside the Moors murderers, Sutcliffe and others, as a continuing menace to our way of life.

The ordinary man in the street has nothing to fear from the Kray brothers. Let me tell you of one instance in the Porcupine, when Ronnie Kray noticed an old lady fiddling for money in her purse.

'Give her a large brandy, Peter, tell her good health from me.'

She accepted it graciously, nodding her head in his direction in appreciation.

After he had gone, I asked her, 'do you know who that was?'

'No,' was her smiling answer, 'but he was a gentleman.'

'That was Ronnie Kray,' I told her.

'My goodness,' she exclaimed, her eyes popping.

That typified the Kray's attitude towards the needy, I saw it time and time again. These men were not the depraved animals they were reputed to be. They had a good caring side to them, which the twins made no effort to hide, or draw attention to.

I say again they have paid their debt to society, they should be released to live out their lives in peace and privacy. As other, far more dangerous, criminals are allowed to do.

I found out after the men's initial visit to the Porcupine that the well-dressed man was indeed a member of their gang. He came into the pub many times after Ronnie's maiden visit, shaking my hand on the first occasion as a token of good-will. I might add I was more than delighted to shake his. I had envisaged having a razor used on me, or some other horrible weapon carving my initials on my innards.

Charlie's cheerful thumbs up, the day after Ronnie had made his call, makes a suitable ending for this truly frightening experience.

'Cracked it,' he shouted with glee.

He certainly had cracked it for me and earned my undying thanks. At no time was I ever given the slightest intimation, what the nervous chap had done. I didn't ask, I had encountered the fear at first hand. My wife's only comment, said without rancour, and devoid of emphasis of any kind, 'thank God, we can go out again now. I have forgotten what the outside world looks like.'

My own reaction was of such intense relief I felt numb.

I vowed from then on in, I would treat all similar occurrences with utter caution. I didn't of course, still having a lot of learning to do. Besides talking about it, I was still managing to keep up with my real abiding, first love, boxing. Living in London I had the chance to see most of the big fights. In March 1965, Billy Walker was down to fight Brian London at Wembley Stadium. As usual Walker was the firm favourite with the London fight fans. He didn't win very often. This, however, did not deter his followers. He was a guaranteed crowd puller at whatever venue.

Billy was a large, good-looking Heavyweight, hard as iron and strong with it. In actual fact that summed him up. He couldn't box for toffee, and led with his face for most of the time. How he retained those handsome features had me, and a lot of other people foxed. They must have been made of iron, too.

Brian London, although never a world-beater, had fought a far better class of fighter than Walker. He, too, was strong and it was there that the resemblance ended. He was a first class boxer when the mood took him.

The ex-British and Empire Champion, he had also fought for the world title. Walker was well and truly outclassed.

I knew Walker did not stand a chance against him, unless London was giving away gifts, highly unlikely. Anything gained from Brian had to be paid for in blood, sweat and hurt. He packed a punch.

Yet the betting was showing Walker a shade in front of London to win. It was going to be like taking candy from a baby. Walker's fans were backing their hero to the hilt with silly money and I intended to have my share of it.

First though, I had to see what kind of fettle my man was in. I went for the weigh-in for the fight, getting close enough to have a few words with Jack London jun., Brian's brother. I had beaten Jack in an amateur fight, we got on well together despite this, always enjoying each other's company.

'How is Brian getting along?' I asked.

Jack guessed the reason for my interest. 'Come with me,' he said, leading the way to Brian's dressing room. Brian, just climbing into his shorts ready for the weigh-in, looked in absolutely tremendous form. He put his dressing gown on and I followed him as he proceeded towards the stage.

The place was packed with Walker's supporters, they really gave Brian some stick as he passed by them. Billy weighed in first to rapturous applause from his fans. He had just made a singing record which was selling like hot cakes. The lad could do no wrong. He had charisma to spare and it didn't just work on the ladies.

When Brian stepped on the scales, it was to verbal abuse from all sides. From the look on his face I wouldn't like to be in Walker's shoes, when Brian got him in the ring.

As London returned through the hostile, booing, cockney crowd, to his dressing room, he suddenly stopped in mid stride. Turning to the noisy, jeering throng, he said in his broad, Lancashire accent, 'if ee feghts alf as good as ee sings, ah waint afto tek this orf fer nowt,' indicating his dressing gown.

This statement made with such vehemence, stopped those rowdy Londoners in their tracks. Whether they had understood his words, I wasn't sure, they certainly had got the message. I sincerely hoped it hadn't reached their hip-pocket. London, at that moment, appeared to me as a very formidable sight.

'The betting seems funny to me,' I remarked to Jack, provoking the answer I was looking for.

'Our Brian at five to four against? Walker at four to five on! It's more than bloody funny, it's hilarious. Our Brian will bloody kill him, especially after the treatment this bloody lot has given him.'

Satisfied, I went to find someone I could take some money off, before the rabble came to their senses and sent the betting the other way. Walker was in for a tough time, somehow I couldn't help feeling chuffed about that. It wasn't only the money, I was envious of Walker.

I had a ringside seat for the event, all the ballyhoo which had promoted the fight, had achieved the desired result. They were to box to a house bulging at the seams.

Throwing caution to the wind, I placed £80, at five to four against, on London. As I had thought, and as it duly turned out, it was virtually stealing money.

Round after round London punched and taunted Billy Walker, funnily enough I felt pity for Billy. It was a match that should never have taken place. A mismatch? That was a word which didn't cover the total ignominy that Brian piled on Walker without let up.

After he had hit Walker with six telling punches, his opponent not responding to any, London was heard to say, 'not very good-looking now, are you, Billy?'

This was an understatement of gigantic proportion, Walker's face was red-raw with the appalling punishment it had taken. The fight should have been stopped long before the final bell. It wasn't a boxing match it was sheer, undiluted mayhem.

London could have stopped him at any time, yet he cruelly kept him on his feet, intentionally not delivering the merciful knock out blow. To Billy Walker's credit, he stood and took this terrible battering from his savage opponent, earning the respect of everyone present, including yours truly.

It was the worst beating the Golden Boy would ever take. I had won a great deal of money easily, yet I had not enjoyed the fight, I doubt if anyone else had either.

I went to watch a boxing match, and saw a blood bath.

Nevertheless I regretted not pawning my shirt to put on London, for if ever there had been a betting certainty, that fight had been it.

Brian London was not the same man a year later, he could have done with some of Walker's courage and willingness to give his fans their money's worth.

On this occasion I was again at the ringside when London was to fight the legendary Cassius Clay (Mohammed Ali). It was he who was out-classed this time . . . He didn't try to make a fight of it. It was plainly then a case of, 'why try when you cannot possibly win'.

Heroism no one expects in a boxing ring, honesty is quite a different matter.

London folded, without giving the spectators anywhere near payment for their support. Mohammed wasn't well pleased, he didn't need to 'sting like a bee', a pat on the head would have sufficed for Brian to make his ignoble exit.

Disappointed I may have been with Brian London's performance, yet that was the night I was to meet George Raft again. As he shook my hand in greeting, I reminded him of our first meeting, when he had said I was good as an amateur boxer.

'I have said that to many fighters,' he smiled. 'If I said that to you, then you must have been good, kid. There would have been no reason for me to say it otherwise.'

That was a double edged remark I didn't really understand at the time. George Raft, not only had a reputation as an excellent actor in gangster movies, it was alleged by some he was an active member of the American underworld.

Years before I had met him, he had been accused of being in league with Al Capone. It was the same kind of innuendo of Mafia connections which still clings to Frank Sinatra, only with George it was apparently more substantial. A few years later I read that he was banned from entering the United Kingdom, a great pity for he was inordinately fond of Britain.

They said it was because of his undesirable gambling interests that the harsh order was imposed. Lordy, lordy, we have enough of those gentlemen in the Old Dart, one more or less would not have been noticed. I only know when you talked with George Raft, you gained the feeling he didn't have to act in his film roles. He was playing himself. Or was it the other way round? However, I for one would not have been at all surprised, if the gangster label had been true.

He had one thing going for him, his perfectly flawless manners. Although a small man, he stood out like a giant in a room full of notables and unlike most of the celebrated personages, he had time for lesser mortals.

I am proud to have met the man and I know the *persona non grata* ruling would have hurt deeply. I once overheard him say, 'I love being over here,' when asked, when would he be returning to the United States.

On the subject of gambling, I had steadily become more and more involved. I was throwing money around as if there were no tomorrow, dog racing, horse racing, gambling casinos, you name it, I was betting on it. Taking off to Sandown Park, Alexandra Park, leaving Shirley to cope as best she could. I was well and truly hooked by the gambling bug. Sometimes things were good. I would win a lot of money on the horses or dogs, derived from good tips given to me by the wide boys. Be that as it may, those same tipsters gave just as many bum steers, then I would lose a packet. Just like most confirmed gamblers, I tried to recoup my losses, getting further and further into the mire. I tried for the riches I hadn't been able to obtain in boxing. Unfortunately for me, I was in a profession where gambling is second nature, part of everyday life, a subject of most conversations. In fact in some public houses there should be sawdust behind the bar, the only things missing were the animals. At least the four-legged variety.

The Pickwick still continued to be our main source of entertainment, the stars just as spellbinding. The females just as beautiful off stage, as they appeared to be on. With one definite exception.

One evening Bert Ireland popped his head around the door, 'Peter, Kim Novak is downstairs,' he said.

In those days she was known as the Bachelor Girl. On this night she was accompanied by her husband-to-be Richard Johnson. She was then at the peak of her career in the film industry, a much fêted celebrity. Pictures of her reclining in a bath tub, ensconced in soft, white bubbles, adorned most cinema hoardings, and peered from newspapers and magazines all over the country.

The exalted position was one she obviously couldn't handle, as all in the Pickwick were to learn later in the evening.

I could not wait to get a peep at her in the flesh. I told my wife, 'I am just popping next door, Shirley. Kim Novak is in the Pickwick, I won't be a second, I must have a quick look at her.'

I bounded down the club staircase and stopped dead, looking around for this breathtaking star.

'That's her,' Bert Ireland said quietly, pointing in the direction of a very ordinary looking woman, seated at a table.

Well, to say I was taken aback, is a definite understatement and far less than the truth, although it is kinder. The lady held little resemblance to her screen image. In fact it tarnished my mental picture of all female stars I hadn't actually seen, for all time.

I reported back to Shirley as promised. When I told her of my first impression of Miss Novak, she said, 'you can cut out the exaggeration, I'm not jealous.'

'You have no cause to be jealous of that, wait until you see her, she is *ordinaire* by any standard.'

When the Porcupine closed, we dressed and made our way to the Pickwick. We were just in time to witness the star's temperament on full show. Miss Novak was in the midst of a right royal argument with a waiter, hardly giving the wretched man time to offer his apology, or rectify whatever she presumedly thought he had done.

She was ranting and raving like a fish-wife. Everyone in the room watched this exhibition of supreme bad taste, with something resembling disgust.

Angelo, the manager, quickly strode into the middle of this awkward situation. He made no effort to smooth the waters. To muffle Miss Novak's piercing voice, he said in a loud, emphatic manner, 'please leave.'

She left, but not before giving Angelo, gratuitously, the same kind of abuse she had been bestowing on the unfortunate waiter.

I expect the press office at her film studio must have had a full-time occupation, papering over the massive chinks in the façade they had created for her.

As you will have gathered, she left us unimpressed. Appearing so totally alluring on the celluloid screen, it is disappointing to find in real life some are the most unforgettable bitches.

A lady most certainly not in the latter category, was the irrepressible lovable beguiler, Sophie Tucker. What an absolute gem she was, and a consummate artist to boot.

My wife and I were given tickets to see her show at the Talk of the Town. Later we went into the Pickwick and were introduced to her. She spoke with us for about ten minutes, stressing how she loved to appear in Old London Town. The audiences were good and she consistently had rave reviews, which was great for her ego and bank balance.

We told her we ran the pub next door, that we had seen her show that night, thoroughly enjoying every minute of her performance.

'Look, you guys,' she said, 'I would love to stay on here, but I finish at the Town tomorrow. I appear in Paris on Monday, why don't you both come with me.'

There was nothing which would have given us more pleasure but there were innumerable reasons why this was not possible. Primarily, we were working people and I could just imagine Chef and Brewer's reaction, to a request for a few days off to nip to Paris.

It was a very nice gesture from Miss Tucker, one we had to regrettably refuse. Offers like that do not grow on trees.

In fact it was the only one of its kind we ever received. She was a big hearted, very kind lady. We would have loved to know her better. The next time she came to Britain, we had left the area so it wasn't possible.

With the unceasing pressure from Chef and Brewer, for ever higher takings, the worry of my involvement at Newport House, and our measly wages, we decided to look for pastures new and hopefully better conditions. Chef and Brewer had nothing larger to offer us than the Porcupine. We did consider we could further our career more advantageously by moving elsewhere.

We told ourselves we were now experienced publicans and caterers who had a lot to offer the right employer.

If only God had granted us the ability to foresee the consequence of that action, it would have taken an army to prise us out of the Porky. Again we scoured the advertising columns of vacancies, particularly in the *Morning Advertiser*. Finally a seemingly suitable one was published in that paper. It was a position with a company named A.V. Elliot and Sons, a firm of City caterers.

They required a manager and manageress for their house, The Olde Cheshire Cheese, in Crutched Friars, at the bottom of Lloyd's Avenue in the City of London.

We gained an interview with A.V. Elliot and I gave Captain B.W. Hemstock my old school teacher, as a reference, which I had always done before. I didn't realize the possible trouble that could cause this time.

At the end of the interview proper, Eliot still hadn't committed himself as to whether or not we had won the situation. Looking at me strangely he asked, 'this Captain Hemstock, what regiment was he in?'

I was completely flummoxed, I didn't know, I couldn't remember Hemstock ever saying. Elliot was now gazing at me in a thoroughly sceptical manner. I suddenly remembered something I had heard at school.

'I am not sure what regiment he was in, I know he was in charge of the lines of Bofors guns, which were placed along the south coast during the war, to shoot down the German flying bombs as they crossed the Channel to enter Britain.'

'Was he now? One of those bounders was he?'

I was taken aback, what the hell was wrong with the man? Shirley looked worried to death and no doubt I did too. Elliot then began to tell us a story about the war. When he was a young officer he had been invited out to Sunday lunch, by a group of American officers.

'There we were on a pleasantly warm day, minding our own business, toddling along in this jeep, on a quiet English country lane, the thought of war and all its dangers far from our minds, when that thoughtless lot down there on the coast shot down one of those infernal machines. It landed in a meadow alongside, just as we were passing. The blast blew us into the opposite field, all three of us and the jeep. We were hospitalized, fortunate to be alive to tell the tale, I suppose.'

Elliot looked at us thoughtfully, before saying, 'I will accept Captain Hemstock's reference, but I never want to meet the man. I might tell him what I think of him,' he finished ruefully. We had won the position, after the usual sorting out of possible candidates.

We were pleased and sad at the same time. Sorrow at the idea of leaving the Porcupine, staff, plus all our friends in the area. Pleased because we had attained what we had set out to do, find ourselves a bigger and better public house.

We had wanted the challenge of a larger establishment, with it the expanded catering side. Well, we had found that.

The Olde Cheshire Cheese was a large eating house in every sense of the world. An à la carte restaurant on the first floor, plus two snack bar carveries, one on each side of the house. On the ground floor there was another table d'hôte restaurant.

Shirley was going to be a very busy girl.

My life wasn't exactly going to be a bed of roses either, in ye Olde Cheshire Cheese.

Chapter 6

THE time came all too quickly to leave the Porcupine, and to leave behind the village we had grown to love so much. So many happy memories and good times, so many staunch friends and characters. Those well worn streets and alleyways, my nightly perambulation of the area with my dog, a thing of the past.

I was to shed bitter tears over this irrevocable decision, and our avaricious, pestilential ambitions. Saying goodbye to Geoffrey de Vere and Ivy were to be among our least envied tasks, for both Shirley and I had grown very fond of those two, so different, individuals.

Ivy eventually retired. We never knew what became of Geoffrey but like to think he may have stayed on at the Porky until he, too, retired. Neither my wife nor I will ever forget the Porcupine. The harsh times and there were plenty of those, and the sheer unrelenting slog are forgotten. Only the good times, the people, and those great places which coloured our thoughts then and now, are remembered.

We were destined never to know again the warmth and the exhilaration of our spirits which being an inhabitant of the village gave us.

After two weeks' holiday, a much needed respite, we took over the management of the Olde Cheshire Cheese in the City of London.

The Cheese was a building of primary historic repute, plus being a recognized leading business man's venue. Lloyd's of London occupied most of Lloyd's Avenue, which ran down the side of the Cheshire Cheese. We were in the heart of the bowler hat, striped trousers and umbrella brigade; a far cry from the easy-going artistic type, we had become used to in the Porcupine. It was a quite different kind of pub in more ways than one, as we were to learn very quickly.

One of the first jobs for Shirley, was to find another school for Jacqueline. She eventually found one which our daughter was willing to accept, fortunately this was close by in Aldgate. Jacqueline had resented leaving her tiny school, yet settle in she did, after a great number of rebellious words and upsetting tears.

The Olde Cheshire Cheese at lunchtime, was truthfully a hive of activity. The beautiful restaurant on the first floor, was named the Pepys Room.

The Cheese, besides being steeped in history, was also the busiest pub in that area of the City. The two bar carveries, and the Pepys Room, were inundated during the lunch period, by the upper echelon of business and management. The import and export traders, stock market heavies, shipping and banking magnates, and most other facets of the City's thriving world of commerce, all were represented. Most used the first floor facilities.

Peter and Shirley Aldridge and daughter Jacqueline, Olde Cheshire Cheese, City of London, 1965.

The ground floor catered for the city worker in general. Here we had the accursed luncheon vouchers to contend with, and the same demands. Not least of the Cheese's clientele, were the Fleet Street representatives, it being the local for quite a few reporters, and others in that profession.

Shirley had her hands full. There were three waiters in the Pepys Room, two carvery chefs and waitresses in the downstairs restaurant. We had seven kitchen staff and I had six bar staff. All without exception had to be supervised.

I had set on two more bar staff on our taking over of the house, also another waiter. Shirley wished she could have brought Ivy and Geoffrey with us, that way she could have turned her back on the kitchen more often. This was an impossible dream. Ivy's descriptive language would have been frostily received, by the crusty customers of the Cheese. They, in their turn would have been anathema to Ivy. Geoffrey was too inexperienced to manage the specialist catering . . . and the ultra high standards of the Pepys Room.

The customers however would have delighted him.

Keeping good stocks in both the food and liquor departments, proved to be a headache of immense proportions in the Olde Cheshire Cheese.

The waiter I had employed went by the name of John. Working initially, with me, he had been at the Cheese for about two weeks when a waitress, Angie, who had worked at the Cheese for around four weeks, complained to me of John's behaviour towards her. She said indignantly, 'he is forever touching me, and trying to tickle me. He deliberately brushes against me when there is no need. Keep him away from me, Guv, I don't like the man.'

This was a very serious matter and couldn't go unchecked, I sent for John, telling him to come to the office immediately.

'Look here, John, Angie is complaining about your conduct towards her. Stay away from her, and I mean that literally, stay away from her. I want no more of this tomfoolery, stop it now, otherwise I will have to take other steps and you know what those are.'

'I didn't mean anything by it, Guv, if she can't take a joke, bugger her. She's nothing to write home about anyway.'

'Stay away from her,' I cautioned again, 'and mind your own business.'

Blimey, that was exactly what he was doing, had I but known.

John, stony-faced, assured me he would do just that, 'believe me, Guv, I wouldn't touch her with a barge pole, after this.'

I had no inkling of what was in store for yours truly, let alone grasp the real reason behind Angie's accusation.

Angie was a married woman, about thirty years of age and, shall I say, of medium attractiveness. What should have warned and didn't, was the fact that she always appeared to be in full control of herself, and the situation.

I did wonder why she couldn't handle mild harassment, as the feminists call it today, without having to resort to an official complaint. I know this incident apparently made them deadly enemies. Still, apart from the odd sarcastic remark to each other, it didn't affect their work, and so was no business of mine.

I was relieved about that, having more important things to worry about. Bickering staff, as long as it was out of earshot of the customers, was the least of my problems. Or so I innocently told myself.

My stocks were all to hell, I had lost £300 on the last two stocktakes. London companies are less likely than others to stand for bad stock results. A.V. Elliot was no exception to this rule, they were as hard as nails. Mr Venny, the stock-controller, was not an easy man to get along with at the best of times, now he was under pressure from A.V. Elliot junior the managing director, and a Mr Borrott, another director of the Company. Venny's flashing smile and open demeanour, hid a man as tough as old boots, a survivor, he was staying afloat no matter who else sank.

He pulled no punches about threatening me with dismissal. Although we had been there only a few months, we knew that no one else would employ us with such a bad record, as far as stocks went. They are the most important, as far as criteria go in the licensed trade.

My wife and I were sick with worry. We both concentrated on trying to catch the thief or thieves among our staff. With so much money involved, it had to be a collusion between two or more of them.

The next stocktaking showed a shortage of £200, the thief was becoming more daring. Shirley came to me in tears, 'oh, why did we leave the Porky,' she sobbed.

I could find nothing to say which could console her. Only to reiterate, 'we have to be on our toes all the time, it's under our nose if we only knew which bastard to watch.'

We both tried to be everywhere, watching, ever vigilant for the first sign of something not quite right.

As well as the fear of being unemployed, there were additional reasons giving us a strong incentive to hold on to the position. The City of London is a six day phenomenon, a prosperous commercial machine that literally died by midday Saturday. The streets are more or less emptily devoid of life, apart from the odd tourist, cleaners, and the occasional red double-decker bus, or open touring bus meandering through the quiet, deserted streets. The pubs closed all day Sunday.

Another sweetmeat which other public houses do not enjoy in London, is the early closing time. The City houses closed at 9.30 p.m., whereas normal closing time in other parts was 11 p.m.

One day I took a verbal battering from Mr Venny. He gave me the blunt ultimatum, 'get it right, or get out, Mr Aldridge.'

I felt numb. We had done our utmost and failed miserably. Heads had to roll and they were going to be Shirley's and mine. Not Venny's. In despair I walked down to the cellars which were very extensive. A.V. Elliot used them as a store house. There were literally thousands of bottles of wines and spirits, mostly aged and of very high quality. Old Joe, the cellarman, was a smashing little fellow, faithful, and a trusted aid.

'Watch those bloody wogs, in the best restaurant,' he cautioned.

We had two Spanish waiters in there. John made the number up to three. Joe called everyone who was even slightly coloured, wogs. This stemmed from the time that he'd spent in the army, when everyone not pink, was a bloody wog. He'd have had a jolly difficult job today, using that bench mark to categorize them, for just about three-quarters of Britons on these isles, would qualify under that heading.

Bearing Joe's advice in mind, I decided to do my paperwork in the Pepys Room. I sat there until almost lunch-time, clearing a backlog of clerical miscellany. One or two groups of customers came in. I gazed aimlessly through the window, feeling as depressed as it is possible to be. Angie was busy behind the small bar.

She had asked for the Pepys Room, saying she preferred it in there, although it brought her into contact with her old adversary, John, whom she ignored unless she was serving patron's orders to him.

'Don't be so bloody clever,' I heard her say to John in an undertone.

'Pack it in, ' I snarled at them.

I was in no mood for their petty squabbling, besides if I could hear it, so could the other people sitting in the room.

Shirley came into the restaurant and signified lunch could be served. 'You can take their orders now, John,' I said sharply to him.

I do not know to this day, why I watched him, as he approached the customers Shirley had indicated. They appeared ready to place their order. Shirley had left the room to return to the kitchens. I made ready to leave for the bar downstairs, when the customers decided to have a drink before lunch.

'Change that fiver,' I heard John demand rudely of Angie.

I was on my feet in a trice, moving towards the till on the bar in a couple of strides. I grabbed Angie's wrist, before she could place the note into the cash register. It was a £1 note.

She fought like an ensnared tiger, but I wasn't about to let go. Leniency was the last thing I had in mind for those two godless criminals. I handed them over to the police. I do not know what triggered the action I took.

PETER & SHIRLEY ALDRIDGE
welcome you to :-
YE OLDE
CHESHIRE CHEESE
48 CRUTCHED FRIARS E.C.3.
Phone :- ROY 1533.
AN A.V. ELLIOTT & SONS.
CHARRINGTON HOUSE

LUNCHEONS & GRILLS SERVED
IN THE PEPYS ROOM ALSO IN
THE SALOON BAR
SNACK BAR
WEDDINGS & PRIVATE PARTIES
CATERED FOR
FULLY LICENSED

Ye Olde Cheshire Cheese.

I didn't see the note as John handed it over to Angie. There was something which wasn't quite right about the scene, one senses things sometimes and this was one of those occasions. The scam was simplicity itself stock served without registering payment, the money thus obtained removed from the till. It takes two people to work this well, one behind the bar and one waiting on.

They had worked this confidence trick all over the southern counties of England. They were wanted from Cornwall to London, having fleeced dozens of hotels and public houses . . . using the same *modus operandi*, systematically robbing and running, before the hapless publican's suspicions were aroused.

They had set me up beautifully with their bogus enmity, their smooth operation still has me gasping over its audacity. Yet I will never forgive the buggers. Need I say John was Angie's husband?

Those two plausible actors missed their calling. The stage would have been better suited to them than the life of petty pilfering they chose. Where the two of them were headed would undoubtedly give them plenty of room for reflection on the error of their ways. Or maybe time to dream up a more successful scam, who knows?

I received a police commendation for my part in nabbing the pair, plus an official pat on the back from the law. Nothing from A.V. Elliot. When I informed Mr Venny of my success, he snapped, 'it doesn't get our money back, does it?'

I knew then things would never improve between me and that man. I admit it was the thrust and cut business part of London, an area where profits will unfailingly be the overriding factor. People cost money, very few in their estimation, were worth that expense. Without exception, all were replaceable. Mr Elliot treated all his employees with singular contempt, the above principle being practised to the last man, or woman.

We were absolutely delighted to learn, that at the time of our bad stock results, he had run his catamaran on to the rocks off Cornwall, thus writing off £7,000. We knew the insurance company would cover the greater, if not all of this, yet we savoured the humiliation it would have caused this arrogant, upstart of a man.

Our bitterness was excusable. Shirley's distress, and the open threat of job loss alone, were sufficient to turn the proverbial worm.

Elliots emulated Chef and Brewer in pushing for higher and higher returns. I began to use the tactics to improve the bar trade, which we had found so successful in the Porcupine.

Good looking mini-skirted, young girls, replaced the old staff, and turned those cantankerous, staid business men, into lambs. Some even into lecherous, mouth-dribbling old billies. They spent up in a big way, trying to impress those hardened, unimpressible, skimpily-attired females.

One of the girls, named Diane, was really something. Her low cut cleavage and smashing legs, made her into a desirable, pulchritudinous bundle indeed. She said she was of Italian descent, believable because of her dark colouring, which added to her sultry seductiveness. She was very aware of her desirability, using her wiles on every male within sight, regardless of consequences.

Shirley was on to her too, and watched her constantly. 'Watch it,' she would say, whenever she saw Diane and I talking together.

Having Sundays free for the first time since coming to London, allowed us to enjoy a normal family life on a week end.

Sunday mornings we would go for walks. Shirley loved to go round the Petticoat Lane trading stalls. Mind you I wasn't averse to this either, the droll humour, the smells emanating from the myriad of snack bars and small cafés, the variety of goods being peddled with artful articulateness. The good natured buyers, tourists and locals alike playing the stooges for the traders playful buffoonery. All this represented Petticoat Lane.

We needed this time for unwinding. The Cheese entailed hard, manual work for both of us. This plus the mental stress, left us truly jaded by week's end. It took a supreme effort on our part to leave the building, and go for this essential, refreshing break.

The bottom end of Petticoat Lane was nearest to the Cheshire Cheese, and close to the beginning of the Mile End Road, and the East End of London. The true home of the cockney.

One Sunday, Shirley and I were wandering alone around that entertaining area, when who should we bump into but Ronnie, the Find-the-Lady school boss. He, as I have said, invariably had two schools running in the Lane. One was at the top end, by Dirty Dicks, the other at the bottom end of Petticoat Lane.

'Cor luv-a-duck,' he said, on sighting Shirley and me. 'Come on in for a drink. I have my wife with me, she is in here,' pointing to a pub close by.

We were delighted to see him and followed him into the hotel, where we stood in a group chatting about old times. We laughingly told his wife the circumstances of our first meeting in the Porky, underlining my stupidity in breaking up the lucrative game. We were interrupted when a man at least six foot tall and very nattily dressed, approached us.

'Hello, Ronnie, I was hoping to find you in here,' he said affably.

'Have a drink.' Ronnie, in this way, invited the man to join the group.

'Don't mind if I do,' the man answered, moving in close to Ronnie.

We all stood chatting for a few minutes, then the man suddenly asked, 'could I have a few words with you in private, Ronnie?'

'Sure,' Ronnie replied amiably.

Leaning over the bar towards the landlord, he asked, 'can I use your snug for a minute, Guv'ner?'

'Certainly, I think it's empty,' the landlord answered helpfully.

The room was vacant, Ronnie accompanied by the man entered and closed the door behind them. They were in there barely two minutes, when we heard the distinct sound of scuffling and furniture being knocked over. I opened the door and moved quickly into the room; that was a big man for Ronnie to tackle alone.

I needn't have bothered, Ronnie had the man by his tie and was busy throttling him, besides banging his head on the oak panelling of the wall.

'You bastard, you weren't there. You weren't there,' he repeated viciously, to the cringing man.

Seeing me he let the man go. Taking advantage of this, the man ran from the Snug, out of the pub into the Lane.

We straightened the furniture, which they had knocked over in their struggle, rejoining our very worried wives. Heedless of their presence, Ronnie said, 'the fucking bastard tried to screw me for twenty quid.'

He went on to explain the man was a C.I.D. sergeant, which was why he hadn't introduced him to us. Apparently he had come for payment of services rendered, claiming he had let one of Ronnie's card-schools run in a plum position in the West End for a goodly period of time. Unfortunately for him, Ronnie was running that particular school on that patch, on the evening in question. The sergeant had underestimated Ronnie by a mile, his own acumen should have told him Ronnie would be no pushover. You don't get to the top of the heap by being a soft touch for every con-artist, be they policeman or crook. It was in this manner Ronnie kept the policemen off his back, handing out liberal back-handers. This way his teams worked unharassed by the law. At the same time he had a short fuse if anyone, be they cop, or any other kind of daring malefactor, tried to make a sucker out of him. This man had, and was no doubt regretting doing so, for if nothing else, he was off the payroll for life.

Really this was just minor stuff, as far as corruption went in the force, bottom of the ladder triviality in fact. The bigger stuff was just as blatant. When I heard of some of the deals that had been struck, my hair stood on end.

I wanted to die peacefully in my bed, so I kept my nose clean. Getting into The Game with the two ladies, during my spell at the Porcupine, was enough for yours truly.

I was in the habit of bringing my mother down to London whenever the opportunity arose. She loved the city. The Porcupine and the Cheshire Cheese, kept her in a constant state of excitement. There was gossip enough to last her for months. She would regale her neighbours with stories of people she had met, or seen. Our excursions to Petticoat Lane on Sundays became the highlight of her visits.

Little did she know, the people I introduced her to were mostly villains and vagabonds. Although this motley collection of reprobates would, given half a chance, rob you blind in the name of business and survival, their hearts were nevertheless solid gold and most definitely in the right place.

It takes the average cockney a long time to accept you. If and when he does, you have a loyal, helpful friend for life.

The best photograph ever taken of my mother, was snapped in the Lane by a photographer I knew. On being introduced to Mam after taking the shot, he generously stated, 'if that is your old mam, Guv'ner, it's on the house. I'll drop it off at the pub for you, when it's ready.'

This is the photo that sits alongside me everyday of my working life.

The Olde Cheshire Cheese clientele separated themselves into two groups, in actual fact it was a voluntary apartheid. Though not racial, it was strictly a class division, one side being frequented by the office worker, mostly clerical and the like. The other side, management and upper classes hobnobbed uneasily. Apart from the odd irreverent Yankee intruder, no one encroached on the latter domain. This extended to the Pepys Room. Both areas being considered sacrosanct.

On this morning I was busy on the office side at the time a group of men entered the Cheese. On seeing them I walked quickly from behind the bar to greet them. It was my old friends from the Porcupine, Ronnie and Reggie Kray, accompanied by their minders.

'Pleased to see you both again,' I said warmly, as I shook their hands. I was absolutely delighted they had bothered to look me up. We chatted for around half an hour, the subject as usual was boxing. Although I must admit, we did have a quiet chortle at the bowler-hatted silly brigade, who were pouring into the Cheese it being nearly lunch-time. They both shook my hand on leaving, Ronnie saying loudly, 'good luck here, Peter,' as he passed through the front entrance. I walked into the class section of the bar. There were a number of people standing around deep in conversation. Unlike the Porky, one didn't greet or interrupt these personages, who were so full of their own self-importance, one waited to be spoken to. They appeared to get some kind of perverse delight in their apparent disregard of one's existence. It didn't bother me unduly, and as far as I was aware the staff of the Cheese were also unaffected by their attitude.

I moved behind the bar to assist Diane during the peak business period. One of the lesser members of the accepted order of things, hurried over to the bar, a concerned look upon his face. He asked in a penetrating voice, 'Guv'ner, wasn't that the Kray twins who just walked out of here?'

The hum of conversation ceased, one could have heard a pin drop.

'Are you a pal of theirs?' he asked, in the same loud derogatory way.

'Well, I know them,' I stammered, unsure of the reception such an admission would receive.

'Cor,' this big-mouthed yobbo breathed intelligently. Then disconcerted beyond measure, unable to find anything else to say, he moved away from the bar area in a distinctly frightened manner.

I received some very peculiar, curious glances from the aloof customers of that wearisome section of the bar; which eventually faded as they became more inquisitive as to how I came to know notorieties like the Kray brothers well enough to have them visit me.

To give you some idea of the mentality of the patrons of the select end, it took at least two weeks before curiosity got the better of them, and one asked, while at the minimum seven listened. 'Peter, old chap, do you actually know the Krays?'

'Yes, I do. I like the pair of them as well,' I added, gratuitously. Then seeing the stunned look on his face, I relented, telling them of my first meeting with Ronnie Kray, and how very afraid I was. I told them of the events leading up to it, and Charlie's assistance in sorting it out. To my everlasting surprise I could hold those men entranced, with stories of my beloved Porcupine, plus other incidents throughout my West End pub career. Not only they themselves enjoyed the anecdotes, they brought their friends to whom I had to relate, in detail, the same stories.

I find it very amusing to think it was the Krays, who in a roundabout manner, had been the means of my acceptance in the Olde Cheshire Cheese. Without their unknowing aid, I would probably have gone on just being the bloke who opened and closed their inner temple.

Often, late of an evening, I would still find myself drifting back towards the West End.

My brother Allan, who had done so much for me during my boxing days, continued to visit me regularly. As I wrote in the beginning of my story, he was a long-distance lorry driver. London was an oft visited port of call. He frequently stayed with us at the Cheese, as he had done at the

Porky. Bringing good clothes to change into, he would join me in my sallies into the village and we would revisit our old happy hunting ground; so sadly missed in the sedate, restrictive City of London. The Pickwick Club was not the least of them. Allan had not seen the like before and in spite of his early morning starts we would linger into the late hours.

I was a member of Joe Davis's Snooker Club just of Piccadilly, quite handy for two lads who were very partial to the game. We would have a quiet game of snooker and talk to the great man himself. It was a small exclusive club which held only three tables, and a bar. What a gentleman Joe Davis was, no edge to him whatsoever. He'd laugh and chat with us as if we were old friends, which indeed I hoped I qualified as, eventually. On occasion we would get a chance to see this wizard with a cue play. He really was the best at the game, bar none, in my humble estimation.

One night Allan and I went to the club for a game, only to find it closed. We agreed to go to the large snooker hall in Great Windmill Street. It had been raining. We were both dressed in white raincoats. The two of us being six footers, I suppose we did stand out a little. When we arrived at the uninvitingly dingy hall we were given a peculiar reception. The man in the kiosk at the entrance, muttered something under his breath as I paid him. Neither Allan nor I caught what he had said, he didn't repeat it.

As the man gave me my change Allan asked me, 'what table is it, Boy?'

'Don't know,' I answered.

I asked the whisperer, 'what table is it, Mate?'

He stared at me belligerently, before curtly replying, 'seven.'

'What's up with him?' Allan asked.

'I'm not sure, reckon he got out of bed the wrong side or something,'

We dismissed him as a surly lout and set up the snooker balls on table seven, more interested in the competitive spirit of the contest, than the players on the other tables. Though Allan had said on entering the room, 'there are some rough buggers in here.'

I didn't tell him the place was used by all of the unsavoury characters you could care to mention, including pimps, crooks, drug pushers and the hard confidence merchants. It was indeed a nest of vipers at its best. We enjoyed our game so much we failed to notice that the two tables in close proximity had finished. After about three more games, I looked around. There was only one table out of the twelve in the room which was still being used. When we had started to play all the tables had been occupied and men stood around watching. Apart from Allan and me, with the other two players, the room had emptied.

'Must be closing, Boy,' Allan said.

We played another game during which time the other two men left. As the place was empty we assumed it was closing time, and called it a day, too. Passing the scruffy looking oddity in the kiosk, Allan said cheerily, 'goodnight, enjoyed that, Mate.'

Halfway down the stairs we distinctly heard a voice say, 'fucking bastards.'

We had donned our raincoats again as the rain recommenced. We stood at the bottom of the stairway waiting for the downpour to ease. A chap rushed by us up the stairs and we heard him ask, 'what's gone bloody wrong?'

'I have just had two bastard coppers in here, they've emptied the fucking place.'

Allan and I erupted into fits of laughter, finally I asked, 'shall I go back and tell him who we are? Wait till he knows we aren't the law after all. That'll spoil his night for him.'

'No.' Allan said, 'let the ignorant bugger think we are coppers. it will help to keep a few undesirables out of the place for a while anyway.' We laughed all the way home about the mistake.

That evening as Shirley prepared supper, she said, 'you two look like cats who have found a basin of cream. What's happened?'

We told her of the mistaken identity and the surly fellow's attitude.

'Well, you two do look like policemen, especially in those raincoats. You've ruined a man's business for the night, possibly for the next few nights. Surely you cannot expect him to be delirious with joy about that. I wouldn't go anywhere near the place again, if I were you.'

That amused us even more, for as far as we were concerned we had no intention of deceit. If two identical white coats could achieve that, he deserved to lose business. His attitude to the law needed some improvement in any case.

We did go back to the snooker hall. About two months later Joe Davis's place was again closed, so we revisited the den of iniquity. We told the untidy character in the kiosk that we were not police officers, just a couple of fellows looking for a game of snooker. His jaw sagged, I am sure he was a bloody sight more unpleasant that visit than he was on our first call.

After a game of snooker we would often stop for a refreshing cup of coffee before making our way home. None of my family drink anything much stronger for pleasure, we are definitely social drinkers only. Faults we have a-plenty, drink is not one of them. I couldn't cope with more than I have already, neither could my wife.

We would use one of the many coffee houses which abound in Leicester Square. Both Allan and I loved to watch the world go by, which it seems to do in the West End. We could always find something to amuse, or distract, as we sipped away.

It is a world apart, omitting the seamier side of the village, there is enough to keep one enthralled for hours. The cockney barrow-boy always one step ahead of the law, the buskers, the naive tourists pointing out to each other the sights, human and scenic, of this ever-changing kaleidoscopic small enclave.

One weekday, at a time when Allan was staying overnight we went for, what had become, our usual game of snooker. As it was a cold, rainy night we decided to settle for a hot cup of coffee and then go home. We ordered our coffee and sat at a table waiting for it to be served. Out of the side door leading to the kitchen, came what I can only describe as the most beautiful woman I have ever seen, Allan echoed my thoughts exactly. He said, 'my God, it's an African princess.'

'It can't be,' I said stupidly, 'she's collecting the dirty pots.'

Allan laughed, as she came to our table. Not having the wit to think of anything else to say, I used the well-out-worn cliché, 'hello, what is a lovely girl like you doing here?'

'I only started this week, but I don't like it. I finish at the week's end,' she answered naively in a beguiling West Indian accent, before flashing the pair of us the nicest smile we had ever seen.

'Would you like to join us for a drink or a coffee elsewhere?' I asked. I knew that particular shop was about to close, they were clearing away all the service area and wiping down in readiness.

She didn't reply, just bestowing a very old-fashioned look on yours truly, before turning to repeat the same on Allan.

'I honestly want to talk to you about a job,' I lied hurriedly.

'Okay, but it had better be true, I'll see you outside in ten minutes.'

I did have a position going at the Cheese, or rather Shirley had. It was for a kitchen hand, I told Allan to quieten his protests, 'it's to help with sandwich making and light snacks, Allan, in the kitchen.'

'Bloody hell! She's far too good looking for that,' Allan swore, 'she won't wear that, Boy. Besides what will Shirley say?'

'She's collecting pots here isn't she? The Cheese is more up-market than this, anyway I think she likes the look of us,' I smirked.

The dazzling lady did join us outside, and we walked on into Soho. She refused a drink but accepted our invitation to have something to eat.

We went into another café we knew and as we were being seated the girl blurted out, 'look, I do not take my clothes off, I am not a clip joint hostess either. I am an ordinary working girl.'

This lady was no fool, she was clearing the air before Allan or I could try any fast moves. I think she thought there was a possibility we might be pimps, trying to enrol her.

I decided to tell her the truth, 'the position I have vacant isn't anything like that, it is in the kitchen of a better class pub.'

'Do I have to wash pots?'

'No, you will be a general help, making sandwiches, coffee and salads,' I assured her. To our surprise she appeared to be quite interested.

Encouraged, I continued, 'you may have to do the occasional collecting of dishes, when our downstairs snack bar closes each day, but there is definitely no washing up. We employ a woman full-time to do the washing up.'

Smiling, she told us her name was Marjory, 'you can call me Marj. Do you want me to start on Monday?' she asked, again giving us the benefit of that brilliant smile.

'Yes, 9 a.m., and bring your P45 tax form, and all relevant references with you.'

'Thank you, do you know I thought you were on the make, or it was just another pick-up. I live in Brixton, it's a fair way to go, so I really must leave you now. I have two small children to care for, too. Good night.'

She left without a backward glance, Allan and I sat looking at each other, wondering how the hell we had managed to talk ourselves into that situation.

'Wait until Shirley sees her,' Allan whistled. 'How the hell are you going to explain how you met her? What will Shirley say when she sees her?' Allan bemused, repeated himself.

I sat stunned too, how was I going to explain to Shirley?

'I could always tell the truth. I can say, "look, I picked up this beautiful black lady in a coffee shop, she was looking for a job, so I offered her one". I think that will be my best approach.'

'Yeah, I can imagine what Shirley will have to say to that. Rather you than me, Boy. I am glad I'm leaving tomorrow.'

'Christ, Allan, even if I tell her the truth she isn't going to believe a word of it, is she? What can I say that will sound plausible?'

'I wouldn't worry too much, I don't think she will turn up for a kitchen job. She has far too much class to do a job like that, and she knows it too. She didn't like the coffee shop, remember?'

I fervently hoped Allan was right and she would be a no show the following week. What a mess I was in.

'What if she does show up? I have got to think of something before then, Allan. Can we say we were just talking to her and the subject of jobs came up.'

'That's close to the truth, and it sounds better to me. Whatever you say Shirley will not believe you. I will back you up for what it's worth.' Allan suddenly chortled, 'wait until she claps eyes on Madam! She won't even believe she worked in a café.'

I didn't feel like laughing. Yet it was such a ridiculous story Shirley had to believe it, no one could dream up stuff like that. Besides, I would have Allan to verify the tale, and really I had no option but to come clean with some explanation.

On our arrival back at the Cheese, Shirley made coffee, asking where we had been as she did so.

Here goes, I thought, better get it over with. I dashed headlong into my account of the evening's happenings. 'Oh, by the way,' I started, in what I hoped was a nonchalant manner, 'I have filled the vacant position you have for a kitchen hand. At least I think I have.'

'Oh, good, who is she?'

'She is black, ebony black,' I answered, waiting for the storm.

'Black? Black?' Shirley looked questioningly at me.

'Yes, she is black, but a very nice person. I think she will do the job very well for you.'

'Is this another one of your foolish jokes, or something?' Shirley asked.

'No, love, it's not a joke. Allan and I spoke to her where she was working, she doesn't like it there, she is looking for another job. She likes the West End and all the lights, but this will suit her here. She doesn't mind work.'

I glanced at Allan, who was intently examining the ceiling. Some help he was proving to be. Feeling my eyes on him, he switched his gaze to the floor, then he decided belatedly to do his bit.

'It's true, Shirley,' he said, then immediately lowered his eyes to inspect the carpet.

'What does she look like?' Shirley questioned, looking hard at Allan.

'Oh, she is quite attractive,' I butted in, 'for a coloured girl that is.'

'Very good looking really,' Allan said, 'and a jolly good worker too.'

I knew he had thrown in the latter bit to appease Shirley after seeing her eyes flash fire at me when he had substantiated my remark about the dark girl's attractiveness. Personally, I thought he had gone over the top a bit, yet it was just as well Shirley was forewarned. The only work we had seen the woman do, was to pick up a few dirty dishes. She may well be the laziest cow on God's earth, I reflected, but I would cross that bridge when I came to it.

Monday morning came around, as all things do which are not longed for. Allan had left the Cheese and quite possibly was in John o' Groats, or some other inaccessible spot.

We used to open the doors of the Cheshire Cheese for the cleaners at 8 a.m., leaving the latch off the door to allow the other staff to enter unaided. We had a West Indian kitchen porter named Sam, a well built, strong, quiet fellow. He possessed a marvellous sense of humour one had to be careful about.

It was his job to answer the door when the bell went. This morning he came up to the flat, 'Madam, there is a lady who would like to see you.'

Christ, I prayed, I hope it isn't her. God, don't let it be her. My mind was stuck on the theme like a worn record. I was in mid-shave and cut myself repeatedly as I mentally panicked. With good cause, for it was indeed Marjory Alexander at the door.

Shirley left the flat to attend to her. I took as long as I dared before bracing myself to face the tempest, which would surely follow. Before I could leave the flat, Shirley returned, slamming the door with enough force to take it off its hinges.

'Who was it?' I asked as innocently as I could, deliberately omitting to tell her I had already inquired of Sam the lady's name.

For my pains I received an ice-cold glare from Shirley, 'quite attractive is she?' Shirley mimicked my previous description of Marj. 'Well, she isn't working in that bloody wig.'

I didn't know the piled bee-hive of a hair style was a wig. The bouffant way of wearing their hair was all the rage at that time. This lady was up to the minute in fashion from head to foot. Trust my wife to spot the phoney first go.

'Are you letting her start then?' I queried, surprised.

That was unexpected, for Shirley did all the hiring and firing of staff employed on the catering side of the business. I had never interfered before. To me that in itself was suspicious.

In an ominous tone, Shirley advised, 'I will give her a week's trial.'

Marj caused quite a stir in the kitchen and everywhere else she appeared. Even in the shapeless white overall she still looked a million dollars. Georgie, the head chef said with some feeling, 'Guv'ner, that is a lovely woman.'

Marjory was not only a lovely woman, she was a good worker, a grafter in the true sense of the word. In less than a week she had got to Shirley, who was always receptive to hard workers. My wife excluded personal feelings when it came to the job, they were purely after hours luxuries. Attractive as Marj was, she did not engender envy in anyone, her infectious laugh, and willingness to crack or listen to jokes, made her a favourite with all the staff. Her exceptional good looks were just an added bonus. Shirley never objected to the hair-piece, or referred to it again. Wig or no wig, it was a part of Marj and was accepted by all. It wasn't long before she started to come in early, to take Jacqueline to school, and became a trusted, well liked member of the Cheese's staff. Not least a friend and confidante of Shirley's.

The only fly in the ointment, Mr Venny, was his usual charming self. He stood in the kitchen one day, watching Marj at work. Turning to me, he said with emphasized vindictiveness, 'keep her in the kitchen. Mr Elliot doesn't like blacks on show.'

It was the nastiest piece of discrimination I had ever heard. I have never encountered any racism to match it since. I shrugged it off, Marj hadn't heard it and though others had they wouldn't tell her. It was typical Venny and Elliot bigotry, typifying the men's warped characters. There was no way anyone could change them. I wasn't about to try. Unable to appreciate the girl's beauty, their vaunted business sense was swayed by their absurd sectarian beliefs. Anyway, Marj rarely left the kitchen, only then when the pub was closed and she was helping to clear away.

This was at a period when Shirley was dashing up to Doncaster most weekends. Her father had been hurt in an accident at work. Shirley was very concerned about him, making the long train trip north on her time off despite her utter bone weariness.

This Friday evening Shirley had left for Yorkshire taking Jacqueline. I had volunteered to run Marj home by car, as she had agreed to work overtime to allow Shirley to leave earlier.

Marj had indeed two children although she was only twenty-two years of age. I never knew where her husband was, or if she ever had one. She lived with her mother who cared for the children while she worked. She was pretty reticent about her private life, for which I didn't blame her. Gossip runs riot in pubs.

'What are you doing tonight, Marj?' I asked, mostly from curiosity.

'Not much,' she replied cheerily.

'Get dressed up and we will paint the town red,' I said on the spur of the moment. I was fed up to the teeth at being left alone. Shirley and I couldn't both leave the Cheese at the same time, unless we had an official relief. Thanks to a good tip I'd had, I had won a fair amount, £200 to be exact. I felt like celebrating my unusual good fortune. It didn't happen that often, not on dogs, anyway.

'I will, if you really mean it,' Marj acquiesced.

I looked at this lovely girl and taking her hand in mine, I said, 'let's do it, I will meet you outside the Talk of the Town.'

I gave her the time I would be there as she left the car. Without a backward glance she walked to the house, entering and closing the door, while still not turning to look towards me.

That was a lady who was very sure of herself. I drove back home to the Cheese. I had dated a lot of girls in my time as a single man but this was my first extramarital escapade. I wasn't confident I was ready for it. Too late to back off now, I convinced myself what was the harm in it anyway? A show or a film, a meal and a drink maybe, then home alone to the Cheese.

Who did I think I was kidding, she was an outstandingly beautiful female. I was a red-blooded male. I had fancied the girl since first setting eyes on her in that café.

To get away with this I had to surmount one hell of a problem. Shirley and I were well-known in the village. Where could I take her? The Pickwick was out, so was the Talk of the Town. A lot hinged on how she would be dressed. Why the devil hadn't I said formal? I dwelt on this as the tube train raced towards Leicester Square. I was getting cold feet up to my armpits and beyond.

Still worried I emerged into Leicester Square, it was five past the hour I had suggested for our meeting. Finding a gap in the traffic, I hurried across the road and into the front entrance of the Talk of the Town. There I stood perfectly still, staring at Marj and the clothes she wore. A magnificent white satin gown enhancing her dark colouring incredibly was topped by a short fur jacket. An obviously expensive, tall wig completed her smashing ensemble. The gown was split high on both sides, exposing two legs which would have put Marlene Dietrich's on the back burner. Again the question came to mind, what the devil was she doing working in my kitchen? Or anybody else's for that matter.

As I have said before, she looked like a million dollars, this time it was all in large denomination notes. All my fears instantly swamped, I went forth to greet her. The formalities over, throwing caution to the wind, I asked, 'anywhere you fancy going?'

'Wherever you want to go, will be all right,' Marj let me off the hook, flashing once again that bobby dazzler of a smile.

We went to a quiet Greek restaurant I knew in Soho. After a superb meal we headed for the Latin Quarter. I knew the doorman Ken, who was a friend of Bert Ireland, the doorman at the Pickwick Club. As we walked down the stairs into the club, Marj stepping daintily in front of us, Ken whispered in my ear. With something like awe in his voice, he asked, 'Peter, where did she come from?'

'She is my kitchen hand,' I said truthfully.

'Ah, ah ah,' was all he mockingly answered.

Taking Marj's arm to enter the room, I turned to look back at Ken on the stairs where he stood on the same step staring at us, then he shrugged, turning away grinning. He didn't believe me then nor would he ever. Marj was a wine drinker. I ordered a good bottle. We drank that and danced to swivelling heads as we negotiated the dance floor. She was attracting a lot of attention and enjoying every minute of it. As my head chef had remarked, 'she is a lovely woman'.

I told her the dress really suited her. I was surprised by her response yet it answered one part of the mystery. Where did she get the money to dress as she did?

'My mother made it, she makes most of my clothes, she is a dressmaker,' Marj smiled at me. I think she knew I had been curious about that. She would not have been out of place on any film set, she had everything going for her, looks, deportment and classy style. Her self-assurance embarrassed me a little, I felt slightly inferior.

That night I met up with an old friend, a bookmaker's son who could well afford to be in there. His name was Steve. He introduced his girlfriend, a Malay by the name of Sashi. She was beautiful, yet not in the same league as Marj. At our request they joined us at our table.

'Do you fancy a gamble?' Steve asked, 'a casino or something? I know— how about Crockford's?'

'I'm not a member,' astounded I stared at him, 'you have to be a member there, don't you?'

'We can try for nothing,' he laughed.

Drinks talking, I thought, and I decided to humour him. Nobody got into Crockford's that shouldn't.

'I know one of the doormen, I've got in before,' Steve bragged.

I was dressed suitably, so were he and the ladies. Maybe he could get us in, it was worth the try.

Our taxi stopped short of Crockford's, at Steve's request.

'Looks better, gotta keep up appearances, old dear,' Steve counselled.

As we walked towards the club a familiar voice shouted, 'where are you going, Peter?'

It was Tom, John Lennon's ex-chauffeur. He was in full uniform standing alongside a gleaming Rolls Royce. After greeting each other and introducing him to the others, I told him what we were going to do.

'We are trying to get into Crockford's. Personally I don't give much for our chances, but it's worth a go.'

'If you aren't a member, you have no chance,' Tom looked at us thoughtfully, 'hang on a minute, get into the back of the Rolls. These buggers open any door.'

'Hold on there, Tom, don't jeopardize your job for us.'

'It's all right, Peter, my boss has just gone in, he won't be out for hours. Now when I have done my stuff getting you there, it is up to you to get in.'

With all four of us seated in the back, the Rolls purred smoothly up to the entrance, Tom stepped smartly out, standing rigidly to attention after opening the door for us to alight.

'Leave this to me,' Steve said, as we all walked into the well-lit foyer.

'Good evening, this is the Jamaican Ambassador's daughter.'

He rapped out a name which sounded suspiciously like Famballoosie. Oh God, I thought, we are all going to finish up in jail.

We finished up in the singularly reserved Crockford's Club. Whether it was the Rolls backing up Steve's outrageous introduction of Marj, we will never know or care; we spent a night to remember in that most select of all exclusive clubs.

We were ushered inside and spent the evening gambling, and socializing with the upper crust. Marj was introduced to at least a dozen people as the daughter of the Jamaican Ambassador. Steve had the bit between his teeth and was doing all the running. Marj enjoyed herself as never before.

'I don't care,' she whispered in my ear, 'I come from Trinidad anyway.'

On top of all this hilarity, we won enough money between us to pay for the whole evening out. We were on a tremendous high.

Sharing a final bottle of champagne, we toasted Jamaica, before taking our leave of Steve and Sashi. They had decided to stay on at Crockford's for a while.

The doorman called a taxi for us, as we stepped inside the cab, I said, 'Brixton, please,' never giving a thought that there are few embassies within hailing distance of Brixton. We laughed at the idea of Steve trying to explain away my *faux pas*. The doorman had obviously heard me, for he looked like a stunned mullet.

Marj fell into my arms, cuddling up close, her perfume and warmth filling my senses. Gone were all inhibitions.

'Do you have to go home tonight?' I asked.

'I should, but I don't want to.'

She cuddled into my body and we kissed passionately, long and lingeringly. I eased her away.

'Driver, to the City of London please,' I requested.

I didn't care what he thought as he swung his taxi around, London cabbies are pretty resilient characters by nature. He probably watched, or heard, most late night courting couples do their stuff in his back seat.

It was a night out I will never forget, apart from all the intense emotion and wild love making, for she was as good in bed as she appeared out of it. To hold that gorgeous creature in my arms, if only for a short while, seemed unreal, as does the memory today.

Marj stayed with me until Sunday evening, in which time we were mostly sexually active. Food needs were secondary, a quick snack and we were wrapped in each other's arms again. I was to see Marj many times after that weekend, yet it was never the same as that first blissful time.

I picked Shirley up at King's Cross station at 8 p.m. that Sunday. Greeting her and Jacqueline was when the guilt really hit me. I allowed the London scene to get to me, gambling, drinking, and now the women. In Shirley I had a wonderful wife, we had faced more ups and downs that most. Through it all she had encouraged, and done more than her fair share of hard work to put us back on track. There were more ups and downs to come, had we but known. It is a good thing one cannot foresee the future, for if we knew what was in store for us, we would pack the struggle in and join the growing legions of dropouts who sit and contemplate their navels.

I still had the paramount love of boxing, I have kept it throughout my life. Nothing has ever come close to replacing it.

I went to watch Karl Mildenberger hand Billy Walker yet another good thrashing. The latter appeared to get little else from his opponents. However, he was well paid to take hidings, but it did get a bit repetitious after a while. I also saw the first Telstar fight from America, that great performer Mohammed Ali fighting Ernie Terrall. It was held at the Leicester Square Odeon, and was a farce from beginning to end. In fact if it had been live, the booing would have drowned out Ali.

'What is my name?' Ali kept shouting at Terrall.

Ernie Terrall, whether for publicity reasons or otherwise, had refused to call Ali anything other than Cassius Clay. We all know Ali adopted the name of Mohammed Ali when he embraced the Muslim religion. As I say it could have been purely attention getting. Whichever, the fight went fifteen dreary rounds, with Ali continually yelling that inane question at Terrall.

It wasn't all a waste of time, for at the screening I met Dick Richardson, the former European Champion, whom I knew well. Accompanied by him, I was able to enter the V.I.P. Lounge, where nearly all the living Boxing Champions had congregated. They had all come to see this historic Telstar event.

Dick introduced me to Tommy Farr, another acclaimed giant in boxing. What a thrill to clasp that man's hand, popular beyond belief he, too, was an unassuming fellow. I did speculate to myself what would be running through his mind, as he had watched the load of garbage we had just endured. For that was what it was, there was just no other way to describe the fight between Ali and Terrall, it was sheer unadulterated rubbish.

I was close enough to catch Tommy Farr's response to a news reporter's question.

'What is your opinion, Tommy, of the outcome of a fight between Joe Louis and Ali?'

Tommy looked at him with disdain, then came out with one of the best statements I have ever heard on the condition of the boxing game.

'Ali? Clay would not have hit Joe Louis up the backside with a bag of rice.'

I remembered that sarcastic remark every time I watched Mohammed Ali box. When you saw the quality of most of Ali's opponents, I was more apt to agree with Farr's 'bag of rice' comment. The shuffling Brown Bomber would have killed Ali, in fact the sting would have been on Mohammed's person.

Everyone who ever watched no-messing Joe Louis box, and knew the fight game, would be forced to agree with Farr. Who should know better than Tommy Farr? He took Joe Louis to a battling full distance, the verdict being almost too close to call. Joe Louis won.

The Olde Cheshire Cheese, as I have already made clear, had a goodly assortment of customers—Lloyd's of London employees and brokers, ship-ping agents, newspaper employees, shipping company staff and executives, private brokers and shippers, et cetera. The Cheese had three public telephones all in constant use. It was commonplace for an order of champagne to be placed on ice. The shippers could make hundreds of pounds with just a few phone calls, simply by using the phone to shipping agents to find cargo space. Or the reverse, finding cargo to fill a space aboard a vessel.

A customer had, say, freight to occupy 1,000 cubic feet of cargo space, destination maybe Argentina or Africa. Finding the ship going there, with that space to fill, was the shippers' stock in trade. Not a hard way to earn a living, standing at the end of a telephone in one's favourite watering hole. Not bad at all to sustain a most comfortable life style.

Forgive my green-eyed envy. There we were working our butts off, running a large, busy establishment, expected to be forever vigilant, all for the princely sum of £30 a week. While those men indulged in an obvious flaunting of their not too intellectual abilities, merrily making a fortune to boot.

The evening trade at the Cheese varied considerably from the daytime business. No less troublesome, yet certainly more entertaining from my side of the bar.

There were two men who, beyond all contradiction, contributed a great deal to this convivial atmosphere of the Cheese. One was an ex-sea captain who we nicknamed Captain Morgan because of his ability to consume a bottle of rum a day. The other unforgettable character was Mr Pudd, a very wealthy man, who loved to brag that he owned four priceless acres of land next to the Royal Mint.

'Beat that if you can,' I used to think, as I watched the still, listening figures assembled around the bar.

Captain Morgan consumed rum as if he were drinking water. However, one could always tell when he had reached the end of his facility to handle it. He would begin to dribble from the sides of his mouth. A tell-tale sign to watch for because, when Morgan was drunk, all he needed was a cutlass and he would have run amok; fortunately, it was always after the majority of the select end had left, when he lost control.

The Captain and Mr Pudd invariably became involved in conversation which, without fail, ended in a nasty row. I had constantly to be on my toes for the first sign of impending altercation. One could consistently tell when the tide was turning from a placid stream, into a raging river of invective. Pudd would set the ball rolling always, 'he couldn't skipper a coal barge.'

This aspersion of Pudd's, was reiterated daily, five nights a week. Morgan would counter with his usual, less than truthful, disparagement, 'he is a twopenny-halfpenny poof.'

Trying to get between these two at this time was, to say the least, hazardous; yet I can honestly say it was great fun.

Shirley would lose her temper with me and say crossly, 'if you stopped laughing at them, you might get them under control.'

I didn't want to get them under control, they were fabulous characters. Who would be incapable of being amused by these men, one was sixty-five the other seventy. Throwing vitriolic abuse at each other made their night—great friends in spite of appearances. It really was a comedy act they had perfected over the years, which could turn quickly to violence if left unchecked when the demon drink took hold.

I knew that when their brains became too befuddled the performance developed into reality for both of them. Bloodshed was on the cards unless I stepped in.

Regardless of this, their night was spoilt if one or the other didn't appear. Years later I learned that Captain Morgan had died. They said Mr Pudd had taken the news very badly, in fact the man was heartbroken. They were one lovely part of running the Cheese.

Alas, most of the time it remained unremitting hard slog, as I have previously said. When our day and a half came around at week's end, we were usually too done in to enjoy it. We slept most of the clock usually only stirring for meals and to satisfy Jacqueline's demands. At the Cheshire Cheese we spent less time with our daughter than we had at the Porcupine. One of the main underlying reasons for leaving that pub, was the mistaken belief we could devote more time to her.

My continued interest in the fight game now took another course. When I was going to watch a boxing match, Joe, the cellarman, would often ask, 'can I come with you, Guv?'

I did take him with me a few times. We were together when we met a city policemen, Len Sharp, who was interested in boxing. We talked him into entering the Metropolitan Police Championships. Old Joe was so enthusiastic, he'd say with conviction, 'he is a world beater, Guv'ner.'

Stripped off for action he certainly looked the part. We rigged up a punch bag in the cellar at the Cheese. I worked bloody hard on this six feet four inches tall, sixteen and a half stone giant of a man. I planned out the roadwork and his diet. He was eager to succeed, doing all that was asked of him and more. He tried his hardest, slamming the bag around, with Joe doing his utmost to hang on to the wildly swinging punchball. I taught him how to throw a big right hand, and we practised ring-craft for hours.

By the time the Championships came around, we had him in what we considered to be tip-top shape. Although he hadn't fought before, he was sure of himself and looked good enough to eat anybody in his class. There would be some classy contenders too, for this was the London Metropolitan Championships. They are not exactly sissies by anyone's standards. However,

Len had the power, the reach and, I hoped, the know-how to more than hold his own.

We had to wait until the last on the Bill, which is where the Heavyweight preliminaries are placed. Len was drawn to fight a man called Shaw. We both climbed into the ring, Len absolutely brimming with confidence, not at all nervous. If he had any butterflies he was doing a bloody good job of hiding them, I for one being fooled.

Seconds out and I hurriedly left the ring and the bell went for the first round. Before I had time to seat myself properly or gather my thoughts, it was Bang—Len flat on his back, all six feet four inches of him sprawled there, out for the count.

To say I was too stunned to move, is a massive understatement. We had honed every inch of that perfect specimen of manhood, with the exception of one area, his jaw. Poor Len had a glass jaw.

'I don't believe it,' Joe repeated continuously.

Tired of the repetitive disbelief, I was forced into giving some sort of an answer, when all I wanted to do was wallow in self-pity. I wasn't going to get a chance to train a Champion in compensation for failing to reach those coveted heights myself.

'Believe it or not, Joe, a boxer can survive in the game with a glass jaw, he just has to be a damn sight slippier than the norm, and a bloody good boxer. He can't afford to get in and slug it out.' I added caustically, 'not that Len had a chance to do either.'

We did try again with Len, after much ring tuition, the emphasis this time being on defence and the protection of that vulnerable jaw.

The second fight was just as inglorious as the first. Len was knocked out in the first round again. His fighting days were over before they had begun. I took the only step I could in the circumstances, I advised him to give it away.

'Sorry, Len, it's disappointing for both of us, better to face it now than get seriously hurt in the ring.'

'Bloody hell, Guv, he was built like Mr Universe. How did it happen again? Couldn't he see it coming?' Joe asked sadly.

'Size had little to do with it Joe. You either have it or you haven't. Len hadn't and never would have.'

We had heaps of tourists visiting the Cheese, mostly Americans eager to view the room where Samuel Pepys was reputed to have written his diaries. The age of the building, also, was another reason for their interest. I used to act as tour guide on many instances, showing them the main rooms, plus giving quite a reasonable spiel on the subject too. Joe was a wonderful little man, with a sense of humour as big as himself, mischievous as an imp too.

One day I had just finished showing a group of Yanks round the house, when Joe emerged from the cellar, 'Guv'ner, the next time they ask about Samuel Pepys, tell them he is still here. Shout Sam down the cellar and I will do my stuff.'

One had really to see this likeable tiny figure, to appreciate the humour and pathos of the situation.

Joe was a wizened dwarf of a man. Riddled with terminal cancer, he appeared to be at least 100 years old. How very like this self-effacing man, to point the finger of ridicule at himself and his pain-wracked body.

He was to die twelve months later and break the heart of everyone who knew him. Rest easy, Joe.

We lost a fantastic cellarman as well as a friend. He was also an expert on rat extermination. The Olde Cheshire Cheese was close to the Thames and we used to get some huge monsters of rats from the Thames sewers. Joe knew how to deal with them as he dealt with everything else. Rats were annihilated by way of poison and traps, thus kept under control without outside assistance. He was a dreadful loss to us, not only had we lost a trusted, able employee, but an irreplaceable human being. Even the most toffee-nosed of our Select End customers, respected and liked this humorous, colossus called Joe.

He had a huge funeral, masses of people turned out to say goodbye. I have him locked in my memory, as one of the personalities who lightened my life. He set me an example of fortitude and is up with the best of them in stature. In adversity, I hope I can stand up to it in the same way as Joe.

We became more and more disillusioned with A.V. Elliot and Sons, as time went by. The increased pressure from Venny for larger and larger returns, in spite of consistently higher takings, wearing us down beyond reason. We were ripe for picking by any other unscrupulous employer who cared to make an offer.

One day I was approached by a man called Weinburg who said he owned a number of good public houses. He told me he had a large pub in Merton, on the fringes of South Wimbledon, London. He was searching for an experienced manager to run the house for him. The largest carrot of all was dangled before our trusting eyes, we could have the catering rights if we paid him a rent for the equipment. He made it clear that all the profits from that side of the house would be ours with no interference whatsoever from him.

My salary would be for the managing of the pub and its five bars. With the everlasting, thinly disguised threats from Venny to increase trade or else, Shirley and I talked at length about the offer, weighing up as best we could the fors and againsts. It meant going back to a seven day week and a much larger house to manage, with all the risks that entailed. It showed the measure of unhappiness and insecurity we felt with Venny and Elliot as bosses that we would even consider such a backward step.

We went out to Merton to see the place. It had an enormous dance hall type of room on the first floor which, with an off-licence, restaurant and five bars made up the whole. Shirley took a deep, pensive breath, saying, 'you know of course, we are leaving the inner city and going into the suburbs for the first time? That is if we accept. It will be far from easy with a pub of this magnitude, plus having to work much longer hours and far more bars to keep our eyes on.'

I knew Shirley wanted to get me away from the temptations of the village. Even though I knew the gambling and the women, were the motivating force behind any decision she might make, if it meant leaving the classy Cheese it would be an outcome which she'd accept in exchange.

The result of all this deep thought ended with our agreeing to take on the King's Head, regardless of the fact the place was built like a bloody castle, and had almost the same proportions.

None of the staff at the Cheese were willing to leave the City. It meant a complete change of personnel for Shirley and me once more. Not only that, the numbers would be much greater; which spelt trouble. Nevertheless, our notice was duly given to a considerably deflated Mr Venny and another chapter of our lives was finished.

A far, far different one was about to begin.

Chapter 7

S HIRLEY and I developed a saying used whenever we were beset with the powerlessness to dictate our own future. 'We should never have left the Porcupine.'

We were to wear that phrase out in the King's Head, a living nightmare to manage confirming our worst fears. Within a few months we realized we had been well and fully conned by Mr Weinburg in respect of the catering, or rather the lack of demand for the same. By the time we had paid him the rent for the equipment, there was very little left over for yours truly. Running all those bars and the off-licence was truly horse-work. Be that as it may, we decided to get stuck in, and stop bemoaning our lot. I could see the potential for the dance room on the first floor, and the concert room, which we had downstairs. We hired a group for the concert room and the place was transformed from a dismal den, into a lively money spinning popular spot. I had employed a chap, Andy, who was quite a good singer, backed by his group of four who were fairly commendable musicians. In no time at all they had built up a goodly number of fans too, which helped the beer and liquor sales no end.

Shirley was catering for the occasional wedding and social event, while I would hold a weekly dance night up there. With the resultant dramatic increase in turnover our stock went up with Mr Weinburg.

The King's Head was a Youngs of Wandsworth Brewery owned house. They had won many awards for their beer and were one of the better southern brewers. On occasion they would deliver the beer order using their famous horses and dray. This was mainly for publicity reasons, of course, as everyone is aware horses and cart have long outlived their usefulness. All the same their horses had won every prize there was to be won. They had sent their Shires as far north as Yorkshire, to the Great Yorkshire Show at Harrogate, winning first prize against the fabulous Shire horses of that county, to the everlasting mortification of the average Yorkshire farmer.

With their outstanding Special Bitter Ale, they were laughing all the way to the bank. It was an unbeatable combination. They were not the only ones beating a path merrily to the bank. Mr Weinburg wasn't doing too badly either with the aid of Shirley and Peter Aldridge who, as per, were doing the hard bit.

Youngs were a family owned brewery, one of the last in Britain, most having been taken over by big combines with little or no interest in brewing, only in the lucrative turnovers of that trade.

John Young, the head of this empire, made a point of visiting all of his houses. He was a charming man who could afford to be that way, a multimillionaire nonetheless giving a firm impression of being a very down to earth fellow. He'd stand at the bar and shout drinks for anyone in the vicinity, including me, holding your attention with his conversation and not just because he was the boss.

Whenever he won a first prize for his beer, every house he owned in London or the south of England, would receive a telegram, 'congratulations we have won first prize again.'

It must have cost a fortune to send all those wires out. At that particular period Youngs owned in the region of 300 houses. This was a typical John Young gesture, to draw his employees into the firm's success, thereby making them feel a part of it. It certainly paid off.

The patrons of the King's Head were as different as it was possible to be from those of the Cheese, though they were equally as good in their spending. Their tastes ran along different lines, beer and not champers being their tipple. The conversation was less guarded and restricted than at the Cheese, although I thought on many occasions it should have been. The clientele included some real hard-bitten characters, not least among these Bruce Reynolds, the infamous leader of the Great Train Robbery.

Reynolds had lived just a few doors away from the Head. According to the regular customers he was a very close friend of the then manager. In addition, they told me they were convinced part of the haul was still stashed somewhere in the King's Head, urging me to get searching with, 'go on, Peter, get looking. There's a bloody fortune here waiting to be found.'

If there was, I couldn't find it. It's still waiting.

I searched that blasted castle from end to end, from the rafters in the roof to the cellars and back again. There was an outside chance of its being

The King's Head, Merton, South Wimbledon, 1967.

there, £2,000,000 to be precise, the amount still unrecovered from the Train Robbery spoils.

Doug Goody and Buster Edwards, two other members of the gang, also used the King's Head as their local watering hole. I would have loved to have been a fly on the wall during those tête-à-têtes between the ex-manager and the leader of the pack.

One customer of mine, whom I knew to be a villain and a possible gangster, told me the get-away cars were tuned up in the extremely large car park and garages at the rear of the Head. I believe him. Roy James, who received a thirty year sentence for his part in the robbery, hired one of the garages prior to the crime.

The King's Head main bar did a roaring trade. It was a tremendous money-spinner, patronized by a mixture of ordinary working men and villains, plus those who made a doubtful livelihood by using their brains to the detriment of others. This motley crowd made the King's Head what it was. Shirley set about cleaning up this cavernous place. The cleaners, bar staff and the catering side quickly learnt that this Yorkshire couple could work and expected no less from the rest of the employees.

When we took over the Head, it wasn't filthy, yet it was far from what one would call clean. By the time Shirley had worked her magic, the place shone.

With the growing respectability of the pub, the numbers of working men using the house steadily increased. I formed a darts team. It was the first time Shirley and I had tried a darts team, none of the pubs we relieved or managed ran them. They were hardly the type of clientele who would participate in such a game. And can you imagine the nefarious crowd which regularly filled the Camden Head in Islington having what one calls a friendly game of darts? Mayhem was more in their line, good at it, too, they were.

The public bar soon outstripped the lounge bars in takings, apart from the weekends when the music was laid on. I preferred the public bar. It had a marvellously warm feeling to it, friendly and inviting, holding at least as much of the milk of human kindness one could expect, considering the odd mixture of mankind's frailties which frequented it. Among the regular bar customers was a man named Reg Swinfield. He was a big man, around fifty years of age. Invariably well dressed in expensive clothes, he had the ability to wear them to good advantage. I could talk to this man at length. Adding to his attraction, he had an interest in my favourite topic, boxing. We were to have many discussions, besides friendly arguments about the fight game and fighters in general. He was well up on the sport, knowing several boxers.

Reg had been, and still was then, a bit of a lad about town. He claimed he had been Jack Spot's personal bodyguard, being more than handsomely paid for this man's bodily protection. Once he got to know me, he could hold yours truly enthralled with stories about the famous gangster, telling how he had lost three fingers in defence of Spot, bringing to an end his bodyguarding days, and the protection business.

He related an incident which occurred during a visit with Spot to America. They had gone there on business and a certain American syndicate had threatened Spot with his life. Even prior to this Jack Spot always liked to feel Reg's shoulder brushing against his. He had to walk that close to his boss. Spot had to feel actual physical contact of their bodies all the time.

They landed at La Guardia Airport, New York. Heading towards the customs area, there was a fairly large crowd of pushing, jostling people. In this unruly confusion, Reg said:

'I was bundled, big as I am, to one side away from Jack, I found myself at least twenty yards behind him. Spot was terrified, he stopped dead in his tracks, shouting at the top of his voice, "Reg, Reg, where are you?"'

'Forcing all my six foot three through the packed, milling mob was almost bloody impossible but I finally managed to get close to him, near enough in fact to assure him, "It's all right, Jack, I'm here".'

'The poor bugger had had the shit knocked out of him, he was a badly frightened man. He clutched at my arm, hugging it close to him, ashen-faced he turned on me and bloody venomously he said, "Don't ever leave me like that again."'

'He told me I had to sleep outside his room for the rest of the American trip, and I did, bloody uncomfortably outside his bedroom door. Christ, I was never so glad to be back in London, and Spot voiced my thoughts exactly, when he said shakily, "thank fucking Christ, we have made it. I could kiss the bloody ground."'

I once asked Reg how he received his wages, and was there a set scale for bodyguards?

'I would just say to Jack, "I am down on money", he would open his safe and give me a bundle of notes without question,' Reg replied, before continuing with his explanation of how he was paid.

'He was amazingly generous with me. I was allowed to go to his personal tailor and have the best Savile Row suits made to measure. Jack paid regardless of cost.'

This accounted for Reg Swinfield's excellent taste in clothes in general which had first attracted my attention to him.

There had been a murder committed, headlined in all the daily newspapers, a mystery which, to all who were following the case, appeared to be baffling the police. A case of the missing body.

'Whatever happened to Ginger Marks?' the tabloids screamed.

Not that they cared. One less villain could only sweeten the atmosphere but it sold newspapers by the thousands.

Ginger Marks had been riddled by bullets, dragged into a car, and to all intents and purposes, disappeared from, to quote Shakespeare, 'the mortal coil'.

On one Saturday morning, Reg Swinfield took his usual place at the public bar.

'Morning, Reg, what do you make of this Ginger Marks caper?' I asked, purely to start the conversation going.

Reg looked at me quizzically, 'Marksie went down Streatham,' he answered quietly.

I was busy at the time serving customers and I continued with what I was doing, thinking to myself, that's a bloody funny reply.

It quietened down a bit, and I had a job to do in the cellar. With this completed, I rejoined Reg in the bar, still puzzled over his reply. He could know something everyone else didn't, he had the contacts still. 'What do you mean, Reg, Marksie went down Streatham?'

Reg considered that question, before answering in a muted voice, 'the cremmy, the cremmy.' (The South London Crematorium, Streatham.)

Still no wiser, I was about to ask Reg what the hell he was on about, when the penny dropped. What Reg was trying to tell me was, Ginger Marks had indeed disappeared, permanently, to the crematorium in Streatham. I was so intrigued by this whiff of the real underworld, the silver screen villains paled into insignificance by comparison. I forgot my fear of knowing too much, this was better than any thriller I'd ever seen, or was likely to see. I wanted to know why Ginger Marks had met such a nasty end.

That Saturday night after we had closed the Head, Reg and his wife, Shirley and I sat in the best lounge, having a sandwich and a drink. I brought up the Ginger Marks story again, determined to find out what had earned the death sentence Marks had received, in spite of the fact it could be dangerous to have that knowledge.

'Now, Reg,' I began, 'do you really understand why Ginger Marks was killed?'

'Don't you know why Marks was done for?'

'No, Reg, I honestly haven't a clue.'

'I'll f'ing tell you,' Reg swore, 'I'd forget it too, if I were you.'

The story I am about to tell you I have kept to myself ever since that night Reg Swinfield took me into his confidence on the promise I would never repeat it. That was twenty-five years ago, I hope Reg wherever he is will forgive, for I have never divulged the story to a living soul before. My lips did remain sealed on the subject. I firmly believe in its authenticity, as I am convinced Ginger Marks was reduced to ashes at Streatham. This is how Reg told me the story.

The Great Train Robbery was performed with military precision, accuracy of timing, every move pre-planned. All the what ifs answered and covered. Each member of the gang had their own job to do. Leatherslade Farm was acquired weeks before the robbery was to be pulled off. This was to be a temporary hide-out during the initial cooling-off period. It was a masterly professional hold-up from beginning to almost end, achieved with a minimum of fuss and a bloody great deal of know-how, by a group of men skilled not only in crime. Though one has to admit they were bloody good at that.

After the perfect *coup* they retired to the farm as planned, where they lived quietly for a few days, undetected by the law.

What threw the police and public into a tizzy, and I believe still puzzles the law . . . Why did such thoroughly competent crooks commit so many gaffes at Leatherslade Farm? A group of school kids could have done better at covering their tracks.

Why had they left all the incriminating evidence? Stupid amateurish things, like fingerprints on beer cans, mail bags scattered around. In actual fact they had left their calling card in so many places, it was an open invitation to the police to pick them up. From the beginning they were aware that the farm only offered a brief sanctuary, a clever subterfuge, knowing the police would run road blocks from the scene of the crime. Who would guess at their staying in the vicinity?

When the police found Leatherslade, they couldn't believe their eyes, immediately putting the job down to a bunch of lucky, slap-happy amateurs, who had hit a jackpot beyond their wildest imaginings.

That is, until they checked the fingerprints.

In the tradition of good, well thought out crimes, what happened was: the job completed they had returned to the farm, for either their share of the spoils, or in some cases their wages, for most were only on a guaranteed amount. Everything had gone according to plan, the usefulness of Leatherslade Farm was at an end, it was time to move out.

A professional burner had been hired, his job was to burn the place down to the ground after all the gang had left, wiping out all incriminating evidence, leaving no trace whatsoever of the gang's use of the place or of any of their identities.

The burner was Ginger Marks.

He arrived at Leatherslade in a Land Rover full of petrol cans, to fulfil his part in the robbery. A part for which he had been handsomely paid in advance.

However, as Ginger approached the vacated farm, a helicopter flew low over the building. It was not, as Marks assumed, a police spotter craft, but a helicopter on training manoeuvres from the local Royal Air Force base.

Ginger Marks panicked. Swinging the Land Rover around, he bolted for home. By doing so, he condemned the gang as surely as if he had informed on them. The gang was convicted mostly from evidence collected from the farm. The sentences were unusually heavy, even for robbery with violence, as this was termed—up to thirty years for the ringleaders. Ginger went underground, his life was not worth spit. Inevitably he would be found and vengeance wreaked. As only the underworld knows how. I wonder if the cremating was part of the rough justice?

Like me, you may have assumed Ginger Marks had seen the inside of a concrete box, now nestled at the bottom of the River Thames, or the Channel. The cremmy, as Reg called it, makes a cement coffin sound like old hat. A very secure, final way to dispose of anyone; no amount of dredging will ever resurrect them.

Cold blooded bastards aren't they? No one gets a second chance.

The King's Head became more of a popular meeting spot as the weeks went by. I ran the public bar with the aid of two staff, Shirley managed the other lounge bars with an abundance of staff. Occasionally I'd take a saunter through to the other bars, without exception at irregular intervals, making the odd detour into the lounge rooms themselves, mainly to keep a weather eye on things in general, often to chat with customers we were beginning to know well. One German business man came into that category, a

Shirley Aldridge, 1967. The Kings Head.

frequent patron of the lounge area, sometimes coming in both during the morning and evening sessions. My wife would often have a drink and a chat with him, as would I. At times he'd send a drink through to the bar for me. During conversation he told Shirley about his business mentioning that he was not only in European commerce, but was also an international businessman.

My wife came to me one night and said the German wanted to talk business with her. She was going into the best lounge with him. He had an hotel in Bermuda and apparently wanted us to manage it for him.

Excitedly I grabbed hold of her, saying, 'Shirley, this is what we have worked so long and hard for, it is all we have been dreaming of. Go back and find out all you can from him.'

It was a chance in a million, if it was true. My wife went to rejoin the fellow to gain all the information she could. They sat at a table while he showed her a stack of coloured brochures and write-ups about the luxury resort and hotel. According to the pamphlets he indeed owned the establishment.

Apparently it wasn't a business trip this time. He was over for the Wimbledon Tennis Championships, staying at a very expensive hotel, the Savoy. As Shirley said, 'his business must be thriving, if he can afford *their* going rates.'

I waited impatiently for her to come back with the details about this tremendous offer. She didn't.

Finally unable to contain myself any longer, I walked through to the lounge, where Shirley and this man had been sitting.

Shirley was at the bar, there was no sign of the German in the room. I went over and put my arms around her, saying, 'darling what a chance for us. What did he say?'

'Hum,' she replied noncommittally, 'what a chance? As he said, "sun, sand, and a perfect romantic island." What more could anyone ask for?'

'Yes,' I hugged her close, puzzled by her reticence yet trying to jolt her out of it by humouring her. 'I reckon you and I can stand some of that, don't you, darling?'

'There is only one thing wrong with it. I do not think you will like it one bit.' Shirley looked at me with a twinkle in her eyes.

'What's that? There can't be much wrong with an offer like that.'

'He only wants me, he wanted me to go with him now to the Savoy to spend the night there to, what he calls, "cement the deal". I told him to get lost, and quick, before you find out the kind of deal it is.'

'The bloody swine! I'll kill the bastard, where is he?'

'Long gone, he almost ran out of here.'

No doubt he had gone to pastures new, or a fresh trout stream, with his well-baited fishing line. We never saw him again.

How we have laughed over that incident, in spite of the momentary pangs over what might have been. Sun, sand and a romantic island indeed, but for whom? Now, whenever anyone mentions Bermuda, we burst out laughing, often to the speaker's consternation.

We were stuck with the King's Head for better or worse, and all the hard work it entailed. Particularly for Shirley, for I was often absent.

When we left the West End, we both thought I would be able to curb the gambling bug. Alas, Wimbledon Dog Track was far too close to the Head, and I was a truly compulsive gambler.

I would take off some week nights and stay away most of the night, losing far more than I could possibly afford. On very rare occasions I would win, then I'd head for the West End and all my old haunts. The place was a bloody magnet to me, I couldn't stay away. Moving into the suburbs had achieved little, I had just a longer distance to travel. Shirley became more and more distraught, as I went my own way.

'Here I am, working myself to death, and you are out, playing Jack the Lad all over the place.'

She was absolutely right of course. Although I promised continuously, to both myself and Shirley it would stop, nevertheless I continued down the stupid path to my own destruction. Had I half the brains I was born with, I should have been a wealthy man today. I made the bookies rich instead, chasing the impossible, elusive certain winner.

Round about that time a very disturbing, and potentially dangerous incident occurred in the public bar. It involved Reg Swinfield and me. Reg came in one morning with a newspaper wrapped parcel.

'Put that under the counter for me, will you, Peter?'

I did as he asked, placing it under a back shelf, out of view of anyone. Reg watched me stow it away, nodding his head as I pushed the two foot long, narrow object out of sight.

I don't know why, yet I had a horrible feeling of foreboding. In those days I really think I had developed a sharp sixth sense for trouble. As soon as the opportunity arose, I turned back one corner of the newspaper around the parcel. It contained a Gurkha-type knife as sharp as a razor blade. Christ, I was worried, what was Reg up to?

I went over to where he was standing. Leaning over the bar, I quietly asked, 'what's the cutlery for, Reg?'

'That's for a fucking bastard who is coming in here this morning.'

God, it was the realization of my worst fears. Reg appeared deadly serious. I knew the knife was not for someone else's use, he had every intention of taking retribution on the woe-begotten wretch he had referred to.

'Please Reg, not in here,' I implored.

'I am going to chop his f'ing ears off,' he snarled back angrily.

'Not in here, Reg, don't be hasty.'

'Hasty? I can't wait for the bastard, I'll fix him proper.'

My God, what a predicament to be in. I didn't want to lose Reg and with him a hell of a lot of good will. However, neither had I any intention of being embroiled in that sort of bother. I decided to sit tight and await events, I could act accordingly. Needless to say, I sweated cobs that morning.

Around midday the swing doors parted, a large, extremely obese fellow pushed his way into the pub. He went quickly up to Reg at the bar, who turned to snap his fingers at me for his murderous weapon. I hesitated, deliberately, for I had no intention of handing the bloody thing to him. That way I would have become an accessory before the fact, if nothing worse.

The fat man saved me from committing myself, by saying, 'there's no need for bother, Reg, I have got it all.'

Reg held the flat of his hand towards me, indicating to keep the knife where it was. He needn't have bothered, the knife was staying where it was, the bugger would have to get past me to get it.

The fleshy man gave Reg a bulky packet, which resembled a large wad of bank notes wrapped in cellophane. Reg swiftly stuffed it into his pocket.

'Tell him this has saved his f'ing life,' he growled at the man, who meekly turned on his heel and left the Head.

'Just a little business, which needed tidying up, Peter.' He turned towards me again, saying as if nothing out of place had happened, 'give me a pint, Peter, and get one yourself.'

At no time did I tell him that I had no intention of letting him have the knife. Why rock the boat? As he made to leave, I said quietly, 'don't forget your parcel, Reg.'

'Oh, yes,' he replied, a huge grin on his face, 'I'll need a shave in the morning.'

It would have done that and more, it was some lethal weapon.

Imagine my relief to get it off the premises, and the whole unhappy experience relegated to a bad taste in the mouth.

The King's Head went about its varied business. On the plus side the band continued to pull in the clients to the concert room. The upstairs dance hall which I opened twice a week did good trade. Still more than holding its own was the public bar, with its sometimes dodgy happenings. The only part of the business refusing to respond to our innovations, was the catering side. It was not paying, regardless of all Shirley's efforts. She did the cooking and serving herself to cut costs, but at the end of the day all profits were eaten up by the rent, and the hiring of equipment from Weinberg.

We finally had the inevitable showdown with Mr Weinburg on this issue, in vain. We wanted more money for managing the pub, and a lower rent for the barely existent catering rights.

We were up against a seasoned campaigner. Scrooge would have appeared benevolent by comparison. Despite our more than doubling the original takings, we received neither a cut in rent nor a hike in wages.

Weinburg's secretary travelled with him at all times, she, without doubt was his right hand. I suspected she was also much more than that. She was quite attractive, physically, playing his little games very well, too. He was a born show-off, seeming to enjoy displaying his prowess in whatever form to her. His favourite party piece consisted of tearing telephone directories in half. As you will have guessed, he was a powerful brute of a man. I harboured suspicions, that he had used his vast strength for purposes other than tearing innocuous telephone books to bits. Be that as it may, on the day of the show-down, he had grabbed a phone directory, done his usual trick, then stared peculiarly first at me, then at his secretary. It is anyone's guess what the implication was. I for one couldn't have cared less. I was sick to death of his childish behaviour, and his complete unwillingness even to meet us halfway on either the rent or the wages.

I picked up another telephone directory, quickly broke its back, and tore it in half all the time watching the pair of them. I had learned how to do that trick years before, from a weight lifter friend of mine, for trick it is.

He looked hard at me. I doubt if he would ever forgive me for spoiling his hare-brained act, spitefully I hoped it was spoiled for good.

'Give me another twelve months of progress, and I will look at the wages situation again,' he said suddenly.

We gave it our best for the following twelve months, a rigorous year it was, too. It contained more downs that ups for Shirley and me, though the takings continued to increase.

The minute remuneration for our efforts, bestowed on us by Weinburg, convinced us it was time to move on again.

This was not going to be easy, obtaining a managerial position in London at the time was difficult to say the least.

In the meantime we had set on another barman, who lived in. We had six staff who resided on the premises. Roughly three days after starting the job the new barman took French leave. Taking with him all Shirley's prized, well-loved jewellery, plus the contents of one till. We had not insured my wife's bits and pieces and she cried at the loss of her engagement ring. How could I hope to replace the invaluable item, even if I could raise the money. We had £80 to make good, money the bastard had taken from the till. Our chances were zilch of Weinburg foregoing that loss, it was all ours. The barman was never traced, he probably made his living doing-over unsuspecting publicans.

We hadn't had to contend with live-in staff before, the security risk was understandably increased a thousandfold, but it had invariably been the custom at the King's Head to use such staff. It was an unceasing cause of headaches. They would come in at all hours of the night. The women would try to smuggle men in, the men determined to bring women inside, I was just as determined the buggers wouldn't.

Our hard-earned rest was shattered thoughtlessly on countless nights, as giggling women and drunken men created their own imbecilic cacophony. On one occasion I caught a fellow climbing the fall-pipe to a waiting girl's window. A modern day Romeo and Juliet, only at 1.30 a.m. one doesn't feel romantically for them, in fact the bloody opposite. I crept quietly into the laundry room, which was adjacent to the girl's bedroom, connected up the hosepipe and drenched the man with freezing, cold water. He fell off the pipe yelling blue murder and bolting like hell for cover.

I doubt very much if he would repeat the exercise, for it must have cooled his ardour more that somewhat, it being dead of winter.

There was another instance of forbidden love being enjoyed out of bounds. We were awakened by an unholy din coming from one of the girl's rooms. I opened the door not knowing what to expect and was confronted by two naked, heaving bodies, loud squeaking bedsprings, grunts, squeals and the squelch of sweaty flesh as it met and parted. They were having one whale of a time. Underneath the surging male on the bed was my barmaid. How the hell she had managed to get him in I do not know, for we were two floors up. Another one who had shinned the drainpipe? I had seen this girl come in alone, earlier in the evening.

'Out,' I yelled at the perspiring lover, unable to control my anger, though we were to see the funny side of the whole incident later. I gathered up all of his clothes which, tidy lad that he was, he had placed carefully on a chair. Opening the window I slung the lot out, into the car-park two storeys below.

Grabbing him by his long hair, I hauled him down the stairs to the bar door. As I shoved him outside, I planted a mighty kick up his arse. I bet he wouldn't sit down for a week.

I relocked the door still fuming and turned around. There was Shirley sitting on the stairs doubled up. Hardly able to speak, she spluttered, 'that was the funniest thing I have ever seen, he had one hand covering his privates all the way down the stairs.'

'Well, tell Madam up there to get somebody who needs two hands to cover them next time. It's a bit late for bloody modesty now.'

Mary, as the barmaid was inaptly named, didn't indulge again, at least if she did it was a quieter less active orgy. I allowed her to stay on for she was a good barmaid, and good barmaids were harder than hen's teeth to come by, so I really wasn't being too lenient with her.

We had enough to contend with, we didn't need nocturnal lovers adding to our security risks and chronic sleeplessness.

Disheartened by the arrogant treatment meted out by Weinburg, who thought he had us tied into the Head until our usefulness to him was over, it was truly time to say goodbye to the King's Head.

I decided we needed help in getting out of there. Weinburg would not take kindly to our intention to leave. He was a spiteful man, considering it a loss of face to lose his manager, besides the possible downturn of the

Head's takings. Any references we got from that source would more than probably be biased against us.

After long consultation together, it was agreed I should go and seek advice from our friends in the village.

Mr Boncey had retired from the Holyrood, Mr Verrell had left Snows to take over the Holyrood in his place. Sorrowfully Verrell greeted me with, 'the West End is finished, the class has gone.'

He was so right, the hippies and society's drop-outs had invaded the village. As true vandals have done for centuries, they set about destroying the established order of things. The people who had made and kept the area respectable for all, ran for cover, and who could blame them. Filth was the order of the day. Eros a resting place for drug-crazed dregs of humanity.

Mr Verrell listened to my tale of woe about the King's Head. Good friend that he was, he promised to keep his ears close to the ground for us. We liked the King's Head in spite of the killing work it entailed. It was far too large to police properly, to keep an eye on all the bars was a physical impossibility, ultimately we were being robbed blind by dishonest staff.

The more we increased trade, the more staff we required, it was a Catch Twenty-two situation. Keeping good stock results was a hilarious non-starter from the very beginning.

Liking the King's Head was a different matter from trying to run it. With tired bodies and blank minds we became almost zombies. Worry led to sleeplessness again. We just had to get out of there.

'Oh hell!' Shirley would exclaim, 'we should not have left the Porcupine. Why did we do it?'

As I have said before, this was a well used type of self recrimination often found to be a good safety valve for our suppressed feelings. Running a pub I know is the ultimate ambition for many men. Take my advise, don't. I would like a penny for the many times I have listened to men saying, 'when I retire, I think I will take a pub.'

Believe me, retirement is hardly the time to cope with a seven day working week, and a fourteen hour day, which more often than not makes up a publican's life. Always having to appear clean and tidy, with a friendly smile and cheery word, even when confronted by the same story, word for word, that you hear for the umpteenth dozen time from the pub bore who seems to enjoy picking on you.

You will never work so bloody hard for your meagre pittance in the cities. In the country you won't work at all, then worry where the rent is coming from. Unless you feel philanthropic, remain a pub user.

One evening I arrived back at the King's Head, after a night out at Wimbledon Dog Track, losing, as had become the norm. It was just before closing time. Shirley said crossly, 'there has been a phone call for you from Mr Verrell, he wants you to call him back in the morning.'

'I will do better than that, I will go to see him in the morning.'

The next day I caught the tube train to Piccadilly, changed for Oxford Street and walked down the road to the Holyrood, which stands fifty yards down the side road of Bourne and Hollingworth's department store. I entered the immaculate Holyrood, as it still was in those days. Memories crowded my mind of the days when Shirley and I were relief managers, and that smashing chap, Mr Boncey, was the manager of the house. Those happy times when we were asked to relieve the Holyrood, how very nice it was to relax in this beautiful place.

As I approached the office door, Mr Verrell came out.

'Hello, Peter,' he greeted me warmly, 'sit down, I won't be a moment.'

He came back a few seconds later, shouting to a waitress to bring two coffees and closed the office door behind him.

'Look here, Peter, I heard you are being worked to death where you are. I know a man whose brother owns two pubs, one in Putney, the other in Porchester Road, W2. He is looking for a manager for the latter house, do you want me to phone him for an interview for you.'

'Do I? Indeed I do, Mr Verrell.'

It actually sounded too good to be true, back on the fringes of the West End again. But I wondered would Shirley be as enthusiastic about the prospect as I? No, I knew the answer to that one.

As I sat sipping coffee, Verrell phoned his friend, to arrange an interview for Shirley and me with his brother.

I couldn't thank Verrell enough for his kindness towards us. Beyond any question he was a very good friend in need.

The friend's brother was named Mr Francis, an interview had been organized for the coming week, at The Albert, the Porchester Road public house. I had two problems to surmount to reach the goal, I had no fears that we wouldn't get the position. My obstacles were Shirley and Weinburg.

Without informing Weinburg, Shirley and I attended for the scheduled appointment at The Albert. We would tackle Mr Weinburg with our next job in the bag, he could do his damnedest then.

Mr Francis was a very large, fat man, a nineteen stone extrovert. Once again we were to be ruled by a bully of a man. He was an ex-racecourse bookie, with none of the finesse of the better of his breed.

During the interview he gave us a preview of what to expect of him, yet my wife and I were in no position to walk away.

Nevertheless, there was one thing which had to be cleared up, before we accepted the position he had offered as managers of The Albert. The stumbling block being, who was to hold the licence?

There was no way I would manage any public house, unless the licence was held in my name. Francis had other ideas, and took some convincing that, regrettably, we would have to turn down the offer of running The Albert if he wouldn't concede this point.

Pure unadulterated bluff on our part, for we wanted desperately to be out of the King's Head and into The Albert.

We won that round. I believe it was the only one we did win with him. We were to take over The Albert one month later. The next bully in line to tackle was Weinburg.

I had to give him one month's notice, the accepted norm for both sides to terminate the contract. He was far from pleased with the *fait accompli* served to him. He hadn't reckoned on our ability to obtain another position. We had disarmed him without going to battle stations, thank God. We didn't need the hassle. A busy time lay ahead, for the last month in there would no doubt be as eventful, as any we had spent under that roof.

I was delighted to learn, Shirley was as pleased as I that we were to return to the vicinity of the village. She had agreed to the interview, without committing herself. Now she was breathing a sigh of relief, the end was in sight so far as the King's Head was concerned.

The Wimbledon Tennis Championships were taking place and we were very busy, in fact the Head was a bloody mad-house during this event. We had met an American couple who had come over for the tennis, among other things. Apparently wealthy, they had a suite at the Savoy Hotel. They were Mr and Mrs Joe Zanelli, who hailed from Hartford in Connecticut. We had a lot in common for he was a hotelier, albeit far higher in the pecking order of things than yours truly. He had other strings to his bow besides the liquor trade being a restaurateur and food concessionaire operator.

Mrs Zanelli came, originally, from Corpus Christi, Texas and was half Mexican. Whether that accounted for her fiery temperament I do not know. She had a temper which was second to none. I think she was proud of it, for she gave it free rein heedless of her whereabouts. Oh boy, when they had an argument it was all-out war, nothing was held back, it was both barrels front on, full blast.

We met them in the Head. They just walked in off the street and stood at the bar. I had met many Americans over the years in London. It does not take long before you realize the first love of most of them, is the history of this ancient isle. Usually one whiff of the subject means they will remain riveted to the bar, while everyone is willing to hold forth on the topic.

In no time at all I was in conversation with the Zanellis, hitting it off immediately. Even minus the historical bit we were still talking long after closing time. Shirley began making tea for us at 5 p.m. We said goodbye for they were leaving the next day for Gleneagles, Scotland, staying there for a week. Joe was an avid golfer though I do not know if his wife shared his enthusiasm. Whichever, she would certainly enhance any golf links she appeared on, so long as she didn't speak.

A week later a letter arrived at the King's Head, accompanied by the most beautiful bouquet of flowers for Shirley. The letter was an invitation to have dinner with Mr and Mrs Joe Zanelli, at the Savoy Hotel.

What a very nice thoughtful gesture, from two exceedingly kind people. We had been in most of the best hotels in London but we had never had dinner at the Savoy. This was an opportunity we were not about to miss. Fortunately, it was for a Thursday night, one of the quietest nights of the week. We arranged for our trustier staff to keep an eye on matters pertinent. I had a good head barman who could close and lock up for me, and stay around until we arrived home again.

We reached the Savoy Hotel dressed in all our evening finery. At the reception desk we were told Mr and Mrs Zanelli were expecting us, awaiting our arrival in the cocktail lounge. Would we please go through.

Joe Zanelli and his wife greeted us like long lost friends, which to our inbred northern reserve, was a little surprising as we had known one another for little over a week, and spoken together for just about four hours. In the face of this we were still pleased to be put so quickly at our ease.

To our somewhat overstated thanks for the invitation, Joe grinned, 'think nothing of it, it is our pleasure.'

I never thought that I would be ungrateful mentally, even if I tried to hide it. It wasn't your fault Joe, that every time my wife and I remember that night, we curl up a little inside, though now we can smile. We sat through the most embarrassing time of our lives, hoping to God a great hole would manifest itself to allow us to disappear.

Thank you Joe, the meal was perfect with no expense spared. Paula, your wife, was another lady who couldn't handle her wealth. She believed that money was sufficient unto itself, manners and good taste she sadly lacked. Her temper was given a full exposure. A restaurant in the Savoy is hardly the place to reveal one's total lack of reserve. Paula did, and how!

The trigger for the outburst was so minor that any comment should have been superfluous. Paula had different ideas.

An unfortunate waiter had accidentally caught her arm, while she was shovelling prawns into her ample mouth. Contemptuously, she yelled, 'you big bum.'

With no exaggeration, everyone in the restaurant turned to look at us unbelievingly. My God, where's the bloody bolthole, I thought. A chance to dine at the Savoy, and it has to be with a bloody loud-mouth.

Joe leaning across the table towards Paula breathed, 'Paula, shut your mouth.'

Shirley and I looked apprehensively at each other, knowing she would not sit still for that. How right we were.

'Don't tell me to shut up,' she screamed at him, 'I will speak when I damned well like.'

Joe gave up, coming to the obvious conclusion he would only be adding fuel to the fire. Correction there, I mean spitfire.

We were stuck with Paula's company, whether we desired it or not, so we settled down to, as I've said, a splendid meal with ultra attentive service. The latter due, no doubt, to Paula's temper tantrum with the waiter. He wasn't going to risk upsetting her a second time. I would have loved to have been there when that waiter returned to the kitchen.

Throughout the meal Joe and his wife flaunted their wealth. Champagne, only the best was good enough, old wine of the same quality. Throughout, Paula loudly demanded, and received, the attention of a panoply of mute waiters. Head-waiters doing their subservient best to attend to her every whim sickened my wife and me, while Paula lapped it up and queened her way through this devil's feast.

Joe said, for no apparent reason, unless he was trying to tell us what we already knew, that he was not of the same cloth as his wife.

'We left Gleneagles a day early.' He added wryly, 'Paula wasn't getting the service she should have had.'

I could visualize the relief of the management of that reputable inn, when Madam Paula took her premature leave. Or was it forced?

She had it all, looks, money and a way of life second to none, yet one was fully aware she considered it was not enough. A very unhappy, discontented lady was Mrs Paula Zanelli.

She did her utmost to disparage everything around her, succeeding only in belittling herself to everyone present. A very common woman, so much so that one felt numb in her presence.

When you imagine how much joy she could have derived with the use of so much wealth, it seemed obscene to expend it as a whip to get her way. After the meal we were invited to their suite for drinks. We were a damned sight happier away from the public eye, and enjoyed the remainder of the night.

Joe and I talked boxing, a sport he was interested in. He told us about the many fighters he had met, among them Joe Louis and Rocky Marciano. He also spoke about his meeting with Marilyn Monroe and Joe di Maggio, the American baseball hero. He said Marilyn was far more beautiful than she appeared on screen. Joe had an eye for beauty which his wife certainly had, but it stopped on the outer side.

Joe had thought we were the tenants of the King's Head, not management. As soon as he realized the blunder, he said, 'I want you two guys to work for me. When I get back to the States I want you to come over and look at a hotel I own. You can run it for me, Peter.'

Paula spent the rest of that night telling us how we would live. It sounded out of this world which, of course, it proved to be. We said goodnight and goodbye. They were leaving for Paris the next day. After treating the Parisians to some of Paula's rough handling, they were returning to the United States. Joe's parting words were, 'I will see you soon, Peter.'

To this day I believe the man meant every word. Shirley and I talked for weeks about the chance of going to America, and working for the Zanellis. Make no mistake we took into account Paula's spitfire temperament. Shirley cautioning, 'if you fall out with Paula, and that will not be hard to do, you are out on your backside, sharpish.'

We still laugh at the recollection of Paula's insensitivity to other people, the embarrassment having long since left us. She could be a very sweet person when she had a mind to be so and that was probably what Joe saw in her. It certainly couldn't have been that hellish temper of hers.

Our month's notice at the King's Head completed, we were having a week's holiday with Jacqueline before taking over The Albert in late October. The year was 1967.

We left a forwarding address with Mam, before going on to Scarborough, the scenic north-east coast holiday resort. We were desperately in need of a rest. Scarborough gave us that with its innate tranquillity retained from the Victorian Spa days when it was known as the Queen of Watering Places.

Holiday over, we called in at Mam's house on our way south to the Albert and our new job. My mother greeted us with, 'a letter came for you from America, it was too late to forward it.'

I quickly opened the letter. It was from Paula Zanelli and it was not the news we wanted to hear, in any shape or form.

Joe Zanelli had been killed in a car crash in Memphis, Tennessee, while on business in that city. It came as a nasty shock, leaving us both very upset for Joe was a nice, friendly and kindly man. In the short space of time that we had known him, he had won a place in our affections. We were sorry to learn of his premature death.

Neither my wife nor I ever heard from Paula again. Minus Joe's restraining influence, such as it was, and probably with all of his wealth, there would be no living with Paula. I hope she found some kind of happiness. Shirley and I always refer to her as Big Trouble. We will not forget our dinner at the Savoy Hotel thanks to Paula when, if all around her were not sons of bitches, they were bums or whackos.

Our take over of The Albert went relatively smoothly, apart from one slight hiccup. Before we assumed control of the house they had had a racecourse acquaintance and two barmaids running the pub temporarily. I need hardly add the stocks were, to say the least, incorrect. The books bore mute testimony to the fact someone had a very fertile imagination. After a brief ding-dong with Mr Francis's stocktaker, the ledgers were altered to show the true amounts actually existing.

The clientele were typically West End, an assortment of businessmen, office-workers, tourists, crooks and con-merchants. Not the least of the norm were the Ladies of the Night. Well, to be more truthful, day and night.

About a week after we had taken up management of The Albert, we became aware of a group of Australians. Seemingly unemployed, yet obviously well-heeled, they used the pub as a sort of meeting place, which did not feel right to me.

I decided they would bear watching, not that holding a meeting to discuss past or future jobs, prohibited them from the house. And, being a crook, sometimes enhanced the joint to others, straight or otherwise. It was only when they involved the house in their shady deals, did a long-suffering landlord ban them as a deterrent to the rest.

The Australians turned out to be a gang of professional shoplifters, pickpockets and thieves in general. The head of this nasty little clique was a woman based in Sydney, Australia, where most of her undesirables hailed from.

If and when, any of these villains were apprehended, they were pulled out of London and shipped back to Australia. After being fined or sentenced they were then of no further use to the gang, in fact they were a liability, drawing attention to the organized band. Another member would quickly be enlisted to fill the vacancy.

One of those not-so-clever would-be gangsters, went by the name of Jerry. He had been caught, imprisoned, then released. However, instead of returning to Australia as instructed, he had decided to stay on in London and freelance, much to my sorrow for a start.

He was a Pommy-hating low life. Probably things were too warm for him down under, and I am not referring to the weather in that sun-lovers' paradise.

This self-employed no-hoper considered himself a hard man. He gave me a fairly tough time, until I decided enough was enough, forcing me into having one of my little chats with him. I invariably finished by reminiscing about whom I had been in the ring with, ending my chinwag always with, 'behave yourself or you are leaving, one way or another. I could do with a bit of loosening up.'

It was sufficient to quieten him. Besides, he stood to lose a lot more than his teeth. Jerry was a ladies' man, God's gift to women in his estimation of himself. There was an abundance of good looking females which frequented the Albert. They were all grist to busy Jerry's overworked mill.

After our small tête-à-tête, Jerry would confide in me the secrets of his methods of earning a crust. That is an understatement to end all others, a very large slice of cake would be a better description. He had been involved in most facets of villainy, not always petty stuff either. It ranged from armed robbery to burglary and shoplifting. Shoplifting was so rife in 1967 that the monetary loss in Oxford Street alone was to the tune of £1,000,000. I do not believe it has improved since. The customer is the loser, prices go up to compensate the shop owner.

Jerry's tools of trade were many and varied; a wire hook which fitted up his sleeve. He was lightning itself . . . shooting it out to hook something back inside his coat. He owned a suitcase; when you pressed a button on the handle the end of the case flew open to be filled surreptitiously by an accomplice, while Jerry held the attention of the shop assistants.

When I say Jerry was self-employed, it didn't imply he worked exclusively alone. Successful shoplifting requires a team effort, working and acting in concert.

An interesting occurrence happened one day to attract my attention. One of Jerry's team came into the Albert dressed in a very heavy Crombie overcoat which had huge patch pockets. Shortly afterwards he was followed by another man dressed like the traditional fanged vampire, covered from head to foot in a black, red-lined cloak. This was on a sizzling hot day in mid-summer. Those two over-dressed and certainly over-done crooks were going on a shopping expedition with friend Jerry who was most conservatively attired.

Overcoat and Cloak would go in through two separate entrances. Furtively, they would pick up and put down goods, in general acting suspiciously to draw the notice of the store detectives. They would steal nothing yet lead the floor detectives a merry dance. In the meantime Jerry and the rest of the legitimate shoplifters moved in to make a killing.

They pulled this stroke for a long time, unbelievable as it may seem to the layman. The major stores' security either didn't catch on, or they were afraid to leave those two extremely colourful extroverts to their own devices, and watch the seemingly innocent.

The goods this mob garnered? Men's suits and coats, women's fur coats, dresses, jewellery, shoes, one could go on, the list was endless.

My wife and I could have been dressed to kill. I warned Shirley, 'don't be tempted, it could cost us our licence, and our livelihood.'

Besides, being caught receiving earned a bigger sentence than the buggers who actually pinched the merchandise.

Being a publican exposes you to all kinds of temptations, not only of the flesh. One could order and have delivered, anything which is sold. Cashmere sweaters, £150 suits (remember this is 1967), Savile Row gear, you name it and they could supply it. To Jerry and the rest of the sticky-fingered gangs, it was one hundred per cent pure profit, no wholesaler, middleman or overheads of any kind.

Some of the articles made your mouth water, and those bloody Crombie overcoats were my *bête noire* then. It was Temptation spelt Enticement. They spent money as if it was going out of fashion, particularly in The Albert. For the size of the pub the takings were astronomical, most of the profits I am convinced, were derived from ill-gotten gains. The Albert had a really excellent catering trade and not the least of the big spenders in this area were our thieving clientele.

Mr Francis was familiar with most, being on first name terms with the majority of the crooked patrons. I often used to conjecture to myself and Shirley, if there wasn't a little more to it than friendliness. His close relationship to some of the shadier of these characters, lent weight to my supposition; especially when he would go into long, whispering huddles with groups of them, which he would invariably do whenever he visited The Albert. So much so I was convinced they were the real reason for his visits, not The Albert. From where I gained the impression I was by no means aware, yet it clung as glue to my senses. I began to think of Mr Francis as a fence, or at the very least, a middleman. Although I neither saw nor heard anything to substantiate those suspicions.

The Albert was a pub-grub establishment in the typical London mould. Despite its shady overtones it was a bright, well-used house, an accepted place to go in the Porchester Road area for both blue and white collar workers. Things appeared to be going well for us, even our Francis appeared pleased with our efforts. We were increasing the bar trade and the catering side was on the up as well. The pub had been allowed to become a little seedy looking, to match its less salubrious customers. Shirley went to work on that aspect. In no time at all we had The Albert to our liking.

I was forced, unavoidably, to set on more staff to cope with the increased trade, and true to past experience, one or two gave us the usual dishonest run-around.

Shirley and I made up our minds to do what we had done so successfully in the Porcupine, never guessing the trouble which we were about to unleash for ourselves.

While in the Porcupine we had advertised for staff in the *Yorkshire Evening News*, a paper with a very good circulation. This had been quite successful and we hoped to emulate that success in The Albert. The *News* was published in Doncaster, an area with not a lot of work for young people. We asked for young girls to live in to be trained as barmaids, and waitresses.

After this was published, I received a phone call from the producer of a late night radio show. He wasted no time in coming to the point, 'Mr Aldridge, why are you advertising in Yorkshire, for Yorkshire girls to work in London pubs?' They had obtained the information from the Press Association. Sensing a story, they rang me.

I asked truculently, 'is that breaking some kind of law?'

'Oh, no, we just would like to interview you on air and have you give your reasons why you particularly wanted Yorkshire girls for the positions.'

I should have refused. They were obviously muck-stirring, sensation hunting mongrels who didn't give a damn if I hired Zulus.

At the time I thought I had little alternative. Not to grant an interview might cause even more commotion. Oh, the wisdom of hindsight. Now looking back, I see that would have been very difficult to do.

The interview was in the guise of a telephone call. It was done during the afternoon over the phone, and was to be relayed that night after editing, the listeners being led to believe it was a live call. Shirley, staff, customers and I clustered around a radio waiting for the programme to begin. I was more than a trifle nervous. Questions had been asked which were more than a little misleading, quite a few intentionally so. However, it didn't sound half as bad as I had feared. I thought I had fielded some off-sided questions well, and sounded truthful. Ah, the innocence of me then!

I explained my reasons for advertising in Yorkshire, the girls there were on average hard-working, down to earth types. In my opinion good looking, well-mannered females who made jolly fine barmaids.

I certainly did not say they were better then the southern variety, yet this is how it was interpreted by all the sodding women, who listened to that benighted programme.

The vituperation was unbelievable. I was castigated up hill and down dale by women whose vocabulary definitely needed some work. The very

Peter and Shirley Aldridge with some staff of The Albert, 1968.

next morning our first phone call set the tone, for what was to be an ear-assaulting few days.

'You fucking, lying bastard,' this unknown virago yelled, 'clear out of London, get back to where you belong.'

I had all unwittingly put every southern barmaid's back up. We received in excess of two dozen of these highly coloured abusive calls. In fact I was convinced they all knew each other, or at least had been to the same school, four letter words being the common characteristic.

Within a couple of days, poisonous, filthy letters and cards started to arrive. They more or less covered the same ground, in almost identical, monotonous, limited language. One or two were life threatening, which I did think was bloody ridiculous. Nevertheless I was forced to approach the B.B.C. for help against this never-ending tirade, from very sick people.

Shirley pleaded, 'get apologising quick, our lives won't be worth living if this doesn't stop soon.'

I did not go on the air again, but the B.B.C. had the producer go on the programme to tender my heartfelt plea for forgiveness; saying I hadn't meant to be derogatory to the great London barmaid. I also paid for a prominent space in the London *Evening News*, expressing my regret. It really was a knee-scraping exercise. I fumed inside making it, for no insult was ever intended to the London bar staff. Be that as it may, the abuse stopped and we could get on with our lives.

It caused no end of amusement among our customers. One of them, a solicitor, had a ball. I would hate him to represent me anywhere, he was stuck like a jammed record on one sentence, 'oh, yes, good looking, good workers and above all, honest. Oh, yes.'

'Let it go, let it bloody drop,' I was finally moved to say, 'don't you realize I felt a big enough fool as it is?'

I hope that is the last time I made a public idiot of myself, there should be a form of redress against shit-stirring media for damage caused, or a law prohibiting them from malicious mischief making.

I really was an innocent abroad, and oh how I wish I could turn the clock back to my days of guilelessness.

Amazingly the northern advertisement worked. We were flooded with applications from girls wishing to come to London, and work in The Albert. I interviewed them in Doncaster not fancying the prospect of disgruntled, unsuccessful applicants shooting their mouths off in London. I had paid the penalty for naivety.

The two girls I eventually chose, were very good lasses, hard working and full of fun. A sense of humour is a definite requirement behind a bar. Their Yorkshire accent proving a winner, they soon became favourites in The Albert. Some customers, cockneys at that, saying, 'I agree with you, Peter, the Yorkies make bloody good barmaids.'

My wife didn't know whether to be flattered or insulted.

We also needed a bar-cellarman. To my later regret I allowed Shirley to talk me into taking her cousin, Jack Longdon, an ex-Grenadier Guardsman and coal-miner, to fill the vacancy. Jack's marriage having failed, he was living with his mother near Pontefract. Unemployed and desperately in need of work he had approached my wife.

I had had some of that, which went in his favour and despite reservations I gave Jack the job.

He was smart and quick on the uptake, too bloody smart at times. He soon knew his job. After leaving the Guards he had worked at the Gleneagles Hotel as a doorman for two or three years. With deep sighs he remembered the famous people he had dealt with in that time, when most tips were at least a pound, more often five pounds, a lot of money in those days. The exception was Bing Crosby, whom Jack never forgave for his miserliness, 'looked after him like a bloody baby, the most the bugger ever game me was ten bob,' he would often moan.

Jack was a heavy gambler, probably the real reason for his giving away such a lucrative position as the Gleneagles.

In no time at all he had subbed his wages, fully two weeks in advance. He also drank like a fish. I then had to have a word with him about coming in late and he reacted as only relations can, 'give me a key, Peter, there will be no problems then,' cheekily he asked.

'You are the last one who will get a key here, Jack. What do you think I am, a bloody fool altogether?'

I had a straight talk to Shirley about him, either he pulled up his socks, or else he was on his way. We both tackled him as one, finally thinking we had managed to straighten him out a little. Then I noticed he was becoming involved with two real dyed-in-the-wool crooks, nasty pieces of work to say the least of them. They would frequently go into whispering, heads-close-together conversation. I can tell you it worried me. One night after closing the pub, I asked Jack to come down the cellar with me, I made sure all the doors were closed before I turned to face him.

'What's up?' he asked worriedly.

'What is going on, Jack?' I answered his question with another.

'I don't know what you mean, Peter, nothing is going on that I know.'

'Those two villains aren't wasting their time with you for nothing. I hope for your sake you aren't planning anything for The Albert, Jack.'

Jack was silent, looking more than a bit put out, trying to figure some sort of answer which would presumably be sufficient to satisfy me.

'Come clean,' I cut his meditation short, 'I smell a dirty big rat here.'

'Peter, it is nothing like that,' he reproached me, 'it is my own personal business.'

'I don't like the sound of it, Jack. You had better tell me all about it. Those two bastards will eat you alive without spitting out the bones. They will use you and you will pay the penalty.'

Jack went silent, looking extremely apprehensively at me.

'Come on, Jack, I want an answer if we stay here all night.'

'Don't tell Shirley,' he begged.

He thought the world of my wife, always boasting she was his cousin, much to Shirley's amusement.

'I won't tell her, Jack, it will be purely between us two.'

As he related his story, I could hardly believe my ears. How anyone could be so absolutely stupid as to even contemplate, let alone become involved in it, was almost beyond my understanding. As the story progressed I started to swear. 'Get out of this one, if you can, Peter,' yelled my stunned mind.

This is the plot to which Jack had been a major contributor. The problem was, how to get him out of it, for sure as hell he would be the fall guy.

Jack had worked as a manager at a betting shop in Doncaster, this firm having six or seven similar shops scattered around the area. Jack had been fired over a minor misdemeanour and he still smarted over what he considered to be a grave injustice after all this time.

He had just talked to these two no-goods in the beginning. As they encouraged him, Jack told them why he was in London, bemoaning his dismissal from the betting concern and the wrong done to him. They must have thought it was their birthday, manna to feed their criminal instincts.

They pumped him dry about the shop, how the money was collected and the security provided. Clever in their approach, they drew him into the web until even if he wanted to withdraw, which he didn't, it would have been impossible for him to back off.

He had told them one man collected the money from all the shops, his last call was the shop in South Elmsall, a mining village between Doncaster and Pontefract. On a good Saturday or Classic Race day, such as the St Léger or Derby Day, et cetera, the lone driver would be carrying thousands of pounds. He had stressed to these two arch villains how easy a snatch it would be. Hell, they didn't need any encouragement, they would have robbed Jesus Christ if he'd had a bob on him.

Jack was now so carried away with his tale, the presumed cleverness of his plan was to avenge himself on his old employer, leaving him with a self-satisfied smirk on his face that he boasted, 'all I told them, is exactly as they found it.'

On his last day off, the two creeps had taken him to meet the big Boss-man who had congratulated Jack on his accurate information. Jack's chest virtually popped out, as he passed on that last small titbit.

'You stupid bastard,' I yelled at him, 'you shouldn't be let out without a keeper. Don't you realize the position you have placed yourself in? You will be a prime suspect if this is pulled off, in fact I'll give you a thousand to one, the police will pick you up before those two get back to London.'

'I have been promised two thousand quid, Peter. That is worth taking a bit of a risk for.'

'A bit of a risk? I don't believe you! You are taking all the risk. You won't see a halfpenny of that money. Stop kidding yourself, if they decide not to pay you, what could you do about it? You silly bugger, Jack, if you're a danger to them, you will be put six foot under. They are not amateurs taking a swipe at their old boss, they're professional cold-blooded bastards. This is the type of person you have been shooting your mouth off to.'

I had finally got through to the blasted idiot, the blood drained from his face, he was a badly frightened man.

'What the hell am I going to do, Peter, all the job is laid on?'

'Go to bed, that's what you can do. I hope you can't sleep for you've made bloody sure I won't. I will try to think of something by morning.'

'I haven't told you the worst of it yet, Peter. They have done a dummy run, it was cased last week. The Saturday of St Léger week is to be the day of the snatch. That is how they knew my information was correct.'

'Christ, what a bloody awful mess. Let's go to bed I cannot even think of a way out of this.'

Horrified, I dismissed the promise I had made to Jack not to tell my wife. I needed all the help I could get on this one. After all he was her cousin, it had been her idea to employ the bastard, too.

As soon as we were alone I plunged into Jack's revelations with, 'guess what that bloody cousin of yours has been up to?'

'He hasn't got into the gambling again?'

'A hundred times worse than that, love, he's up to his silly bloody neck in a hold-up, with the two wickedest buggers that use this pub. I have to figure a way out, for the life of me I cannot see how, either.'

I repeated Jack's story to a very upset wife, who in spite of employing her stupid cousin, had more common sense than most.

The next morning, as we were dejectedly getting dressed, Shirley suddenly plumped herself on the bed. Without preamble she said, 'why don't you tell them someone else has just tried the robbery and failed? Surely that would stop them trying it on.'

I grabbed at her and gave her a resounding kiss. I told you she had more common sense than most. So simple, it sounded truthful, and it might well work. We could but try. I hadn't had a spark from my grey matter all night. I warned her not to let Jack know that I had told her about the mess. I needed no complications or recriminations, although he was in no position for either. I went quickly in search of the big-mouth.

'Get in touch with those thieving bastards straight away, tell them somebody has beaten them to it. Security will now be that tight, it would be almost impossible to pull the job off. Tell them you have been questioned. The cops think it is an inside robbery, they won't doubt your story then.'

This simplistic stratagem worked, the whole frightening episode fizzled out. Nevertheless, I didn't let Jack off the hook easily. I warned him, 'I will personally bloody strangle you, if you get mixed up again with gangsters, or any other kind of sodding crooks.'

My chat, or the fright, achieved some good. Thereafter, as far as I knew, Jack walked the straight and narrow.

The Albert also played host to two amusing homosexuals who kept the bar, staff and customer alike, in a cheerful mood with their antics. One was named Allan, the other Tony. Those two could halt normal business immediately, as everyone listened to their graphic arguments and personal aspersions.

'That little shit used to live with a man who had one that was half the size of my little finger,' Tony sneeringly alluded to Allan.

'I have never gone to bed with a cucumber, you faggot,' retorted Allan.

However, there was more to these two than was apparent. I discussed them one day with a member of the aristocracy of villains, oh yes, there is a hierarchy, a pecking order of things within the criminal element, one which is as strictly adhered to as in the straight world. Anyway this particular top-of-the-pile crook, enlightened me as to the true character of our two entertainers. They were extremely skilful cat burglars.

I later found this to be true. It explained fully their very affluent life style with, to quote the local gendarmerie, no visible means of support. They lived in the grand manner, a very expensive flat in Bayswater setting the tone. Clothes, plus as ease of bearing when they had the mind, being more typical of their mixed gender than a pointer to their wealth.

Lightly built and very nimble, as one would expect them to be in their profession, they could scale drainpipes to a height of three or four storeys or more, if the buildings were high-rise. Their talents were often called into play by large gangs, just to gain entry, then their part in the robbery was completed.

As I have said, their constant supply of wealth, with all its trappings, bears testimony to their skills and demand for their services.

One story they both told me, was of a scouting expedition into the countryside. I think it is worth repeating.

It was a do-it-yourself job, a small sideline they had developed, both searching the likely areas for easy pickings to pluck on their own. They came upon this large manor house, the blinds were all drawn apart from one window on the third floor.

Tony resembled a small monkey and would have been evenly matched in agility, which at times confounded Allan. He weighed just six and a half stone, so could get in where others would fail.

They approached this house from a field at the rear. In no time Tony was up the very convenient drainpipe, which was close to the open window, and inside the building.

Tony told me:

'Everything was covered in white sheets. It was dark by then and I was using a small pencil light to grope my way around the room. I pulled the sheets off the furniture as I passed each piece. There was a long, low type of cupboard, I yanked the sheet off shining my light on the most frightening sight I have ever seen.' Tony shuddered.

'It was the face of a dead man. Move! I bloody shot out of that house, I tripped over every bloody sheet on my way to the window.'

Allan then took up the story.

'There I was crouched among some bushes, close to the drainpipe which Tony had shinned. All of a sudden there was a piercing scream, and Tony came out of that window as if the devil himself was after him. I swear he barely touched the bloody drainpipe during his descent. Scream! You could have heard it in John o' Groats. He pelted across the field in full flight, with me trying my best to keep up. He was still screaming when I got him into the car. I tore off down the road with the quivering mass that was him beside me. I stopped at the first pub we came to, he badly needed a brandy to pull him together, so I could find out what happened.

'Even after a double brandy he was shaking life a leaf in a full blown gale. All I could get out of him was, "he was dead, he was dead".'

Allan laughed, before going on with the tale.

'I finally got the full story out of him, apparently this fellow was laid out on this long trestle, covered only by a sheet. Fortunately for us, the house was empty otherwise we would have been right in the shit when he started screaming.'

'Well, he was dead, he was bloody dead,' Tony repeated.

'Of course he was bloody dead, you silly bugger. What do you think they covered him up for?'

There was a far less funny side to these two, one could actually say it was sinister at times. One episode comes to mind which hardly endeared them to my wife and me. Allan approached me one day with a parcel in his hands, 'keep this in the safe for us, Guv'ner, the geezer who was supposed to pick it up today, in The Albert, hasn't turned up.'

'All right, this once, and only overnight mind you. It is out first thing in the morning, regardless.'

I didn't know what was in the parcel the size and shape of a shoe box. Whatever it was I wanted no part of it, my only desire was to get it off the premises. It could have been something quite legal but knowing those two individuals I wouldn't have put any money on it.

That night after closing up, curiosity got the better of Shirley and me.

'Go and get the parcel,' Shirley urged, 'let's have a look at what they are up to.'

'I suppose you are right, it's better to know than to bloody guess.'

'At least we will know what it is all about, if we are caught with whatever it is,' Shirley said illogically.

If truth be known we were both being unwisely nosey, men have died for a lot less. We should not have accepted the parcel unless they unwrapped it, yet when you have to run a pub, one does a lot of stupid things. I agreed with my wife we were running a risk. At that moment in time we had no idea what the parcel contained.

I brought the package from the safe into our private lounge. It was extraordinarily heavy for its size. We carefully untied the string, removing the coverings painstakingly on Shirley's lap, until the last chamois cloth parted to reveal a veritable Aladdin's fortune. There, in a great glistening heap, flashing and shimmering as my wife moved, lay splendour in jewellery and gold, such beautiful ornamentation as we had never seen before.

A lady's gold watch encrusted with diamonds, necklaces heavy with precious gems, bracelets, rings, diamonds which had a life of their own, a sparkling, pulsating scintillation of spectacular colour.

We sat there mesmerised by all this magnificence, until Shirley broke the spell. 'to think this was some poor woman's loved possessions,' she said.

I knew instinctively she was remembering her own loss in the King's Head. 'I am sorry for her, yet one could hardly classify her as poor. Look on the bright side, they will be insured for more than replaceable value. There is probably no sentiment involved, they are more than likely kept in some bloody vault, being brought out only on special occasions. They were dead unlucky this time, Tony and Allan hit the jackpot. Cheer up, Shirley, they can afford to lose theirs, we couldn't when ours was nicked. Our worry at the moment is putting this lot back, the way we found it.'

'You have become quite bloody heartless, do you know that?' Shirley spat at me, 'some of this is very old, it must be of great personal value.'

She was dead right, of course, on both counts. Those two thieves had robbed someone of their inheritance. There was nothing we could change, or do, except to stay calm, keeping our noses out of it if we wanted to remain healthy. Which I for one did.

The following morning Tony and Allan retrieved their parcel. Where the jewels went, or who had them eventually, I have no idea. When they both left The Albert, it was minus the package.

I later told the pair of them that my wife and I had taken a look inside the packet, deeming it wiser to know the kind of exposure we were up against. That way at least we knew what we were in for, if caught with the goods. I added jokingly, 'how Shirley would have loved a piece of that lot.'

This was met with a stony look, gone were the two affable gents that we had known. Allan said quietly, 'burn your bloody fingers off, Son. Burn your fingers off for sure, they will, Peter.'

One could take that several ways, I decided not to push it. I truly did not require enlightening.

The Albert had a good lunch-time trade. In the evenings, sometimes, it was all hell let loose it was so busy. Midday one did get a chance to talk to some of the less villainous. I passed many an amusing afternoon this way. As they got to know Shirley and me, and found we could be trusted, they accepted the pair of us into their confidence.

They would give us snippets of their activities, some were hilarious, the rest not funny by a long mile. It was a descriptive picture of their means of livelihood.

One bunch of ne'er-do-wells were skilled pickpockets, so good that one checked one's pockets after being in their company. If they brushed by me, I would grab them, then check myself out. Never trust the buggers, was my motto, it was the law of survival after all. Which of us was the bloody smartest?

Among this group were two Australians, they seemed to find it easy to slot into the fringes of the underworld of Britain. As an instance of this, relations of ours were on holiday in Scotland, booked into a small hotel on the fringes of St Andrews. On arrival they had told the landlady, they were on holiday from Sydney, Australia. Outside their room, she had said loudly, 'I will put you on the same breakfast table, as another guest from Sydney. He has that room,' she pointed to the apartment opposite.

The next morning, the landlady informed them, 'the man from Sydney left in a hurry, in the early hours actually.'

Our relations, ex-publicans themselves, were highly amused. So was the landlady. She and her husband had been on relief management of London pubs. They speculated together about the possible causes for his flight.

The pickpockets who frequented The Albert used the time-honoured methods so to speak, working in groups of three to four. Their main target was the tourist-crowded Tower of London where they would strike in a densely packed area. One would bundle a victim with his shoulder, sending the person spinning into the waiting accomplice whose deft hands went immediately to work and it was all over in seconds. He would quickly pass whatever he had filched to another member of the gang, more than likely a couple arm in arm, walking innocently by.

More often than not the victim was not aware of the theft at the time. If there was a hue and cry, then both the pickpocket and his accomplice were clean. The goods were long gone with the happy sauntering couple. The pickpockets were crafty, clever at their trade and were very seldom caught.

Beware, all you unsuspecting people, read the prominent sign outside the Tower, it has been placed there for your perusal. Be alert to pickpockets and their little games, keep your hand on wallets and purses. That would spoil their day and their fun, besides hitting them where it hurts most, the hip pocket nerve. They are thoroughly professional, discussing ways, means and mode of attack before they leave for their despicable work. Later, they exchange views on tactics, the goods acquired and the people they have stolen from, all in a business-like manner. For, of course, that is actually what it is, a very lucrative business.

Around this time we were especially friendly with another solicitor, who used The Albert. We were invited to a garden party, which was to be held at a large house in north London, owned by this man. Shirley and I managed to work it so that we had the Sunday afternoon off for this do. We arrived at his beautiful home, intent on enjoying every minute we were away from our disreputable haunt, and its less than salubrious clientele.

During the party we were introduced to David Whitfield, the singer. He, too, was a Yorkshireman, so we hit it off straight away. He had once presented the prizes at an Amateur Boxing match in the Hull Boy's Club. I was on the Bill and I reminded him of this occasion. He remembered it but not me. It was the start of a very long friendship between us, only ending with his premature death.

I invited David Whitfield back to The Albert. I knew it would please the customers should he turn up, besides Shirley who was a great admirer of his. Surprisingly, he did come, causing one hell of a stir among staff and customer alike. At that time he had hit the top as a singer, heading the Bills in the West End and on television country-wide. Yet David had retained the common touch, enjoying their company as much as they appreciated his. A very nice uncomplicated man, he had a drink problem and, unfortunately, with the fame had come the women. He became a womanizer, eventually costing him his marriage and inevitably his own happiness.

He was later to become involved in a sex scandal with some kids which almost finished him and his career. Such was the power of his wonderful voice and range, and the lovely charismatic personality of David, he managed to claw his way back to the top.

I would say to him, 'David, my father could sing that song better than you.'

'He probably could, Peter,' was always his thoughtful reply. A nice, nice man.

One day in The Albert I was introduced to a man, named Reg, who was a stockbroker on the Metal Exchange in the City of London. Reg was a pure extrovert, nay a flamboyant man is more apt a description, yet he remained very much an unspoilt person. We soon became firm friends. His regularly used invitation to join him for a drink, I can still hear today, 'I'll Cardhu, if you'll Cardhu?'

He was referring to Cardhu Malt whisky, the malt of malts. We went through many a bottle together, swopping stories all the way, a breath of fresh air. What a change from the misfits and miscreants which filled my life at that time.

Reg had never married, I guess he was around forty-five years of age, a fat ugly little man—with a personality to beat the world. What God had neglected in his appearance, He had made up for in charm. His resonant, well-educated voice coupled with his rapier fast wit, endeared him to most who met him.

We were standing in the bar together, listening with only an ear to a man boasting about his gold Omega watch and bracelet. He was a thorough pain in the bum. That is one of the penalties one pays as a publican, one has to be a good listener as well as an unpaid entertainer. Reg suddenly drawled to the man, 'what does it do, Old Boy?'

The man stared mystified at Reg, who was obviously waiting for an answer, 'well, it tells the time,' he lamely replied.

'So does mine, Old Boy,' Reg chortled, 'and it only cost me forty quid.' He had effectively muzzled the bloody show-off, putting the man down with ease and little effort.

Reg was born and educated in India, his father had been a colonel in the Indian Army. He would have taken the same career path, unfortunately poor eyesight prohibited this. So he entered the City Army instead, an umbrella and bowler hat, replacing the uniform cap and baton. He appeared content enough to all around him.

One worrying aspect about Reg which disturbed both my wife and me, he was an incorrigible spendthrift. He threw money around as if he had a bottomless source, to him tomorrow could look after itself.

Jacqueline got on well with him. She'd present him with a picture she had drawn and he would delight her by opening his shirt to place it inside, telling her seriously, 'it is next to my heart.'

The trouble with this action was that he'd give her a £1 note every time. Jacqueline went back upstairs like a flash to draw another, there were no flies on her. Shirley always had to step in and say warningly, 'that is enough, Jacqueline.'

Otherwise, my daughter could have opened up a picture gallery, with the amount she would have produced.

Reg was a lonely man who liked the bright lights of the West End.

With his features and misshapen body, his chances of attracting members of the opposite sex were almost nil. He had to pay for all pleasures of the flesh, and how he paid. He was taken to the cleaners regularly in my presence, God knows what they took him for when I wasn't around.

One evening Shirley and I accompanied Reg up to the West End. It was a rare night off for the two of us together and we intended to make the most of it. We went to the Latin Quarter for a meal where it became very embarrassing because he wouldn't let us pay a penny towards the cost. We felt most uncomfortable. He paid the bill by cheque and as he wrote that first one out I almost passed away at the size of account. Thank God, he had insisted on paying or we would all have been washing up.

Then he told the head waiter, Yanik, to add £10 for a tip. He had asked for and got, a beautiful hostess for the evening. After the meal was when he started to pay in earnest, champagne, chocolates, expensive perfume and cigarettes. The girl did her job well, there was nothing she didn't put the bite on Reg for. If they sold it, she wanted it. It was accomplished without a flicker from those heavily mascaraed eyes and cooingly received each time by over-painted pouting lips.

Reg and I often went out together after that, when The Albert had closed. We invariably ended in the Latin Quarter, where Reg paid as usual for a hostess for the two of us. Those girls were obviously chosen because of their outstanding beauty and charm. They had been very well trained in the art of extracting as much as possible from every client, always choosing one of the more expensive meals, emboldening you to do the same. Only the best of champagne and wines, with the extra perks of the finest chocolates and perfume as gifts. No doubt these would be resold to the club at a quarter of their cost.

If you desired more of the girl, it was available at a price. She was a free agent to do as she wished once she had accomplished her task of encouraging the customers to spend big. Most had been show-girls who had not been good enough to make the grade. They were far from the lower order of prostitutes. Some had more edge than a reigning monarch, still, ladies of the night they were, without exception.

The Latin Quarter and other top-notch night clubs in the area employed these women to entertain and to cajole customers into spending lavishly, not as prostitutes which would have been decidedly against the law.

They sat around until chosen by a customer. Their title hostess, their jobs to induce the mugs, business men on a buck's night out, visitors to London of all nationalities to spend and spend. Americans were by far the most popular clients. They always were the last of the big spenders. At the end of the evening's entertainment, the ladies wanted from £25 to £50 for their other services, a lot of money in the sixties. Notwithstanding, without exception they left with that night's customer.

Reg was something of a regular there, always receiving a good reception from Yanik, but then who wouldn't be agreeable to a customer who spent as he did, besides handing out £10 tips?

This specific night, the Latin Quarter was very quiet. Yanik produced two lovely hostesses for Reg and me, one named Marie, with whom I became very well acquainted.

We were well into our meal when three men came in and sat at the table next to us. They took one look at the gorgeous line up of girls sitting alone. They couldn't resist. Like thousands before them they waded in. Three ladies were soon seated at their table. A whale of a time got underway.

I had picked up their accent earlier, when they had first arrived. Here were three Yorkshiremen out to paint the town red. Now Yorkies are a lot of things and all are different no matter what people tell you. However they had one thing in common which is sacrosanct to the breed—tightness of the purse strings. It is a major character blemish, one which should never be taken lightly. They do not take kindly to anyone who tries to correct this inbred, far from lovable, peculiarity.

I sat back and waited for the inevitable outcome of this frivolity. I knew fun and games would start when they received the bill for this meal, the food and drink being extravagant by anybody's standards. The champers and wine flowed, the ladies pushed their luck to the limit.

I thought I would let Reg into the source of my amusement. I had noticed him watching me, as I surreptitiously kept the Yorkies under observation. I leaned over the table to whisper to him, 'there will be a right royal bill coming at the end of that feast.'

'Not half, Old Boy,' Reg replied gleefully.

These professional ladies were on to a good thing without whoredom, piling up the goodies which would be resold to the club later. Although cigarettes were sold only in packs of two hundred, I had yet to see any of the girls break into these packages. During the many times I visited the club, they smoked only the client's fags.

The bill eventually arrived. Reg and I waited with bated breath for the inevitable explosion from the Yorkshire revellers. Yanik, with his customary aplomb, placed the account on the table in front of the obvious head of this merry little band. I had heard him telling his female companion, he came from the City of Sheffield. As I have said, a Yorkshireman is careful with his money, a West Riding Yorkshireman puts the proverbial Aberdonian into the carefree philanthropic class.

The Sheffielder picked up the bill, his jaw sagged, his face deepened from pleasantly flushed to mottled purple. Swallowing hard, he jumped to his feet. 'Jesus Christ, I haven't bought the bloody place!'

He glared across the room at Yanik in stunned incredulity. Speechless after his initial outburst he now reopened his voiced protest, 'you must be bloody joking.'

That was the last thing they did in the Latin Quarter, when it came to paying the account. We had seen this happen before, in seconds three tuxedoed giants preceded Yanik to the men's table.

'If you will accompany me to the manager's office, gentlemen,' Yanik requested politely.

They had little choice in the matter, those money-suited men were genuine bruisers, I doubt if I would have given them an argument.

The Yorkies were of the same mind as me. They went, followed by the giants, giving no further vent to their injured feelings, at least not within our hearing. As they passed our table they all looked similar to refugees from the Somme, shell-shocked into sobriety.

That night I asked Yanik quietly, 'did they overspend a little? Could they cover the amount?'

He looked at me ruefully, 'close to £800 was the account. It wasn't padded, they had spent every penny of it,' he assured me.

'The Club always gets its money. As a rule men are afraid of their wives and their bosses finding out what they have been up to in the Big Smoke. Those lads hadn't required much persuasion. Taking one look at our overdressed bouncers with no further ado they paid up.' Yanik smiled mirthlessly, before continuing, 'they'd had their money's worth. They had had the time of their lives with three beautiful ladies. They would be able to reminisce about the episode for years, besides being taught a salutary lesson.'

I hadn't taken Yanik for anything other than a hard man. A philosopher he was; one can never tell.

Talking of wives, Shirley had begun to nag me about my increasingly frequent outings with Reg. She confided in me exactly what she thought of him and it didn't surprise me.

'Peter, I am telling you, Reg is not all he says he is. I have an awful premonition he is using you, I am very worried.'

'How the hell can he use me? He is a wealthy, lonely person seeking company, that is all he is.'

I dismissed her fears as concern at my possible womanizing, what do they say about women's intuition? She was right on all counts.

That week I was asked to go with Reg to the Hay Hill Club, in Berkeley Square, an ultra exclusive, high-priced establishment indeed. Reg was to meet a chap there. He introduced me to him, as the man who would run his hotel for him, on Paradise Island, Tobago, in the West Indies.

This came as a bloody shock to me, I immediately thought of the fellow who'd propositioned Shirley, then of Shirley's warning. Why had Reg been so secretive about this hotel, if it existed?

Reg left me to talk to this man alone. I watched them as they sat in close conversation. Nothing felt right.

After this very private chat, Reg and I left the club. Once outside I asked straight out, 'what is going on, Reg?'

'I am going to buy some land in Tobago and build a hotel on it. I want you and Shirley to run it for me. You will be made for life, Peter. I will put Jacqueline through private school, she is a clever girl, Roedean is possible, that's if we can get her in.'

He was genuinely fond of Jacqueline, this latter statement helped assuage the nagging caution at the back of my mind. But, it was only three hours since we had left The Albert and Shirley's renewed warning. Since that time I had received an offer I couldn't refuse and my daughter might have the chance to attend the most élite school in the world. To hell with prudence, I liked a punt. Besides, what had I got to lose? If I had only guessed at half the answer to that question, I might have saved myself and my family, a lot of grief.

On arrival back at The Albert, Reg sat in our flat above the pub and said quietly, 'Peter, I want you to cash me some cheques.'

'No problem, Reg, of course I will.'

'Not my private cheques, these will have other people's names on them.

They have signed the back of the cheques, so you can pay them into The Albert account quite easily.'

'Oh, I don't know, Reg,' I immediately started to back-pedal.

'Do not worry, Peter, it is just a tax dodge for me, nothing can or will, rebound on you.'

I am similar to everyone else in this world believing taxation is an iniquitous burden on all who are liable to pay it. It is a fair game for avoidance, so long as it's legal. In my career as an employee, subject to the Pay As You Earn scheme, chance to evade or avoid would have been a fine thing. The very next day Reg produced a cheque for cashing.

'Bloody hell, Reg!' I gasped, 'fourteen hundred quid? I cannot cash that even if I wanted to. I daren't put it through until the weekend. A cheque of that value, the bank just wouldn't honour it.'

'Peter, bank the cheque, let it go through to be cleared, then give me the money. All right?'

That was quite a different matter, I would be taking no risk whatsoever. In those halcyon days who had ever heard of laundering money. Apart from my wife, no one had ever told me to beware of Greeks bearing gifts, or as in my case, standing free dinners and champers.

On the Monday I banked The Albert's takings, including the cheque made out to a W.T. Stevenson . . . I retained £1,400. I asked the under-manager, whom I knew well, to let me know when the cheque had been cleared. Three days later he rang to inform me the cheque had been cleared for payment.

That evening when Reg came into The Albert, I gave him the money I had held back. He counted the cash, then pressed £40 into my hand saying, 'that's for you, for your trouble, Old Boy.'

Forty pounds was more than I earned in a week. I was well and truly hooked.

Thereafter, Reg would ask me to cash a cheque, sometimes two or three times a week, brimming over with confidence and always with the instruction, 'let them clear the bank, Old Chap.'

This they continued to do. I duly paid him the money each time, in return receiving a substantial backhander. The amounts of the cheques varied from £300 to over £1,000. All were drawn against the International Ore Company of America. The names of the payees differed from the much used, suspicious sounding, E. Smith, to the intriguing Mexican sounding name of J. R. Valaquez.

Shirley remained uneasy, constantly whittling, 'you can get into trouble, I know you can, it can't be legal. There is something fishy about the whole thing.'

'How can I get into trouble? I am not breaking any law. All I am doing is cashing cheques for him, he doesn't get a penny until the cheque has cleared the bank. It is not costing Francis, us, or anyone else one penny. Why Reg is doing it is not our business. The less we know, the better it will be in the long run.'

'If it's so legal, why do you say that?' asked a still unsatisfied wife.

I stuck to my guns, continuing to accept cheques from Reg, paying out only when the bank had passed payment.

This went on for months. I asked no questions and was given no other explanation than the one proffered at the start of the transaction. On rare occasions Reg would invite Shirley, Jacqueline and me out to dinner, our regular nights out had gone by the board since I had started cashing the cheques. Always with our invitation to dinner, came the smiling comment, which backed up his previous statement, 'all on the dreaded tax-man, Old Boy.'

He still maintained the Tobago deal was going through, Shirley and I would run the Paradise Hotel, Jacqueline would be attending Roedean. He would repeatedly say of my daughter, 'she is a very clever girl, that child.'

Jacqueline proved him right on that score anyway, she did do very well at school. Unfortunately, we could not afford the fees of that famous girl's school.

About six months later, I was standing in The Albert's lounge during a quiet period of which I was taking full advantage. We didn't get many of those. The doors opened and a very agitated Reg came in, extremely dishevelled and decidedly grubby, which was most unusual for him. He had without exception been a fastidious dresser, so it was all the more noticeable.

'Peter, Old Chap, I have an urgent business deal tonight. I have lost the keys to my flat and the damned superintendent is out. Can I have a shave here, could you possibly lend me a shirt too?'

Although Reg was much smaller in stature than I, being fat he was about the same neck size. Though startled by his appearance, and the rather odd explanation for it, I answered, 'yes, by all means, Reg. You are more than welcome.'

Reg went to shave and change, while I hunted out a shirt and matching tie, for his was as crumpled as the shirt.

As he left The Albert, he gripped my hand tightly, saying 'I am going away on business, for about a week. Give my love to Shirley and Jacqueline.'

He went down the stairs and out of the side entrance of the house, 'see you, Peter.' he called out as he shut the door.

That evening my wife and I discussed the strange incident. I must admit to anxiety, Shirley was equally affected and neither of us could accept the story of Reg being locked out of his flat.

A week passed with no sign or news of him. Halfway through the second week, Shirley said, 'if you are so bothered about him, why don't you ring him at his office.'

'You know Reg told me never to ring him there, unless it was an emergency, you can hardly call this a crisis.'

I was seeking my wife's assurance, it was forthcoming as usual.

'Well I would ring him if I was in your shoes, tell him you were concerned about him.'

It would be no lie, I *was* troubled about him. I liked the man, in spite of reservations regarding his business dealings. It could do no harm to check if he was well.

'I will phone him, we owe him that much, Shirley.'

I felt better having made the decision. I rang his office straight away, to be answered by a woman's voice.

When I asked to speak to Reg, she said firmly, 'hold the line please.'

I waited for what seemed an interminable time, before I heard a click click, then a male voice came on to the line, saying, 'he is busy, can I take a message?'

There was a pause before he continued, 'can I have your name, please?'

I knew instinctively something was very wrong and hung up the phone. I sat frozen to the seat, a deeply frightened man. Why had the girl kept me waiting so long? Why hadn't she told me Reg was busy? Asking me to leave a message, as is the office custom. Shirley came into the room at the moment.

'Have you rung Reg?' she asked.

'I have rung the International Ore Company and couldn't get hold of Reg, some man told me he was busy. There were clicks on the phone, I think the call was being monitored, I was kept waiting far too long to be told he was busy. I don't like the smell of this, Shirley. I hung up without telling them who I was.'

Worriedly, I prattled on to an equally disturbed, now silent wife. The following Monday I opened the doors of The Albert at 10.30 a.m. as was customary. The first two patrons were both men, I knew neither. I turned away as the barmaid went to serve them.

'Mr Aldridge?' one of them asked, 'could we have a word with you in private, please?'

He flashed his card in my direction, they were the police.

'Certainly,' I replied, indicating the saloon bar which was empty.

'Have you living quarters here?' one of them asked, as soon as we were seated.

'Yes,' I replied, wondering what the hell was wrong with the place where we were sat.

'Can we go up there, Mr Aldridge?'

'Follow me,' I said curtly, as far as I am concerned, my home is my castle. The only people who go in there are those I invite to do so. We passed Shirley on the stairs, who looked inquiringly at me.

'It is all right,' I reassured her, 'it's the police, they only want a word with me in private.'

I looked back at her from the top of the stairs. She was standing rooted to the spot, her face a white mask.

We entered the flat, one of the detectives closed the door behind us, then the mood changed.

'Sit down,' one snarled at me, shoving me on the shoulder with some force. I fell back sprawling on to the settee.

'What's the bloody game,' I shouted, clenching my fists together, 'don't start that, or else I am going to start throwing these.'

The other policeman, a C.I.D. sergeant put the brakes on the rough stuff by saying to the one who had seen too much television, 'all right, calm it down.' Giving me a hard look, he asked, 'where is Reginald White?'

'I don't know who you are talking about,' I said truthfully.

'Don't give us a load of crap, Mister,' said the brutal copper, 'you are in enough trouble.'

'I still don't know any White.'

The sergeant studied me for a moment, before saying, 'White, Percival, Robinson, McGregor, just to name but a few aliases.'

The penny dropped, they were looking for Reg.

'Do you mean Reg, the stockbroker?'

'Stockbroker? Stockbroker's clerk would be nearer the mark,' sneered the toughie.

'Clerk? What are you talking about? Are we talking about the same man, Reg Beaumont?' I asked, in a half-baked fashion.

The sergeant, apparently sympathetic to my plight, told me the full sorry story about my likeable friend, Reg.

He was employed by the International Ore Company, on the Metal Exchange, as a stockbroker's clerk. Reg had worked his way carefully into a trusted position, with access to the Company's cheque books. He was a master-forger and had forged perfect signatures of three directors on every cheque he had stolen. He had embezzled the whopping figure of £130,000. Of that amount I had cashed the amazing sum of £52,500 for him. He had also conned two other publicans, a restaurant and a large off-licence, into cashing cheques for him.

I was in over my head, floundering in deep, deep trouble. The kind of dire straits, the magnitude of which, my mind refused to accept. I moved and acted as if it were a very bad dream, a nightmare unbelievably real from which I couldn't awaken.

I called Shirley up to the flat, explaining as best I could the predicament I found myself in. 'You will have to look after things here, tell Francis, we have no other choice. I am going to be arrested.'

Shirley burst into tears, as she realized I was then actually under arrest. She knew it was no good appealing to the policemen, telling them I wasn't guilty of any crime would have been useless. They had a pinch, they might not have the ringleader, but they had the next best thing so far as they were concerned.

Toughie got his handcuffs out. I looked at the sergeant.

'There is no need to put those on,' he told his companion harshly.

'Thanks,' I said, 'my staff are downstairs, my wife is going to need their help.'

I turned to Shirley, I just had time to ask her to get me a solicitor, and to do her best with the pub, before I was led downstairs into a waiting police car, and whisked away to Paddington Police Station. My wife had been left to cope, not only with the busy Albert, but with Francis, who was not going to take kindly to this mess at all. I was attracting unnecessary police attention, to this hot-bed of wrong-doers, besides leaving him managerless. He would show no sympathy towards my wife, being a bastard plainly of the first order. To make matters worse as far as Shirley and I were concerned, the last cheque Reg had given me, I had stupidly handed the money over before the cheque had been cleared. It was for £450 which I would have to cover myself. It actually was about all that we had in the world.

I was not only firm favourite for a stiff prison sentence, I was also stony broke.

Reg was on the run from the law, in fact he was already fleeing, when he called on me for a shave and clean clothes, if you haven't guessed by now. He knew he daren't risk returning to his flat for fresh wearing apparel, the police would undoubtedly be waiting there for him to do just that. So he came to Joe Muggins here, who was so dumb in those days I needed a keeper. Though, I wonder; if he had told me he was on the run, would I still have assisted him to get away? I liked him before I knew he was a crook, I still couldn't hate him afterwards. Some people possess that kind of warmth. Reg could have made it to the top without resorting to crime. Who am I to condemn? I skirted the fringes of the law for years, thank God, I didn't step over.

That night I underwent the longest and most extensive grilling of my life, lasting for hours in spite of my steadfast plea of complete innocence, little realizing that ignorance of the law does not lessen one's culpability. I was convinced by the end of the interrogation it heightened the guilt in the eyes of the police. Probably because this being the most common of claims among the criminal classes.

I repeatedly maintained I had cashed cheques for a man, a regular customer, not paying out on those cheques until they had been cleared by the bank. I had accepted that the man was who he said he was. Why should I think otherwise? I had been extremely foolish, yet not criminally so.

Shirley had obtained Legal Aid for me. A solicitor we both knew, and a Mr Green who used The Albert, plus a local shopkeeper agreed to stand bail for me. They also knew Reg as a stockbroker; he had taken in everybody he had come into contact with.

I learned later this was not the first time Reg had embezzled company funds, he had almost made a bloody practice of it. He would gain the trust of large companies, then strike heavily before taking off for fresher cattle to milk. While he had been living the life of Riley in the West End, he had also been on the Police Wanted List for quite some time. He had so many aliases the law inevitably lost track of him, just as inevitably he was caught. An ugly, exceedingly ordinary man, whom no one would give a second glance to. What still mystifies me is, why splurge all the ill-gotten gains? Why didn't he strike out for the former dominions, New Zealand, Australia, Canada to name but a few? There to live in retired splendour, or was that the true reason for his visit to the Hay Hill Club in Berkeley Square?

After two days of nightmarish existence, I was released on bail and faced up to Mr Francis who listened to my story, before saying coldly, 'the £450 is your loss. If the International Ore Company want the £52,500 reimbursing, that, too, is your responsibility.'

Christ, I hadn't thought of that, where on earth could we find that kind of money? Francis was going to make my life unbearable from now on in. Police interest in The Albert he could live without. I had outlived my usefulness. I couldn't work under the stress of my forthcoming trial and his deliberate attempts to rid himself of me. Again I consulted my solicitor who made no comment until I had related all that had gone on between Francis and me. Fortunately for my sanity he was far more optimistic, saying, 'the International Ore Company's bank cleared those cheques for payment, they will have to stand the loss.'

Two weeks later Reg was picked up by the police in Wales. He was refused bail, although he cheekily applied for it.

The C.I.D. sergeant, whom I learned later was named Wilson, called in to see me one night not long after they had arrested Reg. He came with a proposition.

'Mr Aldridge, if you stand as an innocent man, who has been duped from beginning to end, giving evidence for the police, I am sure you will come out of it all right. Charges will be dropped against you.'

'Turn Queen's evidence, you mean, my solicitor has already forewarned me you may offer this deal, if I stand as a witness against Reg.'

He was doing me no favour, just making sure of a conviction for Reg, plus kudos for cracking the case. However, I was in no position to take a holier than thou stance. I had a wife and daughter to consider plus the loyalty to a man for whom I still felt a great deal of affection.

'Can I go to see Reg before I give you an answer?'

'I am sorry, that is impossible. Even if you refuse to give evidence for us, you will not be allowed to see him before the hearing.'

I agreed to testify against my friend and I didn't see Reg until his trial came up at the Old Bailey. He had pleaded not guilty. How very like him, he was going to be obstinate to the bitter end.

In the meantime, I knew my future with Mr Francis and The Albert was at an end. There was no use crying about it, I had made a bad mistake, and had to pay for that. Although it had not cost Francis one penny, the more than tenuous relationship between us, which had been under pressure before the calamitous event took place, now irrevocably snapped. Again, on the solicitor's advice, I tendered my resignation, once more to lay a search for another position.

This time it would be a formidable task, another bloody mountain to surmount. How I wished for a sunny meadow without obstacles in my path. Shirley and I had climbed quite a few peaks; we faced this one with more than trepidation.

We had a puppy Alsatian dog, we had named Czar. My mother came down to King's Cross Station, to pick up Jacqueline and Czar, to take them back to Doncaster. They would stay with her until we found another home; our furnishings went into store.

I can see Mam now, struggling with an unruly Alsatian pup and an equally fractious child, neither wanting to leave us.

Mam gave us £200, God knows where she got it from, to tide us over until we could find another position. As I have boasted before who ever had a better mother? Until her death she continued to counsel, give aid, or angry reprimand when she thought it was needed. With me I am afraid that was often. There was always a home should it be required, plus that motherly care of her offspring.

We rented a small room in Paddington, the description of which defies me, suffice to say that it was extremely grotty. We sold an insurance policy to eke out our fast diminishing means, the cost of storing our worldly belongings didn't help. This way we sat out a meagre existence, until Reg's trial came up.

Fortunately for us this was brought forward, he came to trial sooner than we had anticipated. I was pleased with one aspect of that, I was dreading having to stand up and give evidence against him. The less time I had to dwell on it, the better. Sergeant Wilson came over to me on the opening day of the trial. Smilingly he said, 'what a character, what a character the man is. I can see why you like him so much.'

Reg had got to him, too. With a personality to beat the world, regardless of his outward appearances, he could have charmed the devil himself.

On the first day there was a hiccup in the proceedings, which could well have exonerated Reg. Alas, the prosecuting counsel was far too good. An American company director, a witness for the prosecution, shown the cheque bearing an alleged forged signature, insisted the signature was his. He had to be publicly assured by the prosecution that it was not. Much to Reg's amusement, who smiled, like a Cheshire cat just given the top off the milk, throughout the embarrassing deposition by the director.

Sergeant Wilson said worriedly to me, 'if they don't get him out of the witness box fast, he will get Reg off.'

They had allowed me to sit in the balcony area of the court, as I would not be required to give evidence on the first day. I had watched all this, bewildered by the astute verbalism of both defence and prosecuting counsels, plus Reg's apparent lack of concern regarding his future. He looked around the balcony. Deliberately catching my eye he gave me a cheeky, reassuring wink. I could not have turned away, I smiled back at him. He answered with an Oliver Hardy roll of his tie at me, as it was my tie he was wearing. I doubly saw the funny side of that gesture. The next day, as I sat outside waiting to be called, the hearing hadn't then begun, Sergeant Wilson gave me the best news I have ever heard.

'Reg has changed his plea to guilty. I have a letter here exonerating you from any part in the crime. It is written by Reg, he states categorically that he used you from start to finish. That you had no idea of anything going on, you fully believed his false story for the different names on the cheques.'

To my everlasting credit, I thought the best part of the news was that I would no longer be required to testify against Reg. A lot of faults have I; they do not include being a Judas. Reg spared me that outrage. For that I thank him. I distinctly remember saying to the sergeant, 'thank God.'

If he knew why I said it, I know not, neither do I care, my concern was for the small, likeable con-merchant named Reg who had changed his plea. I like to think I know why he did it.

The following day I went back to the Old Bailey, to watch Reg receive his sentence for embezzlement. Before being sentenced to prison, he was described as a glib con-man of dangerous proportions. Was it because of the letter clearing me? He was also branded as a master-forger and a man with a wicked, criminal mind.

Not true! My mind yelled at the Judge. Reg wicked? Never. A crook? Yes, yes, with a decided penchant for cunning. Yet always mindful that no one else was hurt in the process.

He took all the condemnation with his seemingly careless, infectious smile. When the sentence of seven years was pronounced he gave a courteous little bow to the Judge, saying, 'thank you, Mi Lord.' then he was gone below stairs, from there to serve his allotted span of corrective imprisonment. I wonder what he is doing now? I hope it isn't more time.

I never saw Reg again. Goodbye, Old Chap, I didn't get the chance to say it before. Now I take the opportunity.

Our lives in virtual ruin, my wife and I sat in that tiny room in Paddington, feeling utterly depressed and more than a little sorry for ourselves. We considered we had every right to be, deprived of home, family and with small hope of a brighter future. I did not help by repeatedly moaning, 'I think we are out of the licensed trade for good, I'm finished.'

Finally Shirley had had enough. She turned on me, 'look you, do you remember what your mother said to you? Stand up, throw your shoulders back, you are as good as anybody.'

She had the meaning right, but not the words, but who cared? Certainly not I then. I was deep in self pity.

Shirley continued with her admonition, 'we are going to look for another pub, but not in London. You will leave here, or I will leave you. You have just missed going to prison by the skin of your teeth, the Big City life is not for you.'

I had plenty of time to ponder on the truth of that, during the next few weeks. Also to marvel at how gullible Reg's employers had been, they had stood the loss of £130,000, a veritable fortune in the late sixties.

With what inadequate security they had run their business, providing the temptation for weak men such as Reg. Personally, I think the loss of their money, insufficient penalty, for creating a situation where they could so easily be ripped off. I maintain they, too, should be charged with wilful negligence, and heavily fined into the bargain. This would lessen the costs of bringing the embezzlers to book, relieving the burden on the long suffering tax payer who inevitably foots the bill.

Chapter 8

MY WIFE and I scoured the *Morning Advertiser* daily in search of a position. We purchased all other newspapers available to us at that time too, which hopefully could hold the key to the way out of our dilemma. For dilemma it truly was, the weeks went dismally by, with them our resources both figuratively and literally. We spent a small fortune on the telephone, all in vain. We were at our lowest ebb ever.

One morning as we sat in our cramped quarters, poring over the employment sections, of those interminable newspapers. Shirley suddenly shouted in excitement, 'Peter, listen to this,' she went on to read aloud a small advertisement, from the paper she had been studying. 'A bar manager, required, for a large Scarborough complex.'

Most Yorkshire people are envious of anyone who resides in Scarborough. Who wouldn't be? This sounded just right for us. if we had to leave the beloved West End, then let it be for a place we were also very fond of. I became as animated as my wife. They didn't give a phone number, only a Post Office box number which did not augur well for us. There would be heaps of applications for the position.

'Quick, Peter! Get writing.' Shirley implored unnecessarily.

The speed with which I wrote and dispatched that application was a true measure of the desperate straits we were in. I gave a full résumé of my past experience in the licensed trade, adding again for a character reference my teacher at Armthorpe School, Mr Hemstock.

Once more it was an insight into my almost total lack of confidence, regarding my chances of obtaining a decent testimonial from my former employers. I had repeatedly quoted Mr Hemstock who had failed to let me down on any occasion and we remain good friends to this day.

It was over a nail-biting week before we received a reply, besides an invitation to attend for an interview at the Victoria Palace, the London theatre where the famous Black and White Minstrels Show had run for at least six years.

It appeared to us to be an unusual venue for a bar manager's evaluation, more so because the coveted position was in Scarborough, North Yorkshire. London's West End was a far cry from the beautiful, wind-swept Yorkshire Dales, where Shirley and I had spent many happy restful hours.

We both dressed very carefully for this so important interview, arriving at the theatre not knowing what to expect. Although the position advertised for a bar manager only, taking Shirley along could but enhance my chances. My God, we kept toes and fingers crossed throughout the entire time we were in there.

After a short wait we were ushered into an office where an introduction was made to a Mr Noon. He informed us our interview would be with Mr Luff, the noted impresario. He gave Shirley and me a short briefing, prior to our meeting with this man.

The position they were offering was in Scarborough. Mr Luff had bought the old Catlin's Rainbow Rooms, which adjoined the Futurist Picture House, on the sea-front promenade of the town. He was in the process of having both buildings renovated, converting them into one huge complex, the eventual cost would be in the region of £1,000,000. Completed, it would contain five bars in this massive entertainment structure. It stood to reason they must have a very experienced, capable person, to run such a labyrinthine enterprise. I assured him we had the experience, plus the ability, to more than cope with the size, and staff which would be needed in the day to day running.

The finished building would be known as The Futurist Theatre.

We desperately needed to impress both these men, yet we dare not show anxiety. Our feelings had to be restrained during both interviews; that is actually what it was. Mr Noon was doing the prior vetting for Mr Luff. Failure to gain this position was beyond contemplation.

On meeting Mr Luff, we were put immediately at ease. I was able to relax to tell him of our not inconsiderable experience, both in the City and West End of London. Leaving out, of course, all the drama connected with those houses I gave stress to the type of trade, plus the top of the range catering, all the positions encompassed.

He listened quietly as we related our knowledge of the trade. I concluded by telling him of our desire to leave London and return to Yorkshire.

Mr Luff astounded us by telling us he had received very good references from all of our previous employers. Astounded? We were struck dumb.

Mr Francis, for one, must surely have had an ulterior motive. Unless, of course, he thought I knew more than I did? Whichever, he came good.

We left Mr Luff's office a lot happier than when we had entered it, convinced we had made it at least to the short list. There was just the fact that we were unemployed, which might go against our application. It was ten exceedingly long days before we heard from them again when they requested us to attend for another interview at the Victoria Palace. We went full of hope, at least it appeared we had made it to the short list. Mr Noon alone was the man we had to see.

He wasted no time, saying, 'Mr and Mrs Aldridge, we would like you to travel to Yorkshire to meet Mr Curtis, the general manager of the Futurist Theatre. We would like you to be interviewed by him for the position.'

We most certainly would go to Scarborough, to see the devil himself should it be necessary.

We left London immediately for Armthorpe and the safety of home, until the day arrived for this most vital of audiences in that seaside town.

It was early March, the bitter end of the Northern Hemisphere's winter. Following its usual custom, the month was coming in like a lion. Scarborough is on the north-east coast of Yorkshire, fronting the North Sea. There the wind does not waste its time going around you, it goes through, chilling you to the bone. However, this in no way detracted from our high spirits, nor diminished the warm glow which engulfed us. The Futurist was an impressive building, standing almost dead centre of the South Bay promenade, overlooking the harbour, besides giving a panoramic view of the Heads and ocean.

Our interview with Mr Curtis proved favourable, we had won the position. Even then we realized there was one possible drawback in the shape of the under-manager, a man named Clarke. He appeared to be a nasty little yes-man, complete with shifty eyes. I took an instant dislike to the creep from the second I clapped eyes on him. Having learnt to trust my instincts, I felt I would have problems with him; rightfully so it turned out.

It wasn't a clash of the proverbial personalities either, for as far as I could gauge, the man was totally devoid of that normal attribute. Insensitive to the umpth degree, he set out to be as disagreeable as possible from square one.

One wouldn't think he had much formal education, yet mystifyingly he spoke with an apparently natural far-back accent with a supercilious smirk never far from his obnoxious features. I could not tell you which I detested the more, the voice or the face.

He wasted no time in drawing up battle stations, stating loudly for all to hear, how he disliked London bods. Of course the particular body he was referring to was mine, bless his warped soul. I went to great pains to point out to him that his bosses, to whom he loved to creep, were in fact Londoners; whereas I was only by adoption. He had better not let Mr Luff or his associate hear his views, they might not take kindly to them. Whether he thought I was cut from the same cloth as he, and would tale-tell I do not know or care. Ever after that day he hated my guts, taking every chance to show it. Nevertheless he watched me like a hawk whenever Luff or the others were around.

We had been given the use of a flat directly behind the Theatre. It was one of our happiest days when our furniture came out of store, and into our own home once again. We went to the railway station to meet Mam, Jacqueline and our dog Czar, cock-a-hoop with joy at the reunion. We soon had Jacqueline into a good junior school. We hoped fervently it would be the last disruption to her schooling. Her education had suffered badly with the constant changes we had been forced to make. She was fast approaching an age when it would be imperative to keep disturbances down to an absolute minimum.

I was sad to leave the London I had loved too well. I'd miss the village, as well as all the friends I had made there. However, I was determined to turn over a new leaf, putting all those temptations behind me, with the memory of my close call with imprisonment. Surely Scarborough, with its sometimes insular inhabitants, could not lead this now worldly fellow astray?

Cynicism aside, the town would be better for us in every way. Healthwise it couldn't be bettered, a mixture of sea and country air being unbeatable by any standards. On the subject of health, the adage that Cold kills Germs, should have made Scarborians bouncing specimens. The North Sea whipped up over the sea-walls and harbour, bursting in a biting salt-laden white spume, which Czar revelled in and left our city-softened bones rattling in our frozen bodies. This approaching seasonal change couldn't arrive fast enough, at least then the sea-mists would not be of the cold, dank variety, but foretelling a warm summer's day.

Spring eventually arrived, bringing with it the opening of the New Futurist Theatre. The well advertised event brought out the crowds, the place was soon packed out in all five bars. It was splendid mass pandemonium as usual. The Aldridges were back in business.

Mr Luff put on the Black and White Minstrel Show; the year was 1969. The rave reviews for its leading stars, John Boulter, Tony Mercer, Dai Francis, plus Margaret Savage, the female soloist, filled the house to capacity the entire season. For my wife and myself it meant long hours, as well as extremely hard work. In spite of this, we got along well with the stars and the cast of dancers, besides all the behind the scenes workers of the Show. This included George Mitchell, the creator of the Minstrels, plus a very funny ventriloquist, named Neville King. He was a natural comic, mischievous in the most harmless manner. His favourite prank was to come up to the bar, picking up the ice bucket lid he'd stand to one side and out of the bucket itself would issue this hilarious voice, asking for, 'a pint please'.

To the bar staff, it was sometimes funnier to watch new attendant's faces, as they searched for the source of the voice—apart from the surprised expressions of the customers who hadn't seen him on stage.

Neville King was a regular with the Minstrels. I never saw him anything but bright and cheery, as was John Boulter, the lead singer. He, too, was a smashing chap with few airs and graces. Both were popular men with staff and patrons alike.

We settled down to our normal routine of hard graft, mixed with a great deal of pleasure. Adding to this in no small way, was seeing my friends and faithful supporters from my boxing days, as they came for a day at the seaside, or their annual holidays.

It felt good to be back among my own kind, I had never considered myself as primarily a Northerner. Yet here I was lapping up every loving moment of being back on my old turf, enjoying the accents of the crowds. Above all else basking in the warm greetings, often from strangers, as I was identified as Peter Aldridge the boxer.

As I had anticipated at the time of my appointment as manager, Mr Clarke, Clarkie as he was know to everyone, proved to be as difficult as possible. Creating as many obstacles to the smooth running of the bars as he knew how, being careful not to overstep the mark which would allow me to nail him to the cross. I had to rely on him to provide all the change the bars required. Did he take advantage of that?

We used an inordinate amount of loose change over those five bars and he would run me short regularly. More often than not, I became convinced it was purposely done. An insolent smile wreathing his face, as he watched the chaos which ensued as customer and staff alike, searched for the necessary coins, removed any traces of doubt that I might be misjudging him. How I kept my hand off the bastard, I will never know, somehow Shirley and I bit our lips until the end of the Summer Season.

It was no use approaching Mr Curtis, the general manager. Clarkie appeared to have some kind of hold over him. Curtis was the only one in the whole complex who didn't show a patent dislike of the odious beggar. At times I wondered if he was a relative of his?

Clarkie's hatred of my wife and myself, was only bettered by his malice towards the Show's bosses. There the feeling seemed mutual, too. They did little to hide it even in his presence, nor were the stars and cast of the Show immune. His sarcasm and snide cleverness being used on all he came into contact with. It was some consolation to know we were not the only ones suffering. As I have said, Curtis appeared to be the one exception.

Summer drew to a close around mid-September, the crowds began to dwindle, the promenade changed from a seething mass of colour, noise and people, to an almost deserted street.

The Futurist Theatre tried to keep open, showing blockbuster films as quickly as they were released. It was in vain, they played to almost empty houses. We tried to keep one bar open to cater for cinema patrons, for no one else would brave the weather on Scarborough's seafront. We had had little time to build a regular clientele, although I doubt if that would have been possible during the winter evenings. Some nights I saw as few as twenty people during the full trading session. It was a financial disaster, boring too, the hours painfully dragged by. You no doubt think my wife and I were workaholics; you would have been right. We had become so attuned to hard work in those days, we didn't know how to unwind; we were automatons worrying when the pressure was off. Jacqueline and Czar were the only segments of our family who appreciated the deserted promenade and sands. They romped about the abandoned foreshore blissfully, impervious to wind or weather. The froth-topped breakers pounding the beach were all part of the fun, as the pair scurried out of reach of the enraged ocean.

Personally, I do not believe there is a more desolate scene than the closed and shuttered shops, the forlorn boarded up stalls and the empty piers and wharves, of a holiday resort's sea-front during winter. To my imagination it is a haunted place which retains the laughter, the smells, the images of the people who have thronged there in whatever era.

We were not looking forward to another season at the Futurist, we had realized by then, it would soon become just a seasonal position. No company could afford to keep a large non-paying complex open, plus pay the staff required to do so, for six months of the year without feeling the hurt. I put feelers out around the town, searching for another position before the roof caved in on us again.

We loved Scarborough and hoped we could make it our permanent home, yet as you can gather, vacancies in the licensed trade were rarer than in London. You already know of our continued difficulties in the Big Smoke in finding other job opportunities of worth.

Then one day we received a phone call from a Mr Ken Goodall he was then reputed to own half of the town; among those possessions were sixteen restaurants and two hotels—The Salisbury and The George. He also was one of the town's foremost real estate agents. At, that point in time he was on the brink of opening the first Bier Keller in the area and wanted a suitable manager to get it up and running. Bier Kellers were an innovation sweeping the country, taking off in most large cities in a highly lucrative fashion. Helped, no doubt, by returning holiday makers from Germany, and the Continent in general, where the Kellers were decidedly popular.

Mr Goodall had bought a snooker hall, converting this into a Bier Keller he had shown great foresight. He also wanted a manageress for his King Richard the Third restaurant on the promenade. The latter was a large establishment spread over three floors, still well within Shirley's capabilities though we were a little perturbed at being separated. It was the first time in years in which we had worked at different venues. We were not overly pleased about that aspect, but needs must. We agreed to take up the challenge, I would manage the Keller, Shirley the King Richard. She started work at 8 a.m., not finishing until 11 p.m. a very long day indeed. I didn't begin until seven in the evening, closing at two in the morning. As you can imagine we saw little of each other. It was a case of hello and goodbye most days. My wife's job entailed not only longer hours than mine, but was a bloody sight harder too, facts of which I could hardly approve. My daughter, again deprived of her mother for most of her waking hours also detracted from the fact that we were both now gainfully employed.

Mr Goodall had provided a decent flat in the town as part of our combined wages. He owned a number of letting apartments in this busy holiday town. A very rich man, he employed somewhere in the region of 500 people during the holiday season, less, of course during the winter. There were scant employment prospects for Scarborough folk, a large proportion of whom relied on social security payments for their meagre existence. Mr Goodall used a sizeable number of these unfortunates, supplying them with work which otherwise would not have been available to them.

As is their wont, people in fear of losing their livelihood will resort to any lengths to curry favour with the boss-man. Scarborians were no exception. Such a situation existed both at the Keller and the King Richard, backbiting and tale-telling being the accepted norm. I found it anathema and still do, probably because as children we were punished equally as much as the wrong-doer for telling tales. There have been many times in my life when subservience has been the order of the day, yet I managed to retain that so important self respect, if at the same time I didn't always keep the respect of others. Again I am not trying to adopt a holier than thou stance, but I would starve before I could crawl to that extent.

To my mind creeping up to the boss in such an ignominious way destroys all vestige of manhood. I cannot help but feel a great contempt for men, or women, who indulge in it. Deep down, however, there is a kind of pity and anger that circumstances can force some human beings to such despicable depths.

Mr Goodall was well favoured with many such people, from where I stood he appeared to detest it as much as I. A directrix of his company, Ann Closs, used it to run the business more efficiently. She ran the catering side of the company, a very attractive woman in every sense, nevertheless a shrewd, watchful person in spite of this. She could be a real charmer when the mood took her, or if she thought the situation merited it. However if you managed to upset her in some way, or for any reason your face did not fit, it cost you your job. Ann Closs would not rest until the offender had been dismissed.

At the time I was employed at the Keller, a man by the name of Spaven used to visit regularly, reputedly a boyfriend of Miss Closs. Poor hapless sod, she publicly walked all over him. He was a man around forty-five years old as you can guess the hen-pecked type, a quiet retiring sort who faded into the background with little or no effort.

Mr Goodall appeared to have very little in common with him, probably because of this weak trait of his.

Mr Goodall went to Manchester and stood all night in a Bier Keller there, watching how it was run, missing not a nuance of the procedure; convinced he could make it work in Scarborough. He was right, the Keller took off in rip-roaring fashion. Never afraid of hard work, he would remove his shirt in the King Richard's kitchen, and work in a vest alongside the staff serving fish and chips, et cetera if they were very busy.

A bright man by anyone's standards, he would stand in the Keller receiving all the management of his restaurants, sixteen in all. As they gave him the number of meals served that day, say eighty-five, he would reply forty-six down or twenty-one up on last year. Astoundingly, the man had these figures in his head. On a warm, sunshiny day, with barely a cloud in the sky, he would say to my wife, 'you will be busy around 4 p.m., it is going to rain.'

Was this tendency towards clairvoyance the secret of his success?

He told me he had no political ambitions, being quite satisfied to be a powerful figure in the town with no strings attached. Talking one day about horse racing—his father owned several race-horses, he said, 'they are gangsters, those trainers, they are not having any of my money.'

A seemingly quiet, well cultured bloke, he was a wing commander in the Air Force during World War Two and he could turn it out with the best of them when pushed; most never came back for a second helping.

One obstreperous would-be customer, a heavy most of the town feared— he had kicked out a policeman's eye earning himself four years in the cooler—appeared one night and was refused entry because of his trouble-rousing ways. He dragged me by the tie off the Keller steps to the pavement outside. I hit him with a volley of short punches, striking him with a good one as he buckled to the floor. An ambulance took him to hospital. Police Sergeant Jobson told me he had seen him in hospital, saying, 'he looked as if he'd gone through a mincing machine.'

Mr Goodall watched the whole incident from the Keller steps. As I walked back inside he said coldly, 'you are a licensed murderer, Aldridge, go and wash the blood off.'

A professional fighter against a street thug, he hadn't a chance. Goodall was right though the man had asked for it.

With Goodall's approval I engaged an assistant manager, Frank Johnson, a cockney who had just arrived in Scarborough. Johnson impressed me in the beginning, when he began to brag of his dealings in London's under-world. I realized I had made a mistake in my estimation of him, the Keller tills and stocks were more in his league than the London gangster.

Weekends, my daughter stayed with me in the flat until it was time for me to go to work, then I would take her to Shirley in the restaurant. Working like this out of the licensed trade was no fun. My wife broke the record for the number of meals served within a day, 1,940 repasts. You can imagine the dashing about over three floors that entailed to ensure the service was kept up to par.

The wages in Yorkshire were much less than in London, then as now. We lost the London loading for a start, an extra payment for workers there to compensate for the alleged higher cost of living in that city.

Regardless of all this, we were determined to stay in beautiful Scarborough for the rest of our working days somehow. Missing the bright lights and gaiety, I was still a damned sight happier than I had thought possible away from the village and temptations of the West End.

My assistant, Johnson, began playing up on the job as I'd feared, showing his true colours as a typical low-life con-merchant, as well as being an habitual liar. In fact I was at the stage where I disbelieved everything the man said. I worried incessantly about my stocks and takings. Finally, I passed on those fears to Goodall and Closs, informing them I couldn't be held responsible for thefts. They made it quite clear I would be held accountable for any losses incurred, obviously not believing in my distrust of Johnson.

I decided to ask for help from Scarborough police Sergeant Jobson. I explained to him my uneasiness about Johnson. Jobson knew of my expe-riences in London, we had shared many a laugh about the funny and frightening episodes, which had filled my life throughout my stay in the Big Smoke.

I had really nothing other than a feeling of disquiet to offer the sergeant who was aware I had known quite a few awesome villains and petty crooks during the years spent in London. He certainly knew I would recognize the latter when I met one.

Jobson agreed to run a check on my assistant, saying, 'I will get back to you in a few days.'

Inside of two weeks the sergeant came back with the information about Johnson. As I had suspected, he was indeed a small time crook with a criminal record having served time in Her Majesty's jail. He also had a wife and four children he'd omitted to mention, being on the run at that moment from the courts for lack of maintenance. In living fact he was a real charmer.

I faced up to Mr Goodall with this irrefutable evidence, to my surprise besides utter consternation this didn't faze him in the least. Angrily, I stated, 'Mr Goodall, you must realize I cannot be held responsible for bad stocks or faulty takings, when I have a man, a known petty criminal, in a responsible position.'

'Come now, I do not believe there is any need for concern. Mr Johnson, I am sure, is not about to rob us,' he replied with an apparent air of indifference.

I could not believe my ears, here was this acknowledged clever, astute, business-conscious man, totally unmoved by the dangers and obvious risks in keeping Johnson around. I could not envisage any circumstance which would induce any of my former employers to keep him in a position of trust. That type of leopard was unlikely to change its spots. Mr Goodall was willing to countenance the chance. So be it, he could afford the luxury, I couldn't. My position there was more than tenuous. I had no licence or contract. Ann Closs's reputation for making short thrift of people who crossed her in any way, weighed heavily on my mind. I had definitely gone over her head on this. She was not the forgiving sort.

Mr Goodall's behaviour throughout this incident had been peculiar, lending more than a little credence to the leering boast of Johnson. 'I am knocking her off you know,' referring insinuatingly to Ann Closs and leaving me with a nasty taste in my mouth. He must have had someone on his side, it certainly wasn't the angels.

Shirley and I had a long talk, our future with Messrs Goodall and Closs was now very insecure. We had to find something with security in the long term, a place where we could work together, preferably in the licensed trade, a position we could fill standing on our heads. Thus determined, we wrote to every brewery in the north of England.

Frank Johnson had become openly gloating, taking every opportunity to show his new found confidence in his irreplaceable position. The bugger was well aware that I had his full measure, and there was nothing I could do about it. His open bragging of his gangster connections among the élite of villainy, plus his constant reference to his sexual prowess, finally got to me. I waited until the manager of the Salisbury Hotel was with him, for they had become quite friendly. I do not believe the manager was aware of Johnson's true past, though he had heard many a story of the top of the pile crooks Johnson professed to be on familiar terms with.

A couple of my staff were also stood close by when I walked up to the miscreant, saying in the best gangster imitation I have ever done, 'stay where you are, don't move an inch. If you do I will drop you where you stand.'

James Cagney and Humphrey Bogart, eat your hearts out. I was good.

Johnson visibly shook, he stood transfixed ashen-faced and trembling while I gave him a factual run-down on who and what he was. I concluded my venomous satire by telling him he wouldn't know a gangster, if one came up and bit him.

I cruelly carried the humiliation further, 'now it is you and me, Mr Hard-man. I will give you a start then I will book you a hospital bed. You are going to need it.'

'Please, please,' he whimpered, 'you know I will stand no chance against you.'

I can only assume it finished his fearsome mobster image, as far as the Keller was concerned. As for me, I had had enough. I went in search of Mr Goodall to tender my resignation.

Before I could do that the manager of the Salisbury came over to me, asking, 'would you have hit him, Peter? You scared the lying bugger to death, me in the process, I might add.'

I laughed, it was the second time I had pulled that one off. The first was back in my apprentice plumbing days, the victim then was Jock Goldie.

Elated I went in search of my employer, it was evening by the time I found him, the start of another day's work for me.

I pulled no punches here either, telling him I could not afford to work there with the risk of bad stocks I would have to make good, airing my grievances real and imagined. No one had ever dared to speak to him like that. He stood speechless, unbelieving as I gave him one week's notice, all I was willing to give. I could not afford to be so self-indulgent, it cost me my hard-earned bonus besides putting me once again in the ranks of the unemployed. The fear of my vulnerability in the job drove me on and I had nothing to lose. I couldn't bear the cost of the bad stock I was convinced would be inevitable as Johnson became more and more sure of himself.

I, for reasons known only to Mr Goodall, had won his respect for many years to come. This bore me in good stead many times in the future, not least quite recently when I approached him for assistance with this project.

Meantime, Shirley had agreed to stay on at the King Richard until the end of the season. Mr Goodall would then have the whole of the closed winter period to replace her. He could not spare my wife during this busy time, nor could we stand both of us being out of work. Besides, this way we kept the flat as it was tied to the position.

Someone up there loved us, for just one week later our fortunes were to change, leading my wife and me to a very happy ten years in a job of our own choice. It was a miracle, if you believe in such things. Among the breweries we had applied to was Joshua Tetley and Son, the well known Yorkshire brewers. A letter arrived from a Mr David Hill their area manager covering the district from Hull to Whitby; a region which held most of Tetley's public houses. I phoned Mr Hill almost immediately to arrange a meeting with him at the King Richard restaurant. There was no way Shirley could get time off to attend an interview. It was justifiable that we should use those premises on this so important an occasion. Cutting two ways, it would allow Mr Hill to see the type of catering Shirley was capable of handling. Also, it could only help our cause, certainly not detract from it, if only because she was conscientious enough not to take time off.

My wife and I waited for this man, our nerves drawn tight, again so much rested on the outcome of this interview. We seemed to have been living in a vacuum, teetering on the edge of a precipice, unsettled and unhappy in our respective jobs. It had intruded upon our private lives, or what infinitesimal piece there had been of that luxury.

I sat sipping my umpteenth cup of coffee. The summer season was nearly over, the promenade being sparsely populated and there were just a few customers in the room. In walked this smartly dressed man who appeared to be in his mid thirties. Very assured, it could be no other than David Hill.

I stood up as he spoke to a waitress. 'I am looking for Mr Peter Aldridge.'

I walked towards him, introducing myself as that person. I asked if he would like a coffee which he accepted with alacrity. We sat down at a window overlooking the placid ocean beyond the harbour. I felt at ease within minutes, I was to learn David Hill had considerable ability to achieve this with people from most walks of life. He had charisma in abundance, charm oozed out of him. Shirley joined us looking extremely smart in a black and white outfit. I caught the appreciative glance Mr Hill gave her as she seated herself at the table.

He leaned back in his chair making an obvious appraisal of both of us, before saying, 'tell me, what have you done in the licensed trade?'

We began our summary with working as a relief management in London, explaining the type of houses plus the trade they covered. We ran the gamut until we came to the Cheshire Cheese, where Hill abruptly stopped us, saying sharply, 'you managed that house? I used that house when I was in the City of London.'

'Yes, thoroughly enjoying every moment of it too,' I replied, pleased that we had scored a very good bull's eye. The Cheshire Cheese had come up trumps for Shirley and Peter Aldridge.

He was clearly impressed as we went on to relate the rest of our trade experience, including our time spent in Scarborough.

'I haven't a manager in my area who has had the all round type of experience that you both have had. You were in top flight company in the West End and the City of London, managing those houses.'

Shirley and I felt our battered self esteem stir. In spite of our outward bravado, the events at the King's Head followed by The Albert's disastrous culmination of all our hopes had left us drained. Unemployment on top of this had also taken its toll, blowing to bits our self confidence. We were badly in need of reassurance of our worth.

My wife provided sandwiches with still more coffee, while we talked of my younger days when I was boxing. It was a sport he was greatly interested in and we chatted thus for a while. I had brought my photo albums, which were full of snaps of all the public houses we had managed. David Hill perused these leisurely. We had been together around an hour and a half, before he looked up from the photographs, saying, 'well, I suppose you would like to know about the house I am seeking the management for?'

We waited with bated breath, there was nothing on this God's earth more important to us at that time.

Mr Hill continued, 'it is the Silver Grid in Huntriss Row, in the centre of Scarborough.'

Assembly Rooms, later Piccadilly Nite Spot, above The Silver Grid, now Pizza Hut.

Shirley and I could hardly believe our ears, it being one of the foremost hotels in the town, owned by the Laughton family before Tetley bought them out. Before, during, and after the Second World War, it held the reputation of having the best restaurant in Scarborough and district. Prior to the Laughton's ownership, it had been a theatre and the Assembly Rooms. Charles Dickens had read there in the nineteenth century. I was to gain first hand knowledge of that later.

It was said the Laughton family had sent their famous son, Charles, to The Silver Grid to learn the liquor trade; particularly the wine import-export side of it. The Grid had extensive wine cellars.

Charles, to everyone's delight, except his family's, had rebelled. This was not in his scheme of things, he had quite a different career in mind. Not for him the mundane, he ran away to London to be an actor, later to be brought back to Scarborough by his father. However, he eventually succeeded in convincing his relations that his talents lay in other directions, thankfully for the pleasure of millions of people. He went on to become Britain's best loved actor, besides Scarborough's most famous son.

We were brought down to earth and harsh reality by David Hill.

'I will put all this information to my directors,' he said. 'If your references check out all right, I believe I can tell you that you will be on the short list.'

We thanked him before he left, grabbing each other the moment he was out of sight, disregarding the watching patrons of the restaurant.

It was a wonderful opportunity, we prayed earnestly that Lady Luck would again smile on us. Over the last two years we had most definitely been on her don't-want-to-know list.

We waited patiently for one week, then as the weeks went by, hopelessly we began to accept the possibility of failure. Depression with a capital D set in, I was unemployed, Shirley would be shortly, for the end of the season was almost upon us.

At last the letter came which was to change our lives, it read, 'would Mrs Aldridge and yourself, please attend for an interview with Mr Forsyth, Director of Joshua Tetley and Son, on Friday next at 9.30 a.m.'

I immediately phoned Mam to tell her the good news, for she was very concerned over my unemployment.

'I am going to pray for you,' she said typically, always religious, she was becoming more involved and committed as the years went by.

We sorely needed help, if it was divine, so much the better; Mam would do her best to ensure we received that blessing. As I sit here recalling those days, I marvel at the blind, staunch faith which she had retained, in the face of all the adversities which continued to mar her life.

That marvellous Friday eventually dawned and we presented ourselves at Messrs Tetley and Sons, Leeds. We had been through this so many times, as you know; we knew more or less what to expect. As we had done before, we arrived in good time. At exactly nine-thirty we were ushered into the director's office. Mr Hill, a secretary and Mr Forsyth were already assembled there. We were seated at a desk in front of Mr Forsyth, whom we gathered was a Scot, as well as being a very forthright man.

'I am not going to beat round the bush, Mr and Mrs Aldridge,' he said, 'We think you are the couple we are seeking to manage The Silver Grid. Do you think you can run it?' He looked searchingly at both my wife and myself.

'Yes, sir, I am sure we can, we will make a good job of it, too.'

'Right, I am going to let Mr Hill take over now, this house is a very special case, he can tell you why that is. He knows all about it.'

Mr Hill then began to spell out to us the history of The Silver Grid. In recent years it had had a succession of managers, slowly deteriorating from being a well known prestigious house, until it was no longer a first-class, centre of the town attraction, a position it had always enjoyed for many years. Now, it was nothing short of a trouble spot. It boasted a discothèque filled with rabble in place of its once fine restaurant, its former commendable reputation now in disrepute with the police and the people of Scarborough.

Joshua Tetley wanted the good name of the Grid, besides the trade, restored. They were more than willing to spend money on the house to help regain its previous respected place in the town.

Shirley and I were told they would give us a free hand to rid the Silver Grid of motorbike gangs, bed-rollers, town drunks and trouble makers in general who, at that point in time, were firmly established regular users of the house.

It was going to be far from easy, bouncers I would need in plenty.

After the interview with Mr Forsyth was over, Mr Hill made arrangements to meet me at The Silver Grid on the following Monday morning. He told me, 'there I will go through everything again with you. We are also to attend an interview with a police superintendent, a man named Shooter.'

This threw me. What the devil had a superintendent of the police got to do with the appointment of a new manager, of a public house?

I was to receive that answer a week later, when we faced up to Shooter.

On the Monday morning I waited outside The Silver Grid for Mr Hill to arrive. In those days Huntriss Row was a through road off the Main Street, now it is a pedestrian only shopping mall.

Mr Hill pulled his car into the kerb side, we shook hands in greeting and walked into The Silver Grid.

Shirley and I had resisted visiting the Grid, opting to wait until Hill showed me round.

What a mess met my eyes. Once expensive wallpaper, now hung in peeling strips from equally grubby walls. The entrance was filthy to say the least. We entered the main bar. The first thing to catch our eye was a massive, solid oak-panelled bar, above which was a round motif bearing the inscription, Silver Grid 1895. The Silver Grid restaurant which had given its name to the building, had flourished under the Laughton's hands.

From this dingy place David Hill led me into a second room, no cleaner than the first. However I disregarded this impression, on sighting the beautiful oak-panelled floor to ceiling walls. This had been the lounge, it now held a juke box, a huge dirty bar filled one end of this once lovely area. The place had the musty smell of age and neglect, yet it still retained a certain kind of dignity because of those walls.

I followed Mr Hill up the staircase to the discothèque. My God, I had thought the public areas were dirty, this room almost beggared description. The lighting was a blue psychedelic visual effect, the walls were adorned with posters of the gangsters of the 1920s, motorbikes, the gangsters' molls and cop cars. Actually, for a disco the theme was good. However, the decorations had been there far too long without renewal. The place stank, and not only of beer and cigarettes.

The public toilets were all downstairs and they made the rest of the Silver Grid appear clean by comparison.

After permission from the resident manager, Mr Hill led me back upstairs to the flat which occupied the whole of the top floor.

It was a very good one, large with plenty of space for Jacqueline, my wife and myself. It housed a separate large kitchen, which I knew would please Shirley. A long passageway connected the bathroom and Jacqueline's future bedroom to our soon-to-be living quarters.

It proved to be a very intriguing passageway, frightening to the more nervous, yet not worrying to me, or mine.

'What do you think to The Silver Grid?' David Hill asked, once we were again on the ground floor.

'Whoever let this magnificent building get into this state?' I asked, countering his question with one of my own.

'It is the result of a series of poor managers. I have only just taken over this area and I intend to bring this place back to its former standing in the community. To attain that I will need your full co-operation, Mr Aldridge.'

'You have got it now,' I looked David Hill straight in the eyes.

We were to become not only the Big Boss and Manager, but good friends in the years which followed.

'All right,' Mr Hill said, 'now let us keep the appointment with the superintendent of police.'

As we made our way to the police station, he explained the reason for our visit. The Scarborough police had complained about the unending trouble emanating from The Silver Grid to the street outside during and after opening hours.

David Hill had never met Superintendent Shooter, neither had I. As we entered his office, we saw a large, imposing man seated behind a desk. He didn't wait for the nicety of introduction. He glared at the two of us, like a schoolmaster with two recalcitrant children to whom he was about to read the riot act. That is exactly what he did.

He slapped his hands down on his desk, with a crack which reverberated around the room and he shouted, 'I cannot afford to have a police van outside The Silver Grid permanently, nor can I afford to have police on duty just for the Silver Grid. Nor will I. I will close The Silver Grid down first.'

He leaned menacingly across his desk towards us, waiting for argument for or against this dictum.

I looked from him to Mr Hill, who appeared decidedly shaken by this uncalled for vicious outburst. I know I must have resembled a fish out of water, wondering where its next drink is coming from.

David Hill visibly drew himself up to his full height.

'Sir,' he said coldly, 'I am the new area manager, Mr Aldridge, this gentleman, is the new manager of The Silver Grid. He takes over in three weeks. If I have not got our establishment to your satisfaction in a matter of months, then you may close it down.'

He glared angrily at Shooter, who stared back at him. They seemed to hold that hard gaze as if waiting to see who was the weaker man. Without a word being spoken, it seemed to be mutually settled.

The super turned into the pleasant, genial man I was to get to know so very well. 'Right,' he said, 'how would you like a cup of tea?'

I breathed a quiet sigh of relief, pleased I hadn't had a part in the proceedings. I had not expected a reception like that, neither had Hill who had given as good as he got, teaching Shooter a few manners into the bargain. I decided there and then I would hate to cross either man. Settling back to enjoy the cuppa Shooter proffered, I listened to the two of them discussing the news in general, as if nothing had gone on before.

Mr Hill and I returned to The Silver Grid, where we sat and talked about his plans for the reformation of the house.

'Peter,' he said, 'Mr Forsyth agrees with me, you will be given a free hand here. We intend to spend a lot of money on the project to achieve this, even then it will be far from easy. You understand now the predicament the Company has found itself in. That is what Mr Forsyth meant when he told you, "The Silver Grid is a special case". Have you any questions you would like to ask?'

'None, though I hope you realize the trade will go down in the beginning. We have to make a fresh start, gaining the customers back who have been lost from The Silver Grid for a long time.'

'We are not concerned about that,' Mr Hill asserted. 'The trade we have at the present, we neither have occasion for, nor want to keep.'

He left no doubt in my mind that he meant every word he had said. His determination was evident. Today, I can surmise his reputation, if not his career, hung on its complete success equally as much as did mine. We sat talking on this theme, planning how to accomplish the desired results as quickly and effectively as possible.

Two hours later, satisfied with our joint agreement, we withdrew from the coming battleground of the Grid, making our way to the King Richard for lunch. Also to tell Shirley of our plans to reshape the Grid's appearance and with it the type of trade we hoped to attract.

Mr Hill told her of the prestige the house had once proudly owned, including a visit by Queen Victoria and her son, Edward VII, who both reputedly graced the Assembly Rooms.

Shirley only had another week to work, before the King Richard closed for the winter. With the restaurant boarded up against the North Sea's annual spiteful anger, we were free to take a week's break in Armthorpe with Mam. She couldn't wait to hear about The Silver Grid, including all the ideas for its projected future.

Its history appealed to her. I believe she was the source for the whole family's interest in the subject and suspecting she would be our first visitor, I wasn't far wrong.

On our return to Scarborough we gave Mr Goodall a week's notice on his flat. We then prepared ourselves for possibly the greatest challenge of our lives, restoring, in more ways than one, The Silver Grid to its rightful place among the better licensed premises of the town.

It was the largest establishment of its kind in Scarborough and deserved to be ranked among the best. The position we had undertaken was on the premise we could make it so.

The day for take-over came quickly. That morning I went to Court to obtain my licence and my name went over the entrance door to the Grid almost immediately as the Licensee. I felt better just as quickly. We were back in business, the only type my wife and I knew, the pub business.

The incumbent manager was leaving, his removal van was parked conveniently outside. He was soon on his way, my van replacing his as I became officially the manager.

I stood and surveyed the mixed crop of customers I had fallen heir to. Some of these I had known from the Keller, the others eyed me warily, apparently word had spread that changes were about to be made in the Grid. Not only in management, but in the way things were run. I do not now think any of them suspected the enormity of those changes.

I didn't interfere in any way with the ordinary day to day business the Grid had become use to, for a full morning and evening session. On the principle of Know Thine Enemy. I wasn't about to make changes for just change's sake, but the larrikin days were numbered in The Silver Grid. They would be forced to move on to other houses willing to put up with their behaviour. The Grid was not one of those places any more.

There were still some decent people who used the house and I gradually sounded them out. One was a man called Tommy Cross who pulled no punches, 'this bloody place needs straightening out, I don't envy the bloke who tries it though, especially upstairs,' he added, pointing towards the stairway to the disco.

'Don't worry, Tom, I have plans for that place,' I chuckled.

I didn't enlighten him, despite his obvious curiosity. Information from the horse's mouth would spread like wildfire among the regulars, reaching every corner of this enormous place in no time. Soon enough when the move was made.

The following day I sent for the main bouncer. The Grid employed three at the weekend. He was only engaged for three nights of the week, as the summer season had ended. His name was Ken Oldroyd, a strongly made fellow, a rugby player for Scarborough. Rugby not being the breeding ground for sissies, I knew that, properly used, he would be the ideal chucker out for me. I asked him, 'how have you been operating, Ken?'

'I walk from room to room, I am always on call. I tackle the troublemaker as well as its cause, if there is one, as soon as the trouble starts.'

The man had been deployed wrongly, now was as good a time as any to alter his modus operandi.

'From now on in, Ken, you will take over the front entrance, vetting every bugger who comes through it.'

'Christ, that's suicidal, Guv'ner!'

'Nevertheless, that's how it will be done. All known offenders are from this moment banned. I will provide a back-up. I am pretty handy with my fists still. If you have any doubts about anyone, entry must be refused. Between us we are going to clean up The Silver Grid, woe betide the bloke who thinks he can stop us.'

'Better get into condition, Guv'ner, we have a bloody tough job ahead, there will be some bloody scrapping to be done,' Ken said grimly.

He wasn't wrong either. Being winter the discothèque only opened on Fridays and Saturdays. That was going to be the toughest job, cleaning out the bloody drop-outs who used it as the ideal arena to start a fight.

The first Friday arrived. I was settling in nicely at the Grid, we'd had no bother to speak of. Outside the main door I had put up a large notice, 'No Bed-rollers. No Unkempt Long Hair. No Jeans in the Back Lounge'.

With Ken on the main entrance, Paul Geoghio, a huge seventeen stone Cypriot, on the bottom of the stairs leading to the disco, a chap named Big George stationed at the door to the back lounge, we were as ready as we'd ever be. Everything went as sweet as a nut, we must have turned easily 150 people away, with barely any trouble whatsoever. Apart from the odd scuffle with the usual soft-brain.

'You are not going to take much money,' warned Ken.

'That's all right, Ken, the money and the right sort of customer will come when we have got rid of this bloody shower of bastards.'

Saturday evening brought the Yorkshire Hell's Angels motorbike gang to the town, and The Silver Grid. Parking all their bikes noisily outside the house, they approached the door where Ken and I were standing waiting.

Ignoring my large well-lit sign-board, they swarmed towards us, their long untidy hair covering their leather clad shoulders. A more scruffy looking bunch I had never had the misfortune to see.

'It's all over, boys, you do not come in here again,' I told them firmly.

'Get ready for it,' Ken muttered.

'If you leave one bike in front of this building again, you will push it home, not ride it,' I threatened them.

A chorus of descriptive expletives from the menacing Angels, greeted this threat. They outnumbered us at least ten to one.

'Face it lads, I am the gaffer here now, you are all washed up. Take my tip, find another place to wreck, spread the word, you are all finished here.'

'He means it,' Ken shouted.

From past experience they knew he didn't mess about with empty warnings. Slowly in ones and twos they began to back off, then with an almighty defiant roar from their huge bikes they were gone.

'Bloody hell, the bloody bastards have gone!' an amazed Ken exclaimed.

'With not a drop of blood spilled,' added George, who had been a back-up with Paul.

They never returned to The Silver Grid. Where they went I neither knew nor cared. The clean-up of the Grid had began. It was a great beginning too. The Bed-rollers were next on the agenda of banned characters. The message had gone out loud and clear, dress decently, be clean, behave yourself and you were welcome in The Silver Grid. Do otherwise, besides a thumping you would earn a banishment for life, or at least for as long as I was the licensee.

Within a couple of months Shirley had cleaned up the dirt, I had cleaned out the dirties who had taken possession of the Grid. Although it was still distinctly shabby, there was a one hundred per cent improvement in appearance.

We were now into our first season. June, July, August and September were, as we found out, to be the busiest months in The Silver Grid.

During July and August, Scots month fell. I knew from my former London experience, plus the two seasons completed in Scarborough, one at the Futurist Theatre, the other at the Bier Keller, this was going to be a trying period at The Silver Grid.

Mr Hill had promised me if I could show a betterment of the Grid's clientele in the first season, he would spend the money the Company had committed themselves to expend. The renovations would then be completed before the start of my second season.

I couldn't afford to let the marauding, holidaying Scots, wreck all my successful efforts to clean the trouble makers out.

My run-ins with the Scots in the West End of London and King's Head during the Wembley Internationals, loomed large in my memory. I couldn't reform that bloody lot, yet I could box clever. I just had to survive the onslaught, or else all my hopes were down the tube.

This was to be the plan of defence I would put in operation.

Taking Ken off the front entrance I put in his place a Scot named Sandy Aicheson. He, also, was an ex-rugby player, not a giant of a man, yet softly spoken, with absolutely impeccable manners.

He dealt with the redoubtable Scots well, his approach being to get them on side. This way they policed their own ranks with his gentle assurance of, 'you will be looked after here, Jimmy. We want no trouble, it's a good guy who runs this spot. He is a great gaffer.'

Mayhem raged supreme throughout the smaller pubs and hotels, but The Silver Grid came out of Scots month practically unscathed. Takings went sky high. Mr Hill was tickled pink with the results of our first year as management of the Grid. So much so that when the Licensed Victuallers' Dinner and Dance was about to take place, in November of that year, 1971, at the Grand Hotel in Scarborough, he phoned me to say, 'Peter, I have placed you and Shirl at my table.'

This was the top table, which would seat Mr Forsyth, plus the rest of Tetley's directors. We were delighted, yet it did create a few problems, for there was jealousy among the rest of Tetley's management. We were their only representatives seated there, nonetheless Shirley and I enjoyed our position among the upper echelon. We also appreciated the acknowledgement shown by Mr Hill, for our efforts in The Silver Grid. He would say with a smile, 'Peter Aldridge took the Grid by the scruff of the neck. He deserves a medal for the job he has done there.'

A very nice tribute, from a very nice man.

I can tell you this with no fear of being accused of exaggeration. I had no skin on my knuckles for the first six months in The Silver Grid. My faithful Alsatian, Czar, more than earned his keep by discouraging the more rebellious . . . As soon as trouble seemed imminent, my wife would run down the cellar to fetch Czar, then she'd pass him to me and I would hold him on a short lead. Although by nature a gentle dog, he knew when I tightened up his lead there was a job to be done. He was my main doorman and deterrent in the afternoons, when I couldn't afford to pay for the services of doormen.

Czar would show a full set of teeth, accompanying this with a low growl, usually this would be sufficient to demoralize the most aggressive lout bent on creating havoc within the precinct of the Grid.

Tetley's Brewery and David Hill were good to their word. At the end of the year the refurbishment of The Silver Grid began. They spent £35,000 on new carpets and furniture, as well as redecoration of all the public areas downstairs. The discothèque underwent a stupendous change. Tetley spent another £30,000 turning that sleazy room into a cocktail lounge, complete with small bar, stage and dance floor. The disco which had attracted the worst of the baddies was gone. In its place stood a classy night spot, where a man could take his wife or girlfriend for an evening out, quite proudly and safely.

What a great thrill the following year, for Shirley and me, as the Grid filled to capacity, the house back to its former standing in the town. Takings and beer consumption hit an all time high. The owners being brewers, beer sales were more important to them than spirit sales, although we sold our share of those particularly in the cocktail lounge.

I had only one disagreement with David Hill. He wanted prostitutes banned from The Silver Grid. I knew from past experience all large establishments and main pubs drew these ladies like a magnet. It also attracted those looking for their services.

Prostitution is a fact of life and prostitutes are part of the assets of any well-run house. Banning them would affect trade adversely. Properly controlled, with no soliciting allowed on the premises, they could, and did, increase the pub's trade. Banned they would take that trade elsewhere.

I won, with the stipulation there had to be strict supervision of their activities, while they were in the Grid. I had no trouble complying with that maxim, none of them wanted anything else but to go about their own business. I allowed only the better type in, making sure they were good looking into the bargain.

The type which paraded the streets, were definitely not on the wanted list, nor were the obvious for-sale-ladies, though I had an exception. I had one instance of a lady bending the rules which I thought so funny at the time, I gave her just a minor rebuke instead of dropping the bomb on her; which of course meant she would have been out as far as the Grid was concerned. The lady in question was named Jenny Cross, a petite, pretty girl who, unbelievably, was the mother of eight children. She was either careless in her work, or had an equally careless partner at home. I never found out which.

The incident in focus on this occasion concerned the picking up of three soldiers from the local Burniston Barracks and bringing them into the Grid main bar. She then proceeded to take them outside one after the other.

Arriving back in the bar following the servicing of the third one, she walked into the centre of the room and with arms held aloft shouted triumphantly, 'BbbbbBoom'.

The soldiers looked shattered, she appeared as perky as ever.

She was completely irrepressible, a person one couldn't help but like. She admired Shirley, probably because my wife chatted to her as she did to all other customers irrespective of their profession. Jenny told me quite seriously, 'if there is trouble at any time, I will look after Shirley, no one will touch her with me around.'

It was a nice thought from this tiny lady, but my wife was by then a seasoned campaigner more likely to protect little Jenny. Sadly, three years after the incident with the three soldiers, impudent Jenny was killed in a car crash. This world is that much poorer with the loss of this appealing character.

Shirley was doing exceptionally well with food, serving bar snacks both in the cocktail lounge and downstairs in the public bars.

There was a need for late night entertainment in Scarborough, the town died with the closing of the pubs, apart from the Keller type of enterprise and local dances. A more sophisticated amusement stood a good chance of succeeding.

I decided to apply for 2 a.m. closing licence for the cocktail lounge.

'No chance,' said David Hill emphatically, 'With the Grid's past reputation, the court would throw it out.'

'Let me try, that is all I ask.'

'You will be wasting your time,' Mr Hill reiterated.

'I do not think so,' I told him. 'Since I took over the Grid, the police have had no bother from here. Surely that must carry some weight with the court.'

'All right, Peter, you have my consent to try,' he suddenly capitulated. David Hill had given in, yet I knew he harboured many misgivings about the whole idea. I also knew it would be on my head if the enterprise failed, and we were landed with a white elephant. Or, worse still, a more subtle type of disco with all the horrors which could follow.

Nevertheless I went ahead with the project and applied for the 2 a.m. licence, through a solicitor. I then asked for an interview with Superintendent Shooter. I was granted the latter and met him again in his office. This time he greeted me amiably.

Shooter shook my hand, expressing his delight at the radical change we had achieved at The Silver Grid. I wondered if he would receive me so warmly once he knew what I wanted, or countenance a late opening for that once so disreputable place.

I went in with both feet, 'sir,' I began, 'I have applied for a licence to remain open until 2 a.m. I intend to change the upstairs cocktail lounge into a night club to cater for the better end of that trade.'

I didn't wait for any objections but continued with my spiel.

'I assure you all the patrons will be vetted carefully, I have no intention of allowing it to disintegrate into anything other than the purpose I have just outlined to you.

'I have come to see you hoping to get assurance that the police will not object to my application for a time extension.'

He knew as well as I, that any opposition from the police would skittle any chances of ever getting the licence. I had gone there trusting I could influence him into proving David Hill's assumptions wrong. I intended to show Mr Hill those fears were groundless and would indeed be granted the late closing I needed to fulfil my plans.

Shooter looked at me sternly before answering, 'right, Son, you have got my assurance, the police will not object.'

I shook his hand warmly, as he added the following caution, 'do not let me down.'

'No, sir,' I replied instantly, 'it will be run in exactly the same manner as we have already found so successful at The Silver Grid.'

I couldn't wait to get back to Shirley to tell her of my victory. In Court the following week, the licence was granted but only after an eternity of deliberations by the magistrates, even though no police objections were submitted. Without a doubt that was the deciding factor.

David Hill could not believe we had the go-ahead, saying, 'you have astounded me, I didn't think for a moment you could get it.'

That gave me more pleasure than actually obtaining the licence, for Hill was an astute worldly man. He went to the top of the pile career wise. He was promoted by Allied Brewers, finally becoming a director with Ansells Brewer Company in Birmingham.

This was a completely different venture for The Silver Grid. The night club would open at 7.30 p.m. and close at 2 a.m. Winter was upon us, the quiet period of the year known as the off-season, yet it suited our purposes, giving us time to assess the enterprise well before the visitors took it over. I decided to run it on a membership basis, still allowing the holiday-maker to pay at the door to cover the summer trade. They would, of course, be the cream as opposed to the locals all year round bread and butter trade.

We won the lucrative business of the local fisherman, most of them taking out membership of the night club. As I have intimated, they were great spenders bringing the better type of customer with them, ensuring the future success of the club.

At the close of business in the main bars, we allowed the best of the patrons to go upstairs if they wished. As I had promised the superintendent, both membership and visitor alike, were strictly appraised regarding entry into the club.

The takings were astronomical. Tetley, and David Hill in particular, were rapturous over The Silver Grid, and its progress from a sleaze hole to a respected, money-making house.

My wife and I decided to take a break from the Grid, now things were running smoothly. Winter was the only time this would be feasible so, Christmas behind us, we set off in February for the south of England. Devon as well as Cornwall sounded good for two much needed weeks away from it all. Shirley's mother and father moved in to the Grid's private quarters to care for Jacqueline and Czar. My daughter was unable to accompany us, it being school term. Enough loss of schooling had already occurred.

The Silver Grid was to be managed by a Mr and Mrs Hart, who'd live out. We closed the night club for two weeks, leaving only the main bars to be run by our relieving management.

As we drove away that day, not for one moment did we suspect the traumatic event, which would take place during our absence.

The first week of our holiday was blissfully quiet. We had rented a small cottage close to the charming fishing village, and resort area of Looe. Being winter, the peacefulness remained undisturbed by the hordes of holidaying adults and children who crowded this part of England during spring and summer.

The second week, our bodies rested, we decided to tour the area. On the Tuesday we had been to the Devon and Exeter National Hunt race. We had just reached a dual carriageway part of the road and I put my foot down on the accelerator of the Mazda sports saloon I was driving. We flashed by an A.A. station where they were displaying a large board. I was going far too fast to read what was written on it.

Shirley exclaimed, 'I am sure that was our car number, I think I saw Scarborough on the placard as well.'

'Don't be silly,' I replied sharply, 'who knows we are in this area?'

Shirley had began to worry about Jacqueline, I thought this was just another manifestation of that disquiet.

I was still flying along the road, when seemingly out of nowhere a police car came up from behind, its blue light flashing.

'Now look what you have done,' Shirley moaned at me, 'we will be fined for speeding for sure.'

The police car pulled in front of us as I slowed and stopped at the roadside. The two officers got out of their vehicle, approaching us with the measured stride, which is so daunting to the average bloke. They ranged themselves at each side of my car, as I peeped feebly to the nearest man, 'we were only doing sixty to seventy, Officer.'

'Mr Aldridge, Scarborough?' he asked.

My heart missed several beats, what the hell was wrong, who was ill?

Shirley white-faced, sat staring at the policeman.

'We have an urgent message for you, sir. You have to phone home at once, I am sorry but I believe you have had a fire.'

The two policemen couldn't have been more helpful, with two utterly stunned and frightened people.

'Follow us back to the A.A. station, you can phone from there,' one said.

With horn blaring they escorted us back to the motoring association's cabin, which we had passed at such a cracking speed we'd missed the board's message requesting us to stop.

'You have this number to ring,' the A.A. man told us, as we entered the hut. 'Use that phone,' he added, pointing to one on a desk.

It was Tetley's Brewery number in Leeds.

Shirley had literally gone to pieces, her overriding concern was for Jacqueline and her parents.

If was after office hours at the brewery, I let the phone ring and ring, there was no answer. My panic was now almost matching my wife's, I phoned The Silver Grid amid the shouts and cries of a distraught Shirley, plus the soothing sounds from the policemen. Again there was no answer.

The Harts—relief managers at the Grid at the time of the fire—
with the Aldridges

I hit on the idea to ring another Tetley's pub, The Huntsman, which was only round the corner from the Grid. Mr Chubb was the manager there at the time.

'Mr Chubb, this is Peter Aldridge, can you tell me what has happened at The Silver Grid?'

'There isn't a Silver Grid any more,' was the horrifying answer I received.

'What has happened? Can you tell me what has happened to my family?' I shouted down the phone.

'No, I have no idea,' the mongrel replied.

In desperation I searched for and found, David Hill's home phone number.

'Thank God,' he said, as he answered my call, 'I have been sitting by this phone for hours, hoping you would call me first.'

'Jacqueline?' I gasped, interrupting him.

'Everything is all right, Peter. Jacqueline and Shirley's parents are all safe.'

I was repeating this to Shirley, as Mr Hill continued, 'your dog, also, is safe, but I am afraid The Silver Grid is gutted.'

My wife calmed down as the good news penetrated her shocked mind. I arranged to meet David Hill outside the Grid on the following day. My family wasn't hurt, there was little point in trying to drive overnight to Scarborough. In any case, looking back, I think it would have been out of the question. I was so completely shattered it took me all my time to drive my car to the nearest hotel. We had decided to accept the policeman's advice, and spend those terrible hours of darkness there.

I tried to take my wife's mind off the worry, as wide-eyed we waited for daybreak, neither one of us being able to sleep.

I asked her if she had heard the policeman's parting words, as we left the A.A. cabin.

'Yes,' she answered, 'I heard him, he said, "it was ninety, not sixty or seventy, sir. We will say nothing this time, but be careful on the way home." I will make sure of that, Peter, we have had enough trouble to last us a lifetime.'

They were two very good coppers.

Dawn eventually broke and in the pale light of a winter's morning we set off to drive those seemingly endless miles to Scarborough. Strangely, not once did it cross our minds we were again homeless. This time was spent in mental gymnastics, attempting to put together some kind of possible future. With The Silver Grid gone, it looked very bleak indeed.

By 2 p.m. we were turning into Huntriss Row, the blackened frame of the Grid standing out from its smoke affected, terraced neighbours. They, luckily, had escaped the inferno, apart from the smoke and minor damage.

As I parked our car the strong smell of burning filled the vehicle, water was pouring out of the main entrance of the Grid. David Hill stood on the pavement outside the wrecked building, a worried look upon his face as he greeted us.

'I have put Jacqueline and her grandparents into a hotel. Czar is in good kennels near by. I have booked you and Shirl into the same hotel as your family. Don't worry about the expense, Peter, we will meet all of those.'

What a great boss, his primary thought had been for the comfort of me, and my family—in spite of the huge task of sorting out the massive losses suffered in The Silver Grid, which he would eventually be responsible for in the long run, after the assessors had done their work. The three of us unhappily entered the sodden shell which just over a week ago had been our pride and joy. Three-quarters of the main bar had been saved, the back and small lounges had been completely burned out. Those beautiful timbered walls, which I had admired so much, were gone. I was heart-broken. Looking up I could see the sky through the three floors above me, it was obvious where the fire had started. It was subsequently put down to a smouldering cigarette.

We climbed the stairs to the night club. We may as well not have bothered. It, too, was a complete write off, nothing remained except stinking remnants. Our flat had also been badly damaged, our furnishings ruined by fire and water.

I imagined how very frightened my family must have been, in the midst of this terrible conflagration.

They had been rescued by telescopic ladder; four flights had to be negotiated to reach them. They were fortunate indeed to be alive, apparently the building went up like a tinder box ready for use.

Going back downstairs to the main bar, I suddenly stopped in mid stride, my boxing trophies? They had been displayed on the mantelpiece of the large fireplace in the small lounge. They had gone, all melted down to nothing in the intense heat. The cup presented to me by George Raft, the statuette given to me by Lady Docker, thirty or forty other prizes won during my amateur boxing days, treasured by me for their irreplaceable, magic memories.

I turned away, openly crying, tears choking me at this last cruel blow. Shirley put her hand in mind, comforting for she knew not what.

We owed a very alert policeman for the lives of my family, he had missed the aggressive bark of Czar as he tried the main door of the Grid. It was 1 a.m. and Czar, who was on sentry duty during the night in the main public areas of the pub, had not responded with his customary warning to the policeman. The latter immediately looked for Czar, detecting the smell of smoke as he did so. He called out the fire brigade straight away, thereby saving all the people in the house.

It was a sensible thing Czar must have done. He'd had the sense to curl up and try to get what air there was coming under the main door, probably saving his own life in this fashion. There must have been little air entering that way as it was. The thick, choking black smoke, could have killed him otherwise.

When the first fireman, a fellow named Norman Grundy, smashed in the door, he moved to enter the building and as he did so felt something big brush past him. He couldn't see what it was for he was clad in full breathing gear. It must have been a very frightened Czar, who had decided retreat was the better part of valour. He was found on the sea-front sands by a policeman who knew him, he had got as far away as possible from the red-hot nightmare, out to the cooling winds and peaceful sounds of the sea.

The friendly policeman took him into custody, to the strange world of a police station, where he fastened the still very frightened dog securely to a chair.

An incident happened then, which delighted all the coppers present.

As the policeman finished tying up Czar to the chair, the police doctor came out of a door leading off the room. He had been taking samples from a drink-drive suspect and was quite pleased with the results as they had proved positive; for the accused had been a pain in the bum throughout the procedure.

As he passed Czar, he bent and stroked his head. 'Nice doggie,' he said simperingly.

As I have told you, Czar was a very upset dog. He had literally been through hell-fire, his dignity hurt by being tethered so ignominiously to this seat and he wasn't about to take this idiot's affectation lying down. There is a limit to what even a dog can stand.

He bit the silly bugger.

Czar didn't bite as a rule, he didn't have to, his curling lip and full set of pearly whites shown to advantage were usually sufficient to deter the most foolhardy. It was a measure of his fear when he bit without any warning.

The drink-drive bloke shouted gleefully, 'serves you bloody right, you bloody bastard.'

It was a story which went the rounds for days, lightening our load as we faced the massive clean up task, for Czar was granted one bite for free. He was released with a caution.

After our tour of the devastated Silver Grid, David Hill invited Shirley and me out to lunch, late for that, yet too early to call it dinner.

'Look,' he said consolingly, 'now is the chance to do everything you have wanted to do in the Grid. When we have finished rebuilding it, you will have a place in a thousand. It will be a brand new Silver Grid.'

His words allayed our worst fears, unemployment, homeless with a bleak future, were just a few of them.

The Silver Grid was to be restored, better than before, and the best news of all, we were to be kept on the payroll.

As David Hill explained, 'the Brewery is covered by insurance, the ultimate cost of the fire is roughly estimated to be in the region of £500,000.'

This in the early seventies was a great deal of money.

'That is a lot of money,' I was forced into commenting.

'It would have been far higher, the fireman saved the building, it is still structurally sound, Peter.'

He turned to Shirley smilingly promising, 'you will have new accommodation, better than before, the good news is, it will be ready for the start of the season.'

So there really was light at the end of our tunnel. Our depression then lifted miraculously as we were reunited with an excited Jacqueline and Shirley's parents. Our daughter was now treating the whole episode as a thrilling adventure, the details of which were related over and over, to the amusement of both of her grandparents, who were no worse for wear either. We were to hear much more of their rescue by fireman's ladder; as far as Jacqueline was concerned that was the best bit.

Mr Chubb, manager of the Huntsman, received his just desert from Hill, 'how dare you give that sort of information over the phone, have you no pity?' he shouted at Chubb, as he added, 'the Silver Grid is still there, it will be for many years to come, I can assure you it will be better than ever.'

We left Mr Chubb open-mouthed and speechless, yet I still felt like strangling the heartless bugger. He had given me a lot of unnecessary worry.

From the army of workers we had seen shoring up and working feverishly, at the time of our return home, we assumed the insurance also covered loss of earnings. Within two months we had moved back into brand new accommodation, while a large assortment of workmen were putting the rest of The Silver Grid back into possible operation.

Shirley and I were given our heads to choose the wallpaper, curtains, carpets, plus all the furniture for the public areas. Working directly with the architects, it was truly exciting to see it all taking shape. Only the best materials were used, heavy red and green flock wallpaper, Wilton carpeting, with leather and oak fittings.

The time came to name the newly completed public rooms, David Hill, my wife and I sat for ages trying different ones out on each other, before the following three were considered the most suitable.

The main bar would be called The London Bar. It had red leather buttoned seats built into alcoves, and coper-topped tables.

The small lounge was to be named the Dickens Room, to commemorate Charles Dickens readings in the old building.

The back lounge was to be named after the policeman, who saved The Silver Grid from total destruction, P.C. Robson. It would be known as the Robson Lounge.

Guess who had the last say in naming the Night Club? It was to be called the Piccadilly Nite Spot. No prizes for knowing the answer to that one.

By the beginning of June we were open for business, being officially re-opened by Chris Dickens, a great, great grandson of Charles, plus being a director of Tetley.

Now I could afford to be choosy about the type of patron we allowed in. The Grid had had splendid publicity, with the media recalling its history at the time of the fire, the extensive write-ups given during its refurbishment, and the well advertised re-opening ceremony.

The whole place sparkled, from our flat down as far as the cellars, it spelt class in every room. Shirley and I were almost bursting with pride. We were responsible for a lot of the subdued glamour.

All of our former staff were reinstated to their previous positions and we also increased the labour force. I estimated this was going to be one hell of a busy season. I wasn't wrong, it turned out to be a fantastic humdinger of a year.

Among the new employees was a man named Gerald Martin McCormack. Earlier, I had engaged him as a caller in for the night club. I know this sounds a contradiction in terms, so far as vetting the public before entry is concerned, yet the only way visitors could be made aware of the Club's existence, as they promenaded Huntriss Row in search of late night entertainment, was by the calling in method.

Gerald was to stay with us for six years. He was always a good reliable chap, a Scot, but unlike his fellow countryman, Sandy Aicheson, he was of flamboyant disposition. A fast-talking, amusing bloke, if the Piccadilly was having a quiet spell he could pull customers off the street with no effort at all, by means of his humorous spiel.

He invariably carried around twenty men's ties. If someone was of acceptable dress, yet was tieless, which is not unusual in a seaside town, then Gerald would come to the rescue providing the necessary formal piece of apparel, to allow entry to the club. This way he increased his income quite substantially, most men being willing to tip well for this added service. In those days few holiday makers sported formal attire in the evenings in Scarborough. I'd turn a blind eye to this extra curricular activity; all the people thus bestowed were of decent dress and behaviour.

A night club must also have live entertainment, cabaret. The Piccadilly was no exception.

I put on a variety of acts to hold the crowds, singers, comedians, ventriloquists, hypnotists, dancers, et cetera. The membership allotment soon filled, members supporting the club well. Most nights we were packed to capacity, sometimes with Gerald's help.

At the end of that first hectic season of the rebuilt Grid, we were fit to drop, more than ready to try to take another break from this stressful labour. Hopefully, this time, it would be a less eventful one.

We went to Malta for the first time, thoroughly enjoying our maiden venture abroad, so much so, we were to repeat the visit many times over the years to come.

It was now winter, we were back in harness, our sanity restored and absolutely fighting fit after our sojourn overseas.

Scarborough had withdrawn into its customary hibernation, as in most holiday resorts, the only on-going amusements were the cinemas and public houses. This town was a very hard place in which to make money in excess of overheads during the off-season. Most businesses fought for the small extra trade conferences brought to the town. There were few businesses which ventured north for their conferences, opting for the southern resorts which offered better facilities then.

Today's more affluent society makes for a less frugal off-season. A warm sun-shiny day will bring the motorized day-tripper, plus the local populace, into the town centre and to the foreshore.

I walked along the promenade the other day . . . a warm unseasonal day it was, too. The usually threatening North Sea was as placid as a mill pond, the sands were crowded, of parking spaces for a vehicle there were none. The ice cream vendors were doing a roaring trade, a sight unknown twenty years previously, when my wife and I despaired at having a job at the Futurist Theatre during the winter.

At the moment my job was to keep the Grid open, besides make it pay its way, at least in the pub part of it.

Christmas and the New Year behind us, we were forced to close the Piccadilly during the week, there was just insufficient trade to merit keeping it open. We now had opposition in the form of two or three other night clubs all, like us, bent on surviving the winter period. Shirley and I put our heads together once more, both aware there was one other club which was more than holding its own. It had a strip show running.

Keeping to the principle of 'if you can't beat them, join them', I plumped for this measure. My wife was unsure of the wisdom of this, but as I went to pains to point out, we had the muscle to deal with any problems which might arise from too exuberant a clientele. It was to be purely an off-season expedient. We would revert to our usual mode of entertainment during the spring and summer months.

Wise or not, I won the day and went into the Girlie trade almost straight away. Sure enough it filled the Piccadilly for the three nights we opened, besides adding to the business in the Grid's three other bars.

We had our ups and downs with the girls, many a belly laugh after some of the hare-brained acts, too.

One stripper, Samantha, was beautifully endowed in every imaginable way. Hers was a fire blowing performance, which she enacted very skilfully while re-moving her clothing. A most popular act it was too, and because of this I used her on many occasions.

An incident stands out which involved this voluptuous female. One evening while blowing a long streamer of fire over her bared shoulder, she set the bloody stage curtains alight. I ran for the fire extinguisher, spraying the material, stage and Samantha in one continuous burst of foam, as her wig had also caught alight.

There was little damage done.

Samantha, the stripper and fire blower.

During the commotion Samantha had run off stage, using the back staircase which led to the dressing rooms.

We quietened and settled down the startled customers all ready to begin the show again. There was one thing wrong with that idea—the star was missing. Samantha hadn't reappeared to do her stuff for at least five minutes. I took the back stairs two at a time to get her, yelling as I went, 'Samantha, you're on.'

'I'm in here,' came the muffled rejoinder from the bathroom.

I burst into the room without knocking, exasperated beyond words, to find the star sitting in a bath of cold water. Amazed, I stared at her belligerently before I managed to blurt out, 'what the bloody hell do you think you are doing in there?'

'You bloody idiot,' she stormed, 'you sprayed that bloody stuff on my minge, it stings like bloody hell.'

I almost fell down the stairs laughing, it struck me as so funny, yet I guess it must have been very painful. For a long time afterwards, the expression 'Minge' was used whenever anyone referred to a lady's hidden asset.

Like a good trouper Samantha finished her performance. As I paid her fee that night, she said plaintively, 'stay away from me with that bloody fire extinguisher in future, next time let me burn, it will be less painful.'

Although I had cruelly laughed, besides telling a lot of the crowd to explain her prolonged absence, I realize now it must have been truly agonizing. Cold water had been the only obvious alleviation for such a sensitive area.

Princess Allisia, another stripper, also used fire in her act. She was a fire dancer as well as being a strikingly good looking woman. She claimed to be of Italian-Hungarian descent. In the manner of the noted film star Zsa Zsa Gabor she, too, spoke with a heavily accented voice, using sexy body language to its fullest extent.

'Darlink', and 'I love you, darlink', were her two more used, or should I say over-used, expressions on all possible occasions.

Peter Pitts, aptly named for a strip artiste's agent, ran the agency from which I obtained my girls. He called in one evening during her act. As he stood watching her performance with me, he suddenly asked, 'do you know how old she is, Peter?'

'No, but getting on a bit I suspect. I guess she is about thirty-one or two,' I answered in my youthful arrogance.

'Forty-seven is nearer the mark, though you wouldn't peg her for it.'

'I don't believe you,' I staunchly defended her.

If it was true she was the most remarkably preserved woman one could envisage. I often wondered what her real age was after that night.

One evening when she was appearing at the Grid, I went up to the dressing room to tell her how many times I wanted her on stage and at the same time collect her music tapes from her. The club's disc jockey could then play the music for her entry and throughout the performance. I always called her Princess, it kept her happy, it didn't bother me any to play along with the game. As I walked into the room, I called out, 'Princess?'

Princess Allisia, stripper and author's temptress.

'Yes, darlink, I am in the bathroom.'

I walked into the bathroom, there she was without a stitch on, one foot up on the side of the bath, painting her toenails.

Averting my eyes skywards, I said, 'two long spots tonight, Princess.'

'Oh, you are so bashful, darlink. These are my working clothes, don't let it worry you, darlink,' she said teasingly, before adding the contemplative, saucy invitation. 'Why don't you send your wife away for a week? What a wonderful time we could have, you and I.'

She had me stammering, trying to beat a hasty retreat for the door. That lovely, seductive, naked lady thoroughly enjoyed every moment of my discomfiture.

Backing out of the room, I turned to meet my wife's stormy eyes as she angrily flounced away, with me in pursuit, protesting, 'she was kidding, don't be silly, she was only pulling my leg.'

'She wasn't kidding, I am not kidding, she doesn't work here again.'

Shirley was furious, yet she eventually relented and we did use the Princess again. Allisia was a good draw card for the night club. Above all else my wife is a consummate business woman. That will always override any personal prejudice she may harbour.

Nevertheless, she remained wary of Allisia, making sure I was never able to speak with her alone. Thank God, I hadn't gone along with the tease, when the Princess invited me to get rid of Shirley for a week. There actually would have been hell to pay, for Shirley would never have believed it was all just a naughty game.

The other strip club in town was called The Fiesta. It was owned by Fred Feast, a Scarborough man who was later to become known as Fred Gee of the long running television soap, *Coronation Street*.

Fred approached me one day in The Silver Grid, with a proposition.

'Look here, Peter, why don't we bring one stripper into town at a time? That way we can both save money, she can do two spots at each club. Say, starting with me at 9.30 p.m., you at 10.30, me again at 11.30 and, say, you again at 12.30. We can always alter the times if, at any stage, they are unsuitable to either of us.'

This sounded sensible, I was bringing strippers from as far afield as Sheffield, Leeds, Bradford, through the agency of Peter Pitts. Fred brought his from the other side of the Pennine Range, Manchester. Although strippers were a big draw, they were also expensive acts to stage, pooling those costs could make them a far more viable project.

All went well with our arrangement, until one very busy Saturday night when a packed Piccadilly Club sat waiting restlessly for the stripper to make her appearance. The girl was named Magic Myra, a Sheffield girl, and a typical no-nonsense female of that city. Her act included a live python and my first thought was something had gone wrong in the show at the Fiesta, although Myra had assured me the snake was harmless. I tried several times to phone Fred Feast at his club, to no avail. No one was answering phones in that establishment.

I ran hot-foot through Scarborough to the other club. On my arrival, Myra was just going on stage to perform her act. Fred had altered the times without our agreed consultation. I was livid. Angrily, I got stuck into him in public.

'You bloody idiot, I have a packed house in the Piccadilly waiting for her to appear, at the advertised time. They aren't happy and neither am I.

We had an arrangement where both had to give consent for alterations to the schedule.'

He wasn't at all apologetic, in fact the opposite. There was a right royal argument following on this, which ended with my walking out, spitting chips and our special partnership blown asunder.

I made my way back to the Piccadilly to face a disorderly crowd screaming for Myra and her writhing companion. I managed to keep them under control, until she arrived to fulfil her two spot contract. She had the python nonchalantly wrapped around her shoulders.

'I haven't had time to put Monty away,' she explained, as she hurried towards the stage, to appease the howling mob, past the hastily retreating people anxious to avoid both her and Monty.

Myra had walked through the town centre, a whopping great python entwined round her body. She must have frightened half of Scarborough to death. I could imagine the reaction of the masses on seeing such a reptile loose. They were not to know the snake was harmless as I had been assured it was. I didn't believe it, neither would ninety per cent of the world's population. Those slithering, cold, reptilian vertebrates, have a right to life equally as much as I, though it would be preferable to yours truly it be as far away as possible.

Later that evening Ken called me down to the front entrance, where two burly coppers stood waiting.

'Has a woman walked in here with a bloody great snake decorating her bosom?' one of them asked unbelievingly.

'Yes,' I answered, explaining the contretemps to the pair. They both thought the story hilarious.

'Please tell her to put the bloody thing away in future,' one of them said between hearty laughs.

His companion butted in with, 'she has scared two little old ladies to death. God only knows what she has done to the drinking habits of Scarborians. None of them will ever be the same again.'

The break with The Fiesta didn't harm me business-wise. Fred was devoting more and more time to acting and finally closed The Fiesta about two years later. We prospered and in those days that was all that mattered. Fred Feast did try a few more business ventures in the town, none of which I knew to be successful, before he settled for the barman's job in *Coronation Street* exclusively.

Shirley would often remark as she watched Fred on the television set, 'he doesn't do much acting. All he does is learn the lines, a very easy way to make a living, isn't it?'

She wasn't far wrong. Wish I had taken up acting lessons, it would be a damned easier job than mine, I bet.

I continued to try different innovations in the Piccadilly, attempting to keep those all important takings on the rise. The basic staples however remained the same. My music group was called the Piccadilly Circus. Television repair men by day, musicians by night, extremely talented besides being very popular, they broke up just over two years later, when two of them emigrated to Australia. More's the pity for they were accomplished enough to have made it to the Big Time.

Another employee was Roy Fletcher, a bus driver by day, moonlighting as a disc jockey among other things, in the Piccadilly Club. As well as playing records plus ad libbing while the group took their breaks off stage, he had further enviable tasks. One of his duties was to play the strippers' music for them. After the completion of the act he collected the discarded clothing from the stage floor and following the star off stage he'd pass it to her before she reached the dressing room.

'I must have the best bloody job in England,' he used to boast, 'I get a good close up view every time, and what a view!'

Ken would then attempt to steal his thunder by saying, 'give me Fletcher's bloody job, I bet I could do a better job of collecting the clothes off the floor than he does.'

'You're not having it, I will do it for bloody nothing before I will let that jealous bugger take it.'

The Silver Grid was a happy place, the staff long serving and content. Back-biting was a thing of the past, for which Shirley and I were grateful; we had had enough of that to last a lifetime. Jacqueline settling in school was proving Reg Beaumont's words true, she was showing every sign of becoming a very clever girl. Reg unfortunately, was still languishing in jail. I knew he would be genuinely pleased about Jacqueline for he was indeed fond of her despite his many other faults.

Everything in our garden was lovely, then Madam Fate decided to deal yet another blow to shatter this idyllic quietude of mind.

Chapter 9

S EPTEMBER, 1972, came around, bringing with it the most traumatic period of my life.

My mother loved Doncaster Race Week, the week when the classic St Léger horse race is run. It had always been for as long as I could remember, the highlight of her year, her annual holiday, for she had known no other. One she enjoyed more than many who spent fortunes chasing the dream. In this week she could pit her wits against the bookies face to face, many of whom she was on first name terms with. Always on the nonpaying section of the course, known as the free course, over the years she had become a familiar figure to many bookmakers; particularly if they hailed from her home city of Sheffield, of which a sizeable number did.

More often than not she would have visitors to her home, to share the pleasure with. One instance Kate recalls, Mam had gone to the large fair which always was a part of race week celebrations in Doncaster. She found Mam sat at a Bingo Stall with friends. Now Bingo was not mother's game, horses were more in her line. As soon as she saw Kate approaching, she waved her card at her complaining, 'I can't play any more all my spaces are filled up.'

She had to share the prize because of her ignorance, someone else calling 'Bingo', as Kate did. My sister felt angrier than Mam, who thought it a funny kind of entertainment anyway, when the winner could be a loser too. The year 1972 wasn't going to leave that kind of happy memory, just a sadness that still lingers all these many years later. That year she suffered a stroke leaving us, without a goodbye, only a whopping great hole in our lives we have found absolutely impossible to fill.

She had been my best friend, a confidante unequalled, had gone hungry so that I might eat. She had pushed and shoved me, often in spite of my diffidence, to make something of myself. Never again would I hear her little giggle, or her chastising, 'get those shoulders back, stand straight, walk tall. Look people in the eye, you are as good as anyone else.'

Beyond any doubt, she had been the inspiration for everything I had ever done which was good. She gave me the confidence I had always lacked, with her comforting assurance of, 'you can do it.'

We were to miss her greatly in the coming years.

Kate returned to Scarborough with me after Mam's funeral. She had busted her ankle after the interment, so couldn't walk. She was to fly out to Philadelphia, in the United States of America, to rejoin her husband there. Which she did, but it was many weeks later before she was fit to travel.

To pass the time, she sat outside the Piccadilly Night Club, issuing tickets in return for the entrance fee. She knew nothing of The Silver Grid's history. It was her first visit to the pub, although her husband is a Scarborian and she knows the town well.

One night around midnight she dashed, hobbling, into the Piccadilly, the place almost full of merrymakers, causing one hell of a din. A less likely place for manifestations of the supernatural, you couldn't find.

'I am not doing that job any more,' Kate exclaimed. 'Something, or someone had just put their hand on my shoulder. There wasn't anyone there to do that, only me. I was quite alone.'

'Now, Kate, Mam had a habit of doing that with me, it will only be Mam.'

'Mam wouldn't do that, she would know I'd be frightened to death.'

I brushed her fears aside, reiterating, 'it is Mam, letting you know she is here.'

I know now Kate didn't swallow that for an instant. She had already buttonholed Shirley about being outside the bathroom door, besides passing the room without speaking.

Of course this wasn't my wife, or anyone else we could hold to account for being in the passageway, which was part of our private quarters. Both Shirley and myself were at times aware of someone being outside the door of the bathroom, or passing along the corridor. This passage used to connect with the old dressing rooms, in the Grid's theatre days. I guess you could say we were haunted, if you believe in such things. We never saw anything in all the years we were there, Kate being the only person I know who was actually touched.

At the time I deemed it wiser to play down my sister's experience, we had all been through enough, without adding things which go bump in the night. Whatever, or whoever it was, appeared content to promenade that passageway, or loiter outside the bathroom door, a possible voyeur spectre, who knows? They are here during their life span. If there is a possibility of return to this world after death, then why not them, too?

The passageway ended directly above the flight of stairs, leading down to the Piccadilly entrance, where Kate had sat to issue the tickets.

By this time my wife and I were firmly established as Joshua Tetley's top beer sales management, easily so in Scarborough. For years after we left The Silver Grid, the brewery's delivery men would talk of the days when they could load a full lorry and trailer for The Silver Grid alone. Shirley and I had more than justified David Hill, the area manager's confidence in us. We were to bask in his favour in recognition of this.

In 1973 Charlie Williams, the comedian, came to Scarborough for the season, as head of the Bill at the Floral Hall.

Shirley adored the man. She would cook a big meal for him most evenings after he had finished his stint at the theatre. He would sit quietly in the Piccadilly, watching the cabaret, until it was time for him to return to his hotel. Charlie was another man I had known from the fifties, when I was boxing and living at home in Doncaster. He was then playing centre-half for Doncaster Rovers, the local football team. He was a good player too, he could easily have made it as a footballer if he hadn't turned to comedy and the stage.

His slow, slyly delivered threat, 'I'll come and live next door to you, that'll bring the price of your property down,' would slay the audience from John o' Groats to Land's End. A jet black man with a broad Yorkshire accent he tilted at the racialist windmill of distrust and fear doing far more for race relations than marches and violence will ever do. Who could be prejudiced when one's sides ached from laughter, as this man undermined all one's bigoted fears and hatred, with barbed, yet good-natured, gentle satire.

Gerald Martin McCormack, or Martin as he preferred to be called, my ebullient Scots doorman, would capitalize on Charlie's presence to the very maximum, remarking to everyone within earshot, 'Charlie Williams is in the Piccadilly Club.'

We would have people queuing all the way up the stairs to see him, the cabaret, a secondary consideration. Such was the extent of this wonderful man's popularity in Britain.

Shirley and Peter Aldridge with Charlie Williams, The Silver Grid, 1973.

I have heard Martin on many occasions tell likely customers Charlie was in the club, long after he had actually left. With a straight face, and an apologetic air, he would answer their complaints on leaving. 'Sorry, I have been busy, I didn't notice him leaving. He will be back tomorrow for sure, he is here most evenings.'

He was one crafty con-merchant, likeable, and a great club caller. When I had to take him to task, this was pretty frequently, he could get round me with little problem, making me forget the reason I was pulling him up. Often I would overhear him telling people, 'great guy, the boss, great guy.'

Who could stay annoyed with a bloke like that?

Notwithstanding, I must stress he was a great fellow, who did a wonderful job for us for in excess of six years. Breaking the ground rules regularly, yet unfailingly perky and never, never sulky. Taking brickbats and bouquets with the same wry grin, then I honestly believe nothing disturbed him for long.

Especially fond of Czar, he would take him for walks around Scarborough, both morning and night, after he had finished work. A few years later when I broke the news of Czar's death to him, he stood and wept unashamed. That almost broke me up, believe me.

The Silver Grid never could shake off the dubious reputation completely. The ghost of its troublesome past kept rearing its ever ugly head. As with every other large public house in the centre of a seaside resort, it was fair game for every visiting rabble rouser and prostitute. It was impossible to police it, one could only hope to control it. Control it we did, the only successful way known to man, by using the heavy iron hand. This required an acute understanding of the workings of those befuddled brains, knowing when to apply pressure, or when to humour the buggers. Both systems work, the secret is knowing when to use what.

How to talk to the crepuscular human species, particularly the ladies, for this was still the age where the males remained in the twilight. The women were becoming more blatant, pushing their wares to both sexes and in broad daylight. A forerunner of the loosening of accepted standards, bringing with it all the headaches which would ensue world-wide.

The troublemakers were harder to contain, their idea of a good day at the seaside was to create anarchy. Forming mobs they roamed the town's streets, looking for a lively spot to invade. Their aim to smash or break whatever fell within their reach, starting fights in the bars being easily the quickest way to achieve this. Cowards by nature, they used their numbers to intimidate other patrons into defending themselves. Before one could say Jack Robinson there was a full scale battle under way.

To counter this type of lawlessness we used differing types of doormen. Sandy Aicheson, who could talk a raging bull into good natured placidity. Ill-fated Sandy, who broke his neck playing rugby for Scarborough, becoming a paraplegic, confined for life to a wheelchair.

The volatile Ken Oldroyd, who could match the destructive elements punch for mastering punch, if needs be. Of course I was never averse to letting them know I was an ex-boxer of some repute, better a deterrent any day, than a wild physical showdown. Regretfully a lot of them were too intent on mayhem, or too thick to grasp the consequences of such action, then force had to be brought into play as expediently and expeditiously as possible, before havoc was wrought.

The ladies of easy virtue were more tractable, thank the Lord. As I have told you they brought a certain type of business. No matter the aversion this may summon up, it is all part and parcel of being a publican. No amount of glossing will remove that fact of life, one could only keep the lower end of the trade out. God knows they were easy enough to spot.

The rest abided by the Grid's code of behaviour, or else they were banned from lucrative pastures. As a general rule they respected this principle apart from the insuppressible, lovable, unfortunate Jenny Cross.

Scarborough was still a port, albeit a very tiny one, timber imported from the Continent was its main function. The seamen off those ships and boats were easy prey for the street walkers and the Grid's variety of prostitute. One of those women we knew as Woodboat Winnie. She and Jenny Cross made good pickings taking the sailors for all their cash, cigarettes, wine and spirits. No doubt with more than willing participation from the seafarers.

There was a most profitable trade for the ladies too, when the boats had gone. The two of them would come into The Silver Grid with all their booty, bags full of whisky, gin, vodka and cigarettes, all export quality. They would be paid handsomely, for none was for home consumption, ready buyers came out of the woodwork in every direction.

Shirley had her own thing going with them, some elements of which I did not quite approve, even though they had more than willing victims for their scam.

On one occasion they brought a Turkish seaman into the Grid, a member of the crew of a German timber boat, berthed in the harbour. They went into the Robson Lounge where my wife was holding the fort as usual. Apparently the Turk spent money as if there were no tomorrow.

Shirley told me later, 'he was peeling notes from a bundle which would have choked a donkey, the women had never had it so good or so easy. He let them have whatever they asked for.'

The scam with Winnie and Jenny was to serve them singles, when the actual order was for doubles. My wife would then chalk this up for them against the time when they were broke. If the liquor was too heavy for them, they would go on a less potent brew, double vodka and coke, more often than not this would be straight coke. The latter applied on this particular day.

I was in the Robson Lounge at closing time, when Jenny asked Shirley, 'what have we in, Shirley?'

'Twenty-two each,' my wife replied.

That was twenty-two nips of vodka each, to their credit. I called Shirley to one side, for in my estimation they had gone too bloody far.

'This is sheer bloody robbery, Shirley.'

'No, it is not, the drinks were bought for them without coercion, they just haven't had them yet that's all. I do not convert it to cash, they must take it all in cigarettes or drinks.'

The dividing line between what she was doing and robbery was very thin, no wonder she got on well with Jenny and the others. They all thought my wife was the bee's knees, there was no doubt in my mind about that either. I let it go, a decision I regretted later.

When we reopened at 5.30 p.m., the first in the bar were Jenny, Winnie and the little Turk. The ladies were loaded with parcels, they had taken the poor little bugger shopping, and Taken was the operative word. He was still being fleeced. I put all the packages on top of the cellar steps for them, in doing so I grabbed Jenny by the arm.

'Don't you think you have done him for enough?' I asked.

'Not yet,' she gave me a crafty wink. 'Don't worry, he's got plenty, he is loaded.'

At about nine-thirty that night I saw the Turk standing talking to Ken by the entrance door. He was alone, there was no sign of the ladies. The Turk waved me over to them, saying in broken, stumbling English, 'Jeeney gone, Weeney gone, mooney gone,' he pointed at himself ruefully adding, 'me gone.'

He walked out of the Grid and I never saw him again. I was so sorry for the poor, unworldly bloke, diminutive not only in stature, he had come up against the two hardest harlots in Scarborough.

The following day I took the pair of unmentionables to one side, very angry at their despicable treatment of the simple Turk.

'You couple of bastards,' I raged, 'you cleaned the poor little sod out.'

'He loved every bloody minute of it too, he can't wait to go and earn some more money and get back to us,' Winnie gloated.

I doubted that, if nothing else the sorrowful Turk had been taught one hell of an expensive lesson.

Although I thought their behaviour beyond description, and still do, the memory of the Turk's parting words, can still summon a wry smile.

Winnie and Jenny both fell about laughing when, relenting, I told them of the man's last comments before departing from The Silver Grid.

It made little or no effect on them, for months the two incorrigible offenders would say to me on leaving the hotel, 'Weeney gone, Jeeney gone.'

They were outrageous, yet somehow I could not stay angry at them for long, or ever hate either of them. The light hearted banter, the repartee, made and cheered even the dullest day behind those bars.

On one occasion I overheard Jenny remark to her sister, 'I've got one like a mouse's ear-hole.'

'Yes, a hippopotamouse,' came the succinct reply.

In 1975, when Jenny Cross died in a car crash, I made it my business to be at the funeral. As they lowered her coffin into the ground, the Turk's stumbling words came to mind.

'Jeeney gone.'

The 1974 season was another good one for the Grid. I had twenty-two people on the staff, including the cleaners, this in itself denoted hard work. Besides the hotel being on normal licensed hours, we had the Piccadilly open until 2 a.m. during the spring and summer months. My wife and I averaged between four to five hours sleep per night, during the season. It was body punishing labour within an establishment which was virtually a powder keg with a smouldering short fuse. The only sanity restoring features were the diverse characters who frequented The Silver Grid. Their antics and humour kept both of us of sound mind.

Though some were apt to give both Shirley and me considerable head-aches at times, they remain among our treasured memories, as will the Grid.

Chris Dickens, the Tetley director, who as I have told you, was Charles Dickens' great, great grandson, was a regular visitor to the hotel. Both my wife and I liked him very much indeed. The Silver Grid did hold a fascination for the man and he would sit for hours in the Dickens Lounge. This was a splendid room, oak-panelled from floor to ceiling. Its walls were adorned with polished horse brasses, as well as pictures depicting scenes · from Dickens' novels. Warmly glowing copper-topped tables, plus subdued lighting lent an old worldly atmosphere, an air of a more tranquil bygone age.

Chris Dickens invariably asked if he could enter our private flat. Once inside, he would head for a central window immediately, to stand staring through it as if in search of something. This window overlooked the old theatre which the Piccadilly false ceiling now covered. In this auditorium great old, carved, wooden heads laughed, or frowned down on what was then just a blank empty space, apart from the original theatre rail, behind which the theatre-goers of the nineteenth century had stood to watch and listen, as the immensely talented Charles Dickens read his own work to cast his spell upon them. Transporting the audience to a world of his making, full of scoundrels, urchins, orphans and the wealthy taking advantage of the poor woebegones. All the ingredients updated to make today's classics and like Will Shakespeare he rules supreme.

The fidgeting crowds had long dispersed from this theatre they, too, belonged to the shadows now, all that remained was a brooding silence and . . . I really cannot believe in ghosts *per se*. Like Kate, I think there is some rational explanation for everything. I stress this before I go on with my story. However, there are times when logic deserts me, leaving me bewildered and not a little unsure of my beliefs.

You will understand better if I tell you of an incident in The Silver Grid, one I cannot explain. You can then make up your own mind. Is there? Or isn't there?

The Piccadilly always had an eerie feel to it when it was empty, a place where no one dwelt long, particularly yours truly. Czar, my faithful, obedient Alsatian dog, refused steadfastly to enter the room at night, or when the place was unoccupied. He would stand at the door, his hackles up, stubbornly refusing to go any further. They say dogs have a sixth sense, I do not know how true that is, I only know Czar used to scare and anger me, when he baulked at entering the room. All the while his eyes beseeched me not to force him inside, my threats and cajolement useless on every occasion.

About this time my brother Allan, came over from Doncaster, bringing with him a lot of my old friends, Tommy Penrice, George Meehan, Pete Platts, Basher Bell, my trainer from my boxing days, and Jack Rutherford. It was a grand reunion, a time for reminiscence. The season was over, we had time to talk, to laugh as we relived the good carefree days of our youth.

Tommy joshed George about the snow-bound bus incident, saying, 'I am glad the car didn't break down, George would have been sure to offer to fetch help, you all know what that could have lead to,'

'Clever bugger,' George snorted, 'I never once heard you volunteering for anything. You were always first off the mark otherwise.'

True enough, George had him there, Tommy was always reticent when it came to offering his services, or anything else for that matter. He sheepishly smiled, taking George's rebuke without retaliation. We reviewed our past into the late hours, but it was of no matter as they were staying overnight.

We hadn't the room to accommodate them all in the flat, Shirley suggested we slept the lot of them in the Piccadilly. We had no qualms about this as there were six men in all. There was plenty of wide, comfortable seating in the club, which we pushed together to form beds, my wife providing a pile of blankets and pillows for their extra comfort. There were a number of toilets and washing facilities in the place too. The arrangements were ideal, they could lie-in without being disturbed by the early cleaning staff, or anyone else for that matter, when we opened the hotel. Czar as usual hadn't entered the room. He lay just outside the double glass doors, a worried look on his face, his ears pricked.

'Leave Czar with us tonight,' Allan said unexpectedly.

'I can't do that, Allan. He has a job to do downstairs at night.'

I hadn't the courage to tell them Czar wouldn't go in there at any price, or for that matter any bribe, at night time. I honestly thought there would be safety in numbers, that they would enjoy an undisturbed night. Fear of ridicule stopped me from telling them of something which may have been all in our imagination. Or so I told myself. If the truth be known, I was well aware how nervous George Meehan could be when confronted by the unusual.

Years before as young men, we were walking home late at night, after escorting two girls back to where they lived. As we passed the low stone wall which enclosed Armthorpe Church and graveyard, a drunk suddenly popped up from behind the wall, pleadingly asking, 'will you give me a hand in helping me over this bloody wall, and off this sodding grave?'

Without a sound George fled, not giving me a backward glance and leaving me to cope with whatever he thought it was. I helped the inebriate off the grave, more in respect of the dead than for his benefit, then I followed George. He was at least half a mile away by the time I caught up with him, sitting at the side of the road, his head in his hands, shaking like an aspen leaf; definitely in a state of extreme shock. Try as I might I couldn't convince him it was only a stupid drunk, and not a ghost risen from the dead.

I guess you will agree with me, talk of the supernatural was categorically not on in George's presence, unless I wanted him legging it for Doncaster. I said goodnight to my guests as they settled down to sleep, turning in myself almost immediately, to fall asleep as soon as my head hit the pillow.

I was awakened by a loud thumping on the bedroom door, my brother shouting loud enough to wake the dead, 'come downstairs straight away, Boy, there is something queer going on in the club.'

As I had only been asleep for about an hour I really wasn't interested in queer happenings anywhere. However, the urgency in his voice penetrated my sleep dazed mind. I scrambled out of bed, following Allan downstairs into the Piccadilly. All the lights were on, the whole group were sitting on the settees in the centre of the room, with the exception of George. He was lying full length, blankets drawn tight around his neck, his face a drawn white mask.

Allan hushed the babble of voices which greeted me.

'Let me tell him what has happened, then you can all have your say.'

Turning to me he started his story.

'Boy, at around 1.30 a.m. it went as cold as hell in here, so cold in fact, it woke us all up. We couldn't understand this for it had been as warm as toast in the room when we went to sleep.' He looked hard at me before adding, 'as it is now.'

Angrily I whipped on him.

'Cut the crap, Allan, the central heating cuts in and out, it does it automatically. It cannot turn freezing cold, the thermostat would cut in to bring the temperature back up long before that could happen.'

'Tell him about the bloody light,' yelled George.

'I am coming to that, will you shut up, George, for God's sake.'

Allan continued with his tale.

'As we sat discussing the cold, you said we couldn't have, wondering whether to wake you up to ask you what had gone wrong with the heating, the chandelier above us started to slowly spin round.'

'All right, you have all had your bloody fun, you lot can stop playing silly buggers.' I stormed on, 'I am losing badly needed sleep, bloody lights going round! What kind of idiot do you think I am?'

'It isn't funny, Boy. At least not funny ha ha,' Allan shook his head, 'I tell you there is something queer going on in here.'

'Peter, I saw somebody standing at the back of the seats. I thought it was you but when I turned to speak there was nothing there.'

Jack Rutherford, unlike Allan, was not a practical joker, always a staid, set in his ways fellow, he actually believed he had seen someone behind those seats. Now he was a very frightened man.

I looked at George, who lay there as if paralysed, eyes open to their fullest extent to match his mouth.

'It is imagination, Lads, this is a very old building. We have lived here for four years and seen nothing. Our Kate claimed someone had put their hand on her shoulder when she was sitting outside this door, yet Czar will lie there without any bother. I will stay with you for the rest of the night, what possible harm can come to us in here? Do be sensible.'

'We don't need you, you would only compound the problem, fetch Czar in here. He should have been in here in the first place, then this probably wouldn't have happened. I tell you there is something bloody funny peculiar about this room,' Allan finished heatedly.

'He won't come into this place at night, or when it is empty,' I finished lamely. Taking a deep breath I waited for the explosion of condemnation, they were too stunned. I hurried on before they could recover, 'we have always thought there was something strange about this room, but we have seen nothing, or ever heard anything to substantiate the perception. What would you have said if I had told you, that I thought there was something about this room I couldn't put my finger on? You would have never let me live it down, besides telling the story to all and sundry.'

I deemed it wiser not to tell them about the upstairs passageway, I was in over my head, without begging for it.

George in the meantime had struggled off the settee, and was now dashing towards the doorway, dressed only in underpants and short socks, futilely trying to wrap his blanket around his body as he went.

'I'm not stopping here,' he yelled.

'Neither am I,' the six foot of Jack Rutherford towered over the group as he stood up. He looked at the faces of his friends before adding, 'I am game for anything, but I draw the line at bloody this.'

'Look,' Allan said reasoning, 'if Czar will not come in here, this place is haunted. You cannot fool animals, they have a much stronger sixth sense than us of anything abnormal.'

'And he bloody put us in here for the night, some bloody friend!' shouted George from the safety of the doorway, pointing his finger at me accusingly.

'All right I was wrong, I apologize. Calm down, George, whatever was here, isn't here now, is it?' I said as soothingly as I knew how.

George looked fearfully round the room, then reluctantly shook his head. I suggested we all went upstairs to the flat for a much needed drink. A suggestion which no one objected to, not so much as the need for a reviver, but to leave the Piccadilly and its unexplainable, spooky experience behind.

George was first up the stairs, heading immediately for the bathroom and toilet. I couldn't resist a quiet smile, for little did he know that was one area where my family and I were convinced something did dally.

I prayed that this would be one night when, whoever, or whatever it was, decided enough was enough. Otherwise George would be a cot case.

A truly perturbed Shirley made coffee for the lot of us. It had been her idea for them to sleep in the club and, like me, she believed nothing untoward could possibly happen. Most used the coffee as a chaser, a much stronger liquid was required to oil their frazzled nerves.

The thought of sleep now driven from our heads, we talked the night away. I addressed a quietened, yet still churlish George. 'I am going to ask you if you would like to spend a week here in the pub. I don't want this episode to spoil our friendship, we go back a long way you and me. I can assure you the hotel is not haunted, it is just that damned room which has something wrong with it.' I watched for his reaction before continuing, 'what do you say? It will make a nice break for you.'

'Forget it,' he snarled, 'I wouldn't stay here, if you paid me a thousand quid for the week. Not on your bloody life, I wouldn't.'

Pete Platts who had been extremely quiet throughout the whole incident, now put in his twopennyworth of obviously well thought out rationality.

'Peter, you need a priest in that room.'

'What are you talking about, Pete?'

'To exorcise the room, Dummy,' Pete explained, exasperated that he had to clarify why one should require a priest.

George, unchanged by the years, dropped one of his gems that only he, quite unintentionally, could do so ludicrously well.

'Exercise? You would get enough bloody exercise running around here, why bring a priest in for that?' he blurted out. That sent us all into hysterical laughter, in which George joined, very relieved as well as mightily pleased that things were back to normality, though he did not take up my offer of staying on for a week.

Later that day he made his goodbyes with the rest of them. Shirley and I watched my friends leave, partly in sorrow; a lot of our life was tied in with those fellows. We re-entered the Grid, tired and not a little shaken by the events of the previous night. I was determined now to get to the bottom of the mysterious affair. There had to be an answer, maybe it was the foundations?

We spoke to David Hill about the whole mystifying episode. Besides the unaccountable feeling we had in the Piccadilly and our passageway, I also told him of Czar's blunt refusal to enter the club when it was empty.

He was as nonplussed as we were and more than keen to find the cause. Against his betted judgement he dismissed a building fault as unlikely. This would not frighten the dog at a particular time, nor would it give a person a sense of strangeness.

He knew of a man who worked for Tetley's Brewery, in Leeds. This chap apparently delved in the supernatural. He came over to The Silver Grid on Mr Hill's instructions. On entering the pub, without further ado, he headed for the Piccadilly Club. He walked around the room slowly for a few minutes, then asked to be taken upstairs to our flat. We showed him the marvellous carved heads within sight of the old theatre, above the false ceiling of the club. He made no comment whatsoever, as he gazed at the still, empty expanse of the auditorium, before returning once more to the Piccadilly. He stood in the middle of the room and with closed eyes intoned, 'I have a strong presence here, a very strong presence.' he repeated.

As far as Shirley and I were concerned, this vindicated the lads.

We really believe, not in ghosts *per se*, but in the lonely wanderings of something. Or, rather, the re-enactment of some long forgotten event, trapped in the ether for perpetuity, because of its strong emotional content. A theatre would be the ideal site to find such a phenomenon.

Later talking to Chris Dickens about the incident, I jokingly said, 'it may be Charles Dickens himself.'

'By Jove, you may be right. I would love to meet my great, great grandpappy,' was his ebullient reply.

Whatever, or whoever, never strayed from the confines of the passageway and the Piccadilly Club. Nowhere in the building, from the cellars up, apart from the aforementioned areas, did one discern anything unusual. We lived there quite happily, accepting the unknown as part of life at the Grid. The word spread among the customers that The Silver Grid was haunted, a few maintained they had known this for years.

One of the old barmaids, a lady named Mabel, as well as the longest serving cleaner, a woman called Anne, both claimed to have seen something over the years. As in Jack Rutherford's case they were unable to say what, the vague image vanishing immediately on being sighted.

It wasn't friendly, neither was it unfriendly. Kate felt a touch, but not the cold. Was it Mary Agnes comforting her, or was it our unknown spectre? Or was it just a figment of all our imaginations? Maybe Czar knew.

He could not tell us, although he tried his best to let us know something was amiss in the Piccadilly.

I didn't call in a priest. Looking back I believe I thought it would be an admission of the paranormal. I wasn't ready to admit that, then or now. Anyway how can you rid yourself of shades which are only encapsulations of previous events, as in a moving picture?

With the end of 1974 came our usual staff Christmas party. The Silver Grid continued to prosper trade-wise as 1975 blustered in. We were saddened to learn David Hill was to leave us early in the New Year. He was leaving Tetley's Brewery to join Ansells, although both were part of the giant Allied Brewers empire. David, of course, had gained a well deserved promotion. Shirley and I always like to think we had played a part in this, through our undoubted success at The Silver Grid. He had been a great boss as well as a good friend and we were to miss him badly.

His replacement as area manager was a Mr Cathcart, an ex-commander in the Royal Navy. Surprisingly, he was a nice, gentle type of bloke, although lacking the charisma of David Hill. Cathcart found it more than difficult, for Hill was a hard act to follow, one which I would not have liked to have undertaken.

Regardless of this, we got on well with Mr Cathcart. He quickly understood the difficulties of running the toughest, busiest house in his area, giving us all the help within his power. However, things were changing dramatically, not only in the Tetley hierarchy, where Mr Forsyth had died, but in the booze business itself.

The summer trade in Scarborough altered slowly but surely. As one of our leaders so succinctly put it, the British working class had never had it so good. Holidays abroad were the order of the day, a quick weekend in Paris, the accepted norm. Costa Blanca and Costa del Sol on Spain's Mediterranean shore, pinched the trade British resorts had always known. Scots month showed a distinct downturn on previous years. Nevertheless, The Silver Grid held its own, while other licensees in the town felt the draught. One couldn't blame the average holiday maker. He could spend his annual vacation in Spain for half the cost of a similar holiday in Britain. Plus the added surety of almost guaranteed sunshine. He could cheerfully leave his umbrella at home, forgetting about rain insurance too, as well as being assured of obtaining his favourite nosh with his preferred entertainment on hand.

The Spanish, with the aid of ex-patriots, had turned that sun-drenched coastline into a high-rise Blackpool. Fish and chips had relegated paella and all other fish stews to the offbeat back alley bistros. English type pubs run by the British abounded, the Cabaret in the many Night Clubs, acceded to the fact this was Spanish territory, by putting on the dancing Gypsy complete with castanets. Thus giving the whole a romantic aura as well as giving the tourist a feeling of being abroad, in spite of being among things familiar. In fact he was having his cake and eating it, while the British seaboard would never be the same again.

To the seaside landlord and landlady, the publican and hotel keeper, it was the beginning of the death of all things familiar. My wife and I were sorry to see the change. Scarborough was our chosen home, all which hurt it, also hurt us immensely.

Shirley and I were now entering our forties. The long hours, as well as the fast pace in The Silver Grid were beginning to take their toll. We were slowing down, no longer did we run instead of walking. The arduous years of London's magical West End began to exact payment too. We needed a less demanding life style, a more gentle tempo to our workload. Putting our heads together once again, we decided a country pub in the vicinity of Scarborough would be ideal. A tenancy would be preferable to management. This eventually turned out to be the impossible dream, disappointment was in store. The tenancy we tried hard to obtain, we failed dismally to acquire. Looking over my shoulder again, I believe it was due to insufficient capital in back of us, as opposed to our competitors.

When 1976 came around, it brought with it a change of luck for the Aldridges. An incident of fate happened which was to lead us into changing our hectic way of life for good.

A friend of mine, a man named Ken Middleton, was leaving the nicest pub in the whole of Scarborough and district. He was about to take up a tenancy about a mile away from this house which he managed. It was going to put The Rosette, for that was what the hotel was named, up for management grabs. We required little debating to agree to go for it with all possible speed.

We would be sorry in a way to leave The Silver Grid, after all the work and pride we had put into the house, but we realized it required much younger, more agile hands than ours. The distance from one bar to another grew daily, the petty molehills became bloody great mountains to surmount. It was undoubtedly time to go.

The greatest obstacle of all was still to come, we asked Mr Cathcart to transfer us to The Rosette. This hotel was also owned by Tetley's Brewery and, as I have almost said, it was the classiest house on their books. Being set between the prestigious suburbs of Newby and Scalby, its clientele were the wealthy and top business people of Scarborough.

Summer of course brought the tourists to admire the wonderful setting of these villages. Our mouths literally watered when we thought about it.

Mr Cathcart brought us down to earth with a bump. 'I do not think Tetley's will want you to leave The Silver Grid, they would find it extremely hard to replace you in that house.'

It appeared we had done too good a job at the Grid, it stood in the way of our fulfilling the now desired move to The Rosette. For all accounts and purposes Tetley did not want the Grid to revert to its troublesome past, nor did they want to lose the increased business we had built up over the last few years. The casual and idle chat that I wished to leave The Silver Grid, permeated even to the brewery's draymen who, on delivering my beer order, told me, 'Tetley don't want to lose you here, they will never agree to your transfer to The Rosette.'

This gossip had come down the brewery's grapevine. Through the same infallible means, we learned there were innumerable applications from existing management of Tetley's, besides others from outside the company; some from as far away as Doncaster and Leeds. All wanted The Rosette, with all it represented to the fed-up town and city publican. It appeared our chances were slim indeed. Something had to be done, and quickly, for I was determined to have my wife out of The Silver Grid.

Shirley looked ghastly, worn out, living on her nerves, she snapped at all within her range, including our daughter. Somehow I had to obtain a much easier house, a place where her presence wasn't required eighteen plus hours a day, seven days a week. If a gun had to be held at the head of Tetley's top brass, so be it.

We agreed on a strategy which could force the brewery into granting us The Rosette. It could also backfire leaving us with no choice except to resign. It was a sink or swim, no-holds-barred plan, far from ethical, yet I had few qualms about putting it into operation. We had earned The Rosette by our unstinted effort in The Silver Grid alone.

I rang Mr Cathcart, asking him to call on us at his earlier convenience.

The man wasted no time nor did I, for on his arrival I went well nigh straight for the jugular.

'Mr Cathcart, either Joshua Tetley gives us The Rosette to manage, or we will leave The Silver Grid anyway, to take our services to another brewery. My wife is no longer capable of co-managing a house on the scale of this hotel. She is an extremely tired woman.'

He looked at me with a concentrated gaze, before answering, 'Mr Aldridge, I will pass your intentions on to the brewery. I will let you know their response in due course.'

It was a massive gamble. Tetley like all other leading companies, would not take kindly to being blackmailed. Our heavy-handed threat of leaving the Grid was precisely that, whichever side of the street you stand on. We could only hope that our abilities and use to them, would be an overriding factor in our favour. We were left to sweat it out once more, to brood, like a couple of worn out hens, on the enormity of our desperate move against the brewery.

It was a full two weeks before we saw Mr Cathcart again, a confusing time when we consoled ourselves with the time worn adage, 'No news is Good news'. It didn't work. We were convinced by the end of this period that Messrs Tetley were about to call our bluff.

Mr Cathcart walked up to the bar, where I was busy serving, his face inscrutably stern, 'Good morning, Mr Aldridge, I will wait until the end of business to see you and your wife.'

He walked away into the Dickens Lounge without another word.

My heart sank. Oh, God, my mind panicked, now what do we do? I had visions of being thrown out on to the pavement. I had burnt all my boats with the attempted intimidation, a threat I was in no position to carry out. Now, having called the stupid tune, I had to pay the piper.

Closing the hotel at the end of the morning session, Shirley and I joined Cathcart in the Dickens room. We all seated ourselves without a word being spoken. To be truthful, I couldn't think of anything to say.

He gazed at us steadily for what appeared to be ages (I am sure senior management must take a course in this disconcerting art), before he said, 'Joshua Tetley are very grateful for all the hard work and great endeavour, you have both put into The Silver Grid. After long deliberation Tetley,' here he paused to smile at us for the first time, before going on to add the most important bit, 'have decided to give you the management of The

Rosette. We all hope you will be as successful there as you have been in The Silver Grid since you assumed management here.'

We remained speechless. We had done too good a job at convincing ourselves that we had gone too far with the brewery, having more or less accepted we would be thrown out of the Grid on our blackmailing ear. Instead, we had won the prize of prizes. Contrarily, we now suffered pangs of guilt for our action. But not for long.

Shirley and I had been in The Silver Grid six and a half years, a large piece of our lives was tied within those walls. We hadn't had the Flood, but by God we'd had the Fire. I suppose one could say we had suffered the flood when they had doused the fire. No matter, my wife and I had gained many friends, besides experiencing immeasurable pleasure during those years. With the Porcupine in London's West End, it would remain forever one of our better memories of the beer trade.

Unfortunately, The Silver Grid did what Tetley had envisaged, reverting to being just a nondescript trouble spot, the beautiful Piccadilly Lounge no longer used. Mind you it would take a bloody hero to work the hours we did, and heroes are thin on the ground in the licensed trade.

Within a few short years the grand Silver Grid, once one of Scarborough's most respected landmarks, closed down completely, to be turned eventually and humiliatingly, into a Pizza Parlour.

The Laughtons, among them the great actor, Charles, must have cart-wheeled in their graves at the very thought of their lovely place receiving such an ignominious end.

And of the unknown, restless presence, watchful of the people who infringed in the top half of the Grid? What of it? Is it gladdened or saddened? Or, as I ask myself on many occasion, did it exist only in our imaginations?

I am pleased I had no part in exorcism. If something existed there, then it meant us no harm. Our fear was of our own making. The revolving light? If they actually saw it, it only proved beyond any doubt, whatever it was it had one hell of a sense of humour.

I'll stay with my original ideas on spooky happenings, it is far less disturbing to think it a past event being re-enacted.

Chapter 10

THE Rosette was a busy Georgian-style country house, with full catering facilities. It had a regular clientele of business men, and wealthy retired people. Then, of course, there were the working bods who frequented the bar. As in London's Cheshire Cheese, there was an unspoken agreement on segregation. The more affluent used the lounge, the others were quite content to stay on their own convivial patch.

The Rosette was the smallest pub we had ever managed, just two bars. The Lord be praised, trouble was an unknown occurrence, for which Shirley as well as I were deeply grateful.

We had wanted a quieter pub. Ready or not for the extreme in opposites that was what we had in The Rosette, a deeply, peaceful, sleepy hollow. My immediate problem was, how to wake it up a little without disturbing, in any way, the nature of things around here. Doubly difficult because of the mistrust I had engendered, through no fault of my own.

Again I had the unmistaken feeling of *déjà vu*. I was from the wrong side of the tracks, the old reputation of The Silver Grid had preceded me, and how! Had I not managed that dreadful place for years?

Surprisingly, a large number of the Rosette's wealthier patrons, knew nothing of the Grid's reformation under my management. Neither had they heard of my London experience, running hotels far superior, by comparison, to The Rosette. Although I must give credit where it is due, I won this lot over far faster than I had done in the Cheshire Cheese.

Man is a funny animal. He, or she, distrusts automatically anything which doesn't fall within his, or her, class range.

My wife had no such complications with her side of the business. The catering picked up under her more than capable hands. Jacqueline was relieved to learn she wouldn't have to leave her school, Scarborough Girls' High. She settled quickly into The Rosette, preferring it to The Silver Grid, where she had seen little of either parent. As well as not being overly keen on the customers of that house.

My beautiful dog Czar, was at last able to walk in his own backyard, to luxuriate on lush green lawns. Six and a half years in the Grid, after London's hard city streets, his only chance to let off steam had been when he was taken on the sands of the foreshore. Czar died eighteen months later, but he gloriously made up for city living in the latter part of his life. He adored The Rosette, the perpetual worried look on his face being left behind at The Silver Grid.

There was a large lawn at the rear of The Rosette which the previous manager had used as a putting green. In my view, it was ideal for a beer-garden, the setting couldn't be bettered. I arranged outdoor tables and chairs on the grass, setting off the whole with gaily coloured umbrella shelters. I quickly assembled a darts team in the bar which we entered in the Scarborough Darts League. This way we were off and running to build the winter trade.

Summer looked after itself there, apart from the garden furniture it truly needed little help. Its position on the main Whitby road, made it a certainty for catching the passing tourist trade.

Whitby, with its centuries old Abbey, as well as its literary connections with Dracula, draws tourists like a magnet. This peaceful, half-rural, fishing and holiday village remains unspoilt by its visiting thousands. Even though Captain Cook's cottage had been transported to Melbourne aeons before (which seemed fitting somehow, for many poor souls had been shipped out to Britain's former colony), the area where Cook was born still attracts the Commonwealth and foreign visitor alike.

This sightseeing trek has grown to enormous proportions since Mr James Herriot began writing his books, notably, *All Creatures Great and Small*, for Whitby is part and parcel of the Dales country.

History-steeped York is the city which, with the aid of my brother Allan and a few jewel thieves, almost landed us all in jail. It, too, draws the tourists in their thousands, with its Roman Wall, Cathedral and quaint, cobbled streets protected by the great gates spanning major routes out of the city. These gates were purely defensive complete with draw-bridges, portcullises and watchtowers as well as guardrooms. The Romans came to York in A.D. 71, the occupation lasting for 340 years. The city was actually raised to the status of a Roman Colony not only being visited by Hadrian, but two other Emperors, Severus as well as Constantius. Under Pope Gregory, York became a seat of learning, its Principal, a Yorkshireman named Alciun, was asked by Charlemagne to head his Palace school at Aachen.

I told you we were all lovers of history, more so when it pertains to fabulous Yorkshire, but this is not an everyday update of classical lore. It is just an everyday publican trying to paint you a picture of the things which affected his business; for the teeming history-hungry people, sated with all past splendour, spilled over into Scarborough and the enchanting villages of the Dales, which of course includes Newby and Scalby. It is only in the last decade that the phenomenon of thousands of people trekking the North Yorkshire countryside, has become so noticeable. Come they do to York, for it has a well earned place on any traveller's itinerary. I am sure the Yorkies can give the Scots and Irish, a run for their money, when it comes to past feuding and deadly bloody battles. York being the place to go to view the almost endless lists of former battlegrounds, as well as historical re-enactments. These people walk the narrow streets of the old city, fanning out into the Yorkshire Wolds and Dales, to discover for themselves unexpected visual delights down winding country lanes. Villages have seemingly slept through all the modern upheavals, alas, it is pure make believe. As the cottages become vacant they are snapped up by the city dweller, at outrageous prices the locals could never afford.

I wish they would adopt the strong parochial instinct of the Derbyshire villages of Hope, Bakewell, et cetera where outsiders were discouraged from owning real estate, even though those outsiders may only be from the City of Sheffield, on the very doorstep of those lovely villages.

The year 1977 was a good one, with spanking summer trade. In that year I was more or less accepted by the regulars too. It was also the year when David Whitfield headed the Bill at the Opera House in Scarborough. I had known David since the fifties, meeting him again in London as he made his first fortune in the sixties. He was then Number One on the Hit Parade, besides topping the Bill in the West End of London. The blond good looks coupled with a melodious voice proved fatal for this masculine charmer. Ladies, gambling and the demon drink all played their part in toppling this talented entertainer.

Kate saw David at the Finsbury Park Empire theatre in London, truly enjoying his voice but not his act. Apparently, he had played to all the young girls in the audience when, actually, he had no need of such ploys to hold his place at the top. His voice alone ensured his recognition. The previous week she had watched Issy Bonn at the same theatre, past his prime, yet still able to stand there, to hold his audience enthralled without the immature posturing of David Whitfield. Today that is part of the act. Then it wasn't necessary. Talent was enough.

During his stay in Scarborough, David had leased a house close by The Rosette. I was absolutely tickled pink to relive old times with him.

He had two spots, 6 and 8 p.m. to fulfil his contract at the town's Opera House. This left the full morning's session free to spend with me in The Rosette. He loved to play dominoes with the men from Low Hall, the Yorkshire Miners' Home roughly three-quarters of a mile away, a place which was to figure predominately in my working life, but we haven't reached that part of my story yet.

David Whitfield had made his home near Hull, the Humberside city where he was born. The German *Luftwaffe* had found the port of Hull an easy target during World War Two, flying in low along the identifying River Humber to bomb this vital port, the heart of Britain's survival. David knew Scarborough well, having been an evacuee to the town during this traumatic period and he still visited the family which had sheltered him. He was a warm, loving human being, possessing a terrific personality and that beautiful singing voice.

David had squandered the largest part of the vast fortune he had made during the sixties, when he was topping the big Shows. In 1977 he was on the come-back trail, well on the way to accumulating his second fortune, for he had lost none of his old charisma, nor his voice.

By this time we were great pals, so much so he used my flat as if it were his own. He would drink in the bar until around 1.30 to 2 p.m. then, if there was horse racing on the television, he would retire upstairs to my quarters to watch the programme, helping himself to drinks from the drink-trolley in the Lounge.

This particular day, David had gone upstairs to cheer on the horses which, no doubt as usual, he had backed too well. We were very busy in the pub until 3 p.m., closing time. We had then to set about cleaning down ready for the evening session. I suddenly remembered David and for some unknown reason I panicked, I bounded up the stairs to the flat in a muck sweat, to find all my worst fears confirmed.

He was flat on his back. A bottle of brandy, which had been full, lay discarded and empty by his side. He was paralytic, stoned, stinking drunk.

All my efforts to rouse him were in vain, David was out for the rest of the day, there was no uncertainty in my mind about that. He wasn't going to make the stage at the Opera House for the Second Show, let alone the first, for it was then 3.30 p.m.

In dismay I rang David's son, who was his manager. Without ceremony I blurted out, 'get yourself over to The Rosette straight away, your father is blind drunk, I do not think he will be sober enough to make the stage tonight.'

When he arrived at the flat, he stared hopelessly at his prostrate father and to my utter consternation he began to cry, tears rolling unheeded down his face, he said brokenly, 'hell, for sure he will get the bloody sack from the show. It will finish him in every way.'

This man truly loved his father, there was no sign of pecuniary interest causing this loss of self control, his father's welfare being first and foremost in his thoughts. He took all the abuse, which David in his drunken stupor, and shame-faced bravado later, would heap on his head. Much, much more than I could ever have stood.

The production at the Opera House was staged by Mr Don Robinson, a most astute businessman, who didn't suffer fools gladly. He was later to become president of the Scarborough Cricket Club, as well as chairman of Hull City Football Club, besides becoming a very good friend over the years.

At that time the last thing he qualified as, was a friend of mine. He phoned me that evening. Without preamble he ripped into me, as if I were completely at fault for the fact of David deciding to go on a private blinder. He finished his tirade with a completely uncalled for, and uncomplimentary swipe at another performer who was to stand in for David. What he thought that had to do with me, I will never know. I tried to explain what had happened, I may as well have saved my breath. So, fed up with his unwarranted condemnation, I changed my tack.

'Mr Robinson, I understand your dilemma. David was in my private quarters, supposedly watching horse racing on television, not getting plastered. I am not his nursemaid or keeper, I am his friend who happens to manage a bloody pub. However, I can assure you I will watch the bugger in future, you can bet your bottom dollar on that.'

Mr Robinson was unimpressed, he didn't want to hear how it happened. Suffice it to say, his only concern was how he was going to come out of that evening's performances. Someone had to take the brunt of his anger,

David was out to this world, that left his son or me. I had been elected. The stand-in couldn't have been that bad, holiday-makers are not the most demanding of audiences in any case. Robinson kept the show on with David remaining at the Top of the Bill, drawing in the crowds too. Nevertheless Mr Robinson phoned me yet again, with what he hoped would be a salutary warning.

'Never let him get into that state again, or he will never sing on another show of mine.'

I watched David like a hawk after that day, removing the drink-trolley from the flat until David had left Scarborough. I couldn't set myself up as his keeper, but by God I wouldn't stand by while he ruined himself either. On the night of his bender, he slept in our flat, as he was in no condition to go elsewhere. The following morning I took him to task, first telling him of the dressing down I'd received from Robinson, going on to admonish, 'behave yourself in future, David, I can live without this sort of hassle.'

'Fuck him,' a less than chastened David snarled at me.

'You let him down very badly, David, besides upsetting your son.'

'Fuck him, too,' he shouted at me defiantly. Then he rushed out of The Rosette, jumped into his car, and with a vicious squeal of the tyres, sped off down the road.

That night as we closed the pub, in walked David Whitfield. Head held high, he walked up to the bar. Under his arm he clutched a package and as he reached the bar he slung it at me over the counter, saying just one world, 'Here.'

It hit me in the chest, yet I managed to hang on to it, as David walked briskly out of the hotel. I removed the paper envelope wrapping. Inside was one of David's own recordings. On the sleeve he had written, 'To Peter and Shirley, thank you for your hospitality'. It was his way of saying he was sorry.

I have treasured that record ever since.

David continued to use The Rosette as if the incident had never occurred.

A couple of weeks later as we sat chatting in the bar, he suddenly asked, 'I wonder if you will do me a favour, Peter?'

'Sure, what's that,' I inquired naively.

'I want you to meet a girl for me at the railway station. I cannot meet her myself, my wife is in town that day.'

David Whitfield, the author and
customers, Rosette Inn.

'Oh, bloody hell, David,' I moaned.

'All you have to do is to collect her from the station, then take her to the St Nicholas Hotel.' He added gleefully, 'I have booked her in there.'

I am certain the bugger enjoyed discomfiting me, he appeared to take a great delight in shaking yours truly. I distinctly remember thinking at the time, this sod will bear watching . . . yet I acquiesced. One always did that with David, he could charm the birds out of the bloody trees, leaving you to wipe their shit up.

'All right, I will do it this time,' I shrugged. He knew I would agree.

'What the hell, what are pals for anyway? There is a proviso,' I told the smiling David, determined that he wasn't going to win without strings.

'Shirley must never be told. If she finds out, we are mates no more. She would never be a party to anything like this, David.'

Notwithstanding, the following Thursday saw me doing my stuff, as well as feeling a right Charlie to boot. There I was, a paper tucked under my arm, waiting at the railway station for some tart to alight from a train. I felt a complete idiot.

David had said, 'I have told her to look for a chap with a newspaper under his arm.'

Have you ever noticed the number of men carrying newspapers, in that position, on railway stations? That day there were at least six within spitting distance.

Christ, I thought, this is a right balls up! How the hell will she know which one of us, is the guy meeting her? How the hell will I know who she is?

I need not have worried.

The train pulled into the station and stopped, the First Class carriages almost level with me. An extremely good looking red-head, in a smart, black, two-piece suit, stepped daintily onto the platform. I advanced like a homing pigeon, no doubt whatsoever, this delectable maiden was David's girlfriend.

'Rebecca?' I inquired, for David had said that was her name.

'Yes,' she replied, giving me the most dazzling smile I had seen in years.

'I have been asked by Mr Whitfield to escort you to your hotel.'

'Thanks, love,' she answered unceremoniously, as I took her luggage in hand.

Off we set for the St Nicholas Hotel in my car, her expensive perfume now filling the air. Bloody hell, I cursed to myself, I hope this lot disperses before Shirley gets her nose in here.

Rebecca was about twenty-five and her fabulous figure tore your eyes from a beautifully sculptured face and gleaming hair. She was of film star quality plus. I felt pangs of jealously, this girl would drive any adult male into an extra-marital relationship, with no bother.

David at fifty years of age, was a very lucky man to have landed such a bobby dazzler of a woman.

I found out later, she was a dancer from one of the shows David had appeared in. They had been friends for a long time.

After I had deposited her at the St Nicholas, I returned to The Rosette with all the car windows fully opened. On arrival I gave the interior of the car a jolly good waft around with my handkerchief. That perfume had staying power; she had obviously bathed in it.

I rang David to let him know the girl had arrived safely, 'She is ensconced in the hotel, you lucky bugger,' I finished admiringly.

'Thanks, Old Cock. I owe you, I will see you soon,' he blithely chirruped.

On the following Sunday he walked into The Rosette.

'Would you like to come to York for the day, Peter?' he asked loudly.

David worked six days, Sunday being a day off.

'I have arranged to meet someone in York,' he whispered, as he nudged closer to my side.

'Go on, I can manage for the day,' Shirley urged generously.

'I will be back for the evening session, I won't be any later than six,' I told my trusting wife.

Without delay we set off for the old city, and what I knew to be an assignation for David. He had recently acquired a new Mercedes car and was putting it through its paces as we tore up the York road. Believe me that bugger could frighten the hell out of the devil himself when he put his foot down. Speeding along, he turned fully to me and asked, as if it were a foregone conclusion, 'Peter, will you come to Australia with me?'

I was dumbfounded, I knew arrangements were being made for him to go on tour in that far-flung country. While I was still trying to unscramble my addled brain to muster an answer, he went on without waiting for a reply to his astounding question, 'you could be my bodyguard.'

I sat stupefied. David actually believed I could up sticks, leave my wife, family and business, to act silly buggers down under.

'You will have the time of your life, Peter. More birds than you have ever dreamed of, all the birds you want falling all over you,' he repeated coaxingly, as if the thought had just occurred to him that I might refuse. Deciding women might not be enough, he threw another carrot on the heap.

'You will be paid a bloody sight more than you are earning now, my Old Son.'

Before you condemn the man as an out and out irresponsible playboy, you have to know the man behind the brash exterior. Here was a fellow who didn't want age to touch him, he loved life, living it to its fullest. Did he have some deep-rooted knowledge that, for him, it would be a short one? Knowing this, had he decided to make it a bloody merry one, for this would have been his reaction had he known. Either way, his end was no doubt hurried by his own profligacy. I reckon he tried to buy youth, encouraging the non-feathered variety of birds, to flock in his direction. He was immensely talented, one of Britain's great post-war singers, a man whom fortune favoured in every way. He once told me:

'The song which made me famous, "Cara Mia", was pure bloody luck—I had gone to the studio to record another song. They were looking for a "B" side for the recording, when someone suggested "Cara Mia" for it.'

He named his home after the song, but he said, 'I hated the bloody number at the time, so did my agent, yet lo and behold it sold a million.'

I remember that beautiful day in York as if it was yesterday. The sun beamed down on David's blond head as we walked up the driveway of a large house on a private estate called Poppleton. As we approached the building, the front door swung open and Rebecca flung herself on to the path, running straight into David's waiting arms.

I thought, oh bloody hell, here we go again.

I didn't know the half of it, otherwise I would have run into my wife's waiting arms. Too bloody right I would, I'm not daft.

Inside the house, Rebecca introduced me to her friend who had just arrived. Her name was Debra and she, too, was one beauteous lady.

'We are waiting for a show in Birmingham to begin rehearsals,' Rebecca said coyly. 'Debra is a dancer too,' she added, as she handed me a cup of much needed coffee.

The house belonged to Debra's aunt, who continually fussed around David. The latter, used to such things, pointedly ignored all the attentions apart from the odd polite rejoinder. He leaned over to me to whisper, 'kept this as a surprise for you, Peter,' nodding surreptitiously towards Debra. 'We are going over to Doncaster, this is too bloody close to home for you.'

Some surprise! I knew there was a girl in it for him, he had made no secret of that, what I hadn't known was, I was to be accommodated too. To my everlasting regret I didn't decline the offer.

We left forthwith for Doncaster and the Danum Hotel, where David had booked us in for dinner, among other things.

David handed me the car keys for departure, with the injunction 'you drive, Peter. Rebecca and I are going into the back seat.'

Debra cuddled up to me in the front of the car as we sped away from York. David had a very strong point, it was too bloody close to home for me. Unlike London where one can retain some anonymity quite easily, York and Scarborough are but villages by comparison. Gossip being the bread and butter of customers in the local ale houses.

The Danum, at that time, was the best hotel in Doncaster. I was unlikely to meet any Yorkshire miners I knew in there. It was 7 p.m. before we were seated in the dining room. I made excuses and hurried to the phone to ring Shirley. There was no way I could be back for the evening session which had already begun in The Rosette. I was going to have to weave one fantastic fairy story to get her to believe it.

'Sorry, love,' I opted for the simple style, 'we have been held up by David's agent. Can you manage without me?'

'I guess I will have to, won't I?' a disgruntled Shirley replied.

'I will get there as soon as I can,' I placated her. 'It could be late on though, they are up to their necks in business arrangements.'

Guiltily, I returned to the dining room, telling myself I was getting too old for such shenanigans; there wasn't any fun in it any more.

I reached the room just in time to witness an elderly man collapsing to the floor, with a severe heart attack.

He had been seated at a table next to ours, when I had left the room and had been chatting amiably to David, whom he had recognized. The waitresses, too, had been making a fuss of the blond good looker and they were still clustered around David. Other diners waited patiently for their services, quite content, as they, too, watched the singer and all the commotion he created by his presence.

As the man fell to the floor, a chap jumped forward quickly clearing a space around the ailing man, saying, 'please move back. Can we move this table out of the way? I am a doctor.'

The waitresses moved the fellow's table, as the doctor attended to everything. An ambulance was called, the poor old fellow was lifted carefully out of the dining room by the ambulance men who'd wasted no time in arriving on the scene.

We all seated ourselves again. Whereas before there had been merriment, now there was just a subdued murmur of voices.

The doctor came back into the room, after seeing his charge safely stowed into the ambulance and away. Passing our table, he paused to shake hands with David who had been identified by everyone including the washer-ups in the kitchen. Bang out of the window had gone all hope of being unrecognized. Worse was to follow. The doctor turned from David to me, 'hello, from The Rosette, aren't you? You are a long way from home.'

I then remembered the man. A casual customer, he was a doctor at Scarborough Hospital. He was accompanied by his wife, a woman Shirley knew very well.

'Give my regards to your wife,' his wife said pointedly.

She glanced curiously at the two ladies seated at our table, leaving us with little choice except to introduce them. They then joined our now not so happy band of conspirators. As far as I was concerned it was a dead duck, the game was over. David, too, was showing the strain.

I whispered to Rebecca in desperation, 'we must get away from here, this is a real bloody mess. David is getting stuck into the bottle to escape and you know what kind of a state he will get into if we stay here.'

'I am so sorry, Peter, about what has happened, it's ruined our evening completely. I agree with you about David, it's a pity the night has been spoiled, but it cannot be helped now. We have to get away quickly.'

After dinner, and at least an hour of protestations from my tipsy friend, who had made up his mind he was spending the night with Rebecca, we managed to persuade him to leave the Danum, and the company of his new found drinking partners, the doctor and his wife.

I drove, for by that time David was incapable of standing, let alone attempting to drive.

We arrived at The Rosette at 11.30 p.m., after dropping the ladies off in York. Shirley, like Queen Victoria, whom she resembled at that moment, was not amused. David stayed overnight, the fact of which kept my wife's temper in check. He was up and about by nine-thirty the next morning, wasting no time in departing, leaving me to explain, as best I could, what we had been doing for all of that time. Always a great believer in discretion being the better part of valour, and with the cellar needing some work, I withdrew to less stormy depths.

By mid-week, in truth it was the following Wednesday, I came downstairs into the lounge room, after changing from working gear in readiness for the morning session.

Shirley was standing talking to the doctor and his wife from the Danum. I swore to myself, they had wasted no time in coming over to The Rosette. That was the least of my worries, I had to break that little conversation up quick. I raced over to them, my heart racing even faster.

'Hello, how nice to see you again,' I lied politely.

'I was just telling your wife of our experience at the Danum in Doncaster, what a surprise to find you there,' the blasted witch of a doctor's wife enthused.

Fuelling an obviously combustible situation, she exclaimed in an assumed wide-eyed guileless manner, 'wasn't David Whitfield good fun? And those two lovely girls from the show in Birmingham. We all had such a splendid time, it's a pity you couldn't have been there, Shirley.'

She had deliberately spilled her guts, I waited with bated breath for Shirley to explode. My wife is too good a trouper for that. Her face remained expressionless.

'Oh yes, I would have loved to have been there,' she said truthfully, 'I believe you all enjoyed yourselves. Peter has told me all about it.'

She smiled at me sweetly. Then, making her apologies for leaving to the confounded doctor and his wife, she joined the staff behind the bar as she always did at that time.

My only consolation was that the mischief-maker had derived no apparent satisfaction. But that was not going to help me out of this particular contretemps. I decided discretion was again called for and stayed away from my wife until after closing time. Then all hell broke loose.

In my defence I could only say feebly, 'Shirley, I was trapped into it, I have done nothing wrong, apart from lying to you. I came straight home after having dinner with them all. I lied to you because I was afraid to tell you the truth, I knew you would not believe me. Ask David he will tell you.'

'I wouldn't believe anything that man said,' she fumed, 'not if he swore before God. He is a born womanizer, you are no better either.'

I phoned David, telling him of the mess I found myself in after the visit from our mutual acquaintances, the benighted doctor and his wife. To give him his due, he came around almost immediately, using all his undoubted charm he tried to extricate me from the web, which he himself had woven.

'Shirley, the ladies were friends of mine, not Peter's. We took them out in my new car for a spin, then had dinner at the Danum, in Doncaster. Ring the hotel, they will verify that we left directly the meal was over. It was all my fault. I wanted to show off my new Mercedes after my agent had gone home.'

'I do not believe you, you are covering for him, you are both as bad as each other. I am not a fool, I won't be treated like one either.'

David left, shaking his head ruefully at me as he did so.

My wife didn't speak to me for four harrowing weeks. It is surprising how devastating that can be. Only a woman can so effectively send a person to Coventry, still expecting at the end of this mental torture, to receive an abject apology.

David remained unbowed and unchanged. He took Shirley's castigation in his stride. Mind you he got of lighter than yours truly, in no time at all he had beguiled his way back into her heart.

On the completion of his show at the Opera House, David left for Australia and his arranged tour of that land down under. He was to die in that far off country two years later. He died from a brain haemorrhage while on yet another engagement there. It took quite a time for us to accept the death of this head-strong, gifted charmer I was fortunate enough to have had as a friend.

Kate has said that I made a habit of collecting such people as friends, none of them despicable cads, yet all captivatingly unprincipled.

That's as maybe, yet I know as surely as night follows day, David will be on Cloud Nine somewhere, warbling to some stunning yet short-lived female, the sun still reflecting on his blond head, his ability to bewitch undimmed by death.

The Rosette continued on its thriving way. The following year I bought swings, roundabouts and children's climbing frames, setting them apart from the tables on the back lawn. The summer trade almost doubled now that parents could go for a drink without worrying about their offspring. They could take them along, knowing they would be kept amused at the same time. The brewery was delighted at the increase in turnover.

That year I organized a Boozers' Walk. A race which started and finished at The Rosette.

I managed to persuade Fred Feast, Gee of *Coronation Street*, to forget our old animosity towards each other, and compère the event. Richard Dunn, a former Heavyweight Champion Boxer of Great Britain, agreed to make an appearance too. Then Shirley came up with an absolutely brilliant idea, of which, in the beginning I was more than uncertain, to say the least.

'Why don't you ask Bruce Woodcock to come and start the race? After all, it is for charity, tell him the proceeds are all going to the Scarborough Hospital. I cannot see him refusing.'

She looked quite pleased with herself for thinking of it.

My wife may not have visualized Bruce turning us down, my oath I could, and a great deal more vehemently too. Bruce was a man who detested the limelight. The adulation, as well as the accompanying razzmatazz was anathema to him. My business instinct, countermanding my better judgement, came to the fore. If I could prevail upon him, what a draw card he would be. Without further misgiving I set off for Doncaster and Bruce's public house.

He had taken this a number of years previously. It had the perfect name for a mining village hotel, The Tumbler, with all its connotations of a tumbling pigeon, a circus clown, a glass tumbler. The hotel stood in the village of Edlington, a mining village adjacent to Doncaster.

When it came to money, or brass, as it is referred to in my part of the world, Bruce forgot his abhorrence of all things public, reluctantly going on show to draw the fans and thereby their cash.

I was greeted as I had feared, when he learned of the reason for my visit. My request was met with a blunt refusal. There were no niceties of excuses offered, a sharp, raspish, 'not on your bloody life,' was the mildest part of the rejection. However, contrarily this gave me new hope, I hadn't been kicked out of there, which was what I'd feared. Nonetheless, I spent an entire evening pleading, cajoling, changing tactics as he dug in his heels. Finally he succumbed, yet not without the characteristic conditions.

'You will have to send a taxi to pick me up, to drive me to Scarborough. I am not driving all that bloody way. You will have to collect our Billie as well, he will enjoy the run and the day out and he can look after me.'

I agreed, who wouldn't? The expense of a taxi was nothing, a mere bagatelle, it could be overwhelmingly compensated for by the number of people his magical name summoned forth. I returned to Scarborough highly elated. Shirley would be over the moon with my achievement.

Mr Cathcart had by now been replaced as area manager by Tetley's Brewery, with a man named Caldwell, a diminutive, yet very nice fellow. A chap similar in make-up to David Hill, if not quite so dynamic. No matter, he was an accomplished professional within the licensed trade, earning the respect of all Tetley's management.

When I approached him about the contest I was contemplating staging, he was extremely enthusiastic about the whole concept, hardly believing as I listed all the celebrities who had agreed to participate in some manner.

'Fred Gee of *Coronation Street* has said he will compère as well as ad lib before the event. That should hold the crowd, if there is a delay in the start of the race. Richard Dunn, Champion Heavyweight Boxer, has agreed to fill in where necessary. The crowning attraction of course is Bruce Woodcock, he has consented to start the race, besides presenting the prizes to the winners.'

There was no need to explain who Bruce was. The absolute awe on Caldwell's face and in his voice, said it all about Mr Woodcock. he exclaimed, 'Bruce Woodcock! Well I never, Bruce Woodcock!'

The other two notables paled into insignificance, underscoring once again the almost unaccountable respect the former British Empire and

Commonwealth Champion still commanded from the general public, in spite of his assumed surly reticence.

I plastered the whole of Scarborough and outlying districts with large posters advertising the forthcoming event. Bruce's name topped the Bill in bold, black capitals. I was going to capitalize on that bugger, thus making sure this occasion would be remembered for a very long time.

An excited Mr Caldwell phoned to say, 'I am coming over for the race, so are some of Tetley's directors.'

I had expected no less, it could only add to the prestige of our enterprise, showing me the brewery appreciated my efforts also and were willing to play along. There was no uncertainty in my mind, the chance of meeting Woodcock definitely had something to do with their decision to attend.

Saturday, 20 May 1978, dawned in sunny splendour, the gods having decided to smile upon our endeavour too.

I had a lorry with a long, flat, open body, parked at the front of The Rosette, upon which we had rigged two huge loudspeakers, and a microphone. Also in keeping with my expectations, an enormous crowd began to gather early, most good naturedly jostling for prime positions. A picnic atmosphere prevailed. Purely because of the numbers involved and the density of the gathering, the police were forced to move in to control them as well as the traffic, for they were beginning to block the main Whitby road.

It augured well for it to be a spectacular show. We had so many contestants, we decided to start them off in relays, timing them to ascertain the winners.

As the time approached for the start of the race, the excitement grew, everyone was there. Fred Feast skilfully keeping the crowd happy with his humorous patter. Richard Dunn playing the straight man for Fred, appeared to be loving every minute of it. Mr Caldwell and the directors of Tetley had arrived in good time. All were present, all that is except the star of the piece, Bruce Woodcock.

The contestants, now stripped down to vests and running shorts, milled around the starting point. Fred observing this, decided it was time for him to step out of the limelight, away from the microphone. As the minutes ticked away with nothing happening, the crowd grew restive. Disappointment was almost visible. They had come to gaze upon Woodcock, a man they had idolized in this part of the country, for he had given them little chance to pay homage since his retirement from the ring.

Boozers' Walk Race May 1978 from the Rosette Inn.

Official timer, Peter Aldridge; starter and prize-giver, Bruce Woodcock; presenter, Fred Feast (Gee), *Coronation Street*.

They wanted to see him again, maybe to speak with him, to tell their children about this man. To boast that they had met this Champion, who had gone down in Boxing Annals, was all they asked.

To understand one must know the background and the reason. After the Second World War, Britain no longer bolstered by conflict to be won, faced only a drab grey future of rebuilding a shattered economy, as well as an even more battered country.

The people broke this desperate tedium by hero-worshipping a man capable of taking of the world's finest, Mauriello, Baksi, Savold, Oma and Lesnevitch, giving more than a good account of himself in the process. They would never forget Woodcock, especially in his home county, where he would never be superseded.

All this apart, I was worried to death, this introverted, reluctant hero was a no show. I had sent the taxi in good time. Had Bruce changed his mind? Chickened out at the last minute? Had the taxi met with an accident? Whichever, I couldn't win, it was going to leave me with egg on my face, worse still, an unruly crowd convinced they had been conned. I already had a sinking feeling besides a sour taste in my mouth. I wondered why the hell it couldn't have rained, thus saving me from total ignominy. Oh, the folly of chasing dreams of grandeur, when would I ever learn?

'Peter you will have to start the race without Woodcock,' the voice of Mr Caldwell broke in on my self-pitying thoughts, he edged closer to me, giving me a gentle prod with his elbow. My agitation must have been plainly written on my face.

Mentally shaking myself, I grabbed hold of Fred Feast's arm, 'come on, Fred, you will have to start the bloody thing.'

Fred and I climbed on the back of the lorry. Tony Phillips, a regular customer of The Rosette, was a very severely handicapped fellow, with only one leg had volunteered to be the adjudicator. Splendid chap which he was, he was now busy lining up the first of the runners, cheerfully turning to wave, indicating they were ready to start.

The contestants had four circuits of the village to race, drinking a full pint of foaming beer each time they passed The Rosette. In all they had four and a half miles to run, as well as four pints of ale to consume. Which, all things being equal, should slow them up somewhat, apart from entertaining the throng.

Suddenly, as Fred paused theatrically prior to firing the starting pistol, there was one hell of a commotion at the rear of the boisterous masses. A policeman did his utmost to clear a path through the reluctant revellers for a well overdue taxi-cab which screeched to a halt in front of the lorry amid a thunderous burst of cheering and clapping. As Bruce climbed out of the car, Billie scrambling after him, Fred's voice boomed out over the loud-speakers, 'Ladies and Gentlemen, the great Bruce Woodcock.'

It was several minutes before proceedings could continue then, to ear-shattering applause, Bruce climbed on the lorry to join Fred and me. Without one word to this worshipping crowd, our hero grabbed the starting pistol from Fred, held it high above his head and pulled the trigger.

'Crack', the shot echoed around this once peaceful village, the runners caught totally off-guard haphazardly took off on the start of the marathon race, at a spanking pace too, once they had got over the initial balls-up of the start. This herculean effort no doubt spurred on by the thought of a foaming glass of beer. It was indeed a warm day. There had, with the delay in starting, been a prolonged drought as far as they were concerned.

It turned out to be a bonanza of a day, in every way, the event a bigger success than we could ever have hoped for, the weather remained perfect throughout. The sun shining down warmly on the massed humanity worked miracles for my beer sales, which in turn added to the directors' enjoyment of the occasion.

I am very pleased to tell you Bruce, also, enjoyed himself, his brother Billie likewise. The latter remarked later, 'I have not seen Bruce enjoy himself like this for years.'

I was thoroughly delighted, for he had come up trumps all the way, freely throwing himself into the spirit of things, thereby delighting the doting crowd. It seemed only fitting he, too, should get something out of this, besides a long taxi ride.

Mr Caldwell bubbled with joy. A photo had been taken of him being thrown into the air by Messrs Woodcock, Feast and Dunn. This had been part of the high-spirited fun during the prize-giving part of the ceremony. 'Get me at least a dozen copies of that photograph, Peter,' he requested proudly.

I was only too willing to comply, I knew it had been a light-hearted point in his life, one he wished to remember forever.

It was the topic of conversation for months in the bar. Their landlord was a friend of Bruce Woodcock, he had persuaded him to attend, not only that, he had participated fully in the event. A post mortem was conducted on every incident held, it is all that could be remembered in the months ahead. It is a memory I treasure too, for my lounge customers were equally involved, in fact just as enthusiastic as my bar clientele.

I was not aware then, it would be my last throw of the dice in the hotel licensed trade. The last big gamble of my working life as mine host. What a perfect master stroke to finish my chequered career as a publican. Today, I look back with prideful nostalgia, I failed to make that elusive fortune, or hit the vaulted heights of fame, yet what a fantastic life I have led. I regret only that I cannot turn the pages back, as if in a book, to relive in actuality the whole glorious, muddled life again. To meet once more the people who have coloured my life in such spectacular fashion. To have the joy of knowing them, even though it would entail the eventual loss once more of loved ones.

Who among us, on occasion, doesn't desire the same as age dims those beloved memories?

Czar, my faithful Alsatian dog, was now ten years old. As with most large dogs he suffered from hip displacement, an ailment common to them as they grow older. We sorrowfully watched as he gradually lost the use of his back legs, his puzzled unacceptance as he dragged himself around, broke my heart and my family's. Full paralysis of his rear end left us with no alternative but to end his suffering. We arranged for the vet to come along, to put him down painlessly. Barry Pine, another regular customer as well as a good friend, worked with me from closing time to 2 a.m., digging a grave in Czar's well loved lawn of The Rosette.

We dug down a good five foot,

The author and Czar, Rosette Inn.

to ensure he would never be disturbed, only calling a halt when we hit wet clay, the water table. I realize now I was attempting to dig my grief away. This is the trouble with keeping pets, there comes a time when we must lose them, then the heartbreak begins. Again, I am faced with the inevitable. Max, my lovely dispositioned Alsatian, is developing the same symptoms as Czar, the dog he replaced all those many years ago.

After finishing Czar's grave, Shirley and I stayed the rest of the night in the lounge bar with him, the vet being due to do his ghastly task at 9 a.m. We took it in turns to cradle him in our arms, as that long, awful night passed.

Some may think this maudlin, I make no apologies for that, to us he was a dearly loved member of our family. We were also losing a trusted, valued friend.

He had been through most of our ups and downs with us, living in London's grassless, building-enclosed streets, his life spent in ever changing abodes, as we moved from job to job. Almost losing his life in the terribly frightening fire at the Silver Grid. Doing his best to master the fear of the unknown there, just to please me. Now, when he was at his happiest, he had to die. It felt as if we were losing a major part of our lives, as indeed we were.

We grieved long. For all three of us there was an aching void which nagged relentlessly at our guts. We had bought Czar as a ten week old puppy, from the reputable Gamston Kennels in Nottingham. He had never let their reputation for good dogs down in any way.

Time passed, then one day a very old friend of ours called in to see us. This was Owen Briscoe, the General Secretary of the Yorkshire Miner's Union, the N.U.M.

I had known Owen all of my life, both originating from the same road in the village of Armthorpe. At one time I almost had him as a brother-in-law, then something must have gone wrong, the courtship ended.

We had spent many happy hours together over the years. Owen had visited me at most of the London pubs we had managed, in particular the Cheshire Cheese, as well as the Porcupine, both houses he liked very much.

He rarely visited the Big Smoke without calling in to see us. These calls continued after we returned to Yorkshire. We were especially handy at The Rosette when he had been conducting some business at Low Hall, the Miner's Home.

This day he appeared at the bar, looking extremely concerned.

'Hello, Owen,' I greeted him warmly, so pleased to see him. I added, 'nice to see you again in Scarborough, long time since you've been in this vicinity, isn't it?'

He remained very stern of face, which was unusual for him.

'I have just been to Low Hall, there is a small problem there I have to solve somehow.'

'It cannot be that bad, Owen, I can't see those old codgers getting into too much mischief,' I quipped, trying to cheer him up.

My attempt failed miserably, there was no sign of a smile as he asked, 'can I talk to you in private, for a few minutes, Peter?'

'Surely.' He had me perturbed by then. 'Wait until I fetch Shirley to keep an eye on things here, Owen.'

I went in search of Shirley, wondering what was troubling him, he was so ominously serious. I couldn't think of one valid reason for his request for a private chat either. I was most uncharacteristic of him, he would normally have a meal and a drink, waiting until we were closed so that we could talk undisturbed for hours.

Owen didn't leave me in the dark for long.

'Some time ago now, the superintendent at Low Hall decided to retire. He had been in that position for twenty-five years, giving us little problem. No longer a young man, he figured it was time to call it a day. We had not found this to be an insurmountable difficulty, in fact we had had a good response to our advertisement for a replacement.

'Out of them all we had chosen a new superintendent, as well as a matron for Low Hall. Unfortunately, before they could take up the position, the man died suddenly. Leaving us with the job of finding a substitute at very short notice.'

'I cannot see why you are so worried, Owen. It appears simple to me, elect another couple from the short list of candidates, you must have short-listed the possibles when you chose the original pair.'

'I wish it was as simple as that, Peter. The position has to be advertised again. That is the rule.'

'Well, I for one, think it is a bloody silly rule, Owen, giving you unnecessary headaches.'

'That's as maybe, Peter,' Owen studied my face closely, before continuing with his surprising proposition.

'You and Shirley would be perfect for this situation. You are the couple we are searching for. Your invaluable experience in dealing with people from all walks of life, your ability to organize, all are the requisites for this job.'

He went on, not giving me a chance to turn him down flat, which I had in mind. What did I know about dealing with the aged and infirm?

'Shirley's nursing experience, together with her knowledge of good class catering, are the ideal requirements demanded to fulfil the matron's position.'

More than a little taken aback by Owen's pushing, serious style of approach and his overly fulsome flattery, I answered cautiously. 'I don't know, Owen, I need time to think, besides talk the whole idea through with Shirley. I can't imagine what her reaction will be to such a suggestion. We have never given a moment's thought to leaving the licensed trade, it is the only thing we know. It would be an adventurous step, to even contemplate, let alone do.'

Then I asked the sixty-four dollar question, 'could my wife and I run an Old Folks' Home? We are comparatively young yet. Would we be able to deal with the whims and fancies of the aged?'

'It is not an Old Folks' Home. It is a Convalescent Home, an entirely different thing altogether. Ex-miners go there for a two week holiday. We need the nursing experience because, I grant you, these are not young men. Neither are they infirm. They are miners who, by tradition, are as tough as old boots, in more ways than one,' Owen smiled at me.

'A doctor is always on call, he must be brought out if there is any doubt at all about a man's health, it is purely part of the care, there is seldom need for a doctor. In our opinion, these men have earned a little luxury in their lives.'

Owen had me interested, I had listened to his explanation without comment. I knew and liked the miner, the fact that I wouldn't have their job for quids, was beside the point. However, there was much more I wanted to know, before I could take the proposal to Shirley for her consideration. The miners from Low Hall used The Rosette, I could find out a lot about the workings of that place without them being made aware of the reason for my curiosity. Owen, for some reason, was too keen to get my wife and me to give us an entirely unbiased view. He would not deliberately mislead us, yet by omission of some fact, we could very well be misled.

'If we decided we would take the job, how do we go about getting it?'

Owen grinned, he was back to his normal self, I think he thought I had nibbled at his bait, and he started to reel me in.

'As I have stated, Peter, the rules say the position must be re-advertised, with no preselection. You will have to apply to be interviewed by the committee. You are managing a good class establishment at the moment, this fact will stand you in good stead. The best of the applicants are short-listed, there is no doubt in my mind that you will be on that list. In my honest opinion you will gain the position. In the meantime, I can guarantee full confidentiality.'

'We will need time, Owen. I will let you know our decision.'

'If you do decide to apply for the post, I will personally give you a run around the Hall and its grounds before you commit yourself further. I cannot do more than that, although I wholeheartedly wish I could. I want you and Shirley in Low Hall.'

He took his leave straight away which, again, was most unusual.

I joined my wife in the bar, to tell her of this possible curious change in our lives. I needed her advice now, not later.

After closing, Shirley and I talked at some length on the subject, in fact, for days we spoke of nothing else. If truth be known, we were probably talking ourselves into the idea, although we did weigh the possible advantages, against the disadvantages, known or surmised.

My wife's reaction had been remarkably similar to mine, cautious yet intrigued by the thought of a different kind of challenge. Caution ruled, we wanted more information, not so much about the position itself, but the security it offered. Was there superannuation? Was there separate accommodation, in other words private quarters, where we could have some form of family life? So many questions we had no answer to.

'Ring Owen, we must know what we are letting ourselves in for, before we can make any decision. He must keep his promise, we want to see inside Low Hall as well. Then, and only then, will we even consider the proposal. We are not jumping off any bridge, without a safety net beneath it,' Shirley ruled wisely.

When I phoned Owen, he immediately agreed to supply any information which could help us to make up our minds. Good to his word, he came over to Scarborough to show us the interior and gardens of Low Hall.

The Low Hall, Scalby, was built in 1902-05 having taken three years to

The Low Hall.

construct. It was sited away from the original Low Hall which dated back
400 years. Old Low Hall stood on the ground which is now occupied by
the Low Hall bungalow and cottage.

Wilhelm Rowntree, the chocolate magnate, who had the latter day
mansion built, took up residence for Christmas 1904, the year before the
building was completed.

The Rowntree family lived there until 1926-7, the middle depression
years, when it was purchased by the South Yorkshire Miners' Welfare
Committee, for use by the miners as a convalescent home, its present usage.
It was passed around several Yorkshire Miners' Welfare Committees, before
being acquired by the Coal Industry's Social Welfare Organization.

In 1978 it was bought by Arthur Scargill, for the Yorkshire Miners'
National Union of Mineworkers, the N.U.M. It is still owned by them,
despite the havoc wrought to the Union's finances during the tragic folly
of the 1984-5 Miners' Strike.

The Hall is a beautiful manor house, set in seventeen acres of landscaped
lawns and gardens, winner of numerous Best Garden awards. It is one of
Scalby village's main attractions. In recent years the grounds have been
opened for a day, during the Annual Scalby Fair Week, a very popular
occasion for both visitor and villager alike.

The building still retains reminders of its first tenants, the Rowntrees.
Notably among these are the children's names embedded in the conservatory
wall, their dog's gravestone in the orchard together with the aesthetically
pleasing library and main lounge, which still bear the original oak-panelled
walls. In the latter room, an inglenook reminds one of a more distant past.
After being shown around this beautiful place, my wife and I were no
longer doubtful as to the wisdom of leaving The Rosette. It would be a
better place in which to rear a growing girl. We could, for the first time
since our early married life, enjoy a family life unobtainable on licensed
premises.

Our years with Tetley's Brewery had been very happy ones, both at
The Rosette and The Silver Grid. By this time we had in excess of ten
years service with them. Now, frighteningly, we were contemplating leaving
this security. And not only them but the trade, the only business we had
known since selling the transport enterprise, which had been so disastrous
an undertaking for us.

This was a massive stride we were about to take. In spite of our fears, as well as our prevailing good sense which still advised prudence, we agreed to take our chances down this new path.

The applications for superintendent and matron of Low Hall were duly submitted to the Union's Committee.

All that was left to do, was sit and wait for them to act—apart from doing our usual thing of having terrible doubts, wondering whether we had taken the right or wrong course.

Misgivings aside, we still had the urge to achieve, to climb another bloody mountain, or venture into uncharted waters. Age had not dulled the spirit of adventure, in fact at times, I think it had only honed the edge.

PART THREE

All for One?

Chapter 11

THE interviews had been arranged to take place at the Miners' Union Office in Barnsley, the building which has since gained Nationwide recognition as well as the nick-name of Arthur's Castle. The President of the Union being none other than Arthur Scargill.

It was with more than a little consternation we were to learn he would be one of the men interviewing the candidates. We had met him on a previous occasion, only briefly and he probably wouldn't remember the meeting.

Mr Scargill's manufactured reputation ran in front of him by a long mile, a larger than life Bogey Man, in a great number of people's minds. A man whom the media had lambasted for years, a popular whipping boy for most news hounds' columns in the national press containing dire warnings of his reported intention of bringing the country to its knees. 'Scargill is a personal friend of Fidel Castro', was a typical example. The latter being the then threat to the Western World's democratic principles. Since superseded by Libya's Gadaffi, then by the latest villain, Saddam Hussein.

A radical Marxist left-winger was only one of the many labels attached to Arthur Scargill. He had been taught Labour's causes at his father's knee. Had his father been a staunch Conservative, Arthur was clever enough to have made it to the top ranks of that establishment. That is not the case, he walked in front of the miners. He defended stoutly their right to work, as their democratically elected leader. He warned of further intended mine closure, since proven undisputedly true. Propaganda, an art well perfected, is a mixture of fact sprinkled liberally with misinformation. This is used constantly by the reporters of current affairs, it also sells newspapers by its very sensationalism. Too close to call at times within the Libel laws, though many a politician all over the world, has become wealthy through the breaking of those codes of conduct. More destructive to Mr Scargill is the latest scurrilous barrage which would, were there any truth in it, be the death knell for him in the close knit ranks of the South Yorkshire Miners.

The accusation concerns money supposedly supplied by Colonel Gaddafi, purportedly used by the President of the Union, as well as his colleagues for personal use.

Other, more damaging, reports say none of this money ever arrived in the Miners' Hardship Fund. The sum quoted was £150,000. Another allegation states $9m. were given to the Libyans after Mr Windsor, the former N.U.M. Chief Executive, visited Gaddafi in his Bedouin Tent in Tripoli. Sounds mighty colourful, conjuring up visions of silks and satins, in the midst of which sits the villain of the piece, dispensing largesse to the poor British coal-miner, in order to bring down the elected government of that country?

Throw in another £1m. for good measure, donated by the Russian Trade Unions to the N.U.M., to help miners in need, which again did not reach these beleaguered men. The battery lined up against the N.U.M. and its leaders seemed invincible.

Arthur Scargill refutes, not only the vast sum of money received by the Union, but also what he considers to be a deplorable smear campaign conducted by the British media. In particular, the accusation of the inter-mingling of N.U.M./I.M.O. funds when monies were held in I.M.O. accounts in Dublin to avoid seizure by the Official Receiver in Britain.

This money was guaranteed to be repaid, with due interest, on demand.

I tend to agree with Mr Scargill that misinformation is the name of the game.

Nothing was said of monies received from non Communist countries, or of the undisputed fact that the true amounts of money received in aid for the miners was placed overseas. Any money brought into Britain which could have helped the miner, thereby in the Government eyes prolonging the strike, would automatically have been frozen. The N.U.M. is decimated now, no sympathy for the average miner from the ordinary public, who also suffered. They had watched in horror too, as a handful of cowboys used violence of the worst sort to stop the Strike Breakers. An action not conducive to good will, even in the miners' own camp. Nonetheless, violence was used by the police to break the union's picket lines.

Many miners have taken the Golden Handshake (severance pay) from the National Coal Board. They still work in the mines as well as paying their union dues. However, they are now masters of their own destiny, hewing coal for Private Contract Mining Companies, higher paid than Coal

Board miners, too. Not so lucky were the majority put out of work. As I have intimated, Yorkshire's coalfield miners stayed mainly loyal to the N.U.M. throughout the strike, as in the years since, while Mrs Thatcher, Britain's then Prime Minister, carried out her avowed promise, 'To Bury Socialism'.

Pits have closed. Men, unable to pay back massive loans taken out in sheer desperation, had no alternative but to accept the Coal Board's redundancy offer, to get out from under the crippling debt. Where there had been strength as well as faith in a mighty union, there is only stark belief in their, and its, fate.

The Prime Minister, unbendably right-wing Conservative, truly earned the title of Iron Lady bestowed upon her by the Russians, met head-on with Arthur Scargill.

I will need some convincing that it was not a North/South, middle class versus the working class conflict more than an outright miners' strike, this north of Peterborough complex which, unlike the old soldier, will not fade away. Oddly enough, Margaret Thatcher herself is a borderline case, her roots are in Grantham, close to the City of Peterborough. She barely scrapes into the lower middle class, yet it did not deter her from placing her allegiance elsewhere, with a vindictiveness unsurpassed in British politics. It besmirches her excellent record of being Britain's finest Prime Minister since Winston Churchill. The victims of this duel to the death, were the miners, fighting to stop the closure of pits and with it the loss of their livelihood.

Unviable collieries were unavoidably doomed, others also face the threat of closure. The bitter among us claim that their position in the Yorkshire coalfields has more to do with their ceasing operations, than their inability to pay their way. I wish it were not so. Maybe with the change of leadership another stance can be taken against those sinners from the North. I must admit when I heard Markham Main, Armthorpe's colliery, was one of the pits on the Hit List, my rage went beyond being reasonable. Kate wept, it seemed unbelievable for its coal seams are far from exhausted. In fact, it was one of the richest mines for miles around.

In my young days they were the vaunted winners of the highest output, repeatedly. The village and school could have been no prouder if they had picked the whole of Britain's Cricket Eleven from there.

My anger will change nothing. A feeling of utter frustration with politics in general is pretty well world-wide. There is a stench of corruption and machination, with no apparent answer for the average Joe Bloggs. We constantly teeter on the brink of war, we haven't learned anything there either. No sooner is one crisis over than another rears its jack-booted carcass. To martial music we step in time, right over our unwilling heads.

I am getting ahead of myself, we are back in 1979. The Falklands, Iran-Iraq War and Iraq's seizure of the neighbouring state of Kuwait, are still nightmares to come.

Mr Scargill's problems, too, are hardly germane at this point of my story. Yet before we turn the pages of time, there are someone else's words I would like to pass on. I hope you will take the same joy in as I did at the time. Arthur Scargill and Mr Heathfield, the N.U.M. General Secretary, paid a visit to Low Hall during the Scarborough Conference in mid 1989. As we sat in conversation, Mr Heathfield recalled an incident which involved both Mrs Thatcher and Arthur. Someone, I forget who, had remarked, 'Mrs Thatcher has her Divine Right, Arthur has his Divine Left.' I think that says it all.

In 1979 my knowledge of Arthur Scargill had been limited to one brief meeting. What I had read or heard, I discounted. Mary Agnes had always drummed a few well chosen, as well as very wise words home.

'Judge people as you find them, do not allow others to sway your opinion. Make up your own mind.' I do not always follow that maxim, more often than not I live to regret doing so.

Loyal to my mother's guidance this time, we set off by car for our first meeting with the committee, with only the usual trepidation felt before any valued job interview. On reaching Barnsley and the Union Headquarters we realized how the building had earned its nickname. It was a turreted castle-like edifice and we were about to learn it was just as impregnable as the moated type. Its electronic doors opened and shut on the press of a button from inside the fortress.

We were ushered into an empty room, although we knew other people were being interviewed that morning. With the look of things we were being deliberately kept apart from the other hopefuls. Or was it as Owen had promised, complete confidentiality? After what seemed to have been an eternity, the door opened and an attendant then led us into a very large room. At one end of this cavernous place stood a row of tables at which eight people were sitting, all were Yorkshire Miners' Trustees.

Among them, surprise, surprise, sat Owen Briscoe. We were seated almost opposite and close to the tables.

Before the interview could begin, Owen rose to his feet, pushing his chair back as he did so.

'I wish to decline to be on the interview panel,' he stared at me without recognition, before adding his reason for withdrawal. 'I have known Peter for most of his life, it would not be proper if I should be among the interviewers.'

Just as I had thought at least one of the buggers is on side too, he turns sanctimonious on us, after talking me into applying in the first place. He left without a backward glance at either my wife or myself.

We were told later that Owen had done all his lobbying before the meeting began.

Owen informed us later, 'I knew you were home and hosed, no other couple had your width of experience. Rules are rules, I had to declare my interest. I would have been asked to leave in any case. I didn't wait for that, I exempted myself before it could prejudice your chances.'

It turned out to be one of the toughest interviews we had ever undergone, probably because of Owen's campaigning on our behalf. Arthur Scargill bored holes through us with his penetrating stare, firing questions at both Shirley and me with the rapidity of a machine-gun. It went on and on, we thought endlessly, going over our past employment, as well as our references in the most drawn out detail. We felt almost as if we had been put through a wringer. Finally it ended. We were told formally and politely, 'you will be informed of our decision in the near future.'

We left that building with a feeling of immense relief. Interview? It had been more in the style of an interrogation.

We heard through the grapevine that quite a number of people had made it to the short list and were officially notified that we were among that selection, as Owen had predicted.

To learn that we were up against a number of people, did not surprise us. It was to be expected, after all it was a rare plum of a position. Home would be Low Hall, valued then at £4m. You can bet your sweet life, Arthur Scargill and his executive, were not about to let any Tom, Dick or Harry, take over the post. I believe it to be one of the largest investments of the Yorkshire Miners and as such it would be painstakingly protected.

On our return to The Rosette, after our second interview, we were less

The Mayor and Mayoress of Barnsley, 1986: Jack Wood, JP, BEM, former Senior Social Welfare Officer, Coal Industry, and his wife Alice.

sure of landing the position than we had been after our first audience with the committee. The examination had been as tough as the first we thought, with less interest being shown by the panel. In spite of Owen's earlier assurances we remained convinced our chances were indeed very slim.

At approximately nine-thirty that same night the phone rang. Shirley answered from the bar. It was Mr Jack Wood, the Senior Social Welfare Officer of the N.U.M., a personal friend of Owen Briscoe, and Arthur Scargill, as well as being a larger than life character by anyone's standards. He told my wife, 'the meeting of the trustees has only this moment broken up, after an almighty struggle because they couldn't reach agreement. You and your husband have been appointed to the post.'

Shirley, so excited could only screech the news to me, despite the bar being as busy as hell, yelled, 'Peter, Peter, we have been given Low Hall.'

Her recitation of the phoned message was so garbled, I had to quieten her down to understand the substance of it. I hoped the rest of the people present, were as wise as I was at that time, for my wife was completely incomprehensible.

I hadn't realized how important it had been to her. I had become so inured to having to accept defeat in one way or another, her intensity of feeling left me dazed.

We were so overwhelmed, each in our own way, we had trouble sleeping that night, still being in a state of flux several days later. Then I could feel grateful to Jack Wood, he hadn't left us to worry for long. He was to be our boss for the next four years, a jolly good one too.

Only after we'd had time to absorb the news, besides getting over the thrill of gaining the position over tough opposition, did the enormity of what we were on the verge of doing, strike us. Now it was reality time. We were about to leave the licensed trade after eighteen and a half years. Precarious as it may have been at times, it was the only job we knew how to do well. Even though I say it myself, we made a particularly good pair of mine hosts. How we would fare at Low Hall as superintendent and matron remained to be seen now.

As we worked out our notice at The Rosette, we had time to reflect on the years spent as managers of public houses, tumbling through our minds as a kaleidoscope of coloured jigsaw pieces, falling haphazardly into place. The good, the bad? The good far outweighed the bad, as in most people's reflections. We had indeed been lucky to land management of London's West End houses, at such an early age.

The Porcupine in Leicester Square had been a joy, we had loved every dear minute of it, even taking into account our fear of the Kray Brothers' assumed retribution. The oh so obvious class of the Cheshire Cheese in the City of London. The pretentiousness of some of its customers, who had provided me with many a quiet titter. Our Sunday strolls in Petticoat Lane, the memory of Mam soaking up the atmosphere in those places. How she had adored London's ever changing scene. The massive King's Head in Wimbledon, our frightening time in The Albert, plus the subsequent horror of being under suspicion. Unemployment, the degradation is just as potent today . . . the benumbing fear, which will probably never leave me. The move back home to Yorkshire, the wisest move I have ever made, The Futurist in Scarborough, getting to know the talented Black and White Minstrels. The Bier Keller, coupled with the subsequent gaining of The Silver Grid, and all those marvellously happy years there.

Now it was the turn of The Rosette to be relegated to memory, I had lost many friends while beneath that roof. Pete Platts, who had died of a massive heart attack. David Whitfield, a charmer of the first order, who had died just as suddenly. My own beloved Czar, still a very live recollection most days.

Yet I have never considered Mam lost to me, I find her presence everywhere. That photograph taken in Petticoat Lane hangs at the side of my desk. Her hackneyed sayings still ring in my ears, as do the warning bells when someone is trying me for size.

As I have repeated *ad nauseam*, we worked beyond the accepted norm, as do most publicans of busy houses. However we did it in style, and in the very best of company.

I sometimes wonder if I would have enjoyed the life so much in any old run of the mill pub. No. I know the answer. It is a whopping great No. To all the people who contributed to making the life my wife and I lived, so enjoyable and diverse, a bloody big thank you. It isn't over yet, not by anyone's yardstick, we still have a lot of hills to climb, though I sincerely hope there won't be too many mountains to surmount. We have had our share of those.

They say we learn by our errors, so far I haven't been too bloody clever at that. There is another axiom which states, Wisdom comes with Age. Enough said.

Everyone in Scalby knew we were leaving The Rosette, to run the Miners' Home. At times I thought the knowledge extended to the whole of Scarborough. Most wished us well in our new venture, others were only interested in filling our shoes at The Rosette. As in our time, applicants for the position were far from scarce. It was of little moment to us. Our bridges burned, we mentally moved on, hoping beyond measurement, we would be able to cope with the momentous task which we had set ourselves.

Eventually, the time arrived for us to throw off the mantle of publican and wife, yet there was still one last fling to be flung. Our official farewell, a going away party, although we were only moving up the road a little way.

What a party it was! Staff and patrons alike threw themselves into the spirit of the thing, some too well, paying full entry price the following day. Needless to say I was one of the latter.

This February of 1979, we became no longer mine hosts, but superintendent and matron of the Miners' Rest Home, Low Hall.

Low Hall, this elegant, palatial house was first inhabited by Wilhelm Rowntree from Christmas 1904, as a family home and Quaker school. As I've already told you, the Hall was not completed until 1905. Wilhelm arrived from York accompanied by his wife and four children, Margaret, Lawrence, Antoinette and Violet. Last but far from least member of this family was their dog, a Great Dane named, appropriately, Hamlet. He it is who lies in the orchard of Low Hall, marked by a wonderful epitaph.

Who knows why Wilhelm moved in a year early, did he want to see his family settled into their new home? For their stay at Low Hall was very brief, as well as being particularly sad, 1904 to 1926. John Wilhelm Rowntree died in 1905 at the young age of thirty-seven. He died not at home, but in York, the city where his family business was based.

Violet died in 1906 at the age of three, Lawrence Edmund, by then an Army lieutenant, was killed in France in 1917, during the first World War, at the wasteful age of twenty-two. Margaret and Sarah Antoinette lived to a ripe old age, as did a fifth child born in 1905, and named Wilhelmina. The latter recently appeared on television, in fact it was in 1988, and spoke on the life of her grandfather, Joseph Rowntree of York, cocoa manufacturer and philanthropist.

Margaret, a retired Civil Servant, died at the age of eighty in York. Sarah Antoinette, now aged ninety, is a retired school teacher, and lives in Harrow, London.

The widow of Wilhelm, Mrs Constance Mary Rowntree, stayed on at Low Hall until 1926, when she moved to the Manor House which she had had built at Langdale End, Scarborough. In spite of the unhappy memories, apparently she was very attached to Low Hall, the mansion her husband had built. At least so I have been led to believe by family historians.

When Arthur Scargill bought the Low Hall for the N.U.M., it was sold by the Coal Industry's Social Welfare Organization, for the very low figure of £45,000, on condition it remained a Miners' Convalescent Home.

Its true value in 1978 was in the region of £4 million. With the seventeen acres of land it holds, it was truly a bargain basement price. An absolute steal for Mr Scargill, who still boasts, and rightly so, that it was the best deal he had ever made for the Yorkshire Miners. Two years later Arthur became the National N.U.M. President, when Joe Gormley retired.

Our life at the Low Hall was totally different to the one we had envisaged, completely unlike the life encountered in the licensed trade. Our customers were now convalescent and retired miners who had to be fed three substantial meals per day. Each batch of miners actually stayed at the Hall for eleven day periods, arriving at Low Hall on the Monday afternoon they left on the following Friday Week. A coach picked them up from their homes to bring them to the Hall, returning them eleven days later, all the cost being borne by the Yorkshire Miners' N.U.M. The two weekly break of three days, when the Low Hall was empty, was the time off for the staff and Shirley and myself.

It was heaven, squirrels so tame they begged for food, birds in infinite variety, park-like grounds to wander at will, as well as the lovely village of Scalby to call home. We could shop together, go out together, take a run into the countryside and stay for an evening meal. We were no longer ruled by the clock. Having to be back for opening time, was now a thing of the past. The pressure was off on those three clear days. We began each fortnight refreshed.

Far from boring, it was considerably more interesting than we had anticipated too. Owen Briscoe, the Yorkshire Miners' General Secretary, based at Barnsley, would send over visiting foreign miner's delegations, to look around Low Hall. We would pull out all the stops for these V.I.P.s, a first-class five course meal and a big welcome was the order of the day.

In our first two years, 1979-80 we entertained the Russians, Chinese, Cuban, Czechoslovakian as well as Yugoslavian delegations, along with the usual entourage of embassy people besides interpreters from London. Shirley used to seat me at the table with these people which could be mighty uncomfortable, too, at times. One instance comes to mind of a Chinese delegation, eight of them excluding the embassy interpreter, the only one who could speak English.

We had decided, as it was Sunday, to serve them the traditional Yorkshire Sunday dinner. Roast beef and Yorkshire pudding with all the trimmings, as the main course.

There was a constant babble of voices, in what seemed to me to be an unintelligible cacophony. To take my mind off this, I watched a huge

The author and his wife, The Low Hall.

Chinese miner, an electrician at his home colliery. (I wonder, if like me, once you are aware of some personal detail, people actually become more human and understandable, apart from their damned language.) I had observed this man clear everything which had been placed before him. Now, I watched mesmerized as he chased a single pea round and around his empty plate.

The interpreter, noticing my interest, leaned across the table towards me, saying smilingly, 'you see it is an insult in China, not to eat everything that is placed before you, when you are a guest in another's house.'

I felt chastened, not only was there a language barrier, but their customs showed such a great regard for their host's feelings. They were truly splendid human beings. I understood a lot better after that.

Three of the working miners in this group had never left their work commune before. I often wonder what they made of us, as well as everything they were seeing. All that luxury spent on men just like themselves, not kept only for the Communist leaders and an exalted few.

Another story about a Czechoslovakian delegation I am sure is worthy of telling.

This group of people was quite large, sixteen in all, including the embassy officials and the interpreters. Among this number was the Arthur Scargill of their Union, the President of Mineworkers.

We had a great time with this group. After the meal they were taken around the Hall in its entirety, besides the grounds. The president appeared very interested in watching some of the English miners playing bowls, on Low Hall's beautiful crown green. He couldn't speak English, so he asked an interpreter to inquire if he could join in the game.

We were only too delighted to show him how to play, I took him on to the green and proceeded to teach him, which wasn't easy as it all had to be done by sign language. I taught him how to make the ball turn the way he wanted it to, using different bias, a bulge or weight in one side of a bowl. In no time at all I realized the man was a natural who, with practice, could become an excellent player.

He was receiving deafening applause as he bowled, from the rest of the delegation, as well as English miners watching, for he played unbelievably well for a novice. We had gone up and down the green several times, when he suddenly stopped in front of a huge crowd of miners and visitors which had formed to watch him play.

Everything was silent as he pointed to me, pointed at the crowd, pointed down at the bowls, then shouted at the top of his voice, 'Francees Drak.'

He had suddenly remembered some long forgotten history lesson of an English nobleman who coolly played bowls while the Spanish Armada loomed ever closer.

Everyone clapped him, for an Englishman loves nothing better than for a foreigner to pay homage to Britain's historic past.

He was so full of himself too, that he had remembered that bit of English history. The applause was well and truly earned as far as he was concerned.

Even on their departure, as he shook hands with all and sundry, reaching me he hugged my body to him, saying again with a wide grin, 'Francees Drak.'

The Czechoslovakian interpreter told me, 'he will tell everyone when he gets home, how he played bowls with the British. Just as Frances Drake had done.'

We had really made that man's day.

The Low Hall, to all outward appearances, was still a magnificent building. However, we knew its plumbing, electrical wiring, and its central heating were grossly outdated. In 1979, the washing facilities in the patients' bedrooms were 1920s style. A renewal and update was urgently needed, if only because of the potential fire-hazard to these far from agile people.

Owen Briscoe made me a promise, 'Peter, before I retire, I will see that half a million pounds is spent on renovations to the building.'

Throughout 1980-81, he reaffirmed his commitment several times to this project, vowing to bring Low Hall up to the standard of a four or five star hotel.

In late 1981, Owen Briscoe's pledge came to fruition. He had managed to persuade the Executive Committee to grant enough money for a complete restoration of Low Hall. As promised, it was to be on a grand scale. The architects moved in to draw up their plans, Shirley and I moved out into a rented bungalow in the village of Scalby, accompanied by our dog, a lovely Alsatian named Max, which we had acquired two years previously to fill the awful void left by Czar.

Max is one absolute character, a photo nut, bring out a camera and Max is there . . . ready to pose. He must be the most photographed dog in Britain. Each batch of miners have their photographs taken on arrival and Max is on all of them, besides the hundreds of others taken privately by the patients.

Jacqueline had left home to do her own thing which included buying a flat in Scarborough, as well as taking up a secretarial position in town. My wife and I hadn't much time to brood on the latter, though I know that Shirley missed her dreadfully.

Things were not going smoothly at Low Hall. Do they ever in the building trade? Shepherds, a long established York building firm, had won the contract for the renovation work. Fletcher, Ross and Hickling, a Leeds company, were the architects. As is their wont, costs were spiralling sky high. From the original quote of £500,000 they were now exceeding £800,000. To say the N.U.M. Executives were not pleased, is a vast understatement of the true amount of feeling in that camp.

Fur and feathers flew between them and the architects and we were caught in the middle of these broadsides. It wasn't pleasant, I can tell you. I felt like an underweight referee, trapped between two Heavyweight boxers. On top of all of this, the proposed height of the new boiler chimney became not just another wrangle, the dispute actually reached the hallowed halls of the Houses of Parliament.

To understand why, I must explain the lie of the land so far as Low Hall is concerned. The Hall is actually built on ground governed by the Scarborough Council and the North Yorkshire Moors National Park. The dividing line cuts right across the centre of the property. The offending chimney stack which would stand approximately fifty foot high, was just on National Park territory, part of an area of 650 square miles which was established as National Park land in 1952.

It has a population of around 25,000 which includes householders, farmers and large landholders. Among them are the Duchy of Lancaster, the Queen, as well as the Duchy of Cornwall, the Prince of Wales.

Two thousand buildings are listed as of architectural value, or of historical interest. As I have told you, tourism is a major factor of the area. Thornton le Dale is only one of the outstanding villages. Conservation sites abound, Cawthorne Roman Camps, Ravenscar Quarries, Hutton le Hole, beautiful Helmsley, Glaisdale, Goathland, Fylingthorpe, Swainby, Kirkbymoorside, one can go on, the list is almost endless. There are 8,000 records of architectural sites in the Park. Of these 350 have statutory protection. In 1974, the entire National Park coastline was defined as part of the North Yorkshire and Cleveland Heritage Coast.

There are 620 farms in the park, forty-three per cent of these are dairy farms. Thirty-seven per cent rear sheep and cattle and only twenty per cent are arable.

It is an area of outstanding beauty in anyone's eyes. The River Esk is the only Yorkshire river where salmon and trout still breed. Otters and colourful birds such as the kingfisher and dipper command undisturbed conditions surpassed nowhere.

I tell you of all this, not only to boast of the county of my origin, but also to give you an idea of what the N.U.M. was up against. One has a better chance of being a Pools winner, than obtaining permission to build on National Park land, let alone erect a monstrous chimney visible to all. Not least in such a conservative area as Scalby, whose inhabitants were appalled at the concept, pledging to fight it tooth and nail.

The entire thing was dumped in Owen Briscoe's lap, probably because the whole idea of renovation had been his from the very beginning. In spite of all of Owen's efforts, the work on Low Hall came to a dead stop. It was estimated the lost time alone cost the N.U.M. £50,000.

Roy Mason, the Labour M.P. for Barnsley, Yorkshire was contacted. Mason still had some standing, even with a Conservative government in power. He was the former Northern Ireland Secretary, not a position which most M.P.s coveted . . . no matter how anxious they were to become cabinet ministers. One cannot blame them for this, it is one sure fire way of being top of the Irish Republican Army's Hit List.

Mason sent a letter to Michael Heseltine, the then Environment Minister who promptly placed it in front of Margaret Thatcher, Britain's then Prime Minister. The oft quoted, yet seemingly unrecorded statement, from Mrs Thatcher was a stark, chilling indication of what the next two years would bring, 'give them what they want. We do not wish for any trouble with the Yorkshire miners at this time.'

In all fairness, one must say those very miners were credited with the downfall of the previous Conservative Prime Minister, Edward Heath. For whatever reason, work resumed on Low Hall, the chimney stack objections were swept aside, as were the local conservationists. Even so, all hope of re-opening the Low Hall before the end of 1982, was just a pipe dream. A new date was set for the end of February 1983.

Gordon Rowley, Mr Wood's secretary, was by now frantic with worry. His problems arose because of the cost entailed in keeping Shirley and me in an expensive rented bungalow, in Scalby. It was costing £5,000 plus for the year. Put in the context of the enormous escalation of building costs, this should have been the least of their worries. Our rental expenses were a mere drop in the leaking bucket.

Everyone on the site was now uptight. Pressure from above bore down on all, including men doing the most menial of tasks. At the end of each working day, my wife and I couldn't get away from the place fast enough. For the first time, we began to question our judgement in leaving The Rosette. We avoided Owen Briscoe as if he had the plague. Not without just cause, for he snarled and cursed at anyone who came within range. I cannot honestly say, or remember a time, when we saw him smile between the stopping of work on Low Hall and the completion of the renovations.

Gordon Rowley came off the phone one day, his face drawn and white. It moved me so much, I asked compassionately, 'what on earth is the matter, Gordon?'

'I have just been talking to Owen Briscoe.' He took a deep breath, before continuing wryly, 'God, is he mad, he has just told me, and these are his words not mine, "I wish the fucking place would blow up, the f'ing chimney and all ". I don't know who has been having a go at him. Whoever it was did a good job. I have never heard him so upset. Needless to say, I got my share of the fall out.'

Unlike most of us, Gordon couldn't avoid Owen, he had to report the day's doings, good or indifferent. I did not envy his position one bit. Eventually, with the dawn of another year, work on Low Hall actually neared completion.

Brand new central heating worked like a charm. There had been an entire electrical re-wiring done, the plumbing had undergone a massive overhaul and re-modernization. Every bedroom now had its own *en suite* wash basin, shower and toilet. The kitchen was a dream, white and spacious, equalling any top class hotel's facilities. One's feet sank into the new luxurious carpets, the whole building sparkled, for there had been a complete refurbishment as well.

Owen's promise of a four or five star hotel for the miners had been well and truly kept. All the trauma of the last few months faded, the blood spilled figuratively, the actual sweat and the real tears, were a thing of the past. Best of all we were back in the licensed trade.

A cocktail lounge had been added, a small bar in one corner, the rest of the room furnished the same as any better hotel's lounge area.

When I say we were back in the licensed trade again, we were, albeit with a restricted clientele, staff and residents only.

This did not mean we would be standing around in there. Fifty miners every two weeks would ensure a damned busy bar. Those men could drink beer unlike anyone in Britain. Probably because of their dust-coated lungs, it is almost impossible to slake their thirst.

The final cost for the restoration of Low Hall, had nearly doubled from the original estimate. It was almost £1 million.

The opening day was a further opportunity for some of the Yorkshire Miners' National Executive to have another swipe at the architects. Some very harsh, strong verbiage was used, which apparently bounced off both parties. It was just as well, for that day, 16 February 1983, was not a day to be spoiled by anyone. Even though £500,000 extra charge was a good enough reason, in anybody's books, to sound off.

In spite of the verbal mayhem, opening day was a splendid memorable occasion. Jack Taylor and Sammy Thompson, the President and Vice President of the Yorkshire Miners attended the ceremony, as well as Ken Homer, the General Secretary, besides Owen Briscoe along with all the rest of the Yorkshire Executive Members. As you know, the project had always been Owen Briscoe's baby, even if at times he would have loved to disown the bloody child. In recognition of this fact, he was to perform the opening ceremonial act. I had ordered a huge, brass plaque, which Neville, the Hall's handyman, had fastened to the wall. A red velvet curtain covered the inscribed tablet, a tasselled pull waited for Owen's hand as he declared the Hall re-opened.

The people clustered around the plaque included, Owen, Shirley and myself, Sammy Thompson and Ken Homer. This was for the official photographs of the opening. Just as Owen pulled the curtains apart, Ken Homer blurted out loudly, 'Bloody Hell, Owen, they have spelt your name wrong!'

The words on the tablet read, 'Yorkshire Miners' N.U.M., The Low Hall, Opened by Owen Briscoe, General Secretary, after refurbishment. February 1983.'

Of course the name had not been misspelt. After verifying this, everyone present began laughing. All except Owen that is, he was close up to the plaque frowningly inspecting same, checking to see if I had spelt his name incorrectly. At that precise moment, the flash bulb went off, the official

Re-opening of The Low Hall, February 1983 by Mr Owen Briscoe, Gen. Sec. Yorkshire Miners.
Left to right: Peter Aldridge (Supt.), Ken Homer (Hon. Sec.), Sammy Thompson (Vice Pres.), Owen Briscoe, Shirley Aldridge (Matron).

photograph had been taken. It showed a deeply frowning General Secretary of the Yorkshire Miners' Union, yet beneath the concentration, lay an extremely happy and relieved man that the whole bloody episode was behind him.

I look at the commemorative tablet now and smile, it was a typical miner's leg-pull, they have little time for ceremony, taking every opportunity to deflate officialdom. I remember one occasion on Doncaster Racecourse, at the beginning of a Classic race meeting. King George VI accompanied by his wife, Elizabeth, was being driven along the course in an open landau. In the quiet stillness, which typified Doncaster's reaction to the appearance of royalty, a raucous, strongly accented Yorkshire voice boomed out, 'taking your Missus for the day out, George?'

One may not necessarily approve, probably George was as heartily sick of all that pomp as the miners and their families were.

The Yorkshire miner is an unwitting pragmatist, yet certainly a practising one. A man of sturdy character, faithful to a high degree and at the same time, deliberately obstinate and bloody minded when he wants to be. Do not underestimate him, he is astute in spite of that quirk of character. The majority are hard drinking, gambling men, who enjoy nothing better than to sit down with a pint of beer, to watch racing on television.

This same man will bring tears to your eyes, as with badly gnarled hands, he proudly exhibits photographs of his children and grandchildren. The older miner can relate stories of times gone by, terrible tales which transport you back in time to the traumatic 1920–30 period, stories of poverty, of a degradation unknown today. Of senseless, cruel death in the mines, the lingering suffering of those smitten by pneumoconiosis, of which most of these men have first hand knowledge.

The modern miner guards against this killer disease. The use of masks, coupled with up-to-date methods of mining, having succeeded in cutting the dust down considerably.

If they have a better standard in the workplace, as well as in their lifestyle, then surely it is not before time. Personally, I think they are bloody heroes for ever going down the mine, let alone working in those still very dangerous, deep black holes in the earth.

Through it all they retain the dour exterior of the true Yorkshireman, hiding a mischievous sense of humour, plus an almost sacrosanct regard for their dignity and independence. Who are we to criticize that?

Before we move on to other, and I think more amusing chapters in my life, let me attempt to pinpoint why my sympathy will forever remain with the miner.

The racking cough which heralds the appearance of most of the older miners, that deadly unmistakeable symptom of pneumoconiosis. The endurance and resolute, wilful strength shown during the ruinous miners' strike of the eighties. Other parts of Britain capitulated, rightly or wrongly I do not know. In the same manner I would not have the temerity to judge the Yorkshire Miners' actions. You must be judge and jury and find peace in your own mind, I cannot.

For good or bad, I love these indomitable men, for I am part of them. My roots lie deep in the South Yorkshire coalfields.

The mundane life inside Low Hall is shattered daily by the banter between patients of both sexes. This often leaves me doubled up, a smile lingering long after the jokers have gone. There are other times when I am not sure whether to laugh or cry. The following incident was one of those occasions, actually I think I did both simultaneously.

A miner by the name of Ken Jackson had forgotten to bring a towel with him (all linen is supplied, apart from personal items such as towels, face flannels, et cetera). When a miner forgets these essential items, or toiletries, Matron, (Shirley) will provide the necessities. Ken was either too shy, or too independent to ask, he was trying to get along with the hand roller-towel, which was changed daily. One of the older miners approached me one day, laughing fit to burst, 'if you want a good laugh, Super, go and watch Ken Jackson having his shower.'

As Shirley is addressed as Matron, I am always referred to as Super, the diminutive of superintendent.

Ken had been placed in a top dormitory, within which there was a second shower. I went upstairs wondering what the dickens the old fellow had seen to make him laugh so heartily? On entering the shower room, an incredible sight met my eyes. There stood Ken, clad in the altogether, trying futilely to dry himself on the loose roller-towel, while it was still on the roller. First one leg raised on high, then the other, on to the tip of his toes twisting his body as a contortionist would, attempting to make the towel reach his bottom to dry that difficult part.

Hopelessly, I struggled to control the splutters, as I asked, 'Ken, why don't you take the towel off the roller?'

'Never bloody thought of that,' he answered, looking at me blankly.

I knew he was far from thick upstairs, it was far more likely Ken would not dream of doing such a thing, he would consider that to be taking advantage of the situation.

Shirley, when told, immediately provided towels, scolding him gently for foolishly not telling her he had forgotten to pack them.

Incidents like this occurred almost daily. One can easily understand Owen Briscoe's reasoning for giving them five star hotel luxury. Most appreciated the opulent style. For a glorious eleven days they wallow in the luxury, for that time they are king of all they survey.

In a short while I will tell you of one bugger who didn't enjoy Low Hall. Then again maybe he had different ideas on how to enjoy himself, for he certainly gave me the old runaround that's for sure.

Firstly we will stay with a man cast from much the same mould as Ken. Every evening at around 10.30 to 11 p.m., I make a tour of the Hall, turning out the lights after I have checked each area. I often open a bedroom door to have a few words with a patient, mostly it is to swap a joke I have just been told, before I wish them goodnight.

This particular evening, having almost completed my round, while passing one of the single rooms, I heard a voice coming from inside. I quietly opened the door to see who was with him, for all patients are supposed to be in their own quarters by that hour.

There, on his hands and knees beside the bed, was this small rotund figure of a man, earnestly saying his prayers. He was as naked as the day he was born, his back turned towards me he obviously hadn't heard me open the door, so was unaware of my presence. He continued his devotion with the Lord's Prayer. 'Our Father who art in heaven, hallowed be thy name.'

Suddenly, a loud trumpeting sound rent the air. The man had noisily passed wind. There was a hushed silence for a second or two, then he bent his head again, before saying humbly, 'sorry, Lord.'

Before he carried on with his litany, from the point where he had left off, I closed the door as quietly as I could, tip-toeing away from the vicinity, almost falling down the stairs in my hurry to reach a place where I could crack up.

Not so touching or amusing is the next guy to feel the weight of my pen. As I put the pieces together for this, my story, I remember him and his confounded typewriter.

His name was Mr Francis, quite a clever fellow actually. Before his retirement he had been a pit deputy. He was also a confirmed alcoholic who was intent on teaching others a maxim he was unable to adhere to. And how. He was busy at that time, putting together his past experiences with the Demon Drink. Had he got something to write about on that subject? From close-up first-hand knowledge, he could have written reams, and for all I know he may well have done so.

At no time did his typewriter ever leave his side. I am not vindictive as a rule, yet I sincerely hope he had as many headaches with his literary effort as I had compiling this.

We lost little time getting to know each other's less than better side. I had to have strong words with Mr Francis, after only the second night of his visit to Low Hall.

Shirley had put him in a room designed for three patients, the only one in the Hall which contained three beds. That was our first misjudgment of the man. There were to be many more to follow.

After the second night, the two other occupants in the dormitory asked if they could speak with me in private. They told me they were absolutely terrified of the man, one of them informing me, 'he paces the room all night muttering, sometimes he even shouts. When we eventually manage . to fall asleep, through sheer exhaustion, he wakes us again by typing on that blasted typewriter of his.'

'Have you had a word with him together? There is safety in numbers you know. I realize the fellow sounds a bit potty, but that doesn't mean he is a raving lunatic,' I blithely told them, thinking to myself, silly old bugger is probably a bit senile and needs gentle persuasion, as to what is acceptable behaviour or unacceptable.

'Potty! You must be joking, Super. The man is out of his bloody mind. He shouted at us when we tried to pacify him during the night, he yelled, "I have got to get out of here. I will kill myself and take someone with me." I tell you, Super, something has to be done about that bloody weirdo. It is a long way down to the ground from our window, if that is what the silly bugger has in mind to do,' one of the men vehemently said.

Immediately disturbed by this forceful statement, I assured them, 'something will be done, and straight away. I will see the man now.'

True to my word, I sent for Mr Francis. Within a couple of minutes of his entering the office, even a complete idiot would have been aware the man was unstable. Belligerently so. I could understand the reason for the two men's fear. I wasn't too keen on him either.

Nevertheless, I talked at length, like a Dutch uncle, yet still placatory, convinced at the end of this long-winded chat that I had managed to settle him down. However, I was still going to keep a close, watchful eye on Mr Francis. Suicides I could live without. Murderers, be they *non compos mentis* or as sane as you or I, were a definite No No in my book.

That evening at nine-thirty, a time when all the patients were supposed to be back in the Hall, after all it is a convalescent home, not a hotel, our Mr Francis was missing. I lock the doors at precisely 9.30 p.m. If the men are late back then they must ring the bell, besides having one hell of a good excuse for their tardiness.

With apparent concern, one of the patients informed me, 'Francis is in a pub in the village, you won't see him back tonight. He looked set for the night when I left, Super.'

During the time in which these men are listed as patients at Low Hall they, for better or worse, are in my care. I am responsible for them until I book them on to the coach which will carry them back to their own doorstep. That night I waited until everyone else was safely settled down in their own quarters. There was still no sign of Mr Francis. That meant I had to go searching for him in the village.

I tried both public houses in Scalby, he wasn't in either of them. No one admitted to seeing him, most can recognize the patients from Low Hall. I set off for my old stamping ground, The Rosette. Reaching there, I walked through the familiar bar room, looking from this vantage point into the lounge. There stood an unperturbed Francis, propping up the bar, pint in hand, typewriter by his side, obviously collecting more memoirs for his book. He appeared not to have a care in the world as he blissfully sipped his beer in silence.

I spoke quietly to the landlord, who was behind the bar in the bar room. 'I have been searching for one of my chaps, I have just found him in your lounge room. Now he could prove troublesome. It is almost closing time for you and as we don't want any bother in here I propose to leave him where he is until then. It will be a lot wiser to pick him up outside as he leaves.'

'He has given me no bother, Peter, apart from mouthing off about alcoholism. Which I must admit, isn't too bloody good for business.'

I had to smile at that, I could picture the scene as men edged away from this spoiler of a good night out.

I had a quick half-pint of beer, with one of my old regulars, a man named Bill Hollingsworth. I explained what I was doing there, as well as the possibility of a slight unpleasantness with my ward, who was undoubtedly a little unbalanced.

'I will back you up, Peter. That will deter the bugger from causing any trouble. Two of us will appear to be one too many for even a crack brain.'

How wrong he was!

At closing time, we stood just outside the outer door to the lounge, waiting patiently for our man to appear. Almost last to leave the room came my recalcitrant pain in the bum.

'Good evening, Mr Francis,' I said pleasantly.

He stared at me for a long questioning second or two, before responding, 'good evening, Super. What are you doing here?'

'I have come for you,' I told him quietly. 'I have got the car outside, I can drive you back to the Hall.'

'I am not going back,' he retorted angrily.

'Be a good chap, and go back with the superintendent,' Bill urged gently.

'I am not going back there,' Francis truculently informed him.

'Look here, Mr Francis, don't be silly all your clothes and belongings are back there,' I reasoned. 'Come on back with me now, I promise you, you can go home first thing in the morning.'

Promise! I would make bloody sure he went home at first light. My idea of keeping the wheels turning smoothly, did not include scouring the countryside late at night, for a man who was not very well upstairs. Without another word, taking both Bill and I by complete surprise, he made his unexpected move.

He pushed Bill violently up against me. Stupidly astounded, we were really caught off balance. As we tried to disentangle our bodies, Francis had shot out of the doorway into the darkness of the street, like a hare in full flight from the starting gate. By the time we had managed to sort ourselves out, there was no sign of the loony miscreant.

I went back inside The Rosette to phone Shirley, telling her, 'Shirley, get on to the police, Francis has scarpered. I found him in The Rosette, I had Bill Hollingsworth to help me, but it wasn't enough, the bastard pushed Bill into me and took off. He could be hiding anywhere. It is as black as hell out here, we will never find him without some help.'

'What do I tell the police, Peter? That he is unwell.'

'Yes, he is all of that and more. Give them his description and identity. The sooner we get him back the better, no telling what he might do.'

Bill and I drove round and round Scalby as well as Newby, peering into every dark alley, touring up and down every street. To no avail, there was no sign of my patient lurking anywhere. We decided to cover the main road out of Scarborough, more in desperation than well thought out sensible reasoning.

After about a mile and a half of shadow searching, we came across my unwilling ward, striding along the middle of the road, typewriter still in hand, happily oblivious, or uncaring of all the trouble he was causing. I slowed the car down behind him, just as a police car came towards him, stopping with its headlights full on Francis. Out of this stepped a lone policemen.

'Come on, Bill,' I yelled to my passenger. Almost in unison, we jumped out of my car, racing towards the naive policeman.

The copper strode up to Francis and stood in front of him, with the two of us now behind him. We had him trapped.

He looked back at Bill and me. The street was well lit in this section, we also had the added glare from the police car's headlights which silhouetted all of us as if we were on a stage.

Harshly, Francis's voice rang out, 'don't come near me.' He swung the typewriter round his head, in a very threatening manner.

'Please, Mr Francis,' I cajoled, 'calm down, we won't hurt you.'

At that precise moment, the handle of the typewriter case came off, the case itself sailed over a high privet hedge into a private garden. Francis's attention diverted, the young bobby dived at him, grabbing him around the waist. Not to be outdone, I grabbed his arm, Bill tried to restrain him too and copped the worst of it, as my patient using his feet as weapons, kicked out wildly at my poor friend.

It was a ridiculous mêlée of arms and legs, then crash, we all went headlong through the privet hedge on to a lawn at the other side. Immediately, all the lights in the house beyond flooded into the garden. An irate male voice emanated from an upstairs window, demanding, 'what the hell is going on down there?'

'It is all right, sir,' the policeman answered, 'it's only the police.'

Hardly the truth, there were two others plus a madman in the man's garden. Besides, I didn't think ruining someone's front garden was all right. Still, the bobby obviously knew his job and how to respond to the questioning public better than I did. I make a point now of never arguing with the police force. I can find enough trouble without, as you will have noted.

For no apparent reason Francis suddenly became extremely rational, 'there is no need for all this nonsense,' he said quietly, 'I will come back to Low Hall with you, Super.'

My mind reacted, as all reasoning minds would. The bloody swine, it yelled. We had woken up the whole neighbourhood, lights shone from most windows, and here was this cretin smilingly climbing through the hedge to get into my car. As he did so, he turned towards me, saying politely, 'don't forget my typewriter, Super.'

'I wish I could shove it up his arse,' I murmured to Bill, as I picked the offending item up off the ground.

Bill had ripped his jacket in several places, the policeman had broken his torch, I would never be the same again. We had done irreparable damage to the privet hedge, as well as disturbing the sleep of almost everyone within earshot. The cause of all this trouble, with a capital T, was now comfortably seated in the back seat of my car, looking exactly like a moggy which has just demolished a bowl full of cream.

Bill sat with the man until we reached his home, Francis was quiet throughout the journey. I then drove the reprobate back to the Hall, and to an acutely worried wife.

Shirley ushered us quickly into the office, before providing two mugs of highly sweetened tea, assuming we were both suffering from shock. As far as I was concerned, she wasn't wrong, the other sod was acting as if all was right with the world.

'How are you, Mr Francis?' my wife asked, seemingly indifferent to yours truly's plight.

'I am very well, thank you, Matron,' the moron replied smugly.

I think he actually was too. He had obviously enjoyed the whole sorry episode, angrily I decided it was time to change all that.

'You realize we cannot keep you here now, we will have to send you home in the morning,' I said sternly.

'I want to go home now, get me a bloody taxi,' he demanded aggressively.

Like a chameleon, he had changed once again, his mind obviously off on its psychotic roller-coaster anew.

There and then I realized my mistake, once more I tried to calm him down. 'Don't be silly, there's a good chap. You come from Wakefield, that is easily eighty miles from here. Go to bed, in the morning you can go home after breakfast, refreshed.'

'I am going home now, you cannot keep me here against my will, I don't care.'

He pulled a wallet out of his trouser pocket, it was crammed with notes. He waved this stuffed purse under my nose tauntingly saying, 'I have enough money to get home, and I am going home now.

I capitulated. I had another forty-nine men under my care and he was bloody dangerous to have around. His rightful place was in a nursing home for the mentally disturbed. We hadn't the facilities to care for men like him, nor did we want them. One brush with a nut, is enough for me.

I phoned a taxi driver I knew personally, for no one else would wear us at that ungodly hour.

'Clive, I have a chap here who wishes to leave, he lives in Wakefield, can you drive him there?'

'Christ, Peter, Wakefield! You have got me out of bed to drive some bloody bloke all the way to Wakefield?' he half-asked and partially complained.

'He will pay you before you leave here, I will make sure of that.'

'O.K., but I must be bloody nuts, Wakefield!' he repeated unbelievingly.

When he arrived at the Hall, the first thing Clive said was, 'Peter, this is a fifty quid job, or I don't touch it.'

One couldn't blame the man. A 160 mile round trip in the middle of the night, was something strictly for the birds, night ones at that, yet Clive did it.

Francis gave him £55, this included a £5 tip. In advance as I had requested of him, for I didn't trust this strange fellow one little bit.

He shook my hand warmly, before climbing into the taxi with the typewriter firmly clutched under his arm. I think he took that machine to bed with him. As the cab pulled away from the front of the Hall, he waved. Then as they drove down the main drive from the house, he called back to me, 'so long, me Old Cock.'

The author and his wife with their staff at The Low Hall.

Was he one patient I was pleased to see the back of! It meant endless paperwork for both the constable and me. I prayed I would not get his like again. Needless to say, Mr Francis was at no time in the foreseeable future to be allowed to convalesce at Low Hall. I had the gut feeling that wouldn't bother him too much.

Miners came to Low Hall repeatedly, as the places are rostered. We have had men return who have convalesced several times before. Today their wives also get the opportunity to enjoy the Low Hall, along with its wonderful grounds.

We get the odd complainer, they wouldn't be human if they didn't complain. It is usually something trivial which we can quickly sort out. The women are more apt to be at odds with each other. Men, God bless them, are far more tolerant. Or so I tell my wife, who does not agree with me. She shows a preference for female company. I tell her she is being illogically sexist, something I could never be accused of.

Chapter 12

GEORGE ORWELL's book *1984* depicted a world ruled by Big Brother, the all-seeing, all-knowing, faceless leader. A place of fear, a government in office who answered to no one. Democracy was relegated to the history books, the ordinary people numbered and stamped into their allotted place, in the then scheme of things. A very dangerous concept, particularly when one dwells on the all-corrupting deadliness of ultimate power vested in a few. No matter the good intentions, or the faults of our democratic system, at least at the end of government's term of office, we have the opportunity to rid ourselves of them.

In actuality, 1984 brought a recovering Britain. A country ruled, for the first time in modern history, by a woman. And what a lady. The Eastern Bloc had dubbed her the Iron Lady. A title well earned as I have said, the truth of which the Yorkshire miners had still to grasp.

Mrs Margaret Thatcher, like her or hate her, was a very determined, clever woman. Alone, she returned Britain to the front of the world's stage, taking its people by the scruff of their necks to do her bidding. No longer were we treated as a second-class nation, once again we took our rightful place among the world's leaders.

It is a great pity that during her eleven years in continuous office, as Britain's Prime Minister, the division between the north and the south of Britain deepened. As did the gap between the have, and have nots. The latter being predominantly in the north.

I very much doubt if George Orwell, when he wrote his mind-boggling literary masterpiece, envisaged anything like the crippling vanquishing of one of Great Britain's most powerful trade unions. Or the devastating effect on my part of the country.

I see 1984 as the year when Arthur Scargill and his legions, marched against a government ruled by a Prime Minister determined to wipe out Socialism, who used their heavy artillery long after the enemy was broken, when an armistice should have been called. Faults lay on both sides, a government who got their wires crossed and forgot who the enemy was. The miners, reluctant to give up the fight to save their jobs, determined to fight on. No glory was gained by victor or vanquished. What I objected to so very strongly was the unseemly posturing over the corpse and the apparent unwillingness on the part of a less than magnanimous government, to allow the miners to go away and lick their wounds. Mrs Thatcher was resolute. No British Government would ever again be held to ransom by a trade union. The miners were used as examples. As I have said, pit closures were hurried along and many that were never on the unviable list were now added. In that year as well as half of the next, much misery and stupid violent acts occurred, to the credit of neither side.

Margaret Thatcher's words to Michael Heseltine back in 1982, during the furore over the Low Hall chimney stack, come sharply to mind. Remember, she told him she was not ready, Now she was.

The Yorkshire N.U.M. had the largest membership of mineworkers in Britain at that time. It has also the largest coalfield, Markham Main being noted for its militancy, according to the newspapers over the years. Oddly enough, I never knew any militants. The men I grew up with attended to their job, and minded their own business. Sufficient unto itself was the responsibility of family life and where the next crust was coming from. My memories are of white, coal-streaked, drawn faces emerging from the bowels of the earth, heading for the pit-head showers, a luxury not known by their fathers. For all of that, the ingrained coal dust embedded in their son's hands is irremovable. The miners' strike began on 15 March 1984 and it was to last almost a full year, ending on 3 March 1985.

It was a period of total misery and discontent, for it turned neighbour against neighbour, split families asunder, tore down their aspiration to keep the pits open. The world watched safely from their living rooms, as through the medium of television the day's events were reported, albeit more than a little one-sidedly at times.

The Low Hall being separately funded, happily remained in a safe, financially secure position, for the trade union's coffers were under attack by the government. However, the anger and sorrow filled those rooms day in and day out for all of those unhappy months. The patients were miners, and would remain so until the day they died. Old, as well as very sick, they mostly were, yet they, too, were at war with an unfeeling government intent on destroying not only their union and its leaders, but their workmates into the bargain. For every argument there are two sides. On this, as on most occasions, both considered themselves to be in the right. Negotiation played no part. It was a duel to the death, reasoning was considered a sign of weakness, a sign neither side was willing to give. The government meant to break the union's power in Britain for, one must admit, it had been terribly damaging to the country as a whole. The N.U.M. was adamant that their hard-won rights would remain intact. The right to work was one of these and the closure of pits was seen as unacceptable.

Mistakes were made, fickle Lady Luck came down on the side of the government. The summer of 1984 was the hottest summer on record. Coal stocks remained high, so the expected added pressure from the electorate on Mrs Thatcher did not eventuate. A shortage of fuel on the home front would certainly have led to a demand for settlement from the electorate who would undoubtedly have pressured their own Members of Parliament. They, in turn, would have to pressurise the Prime Minister. At least that is the way it is supposed to work in a democratic society. With Maggie Thatcher that is a faulty supposition. It is with hindsight I say that, for none of us had the lady's measure then. It was to be those very qualities, which would not allow her to accept anything less than total victory, which ultimately brought about her downfall.

However, that was years ahead. All that can be said now is that the timing of the strike was unfortunate. Maybe, with a long, cold winter, coupled with dwindling coal reserves, it just might have ended more advantageously for the miner.

Owen Briscoe, the General Secretary of the Yorkshire N.U.M. was not yet due for retirement, he watched the whole fiasco helplessly, for his powers were extremely limited as his time drew to a close.

Owen was a crafty seasoned campaigner who backed his leader to the hilt. Entering my office one day, eyeing me unhappily, he confessed, 'things are not going too well for us, Peter. Whichever way you look at it, it's going to be a long bloody struggle,'

We all knew he was right. Later on Owen told me, 'this is affecting my health.'

This proved to be true, as subsequently he retired, prematurely through ill health. He had been one of the longest serving union officials. He died six years later in 1992. A sadly missed friend.

Owen was always a dyed-in-the-wool Miners' Union man, with only the miners' well-being at heart. I remember well his earnest avowed intention of bringing Low Hall up to the best, if not better, convalescent home standards. He would repeat this constantly and as you know he carried out his promise even if at times he was heartily sick of the project.

As we progressed miserably through 1984, the older retired miners echoed Owen's words. They knew from bitter experience that strikes had never ever brought anything except suffering for the working man. Sensible men, who had grown wiser with age, they could see the bitter end to this feud. Passing through the main lounge one day, I overheard a heated argument between an aged chap and a youthful, union militant type, about the closure of further collieries. The old man exasperatedly said, 'tha can't keep a fire int' grate, if tha's no coal int' coal-house.'

His deep, blunt Yorkshire voice reverberated around the room, attracting the attention of all. He was trying to get across to the young hot-head that, if a colliery had run out of resources (coal) it was not feasible to expect the industry to keep that particular mine working at a loss. The old miner continued his berating of the militant probably assuming, rightly, that the fellow hadn't got the message.

'Tha can't have a thousand men stood dooin' nowt.'

That needed no translation, his common sense far surpassed that of the inexperienced union representative, but this maxim only applied to the mines with worked-out seams, not to collieries with ample reserves, as the old miner stressed.

This was a fight to keep the latter pits working and with it their inalienable right to work to keep their self respect.

However, as it stood, luck hung around in Maggie's Corner, the miners were well and truly taking a beating. Britain sweltered in unusual heat, while coal stocks remained undiminished. The weather offered no respite or hope for the strikers.

No one appeared to understand the position of the miner. To give up the fight meant eventual unemployment. To soldier on was the only alternative left open to them. They took all the vilification the press heaped on them and their union, finding food and clothing for their families was uppermost in their minds. Even after all these intervening years, the 1984 strike continues to be a source of complete bewilderment to the average collier. Let us take a look back at it, at least let us examine the salient points with the advantage of hindsight.

Had the Nottinghamshire N.U.M. stood firm, events may very well have taken a different turn.

Stan Orme, M.P., was also Labour's Shadow Energy spokesman and he tried his hardest to get Arthur Scargill as well as the Nottinghamshire leaders around the negotiating table. Leicester, along with part of the Lancashire N.U.M., were of the same mind as the Nottinghamshire Union. All wanted to call an end to the strike. The Yorkshire N.U.M. and the National Executives were not in agreement with them. To cave in would certainly not stop the closure of the mines, the reason for the Strike. Nothing went in the National Executive's favour. There were fifty-four million tons of coal reserves in this unprecedentedly hot summer. Then Mrs Thatcher brought in a Scottish born expert, a man named Ian Macgregor. He had spent most of his life in America, making it the hard way, a tough cookie to cross. He was to become the Coal Board's Chairman. From the outset things did not augur well for the Yorkshire N.U.M. Cortonwood Colliery, under threat of closure, was the first pit to come out on strike. They could not have guessed at that time, no-one excluding the National Executive and its President, Arthur Scargill, anticipated the number of mine closures which could take place over the ensuing few years.

Before the strike began there were 170 coal mines. In 1989 there were a meagre 76 left operating. A loss of ninety four.

The government then played its ace card, they offered an unrefusable carrot to the pit-worker, eroding still further the N.U.M.'s dwindling country-wide support for this pernicious strike. The offered a £1,000 per year of service redundancy packet. The miners could not refuse this offer with ever mounting debts facing them. With twenty-five to thirty years in the mines, some had as many as forty years working underground, the men had never owned so much money. With no future work assured for many, they took the pay-off. Despite Arthur Scargill's assertion that they were selling their jobs, most had no choice. They had families on starvation diets and debts which they had no means of paying, so they accepted the Coal Board's pay-out.

A breakaway Union was formed by the Nottinghamshire Miners part of the catalyst which hit the National Union of Mineworkers.

Although the beginning of the end for the N.U.M.'s official strike was the failure to close Orgreave Coking Plant, it had been Mr Scargill's main objective. Arthur Scargill's win at Saltley Gate in 1972 had brought about

Edward Heath's Government downfall. He had hoped to emulate this victory at Orgreave. Mrs Thatcher was a horse of a very different colour. She ruled her government and kept the dissenters to order. The saga went on long after the strike was over, bitterness prevailed, and the struggle to stop further closures of viable mines continues, long after her demise as prime minister over her refusal to accept defeat on the poll tax issue. Her successor, however, is just as determined. John Major is totally in agreement that cheaper coal can be imported. A short-sighted policy, as with our national industries. But that is another story.

One national newspaper reporter humorously wrote, 'The NUM have lost more contributing members than the Church of England'. Brought about by pit closures and redundancy methods mainly. Yet the hard right Conservatives would disclaim it. This victory, in their eyes, reassured their inalienable right to rule.

The National Coal Board, now under the more descriptive title of British Coal, no longer employs Ian Macgregor, who had returned whence he came, his purpose fulfilled.

Both sides in this misbegotten strike had helpers who were not publicized nearly enough. Arthur's Left Forum and David Hart's Campaign for Working Miners both held to beliefs hardly considered democratic, the latter reputedly funded by the government to undermine the union, worked assiduously with little or no media attention. The same cannot be said for the Left Forum, which did hold the media's undivided attention after the strike was over. In the midst of this machination were the miners. The Yorkshire miners will, as a whole, remain faithful to the good leader of their branch of the N.U.M. That is the nature of the beast, they know the man and his faults, he has worked well for them in the past. Some of his methods they decry, but nevertheless accept. He is one of them, they look after their own in my part of the world, they will close ranks tighter than a drum, tighter than any defending army. They know only too well that if the Union hadn't placed their funds off-shore, those and all other assets would have been frozen. To bring in succour from abroad for the miners had to be strongly resisted by the government, no matter from what source, for this could only prolong the strike. The public spotlight went into action, naming the countries giving such assistance—but only when they were communist governed. The suggested misuse of those same funds filled our national papers daily. All were to be refuted in a court of law. But at that time hungry men and their families could only writhe in suppressed anger as the media stories were unfolded.

There is a lot more to the strike story, I have but scratched the surface. The mindless violence on the picket lines, the vitriolic language, the union bashing by the media, were just a part of the endless futility of it all. There were so many unexplainables. No public reason was ever given for the complete isolation of the N.U.M. by other unions. For the first time the miners stood alone.

The proposed show of strength at Orgreave Coking Plant, became a veritable bloodbath. Unlike Saltley Gate Coke Depot in 1972, where it had triggered other workers from different industries to join the N.U.M. picket lines, there was no such solid support forthcoming this time around.

The Labour Party, also, stood on the sidelines, rumour had it they were afraid of Arthur's political aspirations. Myself, I believe there was more to it than this story the propagandists gave out.

As it stood, it became a match between the Iron Lady and Arthur Scargill, both were out to nail each other in any way possible. It became dirtier and dirtier, personal details of Scargill and Heathfield, the N.U.M.'s General Secretary's private lives became succulent morsels for the general public's early morning perusal.

The outcome of this less than ethical warfare is best illuminated by a meeting held on 23 August 1990, at the Labour Club in Chesterfield, Derbyshire. Tony Benn, M.P., should have chaired the meeting. The speakers were the National President of the N.U.M., Arthur Scargill, and the General Secretary, Peter Heathfield. No invitation to hold this meeting in the Derbyshire Headquarters of the National Union of Mineworkers had been received by the National Executive. The N.U.M. building across the street from the Labour Club, was deserted. This small room would hold only twenty-five people at best, the only accommodation needed as it turned out. This giant of a public figure could now only attract that number outside of his own former enclave. Tony Benn sent his apologies for his inability to fulfil his position as chairman. Odd, when one recalls it was Arthur Scargill, who backed this M.P. during his campaign for the right to represent Chesterfield, in the N.U.M. building now in darkness.

It appeared that Arthur Scargill's own oft repeated saying, 'A slag heap of dreams', was becoming just that; a dream in no way attainable. The

Lightman Report, so called because of the findings promulgated by Gavin Lightman, Q.C., vindicated Scargill and others of any wrong doing. The Yorkshire area voted that they both stay in power and in the leadership of the International Miners' Organization, the recipient organization for the monies donated to the miners during the year long strike; an association in which the N.U.M. see a part for themselves, as an affiliated union.

Nothing can be gained by disturbing the ground further. The body is dead, the spirit elsewhere. Give it a Christian burial.

With the end of the strike in 1985, things gradually got back to normality in Low Hall.

This building, fringing on the National Parkland (at least with its oversized chimney), of course, some of its grounds and appendages are actually a part too, is a fantastic place to live and work.

The Hall lies roughly four miles from Scarborough, set just off the main Whitby road. In such a position it would be almost criminal not to take the patients out into this glorious countryside. To let them see and enjoy the wonderful places which exist in plenty in this part of the world.

So, it is with every intake of patients we organize a bus tour to Whitby, coming back through Pickering, Thornton le Dale, driving over the North Yorkshire Moors to view the spellbinding scenery. A delightful, beautiful journey I never tire of making. I accompany the men, Shirley escorts the ladies, as someone must be there to watch over those fifty people. Not only because of their sometimes delicate state of health, but, as in other walks of life, they are a mixed bunch of characters who, if left to their own devices, could, nay possibly would, get into all kinds of bother. Some are highly intelligent, having travelled life's highway they can negotiate or surmount most obstacles. Others are so naive, it is a wonder their parents ever allowed them out of the house. How the devil they have made it to the age they are, without learning something about Nature's nasties, tricksters, et cetera has me beat.

Others are crafty individuals, who leech on the innocent, those who spend their waking hours figuring out ways to take the other person down. You can bet your life, on every intake there is at least one of the latter. Occasionally, I have to deal with them, more often the miners themselves will sort out the rotten apples, in their own unique fashion. In that case, I make a point of not being around, believing that what the eye doesn't see will not bother it.

Our visits to Whitby are a highlight for the men and women who convalesce at Low Hall. Whitby Jet, a valued semi-precious stone, is keenly hunted in the tourist shops, particularly by the ladies. Whitby Abbey is also an attractive magnet for them, despite the difficulty of traversing the area. This is not only because of its own historic past, but also on account of Bram Stoker using the Abbey in his book, *Dracula*. He brought the ship carrying Dracula into Whitby harbour, with all the crew dead. He then had Dracula make the Abbey his home.

You would imagine this would turn people off the town, not so. The Abbey and its precincts swarm with folk interested more in the man with the overgrown teeth than in the age of this wonderful Abbey.

The first German plane, a Heinkel bomber, shot down in the Second World War, was first spotted over Sleights, a village near Whitby. It was engaged over this small, set in the Wolds, charming settlement and landed in flames about three miles away, just off the main Whitby, Sleights road. A marker has been erected over the spot in commemoration.

An interesting aspect of this incident involves no less a personage than Group Captain Peter Townsend. All in Britain and the Commonwealth heard of him eventually in a completely different set of circumstances to the one just mentioned.

Peter Townsend was the Spitfire fighter pilot, who shot down the Heinkel. We always stop the bus to let the old-timers view this spot in our history. Most can remember the event, too. Invariably, they will tell you what they were doing at the time.

On one such occasion, a miner getting on in years, turned to me and said, 'bloody hell, and the poor sod finished up getting himself shot down, by buggers of German origin.'

He was referring, of course, to the romantic involvement of Princess Margaret, the Queen's sister, with the group captain. Unlike her uncle, Edward VIII, she chose to keep her position in the royal hierarchy, publicly forsaking Townsend. The man left the British Isles to live, mostly, abroad. Little has been published about him since.

Today those standards of behaviour do not apply, she could have married the divorcee, probably living happily ever after.

Thornton le Dale, a picturesque village of Norman origin, is a favourite port of call for the men and women of Low Hall. Why wouldn't it be? It has won the accolade of being Britain's prettiest village which, when taking into account the number of breathtakingly attractive small communities scattered over the length and breadth of the British Isles, is homage enough.

A trout stream gently meanders through the centre of this village of thatched and slate cottages, old world rose gardens and hanging baskets overflowing with colourful geraniums. Tiny footbridges intermittently span the stream giving access to shop entrances. All add their fragrance and undoubted eye appeal, to the inherent charisma the place holds for everyone. In the last few years we have become very insular. I am referring to the decision of the powers that be, to eradicate the Norman 'Le' from the Dale's village names. Thornton Dale, is not a fitting name for such beauty. Thornton of the Dales I will accept, but only after protest. Methinks someone out there is trying to build a monument to themselves.

Among the most memorable of the people who come to Low Hall as patients and whom we have been privileged to gain as friends, are two miners from Grimethorpe Colliery, near Barnsley, Yorkshire. Their names are Fletcher and Buckingham, two lifelong friends, inseparable. Where Buck was Fletch would be in close attendance.

The pair of them had done a fine job for me as captain and vice-captain on a previous visit two years before. With every intake a captain as well as a vice-captain is appointed. They organize outings, social evenings, sort out arguments, generally help out with the patients.

When Fletch and Buck arrived in 1985 for the second time, Shirley and I were delighted, making a great fuss of the pair of them. They were both of retirement age. Fletch had retired two years previously. Buck was on the verge of doing so.

At that time Enid Trueman, the ex-wife of Freddie of cricket fame, used to visit us regularly. We had known her from our early Silver Grid days, when she was a friend and customer throughout our stay there, frequently visiting us in The Rosette as well.

She had been divorced from Freddie Trueman for a number of years and, although extremely charming, she had never remarried. She was the daughter of a prominent Scarborough family, the Chapmans, a family established for generations in real estate and auctioneering in the area.

In her time Enid had been a well known socialite and kicker-up of heels. Still an attractive red-haired woman, as the adage goes, she had a temper to match. It could flare up in an instant. Brother, if you were the target, or the cause of such fiery anger, then duck for cover.

I made the terrible mistake of introducing her to Fletch and Buck.

Now Enid could drink most normal people under the table. By normal I mean the average holder-up of bars, not someone who pussyfoots around knocking back the odd half dozen drinks.

To Fletch and Buck she epitomized all they prized most dear in humankind. Not only could she drink, she stayed lucid throughout, neither becoming tearful nor obstreperous, besides matching them drink for drink.

It was during the morning session in the lounge when I introduced them to each other. By the time I had cleared away and closed down the bar, all three had vanished. I did not know at the time she had taken the buggers home with her.

Fletch and Buck were not back for tea at five-thirty. By six-thirty I was a very worried man. I was not too concerned about Enid taking them home with her, for she was a much younger woman well able to take care of herself; no, my unease was that, all things being equal, those two would by now be distinctly under the weather.

The two men had an insatiable appetite for booze. Enid, unknown to them, made both Fletch and Buck appear as babes in arms by comparison. It was a frightening thought. I was going to have two very sick, as well as extremely sorry, men to deal with. I could only hope for their sakes, Enid would see to it that they were safety returned to Low Hall.

She did. At 7 p.m. a taxi pulled up outside the front entrance and out of it fell Fletch and Buck, the pair of them paralytic, stinking, absurdly drunk. Yet not so much so they didn't realize how much trouble they were in.

Fletch peered at me through half-closed eyes, as if trying to focus on one of the several supers he could undoubtedly see, before he haltingly burped, 'we are as pissed as farts, we tried to drink her under the table, we failed, Super.'

He said it disbelievingly. No one in all his vast experience had ever been able to out-drink him. Now, a woman, a good-looking one to boot, had not only done that, she had sent him home ribbon-tied.

Fletch was an ex-guardsman, a stayer by nature, he had been taken prisoner of war at Dunkirk. With others of his ilk, he had spent the rest of the Second World War cooped up inside a compound. Since then, Fletch had been trying to drown the memory. Unlike his friend, Buck, he was unable to accept this defeat at the hands of a lady.

Buck, on the other hand, was more than willing to concede. All he wanted was his bed, tomorrow was another ball game.

In all fairness to the men, I must tell you they had been defeated by a past master. Enid Trueman was a formidable drinker. It had taken her years of downing the fluid, to reach the stage where, unless you knew her, one couldn't tell she had been on the toot.

Enid phoned the next day to ask after the men's welfare.

'How are the boys, Peter,' she asked blithely. 'They got out of their class a bit, didn't they? They were nice, funny boys though, I thoroughly enjoyed their company. Tell them that.'

'Funny! To put it in Fletch's own words they were, "as pissed as farts". Do you know it is an offence for the men to get drunk while they are on convalescence?'

Enid's only reply was to laugh, saying, 'they are big boys, Peter, more than capable of looking after themselves.'

'It is no laughing matter, it is a sending home violation of the rules. One which the committee strictly enforces. It will take all the persuasion Shirley and I can muster to get the panel to bend the regulations for this one-off occasion. To allow both men to stay for their allotted span at Low Hall some lying must be done. I hope we aren't found out, Shirley and I are both very fond of these fellows.'

I omitted to tell Enid, if we hadn't found them such a pair of likeable rogues, their drinking would have earned them a much earlier banishment. This was another occasion when they got away with it.

About two years after this incident, Buck died of a heart attack, sadly missed he is too. Fletch is cheekily fit and well, by all accounts he is still competitive in the world of drinkers *extraordinaire*, well able to hold what has been rightfully paid for.

Fletch's son, Fred, named after his father, is an actor. He appeared as the bullying brother in the film, *Kes*, besides having parts in the long-running soaps, *Coronation Street* and *Emmerdale Farm*, he also starred in *Queenie's Castle* with Diana Dors. In spite of all this he will never surpass his father in the acting stakes, who was a comedian *par excellence*, which he combined with amusingly harmless confidence tricks.

I introduced Fletch to Mr Tubbs, the staid vicar of Scalby Parish. In seconds, Fletch had the vicar rolling about with laughter at his jokes. One incident he related to the vicar, I will repeat here.

'After Dunkirk I was a prisoner of war for five very long years, the camp was finally overrun by the Russians early in 1945. The Russians were good to us from the word go, we were bloody starving when they arrived, they killed a horse a day to feed us. Do you know I ate that much hoss meat that when I arrived home, if someone cracked a whip I was off and trotting down the road.'

I am very pleased the world has reacted to Russia's plight in 1990, with massive aid, particularly food supplies. Knowing Fletch, he will be as pleased as I, that we, in turn, are feeding the hungry Russians.

Thinking of characters who lighten our lives, my thoughts inevitably turn to my old and trusted friend, George Meehan.

Over the years I had lost contact with George, although my brother Allan, kept me informed of his doings. The last I had heard of George he was still a bus driver, or at least I assumed he was. He had a family of his own now, though they had all grown up. Then, during a conversation with Allan, he mentioned George had left the bus company and now worked on the Doncaster Race Track. I wish I had known, for I'd been to the course on many occasions. I most certainly would have looked up my mate of yesteryear to renew our valued friendship.

Then, one afternoon while watching racing on the television, lo and behold, who should appear on the screen, although admittedly in the background, none other than my old mate, George.

Unchanged by the years in habit, although they hadn't been quite so kind in the age sense, he stood motionless, in such a position that ensured the camera caught him in its encompassing of the scene. His long, once sleek black hair, was now a steely grey. He appeared different somehow, even if I couldn't quite put my finger on it. I hoped the, I-couldn't-give-a-damn, George, was still a part of that immobile figure on the television screen.

I vowed to myself, I would seek him out at the first possible opportunity. I was to hear of him again through the same medium. Shirley and I were watching the television one Saturday afternoon when a racing identity was being interviewed about the event due to take place. My wife and I almost shot out of our chairs as the man said, 'I was talking to the groundsman, George Meehan, this morning. He wasn't satisfied that the lines on the paddock were straight enough. He decided to go over them again before the gates were opened.'

George had made it, not only being seen on television, but also being mentioned on another occasion. I bet everyone within earshot will hear the quote *ad nauseam*, as well as being repeatedly asked if they had seen him.

The day arrived when I could make it over to Doncaster to visit Mary Agnes's grave, and enjoy a day at the Races. I searched the Paddock area, there in the Parade ring stood George. I was so pleased to see him I had to resist hugging the blighter, for I know what his reaction would have been.

'Silly bugger,' is what he would have said, as he fought his way out of my clutches.

Not overly given to outward displays of emotion, his response undoubtedly would have been one of distrust. Our small street of Ash Grove hardly lent itself to shows of affection. Do not get me wrong, Kate was astounded at the reception she received after a ten year absence. It was fondness without restraint, without question. She was one of the family.

George and I talked and talked, forgotten were the races, our animated conversation broken only by George's sporadic token return to his duties.

'Do you like this job here, better than bus driving?' I asked, during a lull in our reminiscing.

'Peter, I have waited four years for the guy who had this job to retire. He has at long last, I have got the job now.'

'What do you have to do? What job is it?' I asked intrigued.

'Best bloody job on the course,' George replied gloatingly. 'I am the man who keeps the Parade ring clean, if one of the horses shits, I get it cleaned up straight away. That's all I have to do.'

It suited him down to the ground, he couldn't make an asshole out of that, no matter how he tried. He was the same George, still not keen on manual labour. What you see is what you get, down-to-earthness. The change was in the ready laugh, it did not come quite so often. Then whose does at our age? The jovial banter so much a part of our youth, was as good as ever. I was sorry to leave, for I shed the years just talking to him. I like to think I did the same for him.

He was happy in the job, as well as it being 'dead easy', as he put it. It gave him the opportunity to see and sometimes meet the famous, to gain information. A few good tips from trainers and jockeys was the cream on the cake as far as George was concerned. I was pleased for him. As I walked away from George, my brother Allan's words rang in my ears, 'I ought to have been his manager and put the bugger on the stage. We could have earned a fortune, he's a natural.'

Allan has repeated this statement over the years. The mention of George's name will always trigger the same response.

I laughed all the way home to Scarborough, as the memories now evoked came flooding back. The time when George accompanied Tommy Naughton (my cousin who was killed in the Armthorpe pit), along with his brother, Jimmy Naughton, went fishing to Barnby Dun, a small hamlet close to Armthorpe. Tommy had been on the night shift at the mine and was very tired. He was sitting on a basket nodding off in the warm sunshine. Suddenly Jimmy said to George, who was sitting next to Tommy, 'quick, watch him, he's going to fall in the water.'

Tommy was slowly falling forwards in his sleep. George dived for him. Tommy went sideways on to the bank, George went headlong into the canal. Everything went wrong for George, with the best intentions in the world, without fail, it turned out the wrong way.

I remembered George spilling the bucket of water over the immaculately clad couple at the ringside, and the pandemonium which erupted. Trapped in the snow on the Snake Pass, George's physical collapse on his return to the bus. The loss of his prized watch in the River Humber, his later fronting up to the two tough lorry drivers. The scene in Doncaster Police Station, as he steadfastly insisted we were being fitted up with the jewellery store robbery. His innate inability to do anything right, fouling up the most simple of tasks.

My sides ached with uncontrollable mirth as I remembered the late Pete Platts with his intrinsic distrust of George and his capabilities.

Pete was always the steadying influence on the crowd of lads we associated with as young men, a well read intelligent man, without exception a friend to all of us. As I have said before, he finished up working in insurance. He had all of our measures. Tommy Penrice he would refer to at Tommy Spendthrift. Of course, Tommy earned the title, he was as tight as a duck's arse in reality. George never lost the nickname of Gunga Din from his water carrying days. Years later when both Pete and George married, they lived just a few houses apart. In 1978 just before Pete died of a massive heart attack, we met up for a drink and he cracked jokingly, 'I wonder if I am safe living so close to George.'

Peter Aldridge and Arthur Scargill,
President of the N.U.M., The Low Hall.

It was the last time I saw him alive, I travelled over for his funeral, which was a very large affair for he had been a well liked and popular man. I can still hear his call of 'good old Gunga', as I made my entrance to the boxing ring, followed by George carrying his water bucket.

Oh, the times we had in my salad days.

The Low Hall standing proudly in Scalby village, is a part of the Duchy of Lancaster estate which, of course, belongs to the Queen.

It seems a very odd situation to me, here the Yorkshire Miners own the largest property locally, and the biggest pain in the side of British politics then, was Arthur Scargill, the man who purchased Low Hall for the Yorkshire Miners when he was their president, before he moved on to become National President.

Arthur Scargill, as I have said, is a dedicated believer in the theory of Karl Marx and Friedrich Engels, that class struggle is the agency for historical change, that Capitalism will eventually be replaced by Communism. Jumping forward to 1991, this hardly seems likely, Communism or Marxism has been found wanting world-wide. Economist though Marx may have been, his followers could certainly have benefited from some of his knowledge in that particular sphere. More so than the above philosophy. As for me I am saddened, as in the rest of the free thinking world. There is a place for all opposition. If only, as they say, to keep the rest of the buggers honest.

Humans, being what they are, one form of bureaucracy answerable to an electorate and opposition parties, is far preferable to a one party state. This is where the Eastern Bloc made their biggest mistake. The Iron Curtain of Churchill's era has rusted away. Can they replace it with a better system or, like us, keep changing from hard right to middle of the road Labour in perpetuity.

I have commented before on Mr Scargill's other side. He is very amusing company. An accomplished mimic, he sat in my flat one day having tea and began to imitate Margaret Thatcher. If I had closed my eyes and listened, I could easily have been convinced she was in the room. One of her greatest antagonists mimicking her so well would not have amused the lady, even though she was accustomed to good and bad impersonations. Looking back, now that Margaret Thatcher has been replaced by John Major, I wonder if God shook his head at the immovable intractability, which both she and Arthur displayed during the strike, as if it was an attribute worthy of note.

Things were not all doom and gloom at Low Hall, it went about its daily business lightened at times by the behaviour of some of the patients. Nevertheless, there were times when I thought the blasted picket lines ran through the centre of this grand building, with strike-breakers resembling extraordinarily some of my patients.

One incident which diverted our attention somewhat at the time, and I hope will do so again now, occurred around this time.

A patient named Mr Sample, went out for the day to Scarborough. While on the sea-front he lost his wallet containing all his money and papers. The news of this calamity was conveyed to me by the Captain of the Intake, on the man's return to the Hall. The distressed fellow had broken down in tears, for he had lost £200, a big blow at any age and to a man in his sixties doubly so. I invited him into the office, where I had one of the waitresses bring him some highly sweetened coffee. However, he was inconsolable, he wept copiously, tears running unchecked down his face. Finally, I managed to quieten him enough to obtain the details, of where and how he had come to lose the wallet. I contacted Scarborough police, giving them all the particulars Mr Sample had given me. I knew it was hardly possible a wallet containing so much money, would be handed in to the police. Still it had been known to occur, if only very infrequently. The odds were long though on Scarborough's promenade in the middle of the summer season when it teemed with holiday-makers, not all of them financially well endowed.

My patient was not one of the fortunate few, there was no news of the wallet or its contents. He was left with little option but to return to his home in the Sheffield area. A grievous pity, for his convalescence had barely begun.

The Captain of the Intake, obviously felt the same way as I. He asked, 'Super, will it be O.K. for me to make a collection for Sample?'

I could raise no objection to that, it would be almost impossible for the man to stay on without money, if only to cover his daily needs.

Indeed far from opposing the suggestion, I encouraged it by donating £2 myself.

During tea-time that night, the captain did his bit for the unfortunate man. By his efforts he amassed a marvellous £55 for Sample. Most of this had been given by old age pensioners, or disabled men unable to earn more. I was very moved and proud to be of the same stock.

It was another example of the warm heart behind the gruff exterior of a miner. Mr Sample, emotionally grateful publicly, accepted the money. To resounding applause he decided then and there to stay on for the rest of his convalescence.

Sunday is the official visiting day at the Hall, when miners can receive their relations and friends on the premises.

One old miner who was rather bad on his legs, roped me in to show his family around Low Hall. It was an extra duty I constantly fell for, although I have never objected to the role of tour-guide, finding their relations and visitors, often as entertaining as the patients could be. The captain who knew some of the miners' guests, was also in attendance, as I escorted them round the building and grounds.

As we entered the main lounge, I noticed Mr Sample sitting smoking, while apparently engrossed in a newspaper. He didn't stir as we passed.

The captain had also spotted him. Pointing to Sample, he said in an undertone which could still be heard by all of our group, 'see that poor man, he lost all his money on the sea-front at Scarborough. He was heartbroken, his holiday ruined, it looked as if he would have to return home. But we made a collection for him and he is all right now.'

Turning to me, he added, 'that's right, Super, ain't it?'

I nodded my head in agreement, a bit embarrassed for Sample's sake.

Immediately one of the visitors, a miner himself, grabbed me by the arm, 'may I have a word with you, Boss?' he urgently requested.

Not waiting for my answer, nor making any effort to lower his voice, he said angrily, 'that guy was on convalescence with me last year, in Wales.'

The N.U.M. had another convalescent home in Wales, at that time. 'He lost all his money there too. We, also, made a collection for him.'

Mr Sample looked up startled from his reading. He shot out of the chair running upstairs without a backward glance. His newspaper lay scattered where he had dropped it in his frantic haste to leave the room.

During this denouncement, the captain had listened with sagging jaw and a disbelieving expression on his face. Then the inescapable truth registered, 'the bloody bastard,' he exploded, 'now I have to tell the men how we have been taken in by that bloody liar.'

If the captain was furious, I was spitting mad at being conned, vowing silently to myself to nail the bugger to the mast, as soon as I had rid myself of the visitors. It was stretching the imagination too much to accept that it could have happened twice, two years running. In any case Sample's bolting for cover more or less confirmed his guilt.

The captain wasted no time in making it public knowledge. It was tea-time, all the patients were present and he started in without preamble. In a slow calculated drawl, he told them of Sample's previous loss in Wales. Now gullible they may have been, idiots they were not. To lose all one's money two years on a trot, while on convalescence, was too much to expect anyone to believe. There was an instant howl for retribution which must have been heard in Scalby. I tried to quieten them down. Fortunately for Sample he had decided to skip tea. I am convinced there would have been a lynching job, had he been present.

The hatred and anger was almost tangible.

Over the uproar, I shouted to assure the men I would find Sample, to bring him to book, a promise I have never been able to fulfil. Although I wasted no time in going to Sample's room, the con-merchant had flown, along with all his belongings. No one had seen him leave. We heard nothing of the man again, or of the money out of which he had cheated so many generous souls who could not afford such benevolence in the first place. I am still angry when I think about it.

Sample must have been prepared for flight. No one could have packed up in the time he had without anticipating the need for readiness.

It was some consolation he could never rest easy.

It was in 1985 we began the intake of miners' wives and widows. Twice a year we were to accommodate them in Low Hall. The home in Wales had been closed down; it had taken all the wives wishing to convalesce.

To replace this, the N.U.M. had opened a new, smaller home, named Lynwood, situated roughly two miles from the Low Hall. However, it was not large enough to house all the ladies, so the Hall had to take the surplus of two or three intakes over the seasonal year.

Lynwood, or rather its management, was to cause us many headaches over the coming months. None of it was foreseeable or able to be stopped. It was a petty niggling argument, which we found interminable. But that was in the future.

Fifty women at a time took a little getting used to, but we managed. They were different from the men in almost every way, apart from their memories of the depression years. Like the men their stories are an indictment against today's moaners, who think they have it hard in this year of 1991, a year of recession.

The women remembered trying to feed and clothe their family on the pittance their husbands brought home, as wages, from the mine. The arduous time when even that ceased, as the mine-owners closed the pit gates, their coal requirements fulfilled. The agonizing fear as they raced to the pit head, when the undulation of the mine's siren wailed its terrifying message throughout their small community.

Was it their man this time?

All black, dark memories of the past, some had lost their men in stomach-turning accidents down the mine, for them the fear had changed into reality. Others luckier, had watched their young men change to old ones in a few short years. Still others saw their men crippled forever, in mind as well as body.

As with the male patients we had our share of comedy acts and others. In one intake we had two extremely large old ladies, Mrs Kear and Mrs Bucktrout both weighed in excess of eighteen stone. We weigh all patients on arrival, again when they are leaving. Most have gained poundage during their stay, due to the three square meals per day we serve up whether they want it or not. Most live alone, eating the wrong type of quickly prepared food, which fattens yet doesn't provide the vitamins their bodies need. The two ladies mentioned could well have done without the extra weight, though I doubt if they would have been so jolly. They shared the same room, putting their false teeth in the same glass overnight, as only one glass had been placed inside their quarters. They wouldn't dream of asking for another glass in case they were suspected of taking liberties.

The first morning they came down to breakfast with each other's teeth in. In all seriousness, one said to Shirley, 'I can't talk properly this morning, and I can't even eat the toast.'

Concerned, my wife looked into her mouth, 'are you sure these are your teeth? They appear to be very badly fitted, I am certain they weren't made for your mouth.'

'Christ, that is what it is, I've got her teeth in,' she pointed at her friend, who apparently was having the same kind of bother with her molars. We watched in helpless hilarity, as the two unwitting comediennes, sorted out their mixed up sets of teeth, to the accompaniment of the following throwaway lines, which would have brought the house down, if they had been performed on stage.

As they swapped their falsies, one said to the other comfortingly, 'there, luv, is that right now?'

'Can't bloody be, my top front teeth is an inch further back than the bottom buggers,' replied the second lady.

'I'y ah feel like bloody Dracula too,' the first lady quipped.

'Tha looks like him as well,' her staunch friend saucily fired back.

For the rest of their stay, those two tossed backhanded compliments to each other, with the ease of a comedy duo. Insults became verbal bouquets as each one played off the other's brickbat, far from ineptly too.

Sadly, a short time after returning home, one was to pass away, leaving the other bereft with grief.

This is the trouble with the Low Hall way of life, one which I have bother coming to grips with. These enchanting people are senior citizens in every way. For admittance to Low Hall age is the top criterion. It is no respecter of persons, it lays us all low in the end.

I would be hard put to name favourite patients, yet these lovely Ladies are among the hundreds who would quality. Of the fifty people who enter Low Hall each fortnight, year in and year out, they single themselves out, standing head and shoulders above the rest. They become the life and soul of Low Hall for the whole time they spend inside those walls.

My wife and I miss them very much when they leave, news of their passing disturbing us greatly. If the following intake is a quiet one, and this does occur at intervals, one after the other influx of patients proving to be highly reserved. Imagine our delight when the run is broken by a droll Yorkshire wit or two.

During the summer of 1989, my sister Kate returned home after ten years abroad. She brought with her unusually warm weather, a climatic condition more fitted to the Middle East than changeable Britain. Kate was hardly to blame, the climate had been warming up all of that year, for the entire winter season it had tried to fool us into believing it was spring. It succeeded with nature, the garden held colour throughout. From autumn to autumn the grass grew, the flowers blossomed, the birds sang. When my sister saw Low Hall for the first time, it was at its most beautiful. The grounds presented a perfumed, floral display which was second to none. Tame squirrels and birds in abundance, entertained the intakes of both men and women.

She was staying with my elder sister in Doncaster, when I phoned to ask her to come to Low Hall.

'I have someone here, I know you would love to meet again,' I told her. 'In fact there is more than one, I have told them you are on your way.' I knew curiosity alone would bring her.

She came through to Scarborough at my request, and was thrilled to bits to meet again people she had known for all of her young life.

The women I wished her to see, were part of that fortnight's intake. I didn't know, until Kate told me, those very women used to wheel me about in my pram. A family of girls, the youngest around Kate's age, all in reasonably good health, apart from the next to the youngest, who was ailing. She wasn't present which was a great pity, for she had been a good friend of Kate's.

Kate also told me these girls would often steal away with me, when Mam put me into the front garden in my perambulator. The back garden, such as it was, being hidden from view of the house by the outside toilet building. In the village all pit-houses had bathrooms even then, but no other facilities inside. When it rained, as it does often in Yorkshire, we all became very wet while making that mad dash to the outside lavatory door.

Those girls reminded Kate of another family who lived close by. That night they had all been to the local picture house, to see a film about Sweeney Todd, the Barber. Returning home with Rosie, the daughter of this family, they found the mother had been extremely busy baking mince pies, she had filled the surface of a long, unvarnished deal table, with plates of shallow, round meat pies. Kate told me Rosie took one look at this display, and said, 'Oh, yuk, Sweeney Todd.'

Now Sweeney Todd, in case you didn't know, murdered people, mincing their remains to fill those pies to sell to the general public. Rosie's father did not see the humour in his daughter's remark. Without a word he grabbed one of those plated pies and let Rosie have it, full in the face. Kate ducked and fled for the safety of home, as did the rest of Rosie's friends. Mary Agnes had another good laugh when Kate told her about it. Obviously the father had seen the film.

I haven't named this family for a reason. Rosie married a local boy, he died on the beaches of Crete during the Second World War. (While on leave, he attempted to show us how to charge the enemy with a fixed bayonet—not very successfully. He stuck his bayonet into my mother's front wall, badly buckling the weapon. I do not know how he explained that away to his superiors.) Anyway, after the war Rosie remarried. Her husband, a demobilized airman, joined the police force. The last time Kate saw Rosie she was the wife of a police sergeant, with a position to maintain, as she stressed to Kate, who found that singularly funny at the time. Bowing to Rosie's newfound station in life, she will remain nameless.

There was another treat in store for Kate, on her visit to Low Hall. She met Arthur Scargill, being both agreeably surprised and impressed by the man. Her knowledge of him had been restricted to newspaper reports, and the television screen, shots of him being hauled away by the police, leading marching strikers, always flanked by minders whenever the camera caught him. All this did nothing to prepare her for the courteous, quiet fellow, who suddenly appeared on my flat doorstep one sleepy weekend. On another occasion she met Frank Vernon, an ex-miner who had written, 'The Day the Earth Trembled', an account of the mining disaster at Barnburgh Colliery where seventeen men had been entombed alive. Vernon was a patient at Low Hall and we talked together for hours about the accident which moved him to write the report.

Kate has more vivid memories than I of the horrors of pit accidents, being the elder by eleven years. She grew up with, and knew well, some of the men and boys who died, or were maimed in Markham Main Colliery. Easily moved to tears, she will defend, to the last breath, the rights of the miner. Most important to remember she is politically Conservative, always maintaining that, human nature being what it is, the theory of Marxism is pie in the sky, a fictional Utopia, replacing one pernicious bureaucracy with one only too willing, once in power, to emulate those they had relieved of office.

In other words the ordinary bloke in the street cannot win. The scales are weighted against him.

In the past we have had many political arguments and there is no doubt there will be many more, for she has reached the age where she can see no point in bucking the system. That is for losers.

As I have already made known, the Yorkshire miner has, as far back as anyone can recall, been a part of the summer scene in Scarborough. Before they purchased Low hall, the union's convalescent home was on the sea-front at South Bay.

Now they are an accepted feature of Scalby.

As one comes down from the Hall to turn left into Scalby village, one crosses the bridge spanning the brook (beck). Here, iron railings surround the local kindergarten. One morning, as my brother-in-law was passing the school, a small child rushed up to the railings asking him hopefully, 'are you going to tell me a story?'

Obviously some of the miners had been stopping to talk to the tiny tots when on their way to catch a bus into town, or to visit the village pub. Yet another facet to this jewel of a man.

The man and wife team who were matron and handyman at Lynwood convalescent home were really very difficult people to get along with. In spite of all our efforts and overtures, we have been continually bombarded by snide remarks to the patients about our running of Low Hall. The miners and their wives frequently visit both homes, most are on side and, of course, they repeat the comments to us. It is silly and childish, we are both here to do a job. I think my wife and I do it well. We neither know nor care how Lynwood is run. Low Hall is a full time occupation. As I have remarked times many, I can find trouble with no apparent effort. Why look for it? In this Eden on earth which is Scalby village, besides the seventeen acres of heaven at Low Hall, who would want to stir the pot?

We have our problems, enough to worry us greatly in regard to the future.

Owen Briscoe retired and then died in 1992. On the 14 August 1988, Sam Thompson died of cancer, while still in office. He had taken over the position of General Secretary, Yorkshire N.U.M. left vacant by Owen. Both were Armthorpe men, maybe this was why I earned the comment from Keith Fieldhouse, the Senior Social Welfare Officer of the N.U.M.

Mr and Mrs Aldridge with Mr and Mrs Arthur Scargill and Mr and Mrs John Maitland,
Australian N.U.M. President.

and my boss. He said intimidatingly, 'you have no friends left at the top
now, have you, Peter?'

Early in 1987, Sam Thompson was voted in as Vice-President of the
N.U.M. second in command to Arthur Scargill. His funeral was massive,
being held at St George's Church in Doncaster, over 2,000 people attended.
He was buried on the 18 August, a great man by anyone's standards, the
first N.U.M. leader to die in office. His funeral was covered by the national
press as well as television. Arthur Scargill said of him, 'in the name of the
song, "I did it my way", Sam Thompson did it his way. I have lost a
comrade and a dear personal friend.'

Sam Thompson visited Russia, France, America, Australia, New Zealand
and Egypt in the course of his duties. After he died, John Maitland, Australian
President of their Miners' Federation, wrote the following eulogy.
'Throughout our history it has been our honour to host visits by numerous
International Trade Union leaders. None worked harder than Sam
Thompson and his attractive wife, Alma, during their arduous trip around
our Continent, during the 1984 historic British Miners' Strike.'

At his funeral John Maitland, President, Tony Wilk, General Secretary, and Barry Swan of the Australian Miners' Federation, as well as Paddy Gorman, Editor of the *Common Cause*, an Australian news sheet, sent this written tribute at the time of the funeral.

'Sam Thompson has carved a proud place for himself in the history of the miners' struggle. Although 12,000 miles away, we were inspired by Sam Thompson's contribution. Born to the working class, he held deep humanitarian qualities. On behalf of all Australian Trade Unions who knew and respected him, we mourn. An Australian ballad says, as long as workers struggle, Joe Hill will never die. So can we say as long as blood runs red in our veins, and miners fight for rights, Sam Thompson will be there.'

No one told me when I took this job that I had friends at the top, I knew I had but it didn't do me any good. I had to be assessed the same as all other applicants. Nor have I ever received preferential treatment from anyone, least of all Owen Briscoe who, when the blasted chimney held up work on Low Hall, treated my wife and me as mortal enemies. For all of that I still reckon he was the greatest thing on two legs, as was Sam. They both worked for the miner, anything else was secondary, which I for one heartily applaud. My role by comparison is minute.

The outcome of the Lynwood affair was hurtful, as well as being distressing. A large exclusive article by Ian Robson, named both Mr and Mrs Matich of the Lynwood home and myself. Metaphorically putting us into separate corners of a boxing ring, my introduction was as the former boxer, Peter Aldridge. Mr Keith Fieldhouse was quoted, 'speaking of intense rivalry between Lynwood and Low Hall', to the Industrial Tribunal. Causes of conflict were mentioned, such as differing bar prices and souvenir post cards! Mr Steve Hudson, N.U.M. accountant, said, 'all efforts to resolve financial and personnel problems between the two homes failed'. He recommended that prices be standardized. I agree wholeheartedly with the bit referring to an increase in salary, who wouldn't?

The rest is sheer unadulterated balderdash. These petty complaints are not worth refuting, yet I believe my wife and I should have been allowed to defend ourselves. Mr and Mrs Matich had themselves instigated the litigation against the N.U.M., for unfair dismissal. They lost their jobs for allegedly disclosing confidential information to a patient, refusing to hand over keys, and general attitude to management. Yet for more than half of the report written by Mr Robson, I am centre stage of the dispute.

Both Mr and Mrs Matich approached Shirley and me to testify on their behalf. We refused. We were not buying into their problems, times are tough enough and our position is threatened without complicating matters. The Matich's won their case, it being settled out of court. I lost my case without even entering the bloody place. Had we known our characters would be under attack, we most certainly would have insisted on being present to answer any charges.

This is all very sad, when I know that I have worked hard for twelve years, with only the good of the miner and the N.U.M. at heart.

To get to more cheerful sections in my life and to leave the worries behind for another day. After relating the above sorry story, my ego definitely needs rebuilding anyway, so here goes, a little self-flattery.

Dr Anderson, a local doctor in Scalby village, is the medical practitioner used by the miners convalescing at Low Hall. They are on what the government term as temporary residency, giving them full medical cover while they are on this restful break.

Dr Anderson was on a train leaving King's Cross Station, London, for the north.

He said, 'I was sitting reading a book, the train started to move, giving a severe lurch as it did so. I looked up as two gentlemen hurriedly sat down opposite me, I was sure one of the men was Arthur Scargill. He noticed me looking at him and eyed me suspiciously. I decided I had better explain the reason for my interest to the man. "Excuse me, Mr Scargill," I said, "I am the doctor who looks after the Low Hall patients, in Scalby, Scarborough."

'He still studied me without speaking, so I went on to make myself clearer. "You know, the Miners' Convalescent Home." His eyes lit up and he extended his hand.

'"I am very pleased to meet you," he smiled at me, "you know Low Hall is a magnificent place, I have had a lot of dealings with it."

'He went on to tell me, "Peter and Shirley Aldridge run the Low Hall, and make a very good job of it, too. I gave them the job you know."'

Dr Anderson was tickled pink to meet Arthur, as many people are, and to relate the story to us of Mr Scargill's warmth of feeling towards my wife and myself.

The Yorkshire N.U.M. have allowed British Coal to use the Low Hall for winter seminars. In previous years the Hall closed at the end of

Shirley Aldridge with N.U.M. Vice President Frank Cave and President Arthur Scargill, The Low Hall.

November, reopening at the beginning of the following April. The handy-man and gardener, Neville and Robert respectively, stay on all year along with a young apprentice gardener. We work together doing all the painting and redecorating of Low Hall. We are given a free hand in this, as we were back in 1981 at the time of refurbishment. The pictures on the walls, prints of Turner, Millais, Baron Gros are all of our choosing. I like to think they will still be there for many more years to come, reminders of Shirley and Peter Aldridge, matron and superintendent of Low Hall.

The three two-day seminars held at the Hall were apparently very successful, more are envisaged for the future, probably week long they tell me. We enjoyed it, the staff were all brought back in, they were pleased about that too. In winter they are normally all laid off until the start of the new season. Of course, there was no curfew such as with the miners, we had a little difficulty sorting out the males from the females, that was all.

By 1989 Shirley and I tended to look forward to the intake of ladies, giving us the much needed break from purely masculine company, even though I thought they were less apt to differ between themselves. In July of that year this particular women's batch, brought a new perspective to the convalescent world we had become accustomed to. As the coach conveying my future wards pulled up outside the main entrance to the Hall, I was at my office window as usual, watching the ladies disembark. One stood our like a flaring beacon from the rest. She was fashionably dressed, a lovely face enshrined by a cascade of long, shining blonde hair. The slim-waisted figure sported a cleavage which would have put to shame Jane Russell, at the peak of her career. Pardon the pun.

I wondered what the hell she was doing on my intake list? We occasionally do have the odd attractive female among the fifty in the group, but this one was truly exceptional.

I was so impressed, I returned to my desk to read the admittance forms. These give all personal details relevant to their stay, age, address, next of kin, what illness they have, or are recovering from, et cetera. Her form was easy to find, she could only be Pauline Gayle, forty years of age (she fooled me, I would have estimated early thirties at the most). She came from Wakefield, in the West Riding of Yorkshire, married. Her husband being a deputy at his colliery, qualified her for convalescence at Low Hall.

I went through into the main lounge to make my customary reception speech, as all the ladies were now assembled in there and settling into their seats in readiness.

One of the women, Mrs Doyle, had been on convalescence at Low Hall before. I made her Captain of the Intake, knowing from past experience she could certainly handle the position.

Now she looked at me with a quizzical twinkle in her eyes, as I was about to begin my address, 'eyes off, Super, or I'll tell matron,' she whispered jokingly, obviously having taken note of my interest in one particular female. This was indeed hard to do, as my speech lasted at least half an hour. I found my gaze continually wandering across the room in the direction of this beautiful lady, who sat there as serene as an angel, seemingly unaware of all around her.

After the welcoming speech was over, Shirley came into the lounge to designate the women's bedrooms, this being one of my wife's tasks. Margaret Shaw, the head housemaid, always accompanied her during this procedure. Each patient is given a number on arrival, as Pauline's number was called, she self-collectedly sauntered forth, towards my wife and Margaret. They both took one look at this unexpected, lovely vision and in unison their heads swivelled in my direction. It took an almighty effort of self control to keep a straight face, for theirs wore the same blank, open-mouthed expression. With an almost visibly determined endeavour, they managed to regain their composure. A single, top-floor bedroom was then allotted to Mrs Gayle, probably on the principle of, out of sight, out of mind.

As she slinkily ascended the Low Hall main staircase, all eyes in the room were rivetted on the tightly fitted, red, two-piece suit, which hugged a bottom gently swaying rhythmically from side to side.

Neville, the Hall's handyman, who had held that position for thirty years, followed her breathlessly wide-eyed, carrying her suitcase. He whispered to Shirley as he passed, 'never seen nothing like it here before, Matron.'

My wife just smiled tightly, looked at me, then shrugged her shoulders. I was to be watched, I had no illusions about that.

After the first day, during which I had passed a few pleasantries, a couple of times with Mrs Gayle, I had occasion to go into the library. She was in there earnestly going through a large volume of classical English literature, she was no dummy either, intellectually.

In actual fact I was to find her quite bright in conversation, as well as being a very nice, friendly person.

On the second evening, the captain, Mrs Doyle, accompanied by the vice-captain, Mrs Martin, came into my office. 'You know, Super,' Mrs Doyle began, 'after a day here, all the girls usually have no problem finding their way about. Not Marilyn Monroe, she has just asked where the toilets are?'

'Really?' I questioned, with less than enthusiasm. I knew they were referring to Pauline. I smelt more than a little jealousy in their interest regarding Mrs Gayle's forgetfulness.

'She didn't know her seat in the dining room at tea time,' Mrs Martin chimed in. 'When you think she has had supper, breakfast and lunch in there, then I think she is a bit thick.'

Every patient has their own numbered seat in the dining room, sitting there for the duration of their convalescence. The information about Pauline was in direct contradiction to how I had read the lady in question. As I have already stated, she struck me as being above average mentally, as well as physically.

Mrs Doyle and Mrs Martin were two lovely ladies, funny, quick on the uptake, besides being good at their job. This entailed organizing games,

Peter and Shirley Aldridge with the President and Secretary of the Nigerian N.U.M., official visit, August 1993.

The author; Kgalema Motlantke, General Secretary, South Africa N.U.M.; Shirley Aldridge; Ken Capstick, N.U.M. Spokesman. Motlantke spent twelve years in gaol with Nelson Mandela.

outings, keeping their eye on things pertinent to patients generally, to keep the wheels running smoothly. Things my wife and I would probably never be aware of, unless told.

As they sat facing me in my office, I felt a little perturbed, maybe my assessment of Pauline had been wrong.

'Mrs Doyle,' I asked, 'would you keep an eye on her for me? Let me know if she gets lost, or still doesn't appear to know her way around.'

I went on to explain the reason for my request, to the ladies.

'We very often have patients suffering from loss of memory, Mrs Gayle's medical sheet states that she is subject to depression. This could account for her peculiar behaviour.'

'O.K., Super,' Mrs Doyle replied, 'we will both keep our eyes open for her.'

The pair of them left my office determined to watch out for the ailing Mrs Gayle. The following morning I was back in the office at my usual time, with the doors wide open as normal, when Mrs Gayle passed on her way towards where morning coffee was being served.

'Mrs Gayle,' I called, 'can I have a word with you, please.'

She came into the office like a ray of sunshine, sitting down opposite to me she appeared absolutely radiant, knowing just how to cross her legs to gain the maximum effect. Giving just a short tug at the high-riding skirt bottom, for modesty's sake.

'How are you finding it here?' I asked pleasantly, 'everything all right?'

'Oh, very nice indeed,' she replied.

'Finding your way about now?' I inquired nonchalantly.

'Yes, thank you. I love everything here, the flowers, the grounds, the elevation of the Hall. The library with all its good books. It is marvellous.'

She stood, straightening her dress fastidiously, before leaving.

I knew that this woman was far from thick in any way, my first estimation had been the correct one. I watched her leave, her long, blonde hair carefully caught up into a shining bun arrangement.

After lunch Mrs Doyle came into the office, 'right, Super,' she said authoritatively, 'Monroe's going out tonight, she went out last night, too.'

'That's O.K.,' I told her, 'so long as she is back by 9.30 p.m. it's all right. But keep watching her for me.'

I do not know why I added the last bit, the woman appeared quite rational. 'Don't worry, Super,' said the good Mrs Doyle.

There was one thing in Pauline Gayle's favour, she didn't appear to be man fond, as many attractive females are. In actual fact I gained the opposite impression. On every instance I had spoken with her, she appeared to hold me at arm's length. I was far from lecherous in my approach, my concern aroused by the two ladies, was with her health. This too was puzzling, why the cool distancing? She obviously knew how to attract men, using this knowledge in every movement of her body, yet unmistakably she warned hands off.

That evening Mrs Martin popped her head around the office door, 'just asked me where the bar is,' she said, 'as if she didn't bloody know.'

I walked down the corridor to the cocktail lounge, where our little bar was situated. Mrs Gayle was sitting on a high stool at the counter. She seemed very different from the lady I had spoken to that morning. She greeted me with, 'I was just telling matron how nice it is outside.' Slipping her arm through mine in a friendly gesture she asked, 'would you like a drink, Super?'

Taken aback by her change in manner, I didn't answer.

'Go on, I have just bought matron one,' she urged.

I accepted half a pint of bitter beer from her, taking stock of this chameleon as I did so. Her hair was now down, untidily so, her apparel not nearly as neat.

By the end of the first week I was a very confused man, there were plenty of others just as bewildered in the Hall. She had blown hot and cold repeatedly to all, one time all over you, the next time you saw her she would ignore your existence. Mrs Doyle remarked in her forthright Yorkshire manner, 'I got, "hello, love," this morning, a bloody curt "good evening, tonight." I think something is definitely wrong with her, Super.'

On the Sunday, the start of the second week, everyone was wary of the capricious moods exhibited by Pauline Gayle, most assuming the poor thing was a bit touched, gave her a wide berth. After all, this was their holiday too.

By the following Tuesday, we would know the reasons for the fluctuation of temperament, thank goodness, for it was getting to be like a 'Peril's of Pauline' saga. Most people in the Hall deemed it wiser to let her speak to them first, that way they would know if it was friendly Annie, or frigid Sally, they were dealing with.

On the Tuesday morning, Robert, the Hall's gardener, came to the office door, 'gentleman to see you, Super,' he said.

'Come in,' I invited the tall, well-built, smartly dressed fellow inside. 'Take a seat.' As he seated himself, I asked 'what can I do for you?'

'I have come to see my wife,' he said pleasantly. 'Mrs Gayle,' he added, before I had time to ask her name.

'Certainly,' I said, ' I will get her on the Tannoy. She is in the dining room, they are just finishing breakfast.'

Without further ado, I went to the public address system. 'Mrs Gayle wanted in the office,' I repeated twice.

As Pauline entered the room, the man leapt to his feet, 'this is not my bloody wife,' he shouted angrily, 'it's her sister.'

One of the housemaids passing the door at the time of his eruption, quickly brought Shirley from the kitchen where she personally checks all meals before they are served.

My wife hurried into the office, closing the door behind her. I stopped the shouting abruptly.

'Now,' I demanded of Pauline's sister, 'what is going on here?'

Not that I couldn't have guessed part of it, I had been suckered by a pair of identical twins, no wonder we were all confused.

'Where's my wife?' demanded the irate Mr Gayle. He was livid with an anger the situation did not merit, as far as he was concerned.

'I'm not telling him,' the sister said defiantly to me.

After about twenty minutes of this verbal toing and froing, the argument becoming more heated with the passing of time. I'd had enough, we were getting nowhere fast. I looked hard at the sister, 'tell me where she is, or I am bringing the police in.' I reached for the phone on my desk.

The bluff worked.

'She is in a caravan about two miles away,' she informed me unwillingly.

'I will take you, but I am not taking him,' she added, pointing at Mr Gayle, who looked positively gutted.

'Will you stay here with me, Mr Gayle?' Shirley stepped into the breach as usual, adding, 'just until Super brings her back.'

'Yes,' he answered meekly, staring hopelessly at the floor.

On the way to the caravan site, the sister sat grinning like the proverbial Cheshire cat.

'Let's have a smile, Super, it is funny really,' she coaxed.

'There is nothing to laugh about, this is a very serious matter,' I replied, trying to keep a silly grin off my face. For when you think how they had neatly conned us, it was bloody hilarious, more than funny. On arrival at the caravan, I parked the car and side by side we walked briskly up the path. I knocked sharply on the door and the real cool Mrs Gayle opened it straight away. She stood there as if transfixed, clad only in a thin dressing gown, before blurting out harshly, 'oh, God.'

'Albert is at the Hall, love,' her sister told her kindly, 'he is waiting for you there.'

A man loomed up behind Pauline, saying domineeringly, 'you don't have to go.'

I shoved the door open wider with my shoulder, saying fiercely, 'oh yes, she does, and now.'

He dropped his eyes, as well as his belligerent manner.

'If I were you, I would make myself scarce,' I advised him gratuitously.

Pauline was dressed and ready to go back to the Hall with us in next to no time, looking as neat and chic as ever. How the hell had I not spotted the difference? The sister, by comparison, was a slap-happy dresser, as well as a definite extrovert. Then who would be expecting that kind of a switch in a convalescent home for miners' wives and widows?

While we had waited for her, I stood outside talking to the man named Ron. 'Think yourself lucky,' I browbeat him, 'if it had been my wife, you would be hospital bound by now.'

He was a complete weasel of a man, saying nothing in his own defence. I still smile at the memory of walking through the main entrance of Low Hall, accompanied by the two beautiful sisters. In appearance, they were the absolute spitting image of each other. One could hear the gasps of astonishment, from the rest of the intake, as we walked towards the office.

Mr Gayle wasted no time in claiming his wife. He grabbed her by the arm, propelling her out of the door. He turned to look back at me before leaving, saying quietly, 'thanks.'

His wife said nothing, remaining distantly aloof throughout the whole journey and confrontation with her husband. I watched from the office window, as he bundled her unceremoniously into his car. Climbing in himself, the car roared off down the drive, leaving the other sister behind. She appeared far from contrite about her part in the deception, in fact it was the direct opposite. She introduced herself saucily.

'My name is Maureen Marsh,' she said before continuing with her explanation of events. 'I live in Blackpool, I only did this as a favour to my sister, it was so daring I couldn't resist doing it,' she laughed heartily.

'You see, my sister wanted a couple of weeks with her lover, so we devised this plan. Pauline applied to come on convalescence, her husband being a miner she was eligible to stay here. I agreed to change places with her at night-time. I was the one who always slept here. We had everyone fooled, we would have got away with it too, if her husband hadn't arrived to spoil it. Did you see his face when he saw me?'

She turned in her seat towards Shirley, 'can I stay for the rest of the week? I like it here, Matron.'

'No, you cannot,' an angry Shirley snapped, 'pack your bags you are leaving now.'

'Pity,' she replied, with a mischievous twinkle in her lovely eyes.

I drove her to the railway station with her and her sister's baggage. On the way she propositioned me quite seriously, 'that caravan will be empty for the rest of the week, Ron will have gone by now. It is a shame not to use it.'

'Don't you think you have caused enough trouble, for the time being?' I asked. She didn't bother to answer.

On arrival back at Low Hall, Mrs Doyle and Mrs Martin were waiting, along with Shirley, for my return.

'Tell the super, what you have told me,' my wife instructed the ladies.

Mrs Doyle sat looking at me like a character from an Agatha Christie novel, before saying, 'the game was up for them anyway, Super. You can't go out in one pair of shoes, then come back wearing different ones.'

Mrs Martin threw in her observations for good measure, 'or go out wearing one colour of lipstick, coming back with a different colour on.'

Mrs Doyle chimed in again, 'we were coming to tell you, but her husband beat us to it.'

Those two elderly Misses Marple had certainly kept their eyes open. Dame Agatha's detective couldn't have done it better. They added yet another lovely memory to my store, as well as one more chapter of my story of Low Hall. It probably made their convalescence memorable too. I could imagine the Tale of Two Sisters, doing the rounds of their acquaintances. By golly it wasn't historical, but no one can deny it was hysterically entertaining at the time.

I didn't tell you that when we are catering for the seminars, Low Hall takes on a different coat. Midnight is the time to be back within the Hall, the menu is à la carte, wines and spirits being served with all meals and buffets. Whereas, with the miner, 9.30 p.m. is curfew, the menu is set, although very substantial, a three course dinner (lunch), a two course tea, as well as a large English type breakfast. Wines, beer or spirits are not allowed in the dining room. Birthdays or special occasions being an exception. The miners' intakes are either male or female while the seminars include both sexes at the same time.

The miners do have it good for all that. Early morning tea at 7 a.m. The bar is open in the morning, as well as evening. Lunch is at 1 p.m., high tea at five-thirty

Shirley and Peter Aldridge,
The Low Hall, 1992.

and we put tea and cakes up for them before they go to bed. No wonder they put on weight, looking like prize porkers, with a glow of health to their cheeks when they leave after eleven days.

Shirley has her surgery that looks after the miners, the doctor being brought quickly to the Hall for any really sick patient. To say it is a full time job is a joke, it is a night and day job if anyone falls ill during the period of darkness. I have seen my wife get two hours sleep some nights, bringing her back from the hospital at 4 and 5 a.m. on many occasions, where she had been sitting with ill patients, too sick and frightened to be left to their own devices in a public hospital.

This brings to mind another miner, a silly bugger who signed himself out of hospital. A very, very sick man indeed. The hospital rang us, asking urgently if we would go to the hospital to see Mr Burns, one of our patients, a man of about forty-five whom Shirley had had hospitalized after a heart attack. When I arrived at his bedside he was fully dressed. He was

Geoffrey Lofthouse, MP for Pontefract and Castleford, Deputy Speaker, House of Commons, with the author's wife, 1994.

demanding to be allowed to sign himself out. He had three doctors and three or four nurses pleading with him to stay. 'Mr Burns,' I almost shouted at him, 'will you do as the doctors say!'

'Not bloody likely,' he replied colourfully, 'I am not staying here, you fucking die in these places.'

It was very embarrassing for all present, yet the doctors and nurses turned not a hair. One doctor took me to one side, 'please, Mr Aldridge, get him to change his mind, he does not realize how very ill he is.'

I returned to Burns trying to reassure him, saying coaxingly, 'be a good lad, get back into bed, they only want to look after you, I promise you, you will be all right.'

'No,' he shouted, 'I'm going back to Low Hall, this lot can get fucked.'

The situation was impossible. Capitulating, the head doctor said, 'I am sorry, you will have to take him out, he is upsetting the other patients.'

I helped him to my car. It was only when I closed the door, with us inside, did I let him have it. 'You big ignorant bugger,' I ranted, 'not only are you putting yourself in jeopardy, you are also giving Low Hall a bad name.'

He had nothing to say now, he was out of the place where men die, he would take all of my castigation in his stride. When we arrived back at the Hall, Shirley refused to admit him back on the register. 'If the hospital has no responsibility for him, then I cannot accept it.'

We explained to Mr Burns why we couldn't assume liability for him, that all sick patients must be sent to hospital, our obligation ended there. He must make his own way home, unless he was willing to go into hospital.

'No trouble, Old Cock,' he said smilingly, 'can I have a pint before I go home?'

'No, you cannot,' I said sternly, 'do you realize you can drop dead any minute?' The doctor had told me that before we left so hurriedly.

'You win some, you lose some,' he said fatalistically. 'They don't know what they are talking about, that bloody lot at the hospital.'

I phoned for the time of the next train to Barnsley, taking him in my car to the station, making him give me a firm promise he would telephone me on his arrival at home. Both my wife and I remained on tenterhooks until around six-thirty that evening, when the phone rang. I answered, it was Burns carrying out his promise to let us know he was safe.

'Back home, Old Cock,' he said cheerfully, 'I'm ringing from the pub.'

The thought flooded my mind, my God, this man doesn't know how very ill he is, as the doctor at the hospital had warned.

Burns went on to give yet another interpretation of his views on doctors, 'I'll tell you what, Super,' he said, 'tell the doctors to get stuffed.'

He hung up before I could give him another ear-bashing, in the forlorn hope of prolonging his life. What a character he was.

This was on the Friday night, two days later on the Monday morning, another patient, a friend of Burns, who worked at the Grimethorpe Colliery with him, came into the office. 'Excuse me, Super,' he said, 'Ted Burns dropped dead while walking home from the pub on Sunday night, his wife has just phoned to tell me.'

I will never forget this silly man, could he have saved his own life if he had stayed in hospital, or was his death inevitable? Did he realize this, deciding to go out with a bang not a whimper, or was he just an obstinate bugger?

I think he knew, he held my hand for a very long time, as we shook hands on his leaving Scarborough Railway Station. He had a quizzical twinkle in his eyes, as he released my hand, when the train pulled away.

It is 1991, the worst winter Britain has sustained for many long years, is behind us. At one stage snow had actually settled on Scarborough sea-front beaches, as well as the precincts of Scarborough Castle

Low Hall became a veritable winter wonderland, magnificent in its snow covered splendour. No matter that it was a formidably destructive fury which unleashed itself over the north-east coast of England, as well as most other areas of Britain. The trail of damage extending from the south of England to John o' Groats in the north of Scotland. Many lives were lost, irreparable damage done to the forests and parks of Britain, homes lost, most receiving damage, if it was only tiles being blown from roofs, others losing chimneys, walls, the more unfortunate their houses.

Hundreds of people braved the icy winds though, to join in the fun of Shrove Tuesday on the foreshore. The inhabitants of Scarborough turn out for the annual skipping, which is preceded by the ringing of the Pancake Bell. Then the citizens take to the ropes for a lively skipping session, a ritual established more than ninety years ago. It is said the people skipped to keep warm, as they watched the Shrovetide activities on the sea-front.

There were many humorous incidents to surface during those bleak months like the story of the couple caught on the Yorkshire Dales during a snow storm. As the snow mounted up the sides of the marooned car, waiting for help they listened to a discussion on the radio about global warming, and its dangers.

Another incident on the same theme caused some mirth, as we watched from our warm fireside, an unfortunate lorry driver trapped on the Snake Pass, being interviewed on television. He said, 'I would like to get my hands on the silly prat who said that through global warming and that ozone bloody stuff, we probably wouldn't see any snow as such again . . . The prat should be here with us.'

Low Hall got off lightly compared to other properties in the village. We lost the television aerial as well as six trees blown down, some damage being done to the gardener's cottage, yet the Hall stood impregnable. Houses were well built in those days of cheaper labour, and pride of workmanship the old masters undoubtedly possessed.

As I come to the end of my story, I look back with nostalgia. The writing of these memorabilia evoked so much depth of feeling at times, I wondered if it wasn't better to let sleeping dogs lie. Then, I came to parts of my life of which I am inordinately proud, Armthorpe, the village I love, almost as much as I love my wife.

The Staveley Coal and Iron Company built this mining village in 1924, each home being occupied by a miner and his family. Everyone knew everyone else, there were no strangers in this camp. After the war Markham Main, the village colliery, employed 3,000 men, all living within the confines of the village. Today the figure is around 600 miners, many of those being brought by bus from surrounding colliery villages. Young men no longer want to know the rigours of working underground, preferring to move to more lucrative pastures down south. So Armthorpe has become just a part of suburban Doncaster, part of a commuter belt surrounding that town. There are vast changes in this village today, once mine-owned houses are now private homes. The owners changing windows and doors, all are different, the colours clashing wildly. The once sameness of these terraces gone, as has the thick, smoke-laden air we all breathed. The houses coated with the coal grime of years remain, washed with the cleansing rain, and more than a decade of clean air.

Yet, if I close my eyes I can still hear the ring of clogs striking the roadway, as miners pass on their way to and from Markham Main.

Mere Lane School was where I became victor ludorum, purely because of want. Mr Hemstock my teacher, a friend and mentor, with his well-worm admonition of, 'Manners maketh man', a saying, coupled with corrective treatment, he used in excess of forty years on the youth of Armthorpe.

They are all there jostling for recognition, friends and foe, a beloved recollection stored with inerasable care.

My move to London and the West End I became so familiar with. Snows of Piccadilly no longer standing, the changing into formal wear for the evening session in The Porcupine. Now it is just a dirty old pub, with a tattooed landlord in shirtsleeves reigning as mine host. The best of London's pubs, besides possibly the worst (The Camden Head being the probably outright winner in the latter category), we managed them all. Some for a short span, others for longer, all the time proudly confident of our capabilities and of the fact we were the youngest to do so.

Returning to Yorkshire to manage the Futurist, getting to know those talented entertainers, The Black and White Minstrels. The season at the Bier Keller before finding our niche in The Silver Grid.

The unknown, or unexplainable, whichever way you like to look at it, that holds court in the upper storeys of the Grid. Is it Charles Dickens intent on gaining his revenge on the people of Scarborough? After all, the critics were hardly kind to the man, one saying he preferred him as an author more than a descriptive reader. Another said he disappointed his audiences with the portrayals of his characters! After all, who should know what his literary cast should do and say, and in what manner? He travelled the length and breadth of Britain by uncomfortable stagecoach, to give his version of his own works. To be told by the tabloids of the day they were given little justice, must have been irksome. I would haunt the buggers too, if it were possible.

The Boozers' Walk, while we were at The Rosette, sharing the joy of that marvellous day with so many notables and the appreciative public.

Then our change of direction, becoming superintendent and matron of Low Hall, with all the ups and downs, humour and pathos it has entailed. The telling of jokes which make our day. The following is a typical example of the miner pointing the finger of fun at himself.

A miner was having a quiet drink in his favourite watering hole, when he was joined by the local undertaker.

'Mr Montague,' asked the miner, 'how much will you make me a coffin for?'

'Well, you aren't very big, Bobby,' the undertaker replied, 'I'll do you for forty quid.'

Quick as a flash, the miner shot at him, 'lend's a fiver now, and charge bloody wife forty-five quid.'

Back in 1988, the Scarborough Cricket Festival was held as usual in September. For the first time Shirley and I received an official invitation, after over twenty years residence in the town. It is a sort of status symbol when the president invites you to lunch and tea in the main marquee. We greatly appreciated the honour. In 1988 the Australian fast bowler, the great Dennis Lillee, was playing for the World Eleven so, too, were Imran Khan, Kapil Dev and Geoff Lawson, the other good Australian player. Shirley and I spoke with Dennis Lillee. He told us he'd had a bad injury in May of that year, and hadn't played cricket until July. He said, 'I've been under the bloody physiotherapist for weeks.'

He had decided on that instead of surgery. He gave me that mean look which has become legend among cricketers, before saying, 'I'm not having the knife, Mate.'

Bob Taylor, the English player jumped in quickly with the crack, 'somebody should knife him.' It caused a terrific gale of laughter throughout the tent.

It was a memorable day in many ways, for both my wife and myself are ardent cricket buffs.

The following year, 1989, on the main day, The Tesco International, Michael Parkinson's World Eleven versus The M.C.C., Shirley won the signed cricket bat. All the players sign this and it is then raffled off for

Shirley Aldridge (left) being presented with a World Eleven signed cricket bat by Mike Parkinson, Scarborough Cricket Festival, September 1989; (right) with the Sylvester Worthy Cup winning for the fifth year running Scarborough in Bloom.

Peter and Shirley Aldridge with the Mayor and Mayoress of Scarborough Mr and Mrs George Tuby in 1987.

charity. Michael Parkinson presented the bat to Shirley and, as he did so, the President of the Scarborough Cricket Festival, Mr Don Robinson, shouted loudly, 'well done, Shirley.'

We had know him for many years, from the time of David Whitfield's escapade in The Rosette. It was at Don Robinson's invitation we were fortunate enough to be at the match, to receive that wonderful bat. The Mayor of Scarborough, Godfrey Allanson, also congratulated Shirley on her win. He told us how he had worked at Low Hall as a builder, and what a wonderful place he thought it was. Kate met this Mayor, at her husband's side, when they visited the Town Hall and signed the visitors' book. She reckons he is a credit to Scarborough. They were most impressed by him and his wife.

Shirley and I, also, visited the Mayor's Parlour. On 11 October 1990, we were presented with the Sylvester Worthy Cup for the third year running. This is an award for the grounds of Low Hall which really deserve this tribute as does the head gardener and his team, including my wife and me.

I have said before, the gardens are a wondrous sight when in bloom, much appreciated by the miners who, themselves, are no slouches at gardening.

Our world goes on. It is 1991 and the start of a new season. On 8 April we opened our doors again for the first intake of the year. We were greeted with the usual spate of jokes. This one, I think, is worth repeating, it gives a picture of the mining village.

Policeman knocks on the door of the house and a burly miner opens it.

'Your dog is always chasing people on a bike,' the policeman complained.

'Well, take the bloody bike off it, man,' the miner quipped.

The scene of the N.U.M.'s disastrous defeat in the 1984-5 strike, the Orgreave Coking Plant, is to be turned into a landscaped wood. A bitter N.U.M. official stated, 'Orgreave is a symbol of N.U.M. power, which British Coal wants to erase from the face of the earth.'

Well, while ever the eyesore stands, there will be acrimony, so be done with it. Let these men forget and live out their lives in hard-won peace. It is not a place to be enshrined by either side.

If you are ever Scarborough way, watch out for these miners and say hello, they are the very salt of the earth, in my opinion, second to none.

Not for one moment do I regret taking this position over, I know my wife is of the same mind. We look forward to a good many years yet at

Low Hall minding the miners and their wives—though we can live without the Samples and Gayles of this world.

This should have been the end of my story. Madam Fate had other ideas.

I have told you how my wife escorts the ladies on their day trips by coach, into this fantastic wonderland which is the north-east coast of England.

It was on one such trip the other day, when terror entered our lives without warning.

After an enjoyable outing to Bridlington and Flamborough, they were on their way back to Low Hall. Having stopped in the tiny village of Buckton my wife, and the driver of the coach, noticed smoke coming from behind the driver's seat. They immediately began assisting the women out of the coach, most needed help for their ages ranged from fifty-five to seventy-five years, also they were all far from agile, some being very sick ladies indeed. Shirley said:

'The bus quickly filled with a thick, black, choking smoke, I was amazed they were so very good really. There was very little panic even though they had to use scarves and handkerchiefs over their faces to breathe. A lorry driver stopped his vehicle and he and two workmen helped us to free the patients. By the time we had the last of the ladies safely out, either through the front door or the emergency exit at the back, the coach was aflame. It was barely seconds after we had the last lady on the pavement that the bus went up in a ghastly fireball of gushing black smoke, searing heat and shooting flames setting alight an adjacent hedge. It looked like those pictures one sees on the television, of the oil-well fires in Kuwait.

'The coach was completely burnt out in short time, only the skeleton framework left. Without the help of those men the ladies would not have stood a chance, we couldn't move them fast enough. We dragged, pulled and pushed them out. I think God must have been on our side. It was horrendous as we stood and watched the coach burn out. There were loads of cracks and bangs as the windows blew out and the tyres burst with the heat.

'The villagers were marvellous to the ladies, they took them into their homes giving them tea and soothing their nerves.'

Four of the women were admitted to hospital suffering from smoke inhalation, all suffered from shock in one form or another, including Shirley who has been decidedly unwell since the incident.

The coach fire.

I am immensely proud of my wife. Apparently, she remained in complete
control of the situation throughout the ordeal. The elderly patients soon
recovered from their frightening experience, enjoying the media attention,
posing for photographs. They are another bunch of satisfied customers,
returning home with a mind-boggling story to tell neighbours and
loved ones.

There were forty-eight patients on that coach, all lived to tell the tale.

This is hardly the way to conclude my life story, a tale of trauma seems
scarcely fitting when so much humour abounds within the walls of Low
Hall. Let us then refer to the latest newspaper headlines on Mr Scargill.

Taking yet another swipe at Arthur, British Coal plan to undermine the
church of St Luke and All Saints at Darrington, near Pontefract. Among
the numbers buried within the church, are the noble Warren de Scargill
and his wife Clara. Warren married his Clara in 1300, taking possession of
several Yorkshire and Lancashire Manors. This vaunted knight fought on
the side of the Royalists at the battle of Boroughbridge.

The church warden is quoted as saying, 'old Warren might turn in his
grave at this. He was a very important knight in the Middle Ages and, just
like Arthur, he was not afraid to do battle.'

But I like better the quote of the vicar who reputedly said, 'the Coal Board have been trying to undermine Scargill for years. Now it looks as if they have succeeded.'

The plan is to gut the church, underpinning the building to allow them to get at a rich seam of coal which runs under the whole village and church at Darrington.

It is a pity that historic sites cannot be fully protected in this day and age of technological development.

Before I leave you, I must comment on the resemblance between Arthur and the face on Sir Warren's effigy. You might have thought The President of The National Union of Mineworkers had posed for it.